MW00709873

CLASSICAL PRESENCES

General Editors
Lorna Hardwick   James I. Porter

Classical Presences

Attempts to receive the texts, images, and material culture of ancient Greece and Rome inevitably run the risk of appropriating the past in order to authenticate the present. Exploring the ways in which the classical past has been mapped over the centuries allows us to trace the avowal and disavowal of values and identities, old and new. Classical Presences brings the latest scholarship to bear on the contexts, theory, and practice of such use, and abuse, of the classical past.

Vergil in Russia

National Identity and Classical Reception

ZARA MARTIROSOVA TORLONE

OXFORD

UNIVERSITY PRESS

OXFORD
UNIVERSITY PRESS

Great Clarendon Street, Oxford, OX2 6DP,
United Kingdom

Oxford University Press is a department of the University of Oxford.
It furthers the University's objective of excellence in research, scholarship,
and education by publishing worldwide. Oxford is a registered trade mark of
Oxford University Press in the UK and in certain other countries

© Zara Martirosova Torlone 2014

The moral rights of the author have been asserted

First edition published in 2014

Impression: 1

All rights reserved. No part of this publication may be reproduced, stored in
a retrieval system, or transmitted, in any form or by any means, without the
prior permission in writing of Oxford University Press, or as expressly permitted
by law, by licence or under terms agreed with the appropriate reprographics
rights organization. Enquiries concerning reproduction outside the scope of the
above should be sent to the Rights Department, Oxford University Press, at the
address above

You must not circulate this work in any other form
and you must impose this same condition on any acquirer

Published in the United States of America by Oxford University Press
198 Madison Avenue, New York, NY 10016, United States of America

British Library Cataloguing in Publication Data

Data available

Library of Congress Control Number: 2013956162

ISBN 978-0-19-968948-4

As printed and bound by
CPI Group (UK) Ltd, Croydon, CR0 4YY

Links to third party websites are provided by Oxford in good faith and
for information only. Oxford disclaims any responsibility for the materials
contained in any third party website referenced in this work.

For Mark

Omnia vincit amor et nos cedamus amori

Vergil, *Eclogues*

Or se' tu quel Virgilio e quella fonte
che spandi di parlar sì largo fiume?

Dante, *Inferno*

Preface and Acknowledgements

'Virgil is too important to be left to the classicists.' Thus begins Theodore Ziolkowski's formative study *Virgil and the Moderns*. Similarly I would begin by saying that Vergil is too important to be left only to Western Europe.

As far as Russia is concerned, the division of Europe into Eastern and Western is an artificial one.[1] The truth is, Russia is not Europe, Western or Eastern. For a country that spans two continents and is as much an heir to the Byzantine Empire as to the legacy of Genghis Khan's hordes, a unifying geopolitical term presents a distinct challenge.[2]

With that in mind how can we approach the Russian reception of the ancient poet who proved to be the most influential presence through many generations of European writers? The Russian Vergil is indeed, using Craig Kallendorf's book title, 'the other Vergil'. And yet, as the reader will see, the Russian Vergil is not altogether foreign to his European counterparts. On one hand, the Russian Vergil to a large extent is based on the European understanding of Vergil, since he serves for Russian writers as a gateway to form a European identity. On the other hand, Vergil in Russia had to and did acquire distinct national features. This study aims at unravelling this palimpsestic character of the Russian Vergil.

My fascination with Vergil goes back over twenty years. I owe a debt of gratitude to many people who along the way helped me understand his poetry. I am thankful to Nikolai Alekseevich Fedorov, my first Latin teacher, who early guided my timid steps into Vergilian verse; to Maria Murav'eva (née Lada Pererva), my scholastic reading companion in Vergil, with whom I spent countless days in the Moscow University libraries reading and deciphering the *Eclogues*, the *Georgics*, and the *Aeneid*; to Kesha and Kseniia Sarukhan-Bek for opening their Moscow home to me; to James Zetzel, whose astute and unmatched sensitivity towards the intricacies of the Vergilian text taught me what it means to read poetry in a sophisticated way, and to Susanna Zetzel, who from the very beginning was an eager supporter of my suggestion that the Russian Vergil is an unexplored terrain; and to the anonymous reviewers for Oxford University Press, whose insightful comments greatly improved this manuscript.

My deep gratitude goes to the Loeb Classical Library Foundation and Miami University's Office for Research Support for their generous grants that enabled me to have a year free of teaching and concentrate my efforts on finishing this book.

I am also thankful to my colleagues at Miami University for their unceasing support of my scholarly endeavours and especially to Denise McCoskey for teaching me how to be a perfectionist (still a work in progress). I owe a special debt of gratitude to Karen Dawisha, the Director of the Havighurst Center for Russian and Post-Soviet Studies, for always supporting and encouraging my interest in Russian Classics; to Gretchen Ziolkowski, for her many years of advice and guidance both in scholarship and in life; to Vitaly Chernetsky, for his encyclopedic knowledge of Russian literature and his willingness to share that knowledge with me; to Scott Kenworthy, for his help with the chapter on the 'messianic' Vergil; to Stephen Norris, for clarifying for me some complicated aspects of Russian history; and to John Jeep, for his infinite patience when working with Viacheslav Ivanov's German. Special thanks go to Pamela Davidson for her generous help and comments on the earlier version of the fourth chapter.

I also want to thank my parents, Dr Sergey Martirosov and Samvelina Pogosova, whose continuous help, support, and encouragement helped me in all my scholarly projects.

As I was writing this book my thoughts inevitably turned to my late father-in-law, Dominic Peter Torlone, whose indomitable Italian spirit, kindness, and fondness for all things Latin continue to inspire me every day.

And last but not least I am thankful to my husband, Mark Torlone, and my daughters, Christina and Francesca, for giving me joy and happiness every day.

NOTES

1. On the controversy over the term 'Eastern Europe', see Munteanu (2009), 1.
2. For more on Russia's peculiar geopolitical situation, see Bassin (1991).

Contents

List of Illustrations

Note on Translations and Transliteration

Unless otherwise noted, all translations in this book are mine.

I have used the Library of Congress system in transliterating Russian words and names, with some modifications. Although for the most part I use -*skii* in proper names, some well-known proper names are given in their most commonly used forms: e.g. Brodsky, not Brodskii. In citing bibliographical works in English I have retained the transliteration as it appeared in print.

Introduction

Vergil in Russia—Texts and Contexts

Природой здесь нам суждено
В Европу прорубить окно.
Here nature has decreed that we
Will hack a window into Europe.

Alexander Pushkin, *The Bronze Horseman*

Мильоны — вас. Нас — тьмы, и тьмы, и тьмы.
  Попробуйте, сразитесь с нами!
Да, Скифы — мы! Да, азиаты — мы, —
  С раскосыми и жадными очами!

Для вас — века, для нас — единый час.
  Мы, как послушные холопы,
Держали щит меж двух враждебных рас —
  Монголов и Европы!

There are millions of you, but multitudes of us.
Come try and overcome us!
Yes, we are Scythians! Yes, we are Asians
With squint and greedy eyes!
For you—the centuries, for us—one hour.
Like obedient slaves,
We held the shield between two warring breeds
Of Europe and the Mongols!

Alexander Blok

In 1739 Francesco Algarotti, an urbane and sleek Italian man of letters, accompanied Lord Baltimore, who had been sent to the Russian court to represent George II at the wedding of Anna of

Mecklenburg, niece of the Russian Empress Anna Ioanovna. The literary result of that trip, *Viaggi di Russia*, which Algarotti published in the early 1760s, was a set of imaginary letters to Lord Harvey and Scipione Maffei evaluating Russia's political and literary standing.[1] The narrative was also generously dotted with classical allusions, which sometimes were not so much a proof of the author's erudition as they were an exhibition of his urbanity and wit. Vergil was among his favourites and Algarotti quoted him often. What was especially remarkable, however, was how Algarotti in his observations equated Russian military power and patriotism with those of the Romans, employing yet again Vergilian allusions. In his prediction of the future of Russian imperial expansion he even went as far as to use Jupiter's prophecy in the *Aeneid* about Octavian Augustus: '*imperium oceano, famam qui terminet astris*' ('he will limit his power with the ocean, his fame with the stars').[2]

When Algarotti and Lord Baltimore travelled to St Petersburg, few European men of letters had any clear idea about Russia as a nation. Most certainly, even fewer of them would have used Vergil as an appropriate source of allusion to express thoughts or observations about Russia. But it was exactly at that time when the Russian literati started to turn to Vergil for political and literary inspiration which they could use on their native soil. Algarotti's Vergilian ruminations on Russia proved to be proleptic and miraculously coincided with the inception of Russian awareness about and appreciation of Vergil.

By the beginning of the eighteenth century many Russians already had ample information and even understanding of Western culture and thought, although these were accompanied by a certain feeling of inferiority. This feeling found its ultimate manifestation in the entire nation-building project of Tsar Peter the Great (1672–1725) since his extensive reforms were directed at making Russia a modernized European country. The external—and for the most part practical—appurtenances of Western culture that were introduced into Russian life by Peter, sometimes forcefully, extended eventually into the appropriation of a European artistic spirit. According to the nine-teenth-century Russian historian Vasilii Kliuchevskii, one of the first Russian poets, Mikhail Kheraskov, whose epic will be discussed later in this study, remarked 'that Peter gave the Russians bodies and Catherine gave them souls'.[3] Although this remark was meant to be flattering to Catherine at the expense of being unfair to Peter's extraordinary achievements, Peter's concerns were indeed largely practical, whereas Catherine wanted a court that would surpass those of Europe in splendour, wit, and artistic talent. Both rulers, however, brought into sharp focus the fundamental question of Russian national destiny and purpose.

Most European men of letters who gave any thought to Russia in the eighteenth century did not think of Russians as a separate people with their own national identity, or of Russia as a land of great promise and opportunity in its own right. Marshall Poe aptly observes that before Peter 'Western Europeans knew practically nothing about Russia', and the first European account of Muscovy, written by Ambrogio Contarini—like Algarotti, an Italian—was not particularly flattering to the Russians. Contarini reported that Russians 'were handsome but "brutal" and inclined to while away the day in drink and feasting', and that they 'were Christians, but not very good ones'.[4] Algarotti's observations, however, cast the Russians in a much more favourable 'European' light, although he branded St Petersburg's architecture as 'bastard' and stealing 'from the Italian, the French and the Dutch', yet again a nod to a vast European influence in a new Russia.[5] As John Garrard notes, 'the greatest compliment a Frenchman could pay a Russian was to say that he behaved indistinguishably from a Frenchman'.[6] The point of reference at least initially had to be European and, as Marc Raeff points out, Peter's reign 'put into motion the complex process bringing about a nation of "Russian Europeans"'.[7] Russian men of letters experiencing the tide of Europeanization in Russia looked for the models that were most familiar and best understood by their European counterparts. Algarotti's Vergilian ruminations resonated well in the emerging Russian literature and thought, and marked the beginning of the modern age for Russia as it turned to classical antiquity in belated imitation and emulation. The creation of a standard literary language also contributed to the ability to bring to the Russian reading public the literary gems of Western thought. The long-standing dichotomy that existed between the two distinctly separate languages Church Slavonic and the Russian everyday vernacular, which Boris Uspenskii termed 'diglossia', finally reached an impasse.[8] The linguistic blend that emerged and became the Russian literary language was quite remarkable and enabled Russian men of letters to become acquainted with their European and by extension classical legacy through translations.

Vergil in Russia certainly cannot be considered in isolation from his European reception. After all, the Russians never had continuous or systematic contact with either Latin or Greek. After accepting Christianity from Byzantium, Kievan Russia was permitted to use a Slavonic liturgy derived from the practices introduced a century before by Cyril and Methodius into Great Moravia.[9] Until Peter's educational reforms and the revival and transformation of the Moscow Academy from a church school to the Slavonic-Greco-Latin Academy (Slaviano-Greco-Latinskaia Akademiia), even the priests in Russia were not required to learn Greek or Latin, the lingua franca of cultivated Europe. That situation put Russia at a distinct cultural disadvantage as far as the classical legacy was concerned. Antiokh Kantemir (1708–44), Vasilii Trediakovskii (1703–69), and Mikhail Lomonosov (1711–65) were essentially the first generation of writers and thinkers who enjoyed the fruits of Peter's reforms. Most of them attended the Moscow Academy and attained a fairly solid grounding in Latin and classical literature. This education enabled them to pursue further studies and ultimately careers in Europe. Regarding the Russian pre-Petrine literary past as a cultural wasteland, they were also the first to turn to classical antiquity and shape the identity of a truly national literature.[10] In a brief period of time Vergilian references became ubiquitous in the writings of these first men educated in a Western manner as the process of genre assimilation became manifest in their literary efforts. The panegyric and ode inspired by both Pindar and Horace, tragedy evocative of Greek tragedians as well as Seneca, and especially the epic were held in the highest esteem and most eagerly adopted and cultivated by Russian writers. In many cases the Russian equivalents of these genres were significantly influenced by the French models of François Malherbe (1555–1628) and Nicolas Boileau (1636–1711) in the ode, and in the epic of Voltaire's *Henriade* (1728). A good example of Russian 'classicizing' is Trediakovskii's adaptation of Fénelon's *Télémaque* (1699), the first Russian epic to employ classical hexameter, which Trediakovskii's contemporaries considered to be his own original work.[11]

However, it would be wrong to conclude that the Russian reception of Vergil was nothing more than a foreign importation or a mere imitation of beliefs and attitudes towards antiquity developed in Europe. A few words may be necessary at this point about the general reproaches levelled against eighteenth-century 'imitativeness' in Russian literature and the disdain for 'servitude to Europe' that manifested itself in Russia's literature as it came to be modelled on the precepts and practices of Europe, especially France, whose dominant movement at that time was classicism.

In his formative if somewhat outdated *History of Russian Literature*, A. N. Pypin pointed out that the borrowings so ubiquitously perpetrated by Russian writers at the onset of the national literature were necessary and constituted the natural development of Russian culture.[12] Similarly, Il'ia Serman emphasizes that 'the creators of eighteenth-century Russian literature went back to classical models and shaped a literature based upon its precepts'.[13] Russian writers, while creating the foundations of national literature, also imitated and adapted the genres and theories of European, especially French, neo-classicism, making them fit Russian conditions.[14] These adaptations of classical models were by no means exceptional to the Russian literary experience and they do not diminish the merits of a distinctly national literature. Furthermore, in the seventeenth and eighteenth centuries, Russian acquaintance with and imitation of European poetics went hand in hand with contemplation of the nature of statecraft and national destiny. After all, Feofan Prokopovich (1681–1736), a staunch supporter of Peter's reforms, composed handbooks on both poetics and politics.[15] In fact Vergil was central to Feofan's *De Arte Poetica* (1705), a treatise on poetry and rhetoric written in Latin. Fashioned supposedly in imitation of French classicism, the new, almost born-overnight literature developed an acute consciousness of Russian statehood and forged a nationally specific way of looking at the past, not necessarily through the lens provided and tried already by Europe but from its own idiosyncratic perspective.

The conclusion then that Vergil in Russia only reflected the Russian claim to Europeanism would ignore the concern of much of eighteenth- and nineteenth-century Russian thought about national identity and values, and neglect important sources of later thinking about the character and destiny of Russia. At the centre of the Russian reception of Vergil is Russia's challenge to define the character and validity of its own civilization. Vergil's poems, especially the *Aeneid*, offered the Russian literati an opportunity to think about and act (sometimes unsuccessfully) upon national self-determination. It comes as no surprise that the beginning of Vergilian reception in Russia coincided with the development of an articulate national and literary consciousness. Vergil became, then, a part of solving the problem of Russian national identity in political, social, cultural, spiritual, and personal terms.

The discussion of Russian national identity, especially in the eighteenth and nineteenth centuries, involves a frequently debated controversy, which needs to be briefly addressed here. Geoffrey Hosking advances an influential argument that in 'Russia the building of an empire impeded the formation of the nation', and that 'a fractured and underdeveloped nationhood has been [Russians'] principal historical burden' because of the empire they built.[16] Vera Tolz also argues that the imperial policies of Russian monarchs caused 'Russians' failure to form a full-fledged nation'.[17] While Russian nationalism should be discussed with recourse to its imperialist history, there is nonetheless no need for such a strict dichotomy that separates nation-building from empire-building. In Russia, nationalism functioned at least initially within an imperial context.[18] Olga Maiorova observes that while 'the rise of national consciousness was in many ways constrained and impeded by the predominance of the monarchical empire', for the majority of Russian intellectuals 'the empire was a stage where the Russian people's historical drama unfolded, and as such, it served to reinforce rather than to obliterate Russian national identity. Indeed, many expressions of Russianness symbolically plucked the nation from the shadow of empire, assigning central significance to the nation itself.'[19] This point of view becomes especially poignant in the Russian reception of Rome in the eighteenth and nineteenth centuries. In particular, the Russian interpretation of Vergil undoubtedly displays a belief that a literary work can in fact 'nationalize the empire'. Russian national self-expression through invoking Roman parallels (especially Vergil) contributed to the notion that empire and nation were not mutually exclusive projects.

In his book on Russian national consciousness in the eighteenth century, Hans Rogger defines national consciousness as 'a striving for a common identity, character, and culture by the articulate members of a given community'.[20] Similarly, Edyta Bojanowska treats nationalism 'as a discourse of educated elites that articulates the *idea* of nation and national identity'.[21] She further elaborates that 'this discourse invokes various social and political loyalties and culls elements from the fields of religion, history, ethnography, and language in order to construct a new national amalgam'. However, such discourse of nationalism 'is not predicated upon the existence of national political movements or national identity'.[22] This discourse among the Russian elite, although rooted in pre-Petrine Russia,[23] began to acquire its definitive contours only in the eighteenth century after

Peter's and then Catherine's reforms extensively introduced Russia to Europe and Europe to Russia. Liah Greenfeld observes:

> Two autocrats can be held directly responsible for instilling the idea of the nation in the Russian elite and awakening it to the potent and stimulating sense of national pride: these were Peter I and Catherine II. It is not our task to pronounce whether Russia was fortunate or unfortunate in having been, within one century, subjected to two rulers of genius . . . But the direction in which the two monarchs eventually led this great mass, which they could mold and shape according to their wishes, was chosen by themselves. The direction was Westward, toward making Russia a European state to be reckoned with and respected. And the model was no longer Poland and Ukraine, as in the days of Peter's father, Tsar Alexis, but England, Holland, Germany, and later France: the Europe of progress, unlimited possibilities, and national identity, which for some time was to rule the future.[24]

However, the process of 'Westernizing' Russia was always fraught with controversy. Russia was not continental Europe, and as Mark Raeff rightly points out, 'unlike most European cultural leaders, the Russians could not easily tap their own roots, for they had broken with much of their early culture to take on foreign models and inspiration'.[25] Peter's reasons to 'hack a window into Europe', and to seek the recognition of 'the haughty, alien West' at the expense of forsaking old Russian traditions, might never be exactly clear. The forceful tsar might have appreciated the new industrial progress and cultural freedoms of the West, but in the end neither was he a missionary nor was he aiming 'to convert Russians into freedom-lovers'.[26] Although in the early stages of these initial contacts with the West new customs were accepted with undiluted admiration, many of the Western values forced on the Russians remained deeply foreign to them. Raeff observes:

> Despite the increasingly active and constructive participation of Russian science, scholarship and artistic creation in the ongoing progress of western civilization, the nagging question remained: are we truly part of that civilization? There also lingered the hopeful wish that the very differences that defined Russia would contribute to the total renewal of world civilization, of which Russians would serve as both the prophets and the architects.[27]

If Russian society was to become 'a semblance of the West', it had to be, as Richard Wortman emphasizes, 'a semblance, Russians acting as Europeans, performing the metaphor and behaving "like foreigners"'.

The key was to 'imitat[e] Europeans while remaining Russian'.[28] It is remarkable, as we will see in the following pages, how the Russian reception of Vergil, from the eighteenth century to the end of the twentieth, reflected these perpetual anxieties about Russia's self-image and national consciousness. Furthermore, the vision of Russia as an architect of the 'renewal of world civilization' also reflected the fact that Russian national identity hinged upon not so much an imitation of but competition with the West, which 'was indeed the motive force behind the early achievements and the formation of national consciousness'.[29]

The dichotomy between East and West was not always so clearly defined on Russian soil, nor did it develop in a linear fashion. The attitude towards the West oscillated depending on the political and social atmosphere. Elite Russians were always extremely curious about the 'mysterious East', its opulence, and its customs.[30] There also existed some awareness about Russia's Eastern legacy connected with Turkic migrations as early as the eighth century CE and most certainly with the Mongols who held Russia under their sway for more than two centuries.[31] That awareness gave sporadic rise to expressions of ambiguity about Russia's geopolitical identity and feelings of resentment towards the West. As Greenfeld observes, 'in no other work of literature has the threat to and the defiance of the West by a Russian been expressed with such striking, distressing beauty' as in Alexander Blok's 'Scythians',[32] which I include as an epigraph to this chapter: 'Yes, we are Scythians! Yes, we are Asians / With squint and greedy eyes!' In the eighteenth century, however, the considerations that would emerge again amid the cataclysmic changes brought by the Revolution of 1917 were swept aside. Lomonosov and his contemporaries knew both Vergil and Ovid. In Ovid's *Tristia* he described the Scythians as a barbaric tribe with savage customs. The great Russian polymath was not eager to liken Russia to such a tribe.[33]

The main source of inspiration for the new, competitive, and pronouncedly Western national image was at least in the beginning drawn from the city of St Petersburg, in Dostoevskii's words, 'the most intentional (умышленный) city in the world' (Figure 1).[34] St Petersburg, as James Cracraft observes, 'was never a purely Russian town' but 'a metropolis of indisputably cosmopolitan dimensions' with a history 'of Russia's struggle to claim, and then to maintain, a leading role in Europe and the world'.[35] Which author ancient or modern could have served that purpose better than Vergil,

Figure 1. One of the landmarks of St Petersburg, the Kunstkammer along the Neva river embankment. Photograph by Sergio Sanabria.

considering especially that Peter and his successors adopted 'a western, Roman image of secular rule'?[36]

From the early eighteenth century, after the foundation of the city of St Petersburg in 1703, Russian writers and thinkers turned to Vergil as they strove to lay down the foundations of a national literature that could rival its European counterparts. As we will see from many examples of Vergilian reception in this study, Russian artists and thinkers were well acquainted with the general understanding of Vergilian reception in Europe. When Russia was first introducing itself to the European family of nations, the *Aeneid* was seen by most of its early modern readers as a poem of praise for Augustus convenient for those rulers who constructed their nation-building in his image. In the nineteenth and twentieth century there was also a noticeable counter-current from those who responded to the cost of imperial achievement as Vergil brooded on it.[37] The same fluctuations in the Russian reception clearly show that Vergil's Russian readers had absorbed the basic European interpretations of the poem and the poem itself, but for every author discussed in this book I aim to illuminate the national specificity of the Russian reception.

Mikhail Gasparov, perhaps the greatest scholarly authority in the study of Classics in Russia in the late twentieth century, surprisingly enough dismisses the importance of Vergil in the Russian literary landscape. He writes:

> Вергилию не повезло в России. Его не знали и не любили: «пере-лицованные "Энеиды"» разных авторов русскому читателю всегда были более знакомы, чем «Энеида» настоящая. Сближению с Вергилием мешало сначала гимназическое отвращение, потом — языковой барьер. Поэмы, в которых главное — рассказ, могут нравиться и в переводе; поэмы, в которых живет и звучит каждое слово (а таков весь Вергилий), требуют переводчика-языкотворца, какие бывают редко. Для Гомера таким был Гнедич, для Вергилия такого не нашлось. Не нашлось потому, что романтический XIX век, мечтавший о поэзии естественной и непосредственной, не любил цивилизованной римской классики и предпочитал ей греческую. XX век, расставшись с романтизмом, понял, что естественность и непосредственность в поэзии — миф и что громоздкая сложность и противоречивая напряженность римской цивилизации едва ли не понятнее нашему времени, — и вновь сумел воспринять и оценить Вергилия. Последние пятьдесят лет в Европе были подлинным вер-гилианским возрождением, и волны его начинают докатываться и до нас. Это отрадно: поэзия Вергилия — это поэзия, открытая в будущее, и всякой культуре, которая не боится будущего, она близка.

> Vergil did not have much luck in Russia. They neither knew nor loved him: 'reshaped' *Aeneid*s of various authors were more familiar to the Russian reader than the real *Aeneid*. At the beginning it was the disgust engendered by the gymnasium education which hindered closeness to Vergil, then it was the language barrier. The poems in which narrative is everything can please in translation; but the poems in which each word is alive and resounding (and that is Vergil) demand a translator who is a language maker, and that is rare. Gnedich became that translator for Homer, for Vergil there was none. None, because the romantic nine-teenth century, dreaming about natural and spontaneous poetry, did not like the civilized Roman classics and preferred the Greek. The twentieth century, upon parting with romanticism, understood that naturalness and spontaneity in poetry are myths and that the bulky complexity and contradictory tension of Roman civilization are closer to our times. That is when Vergil was received and valued again. The last fifty years in Europe truly marked the Vergilian renaissance and its tide is reaching us as well. This is joyful: for Vergil's poetry is poetry that is open to the future, and is close to every culture that is not afraid of the future.[38]

This excerpt emphasizes many crucial issues highlighted on the pages of the present study. Vergil indeed still does not have a canonical translation into Russian equal to that of Gnedich's *Iliad*. However,

I aim to prove that, in spite of this language barrier, the importance of Vergil for the formation of Russian literary identity is beyond doubt. Gasparov titled his essay 'Vergil—the Poet of the Future' («Верги-лий—поэт будущего»), thus ultimately predicting the importance of Vergil for the future of Russian culture while dismissing the past of Vergilian reception. Although this hope for the 'Vergilian renaissance' is encouraging, it underestimates the milestones that Vergilian reception has undergone from the foundation of the Russian literary canon to the end of the twentieth century.

Sergei Averintsev in his formative essay on Vergil also pays mere lip service to the presence of Vergil in Russian letters, calling only Viacheslav Ivanov a 'Russian Vergilian' (русский вергилианец), but omitting any other examples of Vergilian reception on Russian soil.[39] His essay concentrates primarily not on reception but on Vergil as a poet, whom he sees as exceedingly mature (unlike Catullus) and endowed with 'intonations of marvellous seriousness, not destroyed by experience, uncontaminated by even the slightest taste of irony' («в интонациях . . . чудной серьезности, не разрушенной опытом, не отравленной даже привкусом иронии»), yet appealing to the youth of all ages with a 'slightly "boyish", youthful timbre, in comparison with which the all-knowing frivolity of Ovid seems aged and overripe' («слегка «мальчишеский», юношеский тембр, сравни-тельно с которым такой пожилой и перезрелой кажется всез-нающая фривольность Овидия»).[40] Furthermore, Averintsev attributes Vergil's popularity with Schiller and Hölderlin as well as Victor Hugo to that very 'boyish timbre' surrounded by the aura of romantic ideals of friendship (he provides curiously enough the example of Nisus and Euryalus) and of liberty. Both Gasparov and Averintsev express their views of Vergil strongly (at the expense even of other Roman poets) and cast him in the rather idealistic light of national destiny, and as a flattering herald of a new Rome and Augustus (which characteristically they see as the most damaging for the Russian reception), and only slightly touch upon the darker undercurrent of Vergilian poetics.

However, these two very important scholars conditioned and influenced the opinions of at least twentieth-century readers on Vergil's place in the Russian literary landscape. In his entry on Russia in *Enciclopedia Vergiliana*, Ruffo I. Chlodowski, clearly responding to Gasparov's comment, writes: 'While this opinion is justifiable from many perspectives, it does require a more accurate historical assessment: this was a case neither of love nor luck; the fact that Vergil was less fortunate in Russia than in other Western European countries depended entirely on the evolution of Russian literature.'[41] It is perhaps true that Vergil's influence and presence in Russian literature are not as obvious as those of Ovid (although he was disparaged by Averintsev) or Horace, whose love poetry and lyric modes respectively Russian poets found greatly appealing. However, the continuous reception of Vergil in Russia inevitably reflects not only the different phases of Russian literary development, but also ideas about nationhood and the way Russian writers positioned themselves in relation to the state.

The Russian Vergil, like the Vergil of any European literature, is complicated. The complication of his reception in Russia arises mainly from the fact that sometimes it is not Publius Vergilius Maro, the Roman poet of the *Eclogues*, *Georgics*, and the *Aeneid*, that Russian writers are receiving, but a composite construct that has gone through the reception of influential (and at times even obscure) European writers, and in addition has been shaped by the cultural context of Russia. The Russian Vergil is an imperial propagandist, a subversive revolutionary, and an object of parody; a religious messiah on the threshold of the new spiritual era; an isolated artist overwhelmed by his melancholy and his nostalgia. The Vergil of Russian writers mirrors the social, spiritual, and personal quest of each given epoch throughout Russia's literary development. Sometimes his features are easily recognizable in the poetic texts, and sometimes his meaning is buried under multiple cultural layers that have very little to do with the Roman Vergil. But in every case these texts reveal to us something about what it meant at that time to live in Russia, to understand its destiny, its meaning, longing for it, hating it, and desperately trying to change it.

Although the most persistent reception of Vergil does not begin until the second half of the eighteenth century, it is necessary to dwell briefly on the Russian discourse of Rome in order to understand focal points of analysis this study pursues.

RUSSIAN *ROMDICHTUNG*

In Mikhail Bulgakov's famous novel *The Master and Margarita*, the Devil, in the guise of a magician, Woland, visits the venal Soviet city of Moscow and performs the acts of final judgement over the people who persecuted and imprisoned the Master, the author of a masterpiece about Jesus Christ's crucifixion at the hands of a guilt-stricken Pontius Pilate. After punishing the corrupt Soviet bureaucrats, Woland leaves the city, taking the Master and his beloved Margarita with him. While floating up above Moscow he takes a last look at the city and then says to one of his attendants, Azazello: 'Interesting city, isn't it?' To which the latter responds: 'Messire, I rather prefer Rome.' As Woland and his attendants depart from the city they have destroyed, Margarita turns around and sees that the city itself has disappeared and gone into the ground, leaving only fog behind. There are several levels of discourse in this passage taken from a novel that combines two narratives—one taking place in Moscow, another in Jerusalem, a city under Roman domination; one secular and at times carnivalesque, another eschatological and biblical. Both narratives are derived from the centuries-long quest of Russian thinkers for orientation in relation to Rome, its narratives, its history, its religions, and to reconcile the 'opposites' inherent in all of these.

Russia had two Romes to aspire to, but in the end they became closely intertwined. One was the secular Western Rome of imperial grandeur, military conquest, and cultural upheaval. Vladimir Toporov aptly phrases this aspect of the Russian 'Roman text':

> Римская тема . . . обращена не столько к человеку, сколько к государству, к власти, к величию и глубинно и метонимически — к России. Рим и есть образ этой власти-величия во всей ее полноте и славе, образ державы, Империи, мира в целом.[42]

> The Roman theme . . . is directed not so much towards man, as it is towards the state, the power, the grandeur, and deeply and metonymically—towards Russia. Rome is exactly that image of power-grandeur in all its completeness and glory, an image of the sovereignty, Empire, the world in its entirety.

This image singled out by Toporov includes not only the imperial aspirations but also the ideals of republicanism, law and order, and most importantly civic consciousness. As soon as the Russian intellectual milieu began to formulate its own civic and cultural identity, the need for the metonymical expression of 'Russian' through 'Roman' became ubiquitous and frequent. Although strongly supported and encouraged by the Russian monarchy, the mere identification of Russia with the Roman Empire was seen as dubious. Indeed, the pagan empire of Rome fell eventually to the barbarian hordes. The complete self-identification of Russia with ancient Rome would involve not only the grandeur but all the shortcomings that came with it and admitting its perhaps inevitable failure. And that is why the Russian *Romdichtung* developed its other equally important aspect, which was mystical, spiritual, and deeply rooted in Christianity and the eastern region of the Roman Empire. It was this area of the Roman world that provided the Russians with their alphabet and religion. Judith Kalb observes that 'the "first" Western Rome came predominantly to represent secular authority and imperial power to various Russian rulers and their subjects, even as the "second", Eastern Rome, while the inheritor of Rome's secular authority, could function additionally as a symbol of religious piety'.[43] The Russian 'Roman text', then, with Vergil at its centre, came to encompass both imperial and religious discourses.

   The best-known identification of Russian power with Rome in political terms started with the Petrine reforms. However, this was not willed into existence merely by the forceful tsar-reformer but was preceded by several centuries of a Russian quest for identity in which the political and religious *Romdichtung* became entwined. Iurii Lotman and Boris Uspenskii observe that 'to look to Rome as the norm and ideal of state power was itself traditional for Russian culture'.[44] For example, as early as the sixteenth century there arose the idea of a familial heredity between the Russian ruling family and the Roman emperors. In *The Epistle of Spiridon-Savva* and *The Tale of the Princes of Vladimir*, written in the 1520s, the ancestor of Russian monarchy Riurik became connected with none less than the 'brother' of Octavian Augustus, Prusus.[45] This belief was strongly reinforced in the declarations of Ivan the Terrible (1530–84) and later eagerly supported by Peter I and Peter II (1715–30), his grandson, who ruled briefly but was the first Russian ruler to be crowned emperor.[46] In this desire to associate themselves with the house of Augustus, Russian sovereigns were not different from their European counterparts, who were also extremely interested in creating for themselves ancient genealogies and in seeking mythological comparisons. Charlemagne (742–814), the first Roman emperor in Western Europe since the collapse of the Western Roman Empire three centuries earlier, and Maximilian I (1459–1519), the Holy Roman Emperor from 1493 until his death, both constructed their familial genealogy all the way to Priam, Hector, and other Trojans, thus connecting themselves directly with the descendants of Aeneas, the great patrician Roman clan of Iulii.[47] It also became a part of European royal tradition to compare the ruling monarchs with ancient gods, heroes, or generals. The images of Neptune, Bacchus, Augustus, Vespasian, and Trajan decorated the triumphal arches of Charles V of Spain (1516–56), glorifying his conquests in Italy. In panegyrics commissioned for Henry IV of France (1553–1610) and Elizabeth I of England (1533–1603), both of these sovereigns were compared to Astraea, mentioned in Vergil's Fourth Eclogue, interpreted as a prophecy for the pending Golden Age.[48] Wortman points out that 'the myth of the return of Astraea symbolized the renewal, *renovatio*, brought about by a revival of imperial rule',[49] an important characteristic for both Peter and later Catherine, who tried to set themselves apart from their predecessors.

In Russia, Peter and to a greater extent Catherine continued these European associations, tailoring them more to Russian circumstances. What was especially characteristic of this Russian acculturation of ancient imagery and rhetoric was its close and persistent intertwining with Christianity. This feature was not particularly novel per se. When the pagan empire of Rome was transformed into the Holy Roman Empire in Aachen, European imperial iconography began to rest on Christian foundations as well, and even 'Virgil was baptized into the new Christian faith'.[50]

Similarly Russia's *Romdichtung* was almost never articulated within the context of classical Greece and Rome alone, but often in the context of Russian Orthodoxy the 'Second Rome', Constantinople, to the Christian legacy of which Russia considered itself to be even more of a legitimate heir than to the pagan Rome of the Caesars. Thornton Anderson offers the background to such a dichotomous approach to classical antiquity in Russia:

> The secular and speculative thought of the classical age had been diluted and transformed by Asiatic immigration and by an intellectual preoccupation with religious subjects. Byzantium, by that time, saw itself as an isolated citadel of religion and culture beleaguered by surrounding infidels; the ideal of a Roman and Christian ecumene remained, but in practice something akin to the old Greek concepts of civic membership and of distinction from the barbarians had returned. It was this psychology and the attendant almost inflexible ideas that were passed on to Russia, largely through the church. Furthermore, this Byzantine influence in Russia came to a virtual end with the Florentine Union of

1439, just when the Renaissance was reinforcing the connection of the West with the heritage of the pagan Greeks and Romans. The Greek contribution to Russia, therefore, was markedly different from the Western heritage. Instead of the stimulating and controversial writing of long-dead philosophers, it came in the form of living priests and monks bearing a dogmatic and eternal truth.[51]

This dogmatic truth engendered by Russia's embrace of Orthodoxy perpetuated itself during the first steps of a Russian national literature. Even in *The Tale of the Princes of Vladimir* the narrative about Prusus shows the tendency to combine Roman and Byzantine legacies. Prusus is sent to the banks of the river Vistula to organize affairs there; fourteen generations later the Russians invite Riurik, the direct descendant of Prusus, to rule over them; the Muscovite tsars descend directly from Riurik. But then the other dimension of the Russian *Romdichtung* enters the story. Tsar Vladimir (972–1015) received the True Cross and the Byzantine Imperial Crown, and allegedly took the name Monomakh after the Byzantine Emperor Constantine Monomachus. This story, as Robert Wolf points out, is of course as much a fabrication as the tale of Prusus. Constantine IV (1042–55) ruled several decades later than Vladimir, who never took the name Monomakh, while the real Vladimir Monomakh (1113–25) took his name from his Byzantine mother.[52]

However, both fabricated stories are revealing in terms of how the Russian consciousness formed its connection to Rome. One way was through the great but pagan Roman Empire—that was the political claim. Another was via Byzantine Rome and the piety associated with its Orthodoxy. Even Catherine II, who prided herself on her secularism and association with Voltaire and Montesquieu, thought of the leadership of Russia as the religious and political ideal of a unified ecumenical Orthodoxy under which all the Orthodox East would be politically united. It is with that in mind, for example, that she invited Eugenios Voulgaris (1716–1806), the first translator of Vergil's *Georgics* into modern Greek, to emigrate to Russia and become the first archbishop of the newly incorporated diocese of Cherson and Slaviansk in Novorossiia.[53]

Vergil came to be seen as the answer to both discourses and to encompass both the imperial rhetoric and the spiritual quest for a Russian Christian soul. So it comes as no surprise that an image of the Latin poet is conserved on the western wall of the Blagoveshchenskii

Cathedral at the Kremlin in Moscow (sixteenth century)—a life-sized portrait of him in the garb of a Greek pilgrim. He has no halo and his hands (like those of the biblical prophets) are holding a scroll, on which is written: 'Divine nature was not created and it has no beginning and no end.' Vergil is also represented this way on the double doors of the Uspenskii Cathedral in Moscow (also in the Kremlin), and in some Russian churches.[54]

The syncretic reception of ancient Rome in Russia went hand in hand with Russians' quest to seek the confirmation of their belief in 'Russia's elevated soul, defined against the West's pragmatic and orderly reason'.[55] The Russian reception of the Roman legacy then went beyond merely claiming a European identity. As Mark Raeff explains, it enabled Russian thinkers to construct themselves through that reception as 'both the prophets and the architects' of civilization.[56] This claim manifested itself most strongly in the 'messianic' responses to Vergil in the twentieth century, especially in the interpretations of the Fourth Eclogue. However, these messianic tendencies had their roots in Russia's frequently discussed 'Third Rome' doctrine.

This doctrine originated in the early sixteenth century (around 1523/4)[57] when a Pskovian monk, Filofei, explicitly stated the progressive sequence of 'Romes': Rome, Constantinople, Moscow.[58] Until the Petrine reforms Europeans had refused to recognize Russia as an equal, and the result of that rejection was the development of Filofei's view that Russia was the last remaining Rome, the new core of Christendom since the Byzantines had been conquered in 1453 by the Muslim Turks. After the fall of Constantinople, Russia, and more specifically Muscovy, remained the only independent Orthodox community in the world. The political identity, as Martin Malia aptly observes, became 'secondary to the religious one'.[59] In his letter to Tsar Vasilii III (1505–34), Filofei stated:

> The church of Old Rome fell because of the Apollinarian heresy; the gates of the church of the Second Rome, Constantinople, have been hewn down by the axes of the infidel Turks; but the present church of the Third, New Rome, of thy sovereign Empire . . . shines in the universe more resplendent than the sun . . . All the empires of the Orthodox Christian faith have come together in thy single Empire. Thou are the sole Emperor of all the Christians in the whole universe . . . . For two Romes have fallen, but the Third stands, and a Fourth shall never be.[60]

It is easy to see how in this categorical statement by Filofei two Russian Romes merged: *imperium sine fine* and the centre of

Christendom with a religious mission. There is also a definite even if unintentional imperial subtext in Filofei's statement. More importantly such a parallel with antiquity offered the qualitative assessment of Russia's mission in the world. In the Russian society of Filofei's time the statement of cultural, political, and spiritual continuity had to refer to the past as a point of qualitative reference. It may be appropriate to cite here the words of Pavel Florenskii:

> Для философских воззрений всей древности «давность» и «совершенство» столь же тесно связаны между собой, как для воззрений Нового времени «совершенство» и «будущность». Если сейчас у большинства вызывает приятное волнение слово «вперед!», то таким же знаменательным было тогда слово «назад». Поэтому на языке века, когда господствовала теория регресса, слово «древность» имело двоякое значение: во-первых, хронологической давности, во-вторых, качественного превосходства.[61]

> For the philosophical concepts of the entire antiquity 'remote past' and 'perfection' are as closely linked as 'perfection' and 'future' are for the New Time. If most people now get pleasantly excited upon hearing the word 'forward!', the word 'backwards' was received with the same remarkable excitement then. That is why in the language of the century ruled by the theory of regression, the phrase 'remote past' had a double meaning: firstly, of chronological past, and secondly, of qualitative superiority.

Filofei then does not merely suggest that Russia has a place in the succession of Romes, but that such a place is one of superiority, with the attendant ability to decide the fates of the civilization. This approach to the 'Roman' mission of Russia will resonate strongly with the interpretation of Vergil by such religious thinkers as Vladimir Solov'ev (1853–1900), Georgii Fedotov (1886–1951), and particularly Viachelsav Ivanov (1866–1949), who wrote an exultant essay on Vergil as a poet of religious rebirth.

Kalb points out that 'the doctrine emerged in the face of growing Muscovite stature: in 1472 Ivan II married Zoe Paleologue, niece of the last Byzantine emperor, adopted the title "tsar", derived from the Latin Caesar, and added Byzantium's two-headed eagle to the symbols representing the Russian monarchy'.[62] In the idea of the Third Rome, Russia's inferiority complex towards the West and somewhat shaky claim to the Greco-Roman legacy dissipated. The declaration that Moscow and in fact all of Russia was the 'Third Rome' was not made out of misplaced pride or bombastic aspirations, but it was a manifestation, as N. V. Sinitsyna observes in her impressive study of the doctrine, that Russia retained its loyalty to the precepts of an original form of Christianity, 'when the unity of the Christian world was preserved'. It was also an attempt to claim a place for Russia in world history and on the map of holy places and holy altars after the catastrophe of 1453. It was not so much a messianism as it was a mission.[63] Monarchy became divinely anointed and ordained Russian theocracy with a claim to restore Rome to its grandeur through the Russian spirit, whose religious zeal and truly devout soul would save the world. The blending of political and religious discourses regarding Rome became revived with a new force in the unstable times after the Bolshevik revolution, which provoked the feelings of the *fin de siècle*.

Vergil was chosen to convey Russia's double-tiered *Romdichtung*. After Petrine reforms when Russia started slowly but confidently entering the European scene, the questions of national and literary identity became especially poignant. Peter founded his new city on a site that was largely swamps, a city that was supposed to attract and bedazzle the whole world, and transform the face of Russian national identity. The old boyar beards were gone, the wooden capital city was replaced with one cast in marble, the traditional bulky sarafans gave way to stylish European dresses. All of that was accomplished rapidly, almost without any transitional stage. As W. Gareth Jones puts it, 'a man was a bearded Muscovite, or within minutes, a clean shaven European'.[64] The change in appearance rapidly found its way also in literature. The rhetoric of the 'Third Rome', which re-emerged at that time, shifted. If before it was Moscow that was seen as the 'Third Rome' (by Filofei most certainly),[65] or New Constantinople, the idea of the new capital became eventually juxtaposed with the dated 'big village' of Moscow, which represented the hopelessly backward heart of the land.[66] The new Third Rome, St Petersburg, turned its face decisively to the West and was destined to become yet another 'eternal city'. Feofan Prokopovich, an outstanding proponent of the early Enlightenment, articulated the shift in values and priorities in the following way:

> The Roman Emperor Augustus when he was dying felt it to be the highest praise to say to himself: I found a Rome built of bricks and leave behind one of marble. But to say this of our Most Noble Monarch would be no praise at all. It has to be said that he found a Russia made of wood and created one made of gold.[67]

Feofan, a highly educated man, insisted here on several associations which he deemed necessary for characterizing Peter's reign. First, there is again the identification of Peter with Augustus and by extension with his building programme, which contributed to both national and imperial identity. But Augustus renovated the already existing city by making it splendid with marble. Peter started from scratch and built a 'golden city' in a place where, by general consensus, no city, wooden, marble, or golden, even should have been attempted. Peter willed his Rome into existence, while Augustus merely improved on the old one. Second, the association of the new city with gold brought to mind the idea of the coming Golden Age, and by that association undoubtedly the Fourth Eclogue, to which, as we will see in the following pages, Russian monarchs and men of letters returned continually.

Since Peter was repeatedly construed as the Russian Augustus because of his political and cultural reforms, alluding to Vergil as a pivotal point of reference for glorifying the tsar and his new era became almost a necessity. As Russian literature of the eighteenth century became closely connected with ideas of statehood and nation-building, Vergil was invoked as a source for developing this new self-image, an identity that disassociated itself from the 'backwards' past and looked towards the future.

THE TEXTS

This study is largely based on primary sources which for the most part have not yet been translated into English and thus have received little or no attention from scholars in the West. Some of the most important texts appear in print in English translation for the first time here, and two are offered in full in the appendices to this study.

The authors who are discussed in this book are concerned primarily with the *Aeneid*, although some discussion of the *Eclogues* will be included, especially in connection with the reception of Vergil in the twentieth century. The analysis is presented chronologically in order to trace the development of Russian national identity in the context of Vergilian reception from post-Petrine reforms to the late twentieth century.

The first chapter, 'Vergil at Court', is concerned with imperial aspirations as the initial reaction to the text of the *Aeneid* in Russian literature. Antiokh Kantemir's, Mikhail Lomonosov's, and Mikhail Kheraskov's failed attempts at a national heroic epic are analysed in the context of the relationship between the Russian ruling family and the literature that they encouraged and sponsored. In the same way Vasilii Petrov's first translation of the *Aeneid* reflects the tendency to glorify and idealize the ruling monarch as a way to promote national pride.

The second chapter, 'Subversion and Mockery', analyses various examples of literature that originated in opposition to the courtly attempts to glorify the house of the Romanovs through Vergilian reception. Iakov Kniazhnin's play *Dido* and Nikolai Osipov's *Aeneid Turned Upside Down* are explored in the context of subversion and mockery of the laudatory potential of the *Aeneid*. Kniazhnin, who stands at the very beginnings of Russian mythological tragedy, offered his readers an unusual and politicized interpretation of Book 4 of the *Aeneid*, combined with French and Italian influences on his Vergilian reception. Osipov's burlesque poem, influenced by the travestied *Aeneid*s of Paul Scarron and Aloys Blumauer, mocked the reception of the *Aeneid* by the representatives of Russian classicism: the high genre of the heroic epic created for the literati was transformed into the frivolous adventures and mishaps of an everyday man.

With Alexander Pushkin, discussed in the third chapter, Russian literature enters yet another stage of Vergilian reception. The courtly literature is long forgotten, and so are the monumental attempts at epic grandeur. Pushkin refrains from any open allusion to or evocation of Vergil, limiting himself usually to a few jokes in passing. Instead he writes his own diminutive epic of national pride, the *Bronze Horseman* (*Медный Всадник*). This chapter aims at connecting Pushkin's masterpiece with the Vergilian *Aeneid*.

While the connection of Vergilian reception with Russia's 'messianic' Orthodox mission manifested itself intermittently in secular court literature and even in Petrov's translation, the specific and pointedly deliberate articulation of that mission occurs in the literature of the beginning of the twentieth century and is represented by such formative thinkers as Vladimir Solov'ev, Viacheslav Ivanov, and Georgii Fedotov, who are the subjects of the fourth chapter in this study, 'The Messianic and Prophetic Vergil'.

With Joseph Brodsky, the subject of the fifth chapter, the Russian Vergil enters the stage of postmodernism. Brodsky's Vergilian allusions are numerous and persist in Brodsky's poetics through its entire evolution. However, the monumental themes of either imperial pride or messianic mission become replaced in Brodsky by simpler, mundane, and even base themes. Brodsky reshapes Vergil's Arcadia into a snow-covered terrain, and his Aeneas is a man tormented by the brutalizing price of his heroic destiny. As Brodsky reconfigures different episodes from the Vergilian texts through the lyric prism of human emotion, Vergil remains a constant presence in both his poetry and his essays, and requires a multi-tiered interpretation characteristic of most of Brodsky's writings on ancient themes. The poet moves with ease between ancient and modern, between emotion and detachment, between Russian and English, providing a remarkable closure to the Russian Vergil in the twentieth century.

In the concluding sixth chapter I try to understand and contemplate the fate of Russian translations of Vergil's *Aeneid* after Petrov, their viability, ideology, and value. Two translations are of interest in my analysis: one by Afanasii Fet and another by Valerii Briusov. I compare them against the most widely read translation of the *Aeneid*, by Sergei Osherov, and analyse them synchronically, in the context of their own literary epoch, and diachronically, as the tastes and expectations of the readers of Vergil in Russia change.

In sum, this book aims at a comprehensive understanding of Vergil in the context of the formation and development of Russian national literature. Some works, such as Alexander Pushkin's *Bronze Horseman* or Joseph Brodsky's poetry and essays, are largely familiar to the Western reader. However, the other, less known, texts, are also significant for our understanding of the ways in which Russian national literature developed and perpetuated its self-image through a set of appropriations of and resistances to perhaps the most familiar and revered texts of the European literary canon.

NOTES

1. Bufalini (2006), 156.
2. Bufalini (2006), 162.
3. Garrard (1973), 5.
4. Poe (2003), 12. More on foreign accounts of Russia can be found in Poe (2000, 1995).
5. See Figes (2002), 9.

6. Garrard (1973), 3. Later Russian writers such as Novikov and Fonvizin ridiculed Russian Francomania.

7. Raeff (2003), 120.

8. Uspenskii (1984).

9. See Garrard (1973), 8.

10. See Torlone (2009).

11. Segel (1973), 49.

12. Pypin (1902–13), 3.436–7. See also Jones (1976), 95.

13. Serman (1989), 46.

14. See Segel (1973), 48–9.

15. Prokopovich was also a patron of Antiokh Kantemir, the first poet of the Russian language; Tatishchev, the first Russian historian; and Lomonosov, the most prominent representative of Russian classicism and a polymath. For detailed accounts of Prokopovich's life and activity, see Cracraft (1973).

16. Hosking (1997), xix.

17. Tolz (2001), 10, 15.

18. Bojanowska (2007), 7, for example, correctly argues that Nikolai Gogol's works 'functioned within the imperial public sphere, which was sharply attuned to their nationalistic import'.

19. Maiorova (2010), 5–6.

20. Rogger (1960), 3.

21. Bojanowska (2007), 9. Her italics.

22. Bojanowska (2007), 10.

23. Marshall Poe gives a good review of pre-Petrine Russian history in his essay 'A Distant World' (2003).

24. Greenfeld (1992), 191.

25. Raeff (2003), 136.

26. Greenfeld (1992), 192.

27. Raeff (2003), 136.

28. Wortman (1995), 86.

29. Greenfeld (1992), 227.

30. See Allworth (2003) on Russia's Eastern roots and pre-Petrine exploration of Asia by Russians.

31. Allworth (2003), 139.

32. Greenfeld (1992), 272.

33. Vergil also described Scythia as an unwelcoming icy terrain in the Third Georgic (339–83). See Chapter 5 and the use of Scythia by Brodsky.

34. The phrase is from *Notes from Underground*. Cited in Monas (1983), 28.

35. Cracraft (2003), 27.

36. Wortman (2003), 91.

37. Both interpretations of the *Aeneid* will be discussed in Chapter 1.

38. Gasparov (1979), in the introduction to the collected works of Vergil in Russian.
39. Averintsev (1996), 42.
40. Averintsev (1996), 25.
41. Chlodowski (1984), 608.
42. Toporov (1990), 73.
43. Kalb (2008), 6.
44. Lotman and Uspenskii (1984), 53.
45. Lotman and Uspenskii (1984), 53, point out that 'The "Prusus" of these texts has no historical foundation, but may possibly be the historical Drusus.' As Maiorova (2010), 53–4, notes, the tale of summoning the Varangian princes (Riurik among them) to govern Russia 'occupied center stage in the national mythology' and 'played a significant role in Russian political discourse' because it offered an opportunity 'to claim Russia's kinship with the Western world while at the same time leaving room for constructing the country's identity in contrast to it'.
46. Wortman (1995), *passim*, discusses in great detail the Roman iconography the Russian tsars adopted. Especially interesting is that Falconet cast Peter in his famous statue without a sceptre but 'clothed . . . as a Roman emperor' (134).
47. Kallendorf (2005), 576. See also Wortman (1995), 132ff., concerning the similarities between Peter and Louis XIV.
48. Knabe (2000), 102.
49. Wortman (1995), 14.
50. Kallendorf (2005), 576.
51. Anderson (1967), vi.
52. Wolf (1960), 186–7.
53. Pappaioannou (2009), 99.
54. Chlodowski (1984), 608.
55. Kalb (2008), 10.
56. Raeff (2003), 136.
57. See Clark (2011), 2.
58. In the eighteenth century the poet Sumarokov shifted the focus to St Petersburg by naming it 'the Rome of the North', so that St Petersburg, not Moscow, would be seen as the new Rome. See Baehr (1991), 160. On the connection between the Third Rome doctrine and the ideology of Russian absolute monarchy, see Wolf (1960).
59. Malia (1999), 19.
60. Cited in Wolf (1960), 174.
61. Florenskii (1914), 339.
62. Kalb (2008), 16.
63. Sinitsyna (1998), 13.
64. Jones (1976), 99.

65. See Wolf (1960), 186, citing Filofei's depiction of the church as the woman of Revelations 12:1 in which he states that she (the church) 'fled to the Third Rome, that is Moscow in new great Russia'.
66. See Monas (1983), 29. For the fluctuating perceptions of Moscow and St Petersburg as 'cultural symbols', see Monas (1983).
67. In Lotman and Uspenskii (1984), 62–3.

1

Vergil at Court

RUSSIAN NATIONAL EPICS

As Sparta without Lycurgus, so Russia without Peter would not be able to become famous.

Nikolai Karamzin[1]

Peter's reign introduced into Russian culture a consistent self-identification with the Romans. The enforcement of the Julian calendar (1700), the appellation since 1703 of the fashionable new capital as the new 'Third Rome' (instead of Moscow), Peter's own appropriation of the title '*imperator*' in 1721 and then '*pater patriae*' («отец отечества») in 1724, and the great Russian tsar's predilection for triumphal arches and processions—all of these events demonstrated the tendency of the Russian monarchy to be recognized as an heir to the Roman Empire. One of the most salient examples of expressing the Russian through the Roman was displayed on 30 September 1696 when Peter 'staged a Roman advent to celebrate his victory over the Crimean Tatars at Azov'. He made his armies pass through a classical arch, built for this purpose, whose imagery and inscription ('I have come, I have seen, I have conquered') emphasized Peter's self-equation with Julius Caesar and the 'role of human agency in the achievement' rather than divine intervention.[2] Peter's classical legacy was maintained during his daughter Elizabeth's reign (1741–61) and subsequently by Catherine the Great (r. 1762–96), who wanted, as we will see, to be perceived as an enlightened monarch and a patron of the arts.

This imperial rhetoric required an epic poem since, as Susanna Braund points out, 'in Russia during the eighteenth century, epic emerged as the highest form of poetic achievement'.[3] A canonized patriotic text, which would both educate and delight, was needed to reflect national pride and aspirations. Griffiths and Rabinowitz observe that 'writers of epic...have clear and efficient ways of attaching their works to the tradition as it stretches forward from Homer. Virgil's *Aeneid*, as every schoolboy once knew, begins with a proper obeisance to both Homeric epics.'[4] In eighteenth-century Russia an epic was seen as the beginning of a national consciousness, a way to provide legitimacy to an emerging national identity and connect it with that of the European nations that had long established that identity by a similar connection with the classical heritage. Mikhail Bakhtin, when juxtaposing epic and novel, emphasized the national concerns of epic as genre by singling out its 'three constitutive features': a national past, national tradition as opposed to personal experience, and 'an absolute epic distance' that 'separates the epic world from contemporary reality'.[5] While, according to Bakhtin, 'the world of the epic is the national heroic past',[6] for the Russian poets the additional challenge in glorifying this past lay in their desire to rival the canonized Western epics, especially the ancient ones.

Harold Segel points out that '[t]he Russians shared with Western classicism the greater Western familiarity with and regard for Roman culture as opposed to Greek' and that 'Virgil *not* Homer was the model for the classicist epic.'[7] In the eighteenth century the Russian national experience was consistently paralleled to ancient Rome's, but it was not until the nineteenth century, when 'the old arguments about Russia's identity had been largely resolved', that the interest in Rome would begin to flag and give way to interest in Greece.[8] Andrew Kahn also observes that in turning to Roman models the Russian monarchy and the elite claimed much more than belonging to Europe: 'If Russia could match Rome's discourse, if it could transform its own literary language into the language of epic, then Russia could take its place alongside Rome,' which meant 'asserting Russia's new primacy'.[9] Furthermore, as Craig Kallendorf pithily notes, the *Aeneid* 'served for almost two thousand years as a vehicle through which the powerful elites of Europe visualized the culture they wanted and brought that culture into being'.[10] In eighteenth-century Russia the time was ripe for the creation of an epic of national rebirth in the manner of the *Aeneid*, a poem which, in Katerina Clark's words, 'is effectively a political appropriation of Homeric epic that draws on its aesthetic power in glorifying Rome and its alleged past', and thus is a perfect model for any nation-building discourse.[11] Also of interest

Figure 2. Statue of Mikhail Lomonosov on Mokhovaia St in front of Moscow University's old building. Photograph by Maria Murav'eva.

to the eighteenth-century Russian men of letters was the use of the *Aeneid* as 'the ideological prop for the one-man rule of the emperor',[12] a characteristic, as we will see, extremely attractive for the poets who attempted the Russian national epic.[13]

Mikhail Lomonosov (1711–65; Figure 2), Russian polymath and one of three prominent advocates of Russian classicism[14] along with Vasilii Trediakovskii (1703–69) and Alexander Sumarokov (1718–77), found himself in a challenging and peculiar position when he started writing his epic poem *Peter the Great (Петр Великий)*. Lomonosov, 'this Pindar, Cicero, and Vergil, glory of Russians',[15] was by all means a Russian самородок ('a diamond in the rough'), the son of a peasant and fisherman from Kholmogory on the White Sea, who took his first steps on the path of outstanding academic achievement at the advanced age of twenty, when he entered the Slavonic-Greco-Latin Academy in Moscow. Traditionally regarded as one of the founders of Russian classicism, he proclaimed in his *Rhetoric (Риторика*, 1744) the new rules of Russian versification in which he displayed a thorough knowledge of classical literary heritage. Lomonosov's main poetic interests lay in 'high' heroic genres.[16] He started *Peter the Great* most likely in 1756, but never finished it. Only two books ever appeared, one in 1760, the second in 1761.

Other attempts at a Russian national epic were even less impressive. Alexander Sumarokov first brought out his *Dmitriad* about the Muscovite Duke Dmitrii (1350–89), the victor of the Kulikovo battle, a poem of only one page. In 1730 Antiokh Kantemir also tried to write his 'Petriad, or, Verse Description of the Death of Peter the Great, the Emperor of All Russia' («Петрида, или описание стихотворное смерти Петра Великого, Императора Всероссийского»). A son of a wealthy and noble family of Moldavian gentry, Kantemir was broadly educated and later held a diplomatic post in Europe. Considered the 'first Russian "European" poet'[17] and mostly famous in literary circles for his satires in the style of Horace, Juvenal, and Boileau, Kantemir nonetheless tried his pen at the epic genre. A great admirer of Peter and his reforms, Kantemir limited his poem to lamenting Peter's death instead of glorifying the achievements of his reign. The poem, which ended with the first song, was undoubtedly a panegyric to the tsar-reformer, especially in Kantemir's praise of Peter's new capital and the speed of its rise, but it was also far from resembling anything close to a national epic and a literary masterpiece. In the nineteenth century Alexander Pushkin would return to these motifs but reconfigure the form in which they were delivered.

Lomonosov's attempt must be considered as the first serious approach to the creation of a national epic in the likeness of the *Aeneid*. Catherine's suave and enlightened adviser and the curator of the newly established Moscow University, Ivan Shuvalov, might have been partially responsible for Lomonosov's consent to try his hand at epic. The poem itself, with the subtitle 'heroic poem' («героическая поэма»), was dedicated to Shuvalov and, unlike the *Odyssey*, *Iliad*, or the *Aeneid*, did not start with the invocation of the Muses, but with a word of gratitude to Shuvalov for inspiring him in this task:

> Начало моего великого труда
> Прими, Предстатель Муз, как принимал всегда
> Сложения мои, любя российско слово,
> И тем стремление к стихам давал мне ново.
> Тобою поощрен, в сей путь пустился я:
> Ты будешь оного споспешник и судья.

> Accept the beginning of my great endeavour,
> O Muses' Champion, as you always were
> Accepting of my compositions, loving the Russian word,
> And thus providing me with a new zeal for verse.
> Approved by you I undertake this journey:
> You'll be its companion and its judge.

Shuvalov later claimed that it was he who 'forced' («заставил») Lomonosov 'to make this literary experiment for the empress' («сделать этот опыт для императрицы»).[18] Thus in the tradition of the Roman national epic the poem was in fact commissioned in order to celebrate Russia's tsar and through him the enlightened Russian monarchy. The dedication to Shuvalov and the recognition that he was in fact the main driving force behind the work perhaps also meant to signal the worldly impetus of the new Russian epic. Shuvalov's engagement and participation in the creation of the national epic certainly brings to mind Vergil's relationship with Augustus and the question to what extent poetry that is commissioned can be seen merely as a mouthpiece of the government that sponsored it. It is necessary to dwell here briefly on this parallel in order to better understand the Russian context for a national epic. Karl Galinsky aptly observes in his discussion of patronage in Augustan poetry that 'patronage itself does not produce superior poetry . . . nor did it have to lead to poetic submissiveness'.[19] James Zetzel also points out that when it comes to poetry 'it is not the poets who are the clients, but the patrons'.[20] Vergilian commentators such as Donatus, Tiberius Claudius Donatus, and Servius all asserted that the *Aeneid* was directed solely at the glorification of Augustus. That view, perpetuated from the seventeenth century on, persisted even in such important commentaries as Conington's.[21] While the *Aeneid* was certainly a poem that was supposed to please Augustus, it was not confined to the simplistic scheme of glorifying him or his reign. Augustus better than anybody would have known that such poems have no claim to longevity and fully recognized that poets follow their own agenda. However, the discussions of the darker side of the *Aeneid*, while occasionally debated,[22] did not fully unravel until the 1960s and now constitute a largely accepted aspect of the Roman epic.[23] Vergil began to be seen as a 'purveyor of ambivalence, ambiguities, ironies on a rather massive scale'.[24]

Similarly, Shuvalov's (and the tsarina's) investment in Lomonosov's poetic composition should be seen as an expectation of something more than a panegyric of Russian monarchy. In the tradition of Maecenas' support of the arts, Shuvalov aimed at immortalizing the Russian rulers in poetry that had a future beyond the current reign. In order for the Russian epic to become canonical it was vital that it be a spiritual and poetic reflection of the Russian national experience, the way the *Aeneid* was of the Roman. Vergil from the very beginning of the poem emphasized the price of the Roman achievement (*Aen.* 1.33:

'a matter of so much effort was it to found the Roman nation'—
'*tantae molis erat Romanae condere gentem*') and focused repeatedly
on the sacrifice and sorrow that accompany every victory. Similarly,
Lomonosov was also prone to such troublesome contemplations.

Lomonosov astutely understood the impossibility of imitation or
restoration of the ancient epic in a new epoch or on foreign soil.
However, as he was trying to differentiate his goals from those of the
ancient epic, he also kept a close eye on the great complexity of the
Aeneid and on the ambivalent notions inherent in his national epic.
This view will inform our examination of the text of the poem itself.

From the very beginning Lomonosov sets himself apart from his
ancient epic predecessors although he makes them also his ever-
present interlocutors, the benchmark against which he measures his
own literary goals:

> Хотя во след иду Виргилию, Гомеру,
> Не нахожу и в них довольного примеру.
> Не вымышленных петь намерен я Богов,
> Но истинны дела, великий труд Петров.
> Достойную хвалу воздать сему Герою
> Труднее, нежели как в десять лет взять Трою.
> О если б было то в возможности моей,
> Беглец Виргилиев из отчества Еней
> Едва б с Мазепою в стихах моих сравнился,
> И басней бы своих Виргилий устыдился.
> Уликсовых сирен и Ахиллесов гнев
> Вовек бы заглушил попранный ревом Лев.[25]

> Although I follow the steps of Vergil, Homer,
> I fail to find in them a role model.
> I aim to sing not of invented Gods,
> But the true deeds, the great Petrine labour.
> This task of giving to this Hero his due praise
> Is harder than toppling Troy in ten years,
> If only I possessed the necessary talent,
> That fugitive from his homeland, the Vergilian Aeneas,
> Could hardly even be compared with Mazepa,
> And Vergil would have been ashamed of his fables.
> Ulysses' Sirens and Achilles' wrath
> Would be forever silenced by the roar of the conquered Lion.

For someone unfamiliar with Russian history these opening lines of the
poem require as much deciphering as the opening lines of the *Aeneid* for

the novice in Greco-Roman culture. Lines 15–26 of the poem, following the dedication to Shuvalov, were programmatic in the ancient tradition. According to the tastes of that time, the heroic epic was considered the highest genre possible. Lomonosov in fact was one of the proponents of such a genre classification.[26] However, instead of paying homage to that tradition, Lomonosov distinctly and assertively differentiated his work from those of Vergil and Homer. In a sense he adheres to Voltaire's statement on the epic: 'Il ne suffit pas, pour connaître l'épopée, d'avoir lu Virgile et Homère.'[27] Furthermore, Lomonosov presented that difference almost as an aggressive stance: his subject was something much more serious than 'toppling Troy in ten years'. He not only rejected Vergil as an appropriate model of imitation but called him a writer of 'fables' («басни»), which in Russian has an additional meaning of 'lies', an unexpected statement for the presumed follower of French and German classicism. The French classicist authority Boileau and Lomonosov's German mentor Johann Christoph Gottsched left their imprint on Lomonosov's poetic tastes and aspirations.[28] Therefore we would understandably expect Lomonosov's epic work to be composed in accordance with the requirements associated with European classicism. However, it should be noted that Russian classicism, if we may continue using this term, was rather 'eclectic', and in Jones's words 'as capacious and tolerant as English Neoclassicism whose broad characteristics it shared'.[29] Lomonosov, therefore, demonstrates only superficial allegiance to the precepts of French classicism, mostly in the form of the poem (Alexandrine verse). He wanted his poem to be seen as a historical piece rather than an epic work in the ancient tradition replete with divine struggles and allegorical personages. Following Voltaire's *Henriade*, he invoked for his inspiration the 'endless Wisdom' («Премудрость бесконечна»), much as Voltaire appealed to the Truth ('auguste Vérité').[30] For Lomonosov this primarily meant that his epic account was going to be based in history rather than mythology, a distinction upon which he insisted to show the new departure in epic discourse.

Boileau believed that a truly great epic poem required invention, lofty fantasy, and mythological ornamentation, and even warned the epic poets not to imitate the 'haughty historians'.[31] Although dutiful, respectful imitation of the European models was at the core of Russian classicism, Lomonosov nonetheless keenly understood the alien nature of classical mythology as an appropriate subject matter for a Russian national epic. For him classical values were by no means absolute. He aimed at both drawing inspiration from Russian history more than ancient epics and violating most of the precepts of French classicism. We should not, however, view such a stance by Lomonosov as especially revolutionary.

In choosing the historical figure of Henry IV, a promoter of religious tolerance, as the subject of his *Henriade*, Voltaire was perhaps writing more against the status quo in France than Lomonosov was in Russia. For in the Russia of Lomonosov's time, despite all the classicizing tendencies, the debate between the ancients and the moderns that Voltaire also had to contend with was firmly resolved (with some resistance from Trediakovskii) in favour of the moderns. As Harold Segel observes, Lomonosov's adherence to classicism was more in form than in content.[32] Instead of having a heroic legend as the foundation of his poem he aimed at producing a truly historical account of events in verse where the pathos of French classicism would be replaced with a civic, patriotic feeling. Furthermore, it is important to note that Lomonosov was working on his *Peter the Great* at exactly the same time as Voltaire was commissioned by the Russian government to write his *History of the Russian Empire* under Peter the Great. It is well known that Lomonosov took an active part in collecting for Voltaire different historical documents and then editing his work in 1757 and 1760. However, Lomonosov evidently was not completely satisfied with Voltaire's understanding and explanation of Peter's reign.[33] It is possible that a certain degree of national pride played a role in Lomonosov's desire to offer a Russian version of Peter's reign. Besides, how could Voltaire, a Frenchman, really understand the greatest Russian tsar and reformer, who for all his love of Europe represented an unruly and mysterious Russian spirit? That patriotic pride became the driving force of Lomonosov's poem. In that respect Lomonosov's comparison of Aeneas with Mazepa is also noteworthy, and hardly flattering to Aeneas.

Ivan Mazepa (1640–1709), a Cossack in Russian Ukraine, was made hetman ('leader') in 1687 on the insistence of Prince Galitsyn, adviser to the Russian regent, Sophia Alekseevna. In 1689 he aided the prince in his campaign against the Tatars. Mazepa was able for several years to preserve Ukrainian autonomy while maintaining good relations with Peter the Great. Under Mazepa's direction, churches were built and libraries and educational institutions were also established. He did not, however, attain his goal of uniting all the Ukrainian lands within his territory, which lay on the left bank of the

Dnieper river. Eventually Peter's harsh demands on Ukraine threatened Cossack autonomy. When the Northern War between Russia and Sweden began in 1700, the hetman established secret contact with pro-Swedish elements in Poland. Peter, who trusted Mazepa, refused to believe reports of his treason. In 1708, however, Mazepa openly joined Charles XII of Sweden when the latter's army advanced into Ukraine. The hetman found himself with few enthusiastic followers in this risky venture; most Ukrainian Cossacks remained loyal to the Russian tsar. After the Swedish defeat at Poltava in 1709, Mazepa and Charles fled to Bender in Moldova, where Mazepa died.[34]

Thus Lomonosov explicitly compares Aeneas with the traitor of Peter's great mission to advance Russian national grandeur. Aeneas earns only the title of a 'fugitive from his homeland', the same title that perhaps could be applied to the treacherous Mazepa, and both are stripped of any heroic glory. However, even in this comparison the main goal of Lomonosov becomes clear since Aeneas, a mythological figure, is likened to Mazepa, whose name in history could have provoked only a negative reaction from the Russian reading public, since the memory of Peter's great victory over Sweden remains even today one of the pillars of Russian national pride.

In his mission to sing of a real historical figure Lomonosov sees also a path to his own immortality (l. 36): 'I was chosen by destiny' («Я был судьбой избран»). Peter's greatness will confer the immortal glory upon the poet. The prologue in fact contains lines reminiscent of Horace's *Exegi monumentum*, yet another of Lomonosov's nods towards classicism (35–40):

> Желая в ум вперить дела Петровы громки,
> Описаны в моих стихах прочтут потомки.
> Обильные луга, прекрасны бреги рек
> И только где живет Российский человек
> И почитающи Россию все языки,
> У коих по трудам прославлен Петр Великий,
> Достойну для него дадут сим честь стихам
> И станут их гласить по рощам и лесам.
> О, как я возношусь своим успехом мнимым,
> Трудом желаемым, но непреодолимым.

> Striving to commit to their minds the famous deeds of Peter,
> The descendants will read about them in my poems.
> The fertile meadows, enchanting shores of rivers,
> And every land where a Russian man lives,
> And every language that holds Russia in esteem,

And where Peter is renowned for his deeds,
They all will pay their homage to my verses
And will recite them through groves and forests.
Oh, how will I soar because of my imagined success,
Through my toil so welcome and yet insurmountable.

Such a grandiose promise certainly would engender lofty expectations that would not be fulfilled by just the two books that followed. Lomonosov himself perhaps understood that the task at hand was more than he could handle. The last two lines of the passage above testify to the ambivalence about the poetic path on which he was about to embark.

After defining his poetic goals as different from those of his ancient predecessors, Lomonosov in the 'First Song' («Песнь первая») describes Peter's sailing north and his conquest of the Swedish fleet. His song echoes Vergil's *Arma virumque cano*:

Пою премудрого Российскаго Героя,
Что грады новые, полки и флоты строя,
От самых нежных лет со злобой вел войну,
Сквозь страхи проходя, вознес свою страну;
Смирил злодеев внутрь и вне попрал противных,
Рукой и разумом сверг дерзостных и льстивых,
Среди военных бурь науки нам открыл
И мир делами весь и зависть удивил.

I sing of the wisest Russian Hero,
Who building new cities, armies, and fleets,
From a tender early age waged war with fury,
And overcoming fears, extolled his country high,
Suppressed the villains inside and trampled foreign foes,
With his hand and mind he overthrew the arrogant and
    the fawning,
Amid the storms of war revealed to us the sciences
And amazed the whole jealous world with his deeds.

Like Vergil, Lomonosov mentions 'the man and the wars', fears and hardships which Peter, the Russian national hero and one-word cornerstone of the new foundation story, had to endure in his attempt to accomplish his plans for Russia. What is clearly not a Vergilian touch is the penultimate line. Peter brought to Russia scientific progress («науки») and because of that he is to Lomonosov not just a military figure or the founder of the new historical era, but a man of intellectual power. That is why Lomonosov's muse to whom he appeals for help in his endeavour is the 'endless Wisdom' («Премудрость бесконечна»). Lomonosov's preoccupation with Peter's mission as reformer of Russia and a harbinger of its progress and expansion becomes even clearer in Peter's speech in which he encourages his comrades after they disembarked to escape the raging storm, again a nod to Vergil (171–4):

> Колумбы Росские, презрев угрюмый рок,
> Меж льдами новый путь отворят на восток,
> И наша досягнет в Америку держава.
> Но ныне настоит в войнах иная слава.

> Russian Columbuses, ignoring sombre fate,
> Through the ice will open the way to the east,
> And our power shall reach as far as America.
> But now a different type of glory urges us to war.

Aeneas' famous speech in Book 1 of the *Aeneid* delivered amid the raging storm to his despairing comrades is palpable in these lines, as well as Anchises' speech in Book 6 which predicts to Aeneas the future glory of Rome. However, Lomonosov, while evoking the hallmark moments of the *Aeneid*, again distances himself from the Roman epic. His comparison is modern, 'cutting edge', looking towards the future not the past. Christopher Columbus's 'discovery' of America is Lomonosov's point of reference here, not the Roman foundation myth. Vergil is used as an interlocutor, and Aeneas' address to his comrades combined with Anchises' prophecy receives a poetic homage, but the new, exciting world, the real world of geographic discovery, is what attracts Lomonosov. Here, as Liubov' Kulakova notes in her commentary to the poem, Lomonosov ascribes to Peter his own favourite thought about opening new routes through the 'Siberian ocean' into the Far East and India.[35] The Russian polymath reveals his global aspirations in these lines. In Richard Wortman's words, Lomonosov offers here 'a different measure of Russian European identity'.[36] In order to achieve a glory equal to that of the European states, Russia needed to develop as a sea power and establish extensive commerce with foreign nations. Lomonosov saw Peter as someone who expanded Russian horizons both literally and metaphorically. Conquering Charles XII gave Russia an opportunity to build a city near the Baltic Sea ('a window onto Europe', as Pushkin later phrased it). But why stop there? Why not go all the way to India and beyond? The poem that started as a simple account of Peter's victorious march against Sweden acquired a much more poignant message: the potential of our Russia is unlimited, its might untamed. The great tsar knew this, and the mission of his descendants is to continue his undertaking.

In 1762, one year after he abandoned his attempt to write a Russian national epic, Lomonosov composed a memorandum for Tsarevich Paul, 'A Brief Description of Various Voyages in Northern Seas and Indication of a Possible Passage through the Siberian Ocean to East India.' In this work, as Richard Wortman notes, Lomonosov expressed his immediate concern 'to discover and open a northeast passage that would make it possible for Russian ships to sail across the Arctic sea into the Pacific'.[37] What we have in *Peter the Great* is not a poem about the past and not even the 'myth of Peter', but an expression of the same concern about Russian expansion, a pointed didactic address by Lomonosov to his compatriots similar in its goals to some of the rhetoric found in the *Aeneid*. This patriotic didacticism is also coupled with some pessimistic contemplations not altogether unfamiliar to Vergil's readers as well.

The second book narrates Peter's travel over the White Sea to the Swedish citadel of Schlüsselburg and the subsequent siege of the citadel that resulted in a Swedish defeat. On his way Peter inspects the mountains as possible sources for mining metals necessary for his army and fleet. He intends to build his great new city, which will rise on the shores of the Neva river. The main part of the song is devoted to the siege of Schlüsselburg and a quite graphic depiction of the battles. However, Lomonosov does not rejoice in the terrifying graphic scenes of war which he describes to his reader. He concludes the narration of the siege on an entirely unexpected note (1087–1116):

> О смертные, на что вы смертию спешите?
> Что прежде времени вы друг друга губите?
> Или ко гробу нет кроме войны путей?
> Везде нас тянет рок насильством злых когтей!
> Коль многи, вышедши из матерней темницы,
> Отходят в тот же час в мрак черныя гробницы!
> Иной усмешкою отца повеселил
> И очи вдруг пред ним во веки затворил.
> Готовому вступить во брачные чертоги
> Пронзает сердце смерть и подсекает ноги.
> В средине лучших лет иной, устроив дом,
> Спокойным говорит, льстясь здрав пребыть, умом:

«Отныне поживу и наслаждусь трудами»,
Но час последний был, скончался со словами.
Коль многи обстоят болезни и беды,
Которым человек всегда подвержен ты!
Кроме что немощи, печали внутрь терзают,
Извне коль многия напасти окружают:
Потопы, бури, мор, отравы, вредный гад,
Трясение земли, свирепы зверы, глад,
падение домов и жрущие пожары,
И град, и молнии гремящие удары,
Болота, лед, пески, земля, вода и лес
Войну с тобой ведут и высота небес.
Еще ли ты войной, еще ль не утомился
И сам против себя во век вооружился?
Но оправдал тебя военным делом Петр.
усерд к наукам был, миролюбив и щедр,
Притом и мечь простер и на море, и в поле.
Сомнительно, чем Он, войной иль миром, боле.

Oh, mortals, why are you in a hurry to die?
Why do you destroy each other prematurely?
Or is there not another way to the grave?
Everywhere the evil claws of fate pull us with force!
So many, barely out of their maternal prison,
Depart in the same hour into the darkness of the
    accursed tomb!
Some after delighting their father with a smile
Suddenly closed their eyes forever.
A man ready to enter his marriage chamber
Death pierces in the heart and cuts his feet from
    underneath him.
In the middle of his life, someone having settled his
    household,
Confident in his health, says with a calm mind:
'Now I can live and enjoy the fruit of my labours,'
But that was his final hour and he dies in the middle of
    his sentence.
There are so many diseases and disasters,
That befall you, o human!
Apart from the infirmities, sorrows assail you inside,
And on the outside so many are the calamities:
Floods, storms, pestilence, poisons, harmful pests,
Earthquakes, savage beasts, and famine,

Collapse of houses, all-devouring fires,
Hail, and the resounding strikes of lightning,
Swamps, ice, sands, earth, water, and forest
Wage war with you and so does the highness of the sky.
Aren't you, aren't you exhausted by war
And against yourself you take on armour?
But Peter justified your acts with his campaign,
Towards science he was zealous, peace-loving,
　　and generous,
He extended his sword both on sea and land,
And it is unclear whether he is greater at peace or at war.

This is undoubtedly an odd closure to a book that purportedly aimed to ordain a Russian military triumph. Lomonosov the scientist shines through in this passage full of Lucretian overtones. At the end of the depressing litany of the scourges that threaten human existence he attempts a somewhat unconvincing return to his main theme and hero, Peter, by asserting that Peter's war was an example of the occasional necessity of violent resolutions of conflicts. But this recovery of the theme is contrived and what we take away from the second book is that fear of death, man's inability to conquer it, and his defeat in the face of natural disasters are his ultimate concerns. Is this, we might ask, an appropriate 'digression' in an epic poem that was intended to glorify Russia's greatest monarch? If Lomonosov was following Vergil in making the ruler a strong presence in his poem, if Peter is in fact the Russian Augustus, the august inspiration for his poetic talent, then why does Lomonosov introduce into his epic these pessimistic ruminations on human frailty? Isn't Peter an exemplar of an opposing kind of concept, namely, that nothing can stop a great human spirit and that historical progress in the hands of an outstanding individual can overcome years of fear, hardships, and defeat? Perhaps Aeneas' *olim et haec meminisse iuvabit* ('this too will be at some point pleasing to remember', 1.203) would in fact be appropriate for this occasion?

Although the poem was never finished, Lomonosov gave us a key to understanding his view of Peter's reign. All of Peter's reforms and all of his military deeds were directed towards one goal, to usher in the Enlightenment of Russia. In Lomonosov's opinion the goal justi-fied even the bloodshed which was necessary for asserting Russia's authority as an equal among European nations. The poem, it seems, was conceived both as a glorification and as a justification of Peter's absolute, single-minded pursuit of suppressing his enemies and bringing Russia into the modern age. However, this single-mindedness proved to be an insufficient focus to sustain a fully developed national epic. The more pessimistic thoughts started to undermine the panegyric, a rather significant development in literary consciousness, one that would open, as we will see later, a new path for Alexander Pushkin, who would masterfully combine national pride with the contemplation of human frailty.

Shuvalov, Lomonosov's dedicatee and patron, himself wrote that Lomonosov interrupted his work on the poem because 'he was extremely busy, and the time in which his fantasy was to take place was too close for comfort' («был много занят, и время для фантазии было очень близко»).[38] This meant that Lomonosov found himself too close to Peter's epoch to be able to write about it *sine ira et studio*. We have seen that one of Bakhtin's 'constitutive features' of epic was the distance that must separate the events described in the epic from contemporary reality. Despite Augustus' presence in Vergil's poem, the Roman poet was still writing about the foundation of Rome and a mythological hero whose duty and sacrifice he presented as the backbone of the current rule. Lomonosov had to deal with the historical and not the mythological as his subject, and a quite recent ancestor of the present ruler. While this challenge contributed to the poem's failure, it was most likely not the only reason. The difficult circumstances of the final years of Lomonosov's life and his more pressing interests in science might have diminished the zeal and inspiration for the poetic oeuvre.

The unfinished poem, however, received its share of success. Lomonosov's contemporary S. G. Domashnev wrote: 'Lomonosov was the first one who on a harmonious and magnificent lyre extolled the deeds of the Great Peter' («Ломоносов был первый, который по стройной и великолепной лире возгремел дела Великого Петра»).[39] Shuvalov also considered the poem one of the greatest poetic achievements of his age. Even Sumarokov's negative reaction to his rival's poem received a rebuttal from none other than the great writer Gavrila Derzhavin (1743–1816), who wrote an epigram in Lomonosov's defence.[40] Two other contemporaries of Lomonosov, M. N. Murav'ev and K. A. Kondratovich, even translated the unfinished poem into Latin, thus asserting Lomonosov's rightful place within the ancient epic continuity.

Not until the end of the eighteenth century do negative reactions to Lomonosov's attempt at a national epic begin to surface in the press.

Both Alexander Radishchev and Nikolai Karamzin thought that Lomonosov's poetic talent was inadequate for such a monumental task. Karamzin's criticism was harsh: 'for the epic poem of our time he [Lomonosov], it seems, did not possess a sufficient strength of imagination, that wealth of ideas, that all-embracing vision, art and taste, which are necessary for depicting a picture of the world replete with ethical choices and lofty, heroic passions' («для эпической поэзии нашего века не имел он, кажется, достаточной силы воображения, того богатства идей, того всеобъемлющего взора, искусства и вкуса, которые нужны для представления картины нравственного мира и возвышенных, иройских страстей»).[41] In the nineteenth century Lomonosov's poem did not fare any better. The most influential critical voice of that time belonged to Vissarion Belinskii (1811–48), whose nickname 'Furious Vissarion' («неистовый Виссарион») was given to him by his contemporaries for his unrestrained and often ruthless judgements. He called the poem 'wild' and 'pompous' («дикая» and «напыщенная») and saw it as 'a tour de force of imagination, standing on its hind legs' («tour de force воображения, поднятого на дыбы»).[42]

Whatever the quality of the poem, one thing was clear: the Russian national heroic epic remained a dream, as Lomonosov's admirable attempt at rivalling Vergil was short-lived, serving as a warning for poets of subsequent generations. Surprisingly enough, however, this did not deter their efforts.

MIKHAIL KHERASKOV'S *ROSSIADA*

Херасков был человек добрый, умный, благонамеренный и, по своему времени, отличный версификатор, но решительно не поэт.[43]

Kheraskov was a kind, intelligent, and well-intentioned man and, for his time, an excellent versifier, but decidedly not a poet.

Vissarion Belinskii

A subsequent attempt at a Russian national epic, more specifically the *Rossiada* by Mikhail Kheraskov (1733–1807) published in twelve cantos in 1779,[44] was even less successful and by all accounts more tedious. Unlike Lomonosov, however, Kheraskov did not focus so much on a single historical figure but rather on a formative event for Russia's national identity. His poem narrates the destruction of the Kazan khanate by Ivan the Terrible in the sixteenth century, an episode that signified Russia's first step towards independence and a European Christian identity.

Like Lomonosov, the well-educated Kheraskov was also aware of his predecessors in epic. In fact when he published the *Rossiada*, he attached to it his own preface, «Взгляд на эпические поэмы» ('A look at epic poems'), which was a reflection on Voltaire's 'Essai sur la poésie épique'. Here Kheraskov offers his homage to the *Iliad* and the *Odyssey*, and then summarizes the *Aeneid*:

> В «Илиаде» Гомер воспевает гнев Ахиллесов, за похищение его невольницы Бризеиды царем Агамемноном, гнев толико бедственный грекам и Пергаму; кровавые битвы, пагубу осаждающих и пагубу осажденных троян. Патрокл, друг Ахиллесов, убит Гектором — он мстит за своего друга — убивает храброго Гектора, и тем поэма оканчивается.

> В «Одиссее» воспето десятилетнее странствование Итакского царя Улисса; возвращение его в дом свой и страшное избиение любовников Пенелопиных...

> Вергилий в несравненной своей «Энеиде» воспел побег Энеев из разоренной греками Трои, прибытие его в Карфагену, любовь его с Дидоною, неверность его к сей несчастной царице. Другой побег его, в Италию, где, убив Турна, сопрягается он с Лавиниею, невестою сего почтенного князя.

> In the *Iliad* Homer sings of the wrath of Achilles on account of his kidnapped concubine Briseis by King Agamemnon, the wrath equally destructive for the Greeks and for Troy; bloody battles, the destruction of the besiegers and of the besieged Trojans. Patroclus, Achilles' friend, is killed by Hector—he avenges his friend—kills the brave Hector, and so the poem ends.

> In the *Odyssey* the ten-year-long journey of the Ithacan king Ulysses is sung; his return home and his brutal massacre of Penelope's suitors...

> Vergil in his unrivalled *Aeneid* extolled Aeneas' flight from Troy destroyed by the Greeks, his arrival in Carthage, his love of Dido, his betrayal of this unhappy queen. And also [he extolled] his other flight, to Italy, where, after killing Turnus, he married Lavinia, the fiancée of this esteemed prince.

This rather simplistic rendition of the ancient epics is not accidental. Kheraskov simply outlines their main plot without any value judgement or appreciation of the poetic qualities of the compositions. He proceeds in the same manner to summarize Milton's *Paradise Lost*, Voltaire's *Henriade*, Luís de Camões's *Lusiads*, and Lucan's *Pharsalia*. However, the writing style changes once Kheraskov has to face the failure of the Russian national epic that preceded his effort, that of Lomonosov:

> Для тех сие пишу, которые думают, будто эпическая поэма похвальною песнею быть должна. Эпическая поэма заключает какое-нибудь важное, достопамятное, знаменитое приключение, в бытиях мира случившееся и которое имело следствием важную перемену, относящуюся до всего человеческого рода, — таков есть «Погубленный рай» Мильтонов; или воспевает случай, в каком-нибудь государстве происшедший и целому народу к славе, к успокоению или, наконец, ко преображению его послуживший, — такова должна быть поэма «Петр Великий», которую, по моему мнению, писать еще не время. Два великие духа принимались петь Петра Великого, г. Ломоносов и Томас; оба начали — оба не кончили.

> I am writing this for those who think that an epic poem must be a laudatory song. An epic poem contains in itself some important, memorable, famous event that happened in the world and led to a major change relevant to the whole human race: such is Milton's *Paradise Lost*. Or an epic poem extols an event that has happened in some country and that has served to bring about glory, peace, and finally transformation: such must be the poem *Peter the Great*, which, in my opinion, it is not yet time to write. Two great spirits tried to sing of Peter the Great, Lomonosov and Thomas; both started and both did not finish.

There are several aspects of this passage that are noteworthy since it is an expression of Russian 'anxiety of influence'. Kheraskov is significantly more contemplative and expressive in these lines than in his evaluation of preceding epics. His summary of the ancient epic seems in comparison almost dismissive, a mere fulfilment of dutiful homage but without any awe or reverence for the efforts of his predecessors. This was perhaps Kheraskov's self-conscious way of offering an explanation as to why Russian literature was so unlucky when it came to the national epic.

Furthermore, while Lomonosov was a household name, the name of Antoine Léonard Thomas (1732–85) was less familiar because he was a somewhat obscure French writer, an author of panegyrics and poems among which are fragments of his own *Petriad*, a poem in laudation of the great tsar. By grouping Lomonosov and Thomas together, Kheraskov clearly is trying to set himself apart from all the previous attempts at a Russian national epic and prepare the reader for a poem different from a mere encomium of the past ruler. He acknowledges the need for an epic about Peter, but then adds a mysterious comment that the time for it has not yet come. Why? Is he referring to the remark made by Shuvalov about the proximity of Peter's reign, which made it hard to present an objective view? Or did he feel the urge to explain why his epic theme is different? The latter explanation seems to be more accurate. In accordance with Lomonosov, Kheraskov had sufficient support in Voltaire's approach to the epic to move towards historical themes in lieu of mythological ones. Thus he chose a theme that follows his precept that an epic poem must narrate an event that changed the face of a nation:

Горе тому россиянину, который не почувствует, сколь важную пользу, сколь сладкую тишину и сколь великую славу приобрело наше отечество от разрушения казанского царства!

Woe to that Russian who will not feel what a great benefit and what sweet calmness and great glory our fatherland has acquired because of the destruction of the kingdom of Kazan!

In the same vein Kheraskov starts his ambitious poem:

Пою от варваров Россию свобожденну,
Попранну власть татар и гордость низложенну;
Движенье древних сил, труды, кроваву брань,
России торжество, разрушенну Казань.

I sing of Russia freed of the barbarians,
The trampled powers of the Tatars and their toppled pride;
The movement of ancient forces, their toils, bloody battles,
The triumph of Russia, destroyed Kazan.

Instead of appealing to the muse, Kheraskov evokes the 'spirit of versification' («стихотворенья дух»), whom he asks to grant him the necessary inspiration for his 'feeble and humble work'. What follows is a long narrative of Russia's hard-won triumph over the khanate of Kazan, influenced most likely by authentic historical sources such as the *History of Kazan* (*Kazanskaiia istoriia*), composed by eyewitnesses of the historical events that interested Kheraskov, and by *The*

History of the Grand Duke of Muscovy (*Istoriia o velikom kniaze moskovskom*) by Prince Andrei Kurbskii, a contemporary of Ivan the Terrible. The heroes of the poem combined in themselves the character traits collected from all kinds of epic poems: classical was combined with biblical, Homer and Vergil with Tasso. Alongside Eros, Cypris, and Mars we can also find the monsters from Russian folklore Zmei Tugarin and Idolishche Poganoe.

The poem had a well-defined patriotic goal. It was ideally intended to evoke in every Russian's heart a feeling of national pride and awe at past accomplishments. Could have there been a better subject for an epic than one about Russian liberation from the Tatars? This was supposed to be a far-reaching narrative. As Serman observes, 'over against enchantments, wizardry and demonic forces aiding Kazan there are counterposed the Orthodox Russian troops, Christian saints and martyrs who conquer the evil powers of pagan Islam'.[45] As has been discussed, Russia did not always fully identify itself with Western values, but in the eighteenth century many West-defying postures were abandoned: the light had to come from the West. Kheraskov created the narrative of struggle between East and West, in which Russia was supposed to assert itself as a rightful heir both to the secular Enlightenment and to the Christian piety of the West. Casting Russia as a 'Western' force was extremely important for Kheraskov, considering that Russia at least in the eyes of Europe always had, if not fully an Eastern, at any rate a 'dual identity'.[46]

Even Ivan the Terrible was stripped in the poem of all of his uncivilized (perhaps Mongol-like?) brutality unbecoming of a Western monarch and emerged as a philosopher king, magnanimous, generous, and selfless, who shared with one of his subjects his last gulp of water. This epic would serve as the perfect symbiosis of two Russian Vergils: the patriotic and the messianic. Like the *Aeneid* it was, despite its historical plot, directed towards its contemporary audience and its values. The poem was written during a period when Russia was at war with Turkey[47] and not long before Russia's annexation of the Crimea, when the idea of Christian triumph over Islam seemed within reach. The poem contains ample praise of Catherine, who was called upon to make the 'eastern moon' tremble and give people 'divine' laws. The whole poem in fact is dedicated to Catherine, which made the pronounced liberalism of the poem much less credible.

However, despite all the contemporary and well-timed rhetoric, Kheraskov's poem was yet another failed attempt at a Russian epic of national pride. The poem is seemingly interminable. Even the plot line concerned with the love story of the Tatar queen Sumbeka, inspired perhaps by Dido, requires considerable patience. In his foreword to the poem, before listing his epic predecessors, Kheraskov tries to explain his choice of Ivan the Terrible as his epic hero, who was far from the ideal example of piety and heroic behaviour in the minds of Russian readers. Kheraskov rejected all the 'rumours' about the infamous monarch, blaming them strangely on 'foreign writers':

> Иностранные писатели, сложившие нелепые басни о его суровости, при всем том по многим знаменитым его делам великим мужем нарицают. Сам Петр Великий за честь поставлял в мудрых предприятиях сему государю последовать. История затмевает сияние его славы некоторыми ужасными повествованиями, до пылкого нрава его относящимися, — верить ли столь не свойственным великому духу повествованиям, оставляю историкам на размышление. Впрочем, безмерные царские строгости, по которым он Грозным применован, ни до намерения моего, ни до времени, содержащем в себе целый круг моего сочинения, вовсе не касаются.

> Foreign writers, who composed ridiculous tales about his [Ivan the Terrible's] severity, despite that call him a great man because of his famous deeds. Peter the Great himself considered it an honour to follow this monarch in his endeavours. The shining of his glory is overshadowed in history by some horrible tales related to his unruly temper,—but whether one should believe these tales so incompatible with the great spirit, I will leave that for the historians to judge. In fact, the boundless kingly punishments of his, because of which he was called the Terrible, relate neither to my intent, nor to the time which my work encompasses.

It would be hard to believe that any Russian reader would have found this explanation satisfactory. Peter, as an epic hero, was enough of a problem since his autocratic tendencies were well known. He did in fact build his dream city on the bones of millions of serfs, and against all reason. But Ivan the Terrible was altogether a different story. He was the despot par excellence, an indisputable tyrant in the old mould who might have reminded the 'Russian Europeans' of their Eastern roots, and one from whom the Russian monarchy was trying to distance itself. As an epic hero, even under the guise of a truly pious Christian liberator of Russia from the hateful Islamic yoke, he was still far from credible.

Another reason for this disappointing failure in composing the Russian national epic can be found in the later reception of Kheraskov. A. N. Pypin notes that 'Kheraskov's creations were glorified but they were fruitless' («Творения Хераскова прославлялись, но были видимо бесплодны»).[48] Serman also points out that the political and religious aspirations of Kheraskov's epic left little imprint on subsequent generations.[49] Kheraskov's literary reputation did not live long. Belinskii, quite the merciless judge of eighteenth-century literature, considered the fall of Kheraskov's literary fame an indisputable fact. Although Belinskii acknowledged Kheraskov's merits in the development of Russian literature, his appraisal as we can see in the epigraph to this subchapter was nonetheless rather scathing.

No judgement can be harsher in Russian literary circles than that which brands a poet as 'an excellent versifier, but decidedly not a poet'. Poets in Russian literature, most certainly those after Pushkin and during Belinskii's time, constituted a special breed, almost a rival authority endowed with the power to affect minds and effect change. They were a rare, isolated, and very exclusive group, acceptance into which required what the Roman poets referred to as *ingenium*. According to Belinskii, Kheraskov simply lacked the talent of a true poetic genius and was unable to take on the task of creating a Russian national epic because it was not on a par with his *Naturgenie*. Conscientious poetic composition can be skilful but will never be the same as verse truly inspired by the Muses. Russians were and to this day remain strong believers that poets cannot be conscientious, something that can have a damning effect on their creations.

For Lomonosov and Kheraskov, the exploitation of historical themes to enhance a truly national theme in epic did not change the fact that the heroic poem even in the tradition of Voltaire, not Vergil, was ill-suited to Russian letters. Kheraskov's accomplishment must nonetheless be thought of as a significant step, given that he completed twelve cantos and rose above the level of mere epigone tradition.

Further attempts at creating a classical verse epic continued until the 1830s. The most significant exercises in this genre belong to Prince Sergei Shirinskii-Shikhmatov (1783–1837), whose epic poetry was mixed with lyric elements. His best-known works, *Пожарский, Минин, Гермоген, или спасенная Россия* (*Pozharskii, Minin, Hermogenus, or Russia saved*, 1807) and *Петр Великий: Лирическое песнопение в восьми песнях* (*Peter the Great: A lyric epopoeia in eight cantos*, 1810), show his awareness of the preceding epic tradition and are characterized also by a solemn 'high' style and overuse of Slavonicisms in avoidance of foreign words.[50] His insistence on such a style, which he tried to introduce into all of his literary works, met with acerbic ridicule from such literary authorities as Batiushkov and Pushkin, and because of that they are now largely forgotten.

The following chapter will discuss how the epic poem in travesty became more popular in the eighteenth century than the solemnity of the classical epic. However, it is worth contemplating why a national epic in a truly Vergilian mould of the national idea did not become popular or even possible in Russian literature. At the next stage in the development of the Russian verse epic some tendencies come into focus. The Romantic period in Russian letters is characterized by the influence of Lord Byron, especially his 'Eastern Poems'. What the Russian reader found attractive was not an abstract national idea or even a historical milestone, but a plot dominated by a single hero, preferably a brooding, romantic, even mysterious personality, who undergoes exotic adventures in some remote land. Pushkin's so-called 'southern' poems are classic examples. 'The Prisoner of the Caucasus' («Кавказский пленник», 1821) and 'The Fountain of Bakhchisarai' («Бахчисарайский фонтан», 1823), written in iambic tetrameter rather than Alexandrine verse, contemplate, despite their heavy 'Byronism', the cultural and social problems of Russian life in the 1820s. Both of these poems, masterpieces of Pushkin's unrivalled genius, also convey 'a degree of fascination with the aura of the east'[51] from which the attempts at epic painstakingly tried to distance themselves. But Pushkin's poems are most certainly removed from the epic heaviness and inflated grandeur of Lomonosov and Kheraskov.[52] These romantic poems became one of the most prolific genres in Russian literature. The more mature Pushkin evolved them into writings of historical and social import such as *The Bronze Horseman*: finally, perhaps, the true Russian national epic about Peter and Peter's city.

In the eighteenth century, however, the literary landscape was just beginning to take shape and was not yet primed for the arrival of such an epic. The representatives of Russian classicism were taking their first timid steps in shaping a national tradition, which at that time became profoundly conditioned by the ideology and politics of Russian monarchs. This conditioning becomes especially apparent in the earliest attempt at translating the *Aeneid* into Russian.[53]

VASILII PETROV: TRANSLATING DIDO

Посем скажу какой похвален перевод:
Имеет в слоге всяк различие народ.
Что очень хорошо на языке французском,
То может в точности быть скаредно на русском.
Не мни, переводя, что склад в творце готов;
Творец дарует мысль, но не дарует слов.
В спряжение речей его ты не вдавайся
И свойственно себе словами украшайся . . .
Коль речи и слова поставишь без порядка,
И будет перевод твой как некая загадка,
Которую никто не отгадает ввек;
То даром, что слова все точно ты нарек.
Когда переводить захочешь беспорочно,
Не то, — творцов мне дух яви и силу точно.

Now I will say what translation is praiseworthy:
Nations differ in their style of expression.
Something that is very pleasant in French
May appear completely unappealing in Russian.
Do not assume, while translating, that the original
Offers you a ready-made style,
The author rewards you with the idea but not the words.
Do not try to delve into the structure of his narrative,
Seek beauty in the words that are fitting for you . . .
If you arrange your words without any order,
Your translation will appear as some sort of a riddle,
Which nobody can solve, no matter how long they try,
Even if you rendered each word quite precisely.
If you want to translate without a flaw,
Your main goal is to reflect exactly
The spirit and the power of the original.[54]

Background

This assertive instruction is taken from 'Epistola I' by Alexander Sumarokov, a verse composition written in 1747, which played a significant role in the formation and formulation of poetic principles in Russia. Sumarokov, along with Vasilii Trediakovskii and Mikhail Lomonosov, was one of the most prominent representatives of Russian classicism, as their literary epoch came to be called. In 1748 he published the 'Epistola I' and the 'Epistola II' in a separate edition which intended to answer for Russian readers two questions: can the Russian language be used to translate works of literature from other languages, and can it become the basis for the creation of a truly national literature? This new era in Russian translating practices began to distance itself from the influence of the outdated and cumbersome Old Slavonic and to develop the models from which the nascent national literature would draw its inspiration.

The beginnings of translation in Russia, as Maurice Friedberg points out, are difficult to pinpoint, but a consistent and continuous line of literary translations originated in the middle of the eighteenth century, during the era of classicism, which, for at least a brief time after Petrine reforms, became the dominant movement in Russian literature.[55] Most of the earlier attempts at translation were connected with the need for Christian texts as a result of Russian acceptance of Christianity in Kievan Rus' in the late tenth century and the baptism of Vladimir (988 CE), the first Christian Russian prince.[56] Before Peter there were not many secular texts, and most certainly not many translations of Greco-Roman pagan texts that belong to this early era. The shift from religious translations to secular texts was vigorously initiated by Peter, who, as we have seen, became preoccupied with rivalling European nations in every cultural sphere. This emulation also included a dramatic increase in the procurement of adequate translations of Greco-Roman classics. The tsar's energetic actions demonstrate that Russian literary culture was still uncertain of its own status and tended to expend more effort in undertaking translations from the works that belonged to a more confident literary tradition.[57] The great tsar-reformer went so far as to legally formulate translation practices. In 1724 he issued a decree (*ukaz*) according to which the translations from foreign languages must avoid 'high-style Slavonic words', perhaps in order to decisively separate religious texts from secular ones.[58] Furthermore he encouraged translators to study not just the language from which they were translating but also the subject matter of the work. The decree also stipulated that the language into which the work was translated must be the mother tongue of the translator,[59] which would thus avoid awkward and literal translations by the foreigners who at that time flocked to the newly established court in the splendid Petrine capital of St Petersburg. Peter was a strong proponent of non-literal translation and promoted clarity against precision.[60] As we saw in the introduction, in the eighteenth century the Russian literary landscape rather rapidly achieved a degree of sophistication that became fertile ground for absorbing and acculturating the literary legacies of European cultures. As Vladimir Toporov points out, a 'translation often can become that very space in which something bright and entirely new, something opening a different perspective arises' and eventually awakens the dormant potential of the national literature.[61]

In order to appreciate the value and unusual nature of Vasilii Petrov's first Russian translation of the *Aeneid*, we must first put Petrov's translation into the context of Russian translation practices in general and translations of ancient epics specifically. Eighteenth-century men of letters had complete faith in the ability of the Russian language to render adequately any foreign text. As early as 1755, at the dawn of the Russian national literature, and long before any canonized or viable translations were produced, Lomonosov stated with the utmost confidence that the Russian language had 'the magnificence of Spanish, the vivaciousness of French, the robustness of German, the tenderness of Italian, but furthermore the wealth and powerful dense imagery of Greek and Latin . . . The compelling eloquence of Cicero, Vergil's magnificent gravity, Ovid's pleasant utterances do not lose their dignity in the Russian language.'[62] Sumarokov supported that opinion by decisively stating in 'Epistola I': 'our beautiful language is apt for anything'.[63] Greenfeld notes that Lomonosov's comments about the all-encompassing capabilities of Russian show the emerging 'eighteenth-century linguistic nationalism', since both he and Sumarokov understood that 'the greatness of the nation hinged on the greatness of its language'. Russian, in the eighteenth century only 'a newcomer to the world of literary creation', would eventually become 'the language of some of the greatest writers of all ages'.[64] Both Lomonosov and Sumarokov were looking decades or even centuries ahead with proleptic vision, which took considerable time and effort to actualize.

Vasilii Trediakovskii was the first of three literary leaders who understood the necessity of a comprehensive approach to translation practices. He designed the principles of both prose and verse translation, connecting his theory with the overall goal of 'cleansing' the Russian literary language of burdensome Old Slavonic archaisms and creating a new system of versification, which he initiated with his treatise *A New and Brief Method for Composing Russian Verse* (1735). Frolov emphasizes Trediakovskii's assertion in the foreword to his first book, the *Journey to the Isle of Love* (*Езда в остров любви*, 1730), which was a translation of a French novel, *Le voyage a l'île d'amour* (1663), that 'the translator differs from the author in name alone'.[65] Trediakovskii himself showed an example of such a broad approach to translation practices. His verse translation of François Fénelon's novel *The Adventures of Telemachus* is considered in the Russian literary canon as Trediakovskii's own original work (*Тилемахида*) rather than a translation.[66] Friedberg points out that the new era of translation practices in Russia took the path of freely and even boldly revising the texts of the originals with the goal of 'improving' them. Greek and Roman classics regarded 'as having already achieved perfection . . . were to be treated deferentially' and did not allow for textual revisions.[67] However, as we will see in the case of translations of the ancient epics, this precept was not always followed.[68]

In the case of Lomonosov and Kheraskov, the ancient epics became some of the most important texts that the rising Russian authors wanted to emulate as they challenged themselves to articulate their own national literature. As Richard Armstrong observes, this tendency to translate epic goes back as far as Livius Andronicus and his rendering of the *Odyssey* into Latin Saturnian verse. Epic had certain 'primacy' in the hierarchy of genres and was seen as 'the literal *incipit* for any robust literary culture'.[69] Furthermore, in Russia, both the writing of epic poetry and its translation were seen as exercises in literary discipline, a sharpening of the poetic sword. After the publication of Nikolai Gnedich's canonical translation of the *Iliad* (1801–29), N. Polevoi enthusiastically called it 'a treasure house of language . . . [that] exposes the richness, power, and resources of our own language'.[70] However, epic was not important only for the development of literary language. Griffiths and Rabinowitz point out: 'Epic's second plot, its embedded genealogy, brings arguments more powerful than any creed or nationalism or individual career that it briefly serves.'[71] For Russian men of letters translations of the ancient epics provided an opportunity to express national pride and to rival the long-gone glories of past civilizations. 'Rome envy', as Kalb aptly phrases it,[72] became an integral part of Russian renditions of and allusions to Vergil. However, in order to understand fully the value and significance of the first Russian translation of the *Aeneid*, we need to examine the Russian translations of Homer.

The analysis of E. D. Frolov of Russian renderings of Homer will inform us here.[73] The first translator of Homer was K. A. Kondratovich (1703–88), 'a translator and lexicographer, employed for a long time by the Russian Academy of Sciences',[74] whose monumental task was undertaken of his own free will. From the 1750s to the 1760s Kondratovich translated both the *Iliad* and the *Odyssey* from the Latin version of Iohannes Spondanus. His unpublished translations did not influence future generations. However, their language deserves special mention. As Frolov points out, Kondratovich tried to translate Homeric 'high diction' into the everyday Russian vernacular and by doing that completely failed to convey the heroic spirit and diction of the poem. One of the most ridiculous attempts of Kondratovich at 'Russianizing' the Homeric epic was his use of the Russian patronymic practice in relation to the gods and heroes. Frolov cites from another critic of these translations, A. N. Egunov, '"Iupiter Saturnovich" ("Jupiter, Saturn's son"), "Diomed Tideevich" ("Diomedes, son of Tydeus") and (sic!) "Agamemnon Andreevich" ("Agamemnon, son of Andrei")'.[75] It became clear from this first attempt that the Russian language was still struggling to find an appropriate vernacular equivalent, not to mention the prosody, necessary to translate the ancient epic. More importantly, however, this attempt revealed a tendency to put the foreign text into a native context, to make it accessible to a reader in the receiving culture.

The next translation, accomplished by the end of 1770s by Peter Ekimov, a humble cleric from Novorossiia, showed more sensitivity to the complexities of such an enormous task. Commissioned by Catherine's favourite at that time, Grigorii Potemkin, Ekimov translated (in prose) both poems as well, but unlike his predecessors directly from the Greek original. This translator chose an elevated language, replete with archaic usage, and even evangelical terminology. But this final feature again betrayed the quest for the appropriate heroic and lofty diction which Russian readers would not find completely alien. Ekimov, however, went in the opposite direction from Kondratovich and made the translation unreadable by the excessive use of archaisms and obscure terms. Frolov observes that A. N. Egunov, who studied those translations in detail, noted that these diametrically opposed translations defined two approaches to the translations of the ancient epic. One was that 'Homer must be translated in the most mundane, modern language thus making him accessible to the reader'; the other suggested that the translator should not be afraid of scaring off the reader and has to convey 'through the unusual, strange language of the translation that the reader is looking at something extraordinary and magnificent, and thus must be withdrawn from the sphere of the mundane and moved closer to Homer.

In other words, either make Homer a contemporary of the reader or the reader a contemporary of Homer.'[76]

It was not until Nikolai Gnedich's translation of the *Iliad* that the Russian language achieved a kind of equilibrium between these two extreme approaches and confidently accommodated both Homeric diction and metre. Previously only one other translation is worth mentioning, by E. I. Kostrov (1750–96), whose first verse rendition of Homer paved the road for future translators. By 1787 Kostrov had translated and published the first nine books of Homer's *Iliad* in Alexandrine verse. His style was refined and polished, his imagery crisp and vivid (many of Kostrov's formulae were later employed by Gnedich). It is Kostrov's translation, as Frolov rightly observes, that must be considered a true ancestor of the Russian school of translation of the ancient epic poems.[77] This translation also indicated that Russian language and versification were fully prepared to render adequately Greek and Latin texts.

At about the same time that Kostrov published his translation of the *Iliad*, Vasilii Petrov completed the first translation of Vergil's *Aeneid*. It was important for Russian literature at that time to conquer a translation of the *Aeneid*. There are compelling factors which may have steered Petrov towards the project. Colin Burrow has similarly made this point in relation to the English translations of Vergil: 'Virgil tends to be adopted into English by poets who need the consolation of his authority or the sustaining dream of his imperial vision. . . . [Thomas Phaer] is an example of how writers on the margins of England have turned to Virgil in order to persuade themselves that they are at the nation's centre.'[78] This 'imperial vision' of Vergil's epic undoubtedly attracted Petrov, who was eager to please his tsarina, Catherine. Another equally compelling factor for him in his task was Russia's insistence at that time on not being marginalized by Europe, but on being included among the family of the most powerful European nations.

In the following pages I will examine Petrov's monumental accomplishment in order to understand better its reception and purpose. I arrange my argument accordingly: first, after discussing the divided reception of Petrov's translation, I analyse the verse prologue and prose foreword to the poem, in which Petrov himself explains his translation techniques; next I discuss several excerpts from the text by comparing them with the Latin original in order to assess the quality of the translation as a whole. This discussion leads to a textual analysis of those books of the *Aeneid* where the presence of Dido is prominent, since I would like to suggest that the figure of Dido was meant by Petrov to be compared to Catherine the Great. I specifically offer comparisons between the Russian text and the Latin original in pursuit of that argument. In the last part of this study of Petrov's translation I pursue an examination of the cultural context in which Petrov might have expected his readers to compare Dido to Catherine.

The First Russian *Aeneid*

When Vasilii Trediakovskii, the first reformer of Russian translation practices, stated that 'the translator differs from the author in name alone',[79] this was not meant as an eloquent turn of phrase aimed at elevating the status of the translator and attracting attention to his arduous task. Irina Reyfman suggests that 'in the eighteenth-century theory of literature, the notion of talent was a rational notion, subject to sober analysis'.[80] Translations in Russian then were not viewed as much different from authentic works written in Russian because both required an equal measure of talent that was seen more as a result of diligence rather than of divinely inspired ability. Friedberg emphasizes that 'Russians regarded them [translations] as equal components of national literature, naturalized citizens recognizable as such by foreign-sounding names and faintly foreign accents, but in the final analysis just as indigenous as writings of the native origin.'[81] This may seem a somewhat cavalier approach, and it most certainly had its opponents, for example, the minor author Mikhail Chulkov (1743–92), who bewailed the Russian tendency to freely 'borrow' from foreign works without citing the original.[82] However, this attitude helped the translator to view his task not as a mere imitation, but as a striving for a new type of literary excellence, where he (the translator) would create a new masterpiece that possibly could rival the one he was translating.

This approach, while encouraging translators to revise and even boldly 'improve' the original text, gave them also a certain degree of freedom, which would enable and even empower them to adjust the text of the original to the tastes, demands, and even ideology of their own epoch.[83] Vasilii Petrov, as he embarked on the first Russian translation of the *Aeneid*, strove to make his translation both worthy of Vergil's legacy and relevant to his own times.

A son of humble parents and later a fledgling of the Slavonic-Greco-Latin Academy in Moscow, from which he graduated in 1760, Petrov came to be known as 'Catherine's pocket translator'[84] when he secured in the mid-1770s a position at Catherine's court as a translator and librarian, and enjoyed the patronage of the dashing Grigorii Orlov, then Catherine's favourite. Georgii Gukovskii, a long-time scholar of eighteenth-century Russian literature, called him 'the last formidable representative of a tradition that derived from the courtly baroque of the early eighteenth century in Western Europe, and which in the final analysis descends from the scholastic Latin poetry of the Renaissance'.[85] Petrov ingratiated himself at Catherine's court by composing in 1766 the ode 'To the Carousel' («На карусель»), written on the occasion of a jousting tournament modelled by Catherine on the famous *Le Grand Carrousel* staged in 1662 by Louis XIV.[86] He also became extremely close to Grigorii Potemkin, another favourite of Catherine, whom he extolled in his odes and who for a short time took from him some instruction in ancient Greek.[87] The first six books of his translation of the *Aeneid* in Alexandrine syllabic verse, titled «Еней. Героическая поэма Публия Вергилия Марона» ('Aeneas: A heroic poem of Publius Vergilius Maro'), Petrov published in 1770 (Figure 3); the complete translation was published between 1781 and 1786. The then newly established Russian Academy (1724–5) and its vice president Domashnev gave Petrov's accomplishment a very laudatory and oddly ebullient assessment: 'Vergil found in Mr Petrov a formidable rival, and the beautiful accomplishments of this outstanding Roman poet became our property through such a wonderful rendition.'[88] Catherine also took upon herself the task of extolling the achievement of her librarian, stating that 'this translation will immortalize him'.[89] The literary milieu, however, was not as kind, and bombarded Petrov with humiliating criticism. Frolov cites the acerbic quip of the poet V. I. Maikov (1728–78) as an example of the negative reaction:

> Сколь сила велика российского языка!
> Петров лишь захотел — Вергилий стал заика!
>
> So great is the power of the Russian language!
> Petrov only willed it—and Vergil started to stutter![90]

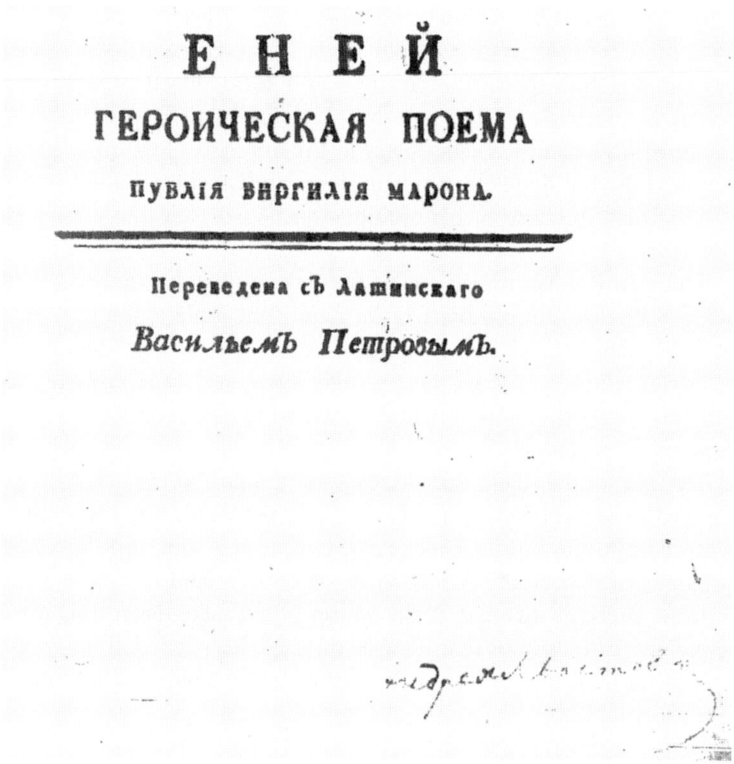

Е Н Е Й

ГЕРОИЧЕСКАЯ ПОЕМА

ПУВЛІЯ ВИРГИЛІЯ МАРОНА.

Переведена съ Латинскаго

Васильемъ Петровымъ.

Figure 3. The title page of Vasilii Petrov's first translation of the *Aeneid*.

Maikov went so far as to compose a parody of Petrov's *Aeneid* which along with the epigram came out following Petrov's first publication in 1770.[91]

Petrov was appalled by such an unkind reaction since he expected accolades, especially from his literary peers.[92] He left Catherine's court in indignation and lived the rest of his days in the countryside. The contrasting reactions by the Academy and by Petrov's literary peers show that the translation failed to fulfil the expectations of an essential audience. The Academy hailed it as a great achievement because in effect it was: nobody before Petrov had undertaken it and brought it to completion. Catherine undoubtedly, as I will demonstrate later, saw also its ideological value for the glorification of her reign and her person. Petrov's literary peers, as demonstrated by Maikov's reaction, saw the translation as a distortion of Vergilian refinement and subtlety. No translation at all, in their opinion, would have been better than doing a disservice to the greatest Roman poet by bringing him to Russian readers in a form which reduced the beauty of the original to its pale and weak echo. Alexander Pushkin, the most important voice in poetry in the first part of the nineteenth century, also recalled Petrov only in ironic and mocking contexts, and it is partially because of his opinion that Petrov fell into complete obscurity.[93]

This first Russian translation of the *Aeneid* most certainly did not achieve literary canonization in its own right, unlike, for instance, John Dryden's translation in English, which will be discussed later. However, we have to look more closely at the text to appreciate the difficulty of Petrov's monumental undertaking and to understand the reasons for its failure.

The goal of the poem and Petrov's main focus become clear from the dedication and subsequently the verse prologue. The translation was dedicated to Grand Duke Paul, Catherine's son, and the verse prologue was basically a laudatory ode to Catherine mixed with didactic precepts directed at the young grand duke. From this prologue we can deduce that Petrov deemed his undertaking more important than that of Vergil and considered his patron above even Augustus himself:

> Я мыслей в высоте Марону подражая,
> И большим, нежель он, усердием пылая
> Потщился бы пред всей вселенной показать
> Чем выше Августа твоя Августа мать.
>
> I, imitating Maro's sublime thoughts,
> And burning with a zeal greater than his,
> Strove to show in front of the whole universe
> Why your august mother is greater that Augustus.[94]

The last line of this excerpt might strike the reader by its obvious exaggeration. However, there is no reason to believe that Petrov did not sincerely consider Catherine above even Augustus himself and was not excited and eager to support her reforms. This remark thus should not be taken merely as a hyperbolic attempt to elevate the reigning sovereign by means of an epic and historical comparison. We might wonder, however, if Maikov's contemptuous remark and the rejection of the translation by Petrov's educated peers were in part influenced by such unbridled laudation of Catherine.

The didactic prologue addressed to Paul is followed by another foreword, this one in prose, which aims at explaining to the young royal the circumstances and the historical background of the *Aeneid*. At the very beginning of that explanatory foreword we find Petrov's peculiar statement that Vergil's *Aeneid* serves as proof that even 'imitation can achieve perfection' («до какого совершенства можно достигнуть подражанием»). Here Petrov curiously remarks about the quality of the Vergilian epic as a whole. He begins by praising Vergil's 'power of imagination' («сила воображения») and the 'ardour' («огнь») that inspired his writing of the poem.[95] Then rather judgementally he remarks: 'In truth, in the last songs he [Vergil] grows weak, but through all the weakness the zeal of his verse composition is apparent' («Правда, в последних песнях он ослабевает, но сквозь всю слабость виден жар его стихотворства»). Petrov in a footnote elaborates on this thought by adding that Vergil's fame would have been even greater if he had limited the *Aeneid* to only the first six books.[96] While taste in poetry is often subjective and some readers today might prefer the first six books of the *Aeneid* to the last ones, further scrutiny of this opinion will help clarify Petrov's own agenda in his translation of the *Aeneid*.

One explanation for Petrov's choice of the first six books of the *Aeneid* can be found in the footnote to the foreword. He suggests that Mikhail Lomonosov's first two books of the incomplete but much talked about epic, *Peter the Great*, showed great zeal and inspiration, but left the author ambivalent as to whether the poem, if finished, would have maintained the same momentum. In this commendable defence of Lomonosov's attempt at a national epic resides perhaps the underlying reason for Petrov's suggestion of abridging the *Aeneid* as well. According to Petrov, poetic imagination and ardour cannot remain unchanged because poetic labour, like any other artistic toil, eventually loses its novelty and thus freshness and sincerity of expression. These gifts of the muse are bound to weaken as the poetic task progresses. Hence Lomonosov, by choosing to limit his epic to only two songs, did better than Vergil because he understood the impossibility of sustaining poetic inspiration indefinitely. Here Petrov's national pride took priority over the truth. He felt a need to explain why Lomonosov's attempt at a Russian epic featuring the great tsar-reformer was unsuccessful and defended his predecessor's failure.

The next factor is decidedly more complicated. Petrov himself, it seems, felt rather intimidated by this daunting task. His adverse reaction to his peers' ungrateful reception of the translation also shows that he was extremely proud of the fact that his was the first full translation of the Roman epic into Russian.

So why did Petrov's accomplishment fall short of its mark?

Petrov compared the difficulty of his task with that of de Vogelas, whose French translation of Curtius Rufus appeared in 1712. In Petrov's opinion the translation of a mere four lines of Vergil equals a whole chapter by Curtius because of the complexity of Vergil's poetic devices.[97] He also admits that a translator of Vergil must be allowed a certain licence in replacing the Latin idiom with one that would be more understandable to the audience of the translator. As a proof of that licence he cites the Vergilian phrase '*et terris iactatus et alto*' ('he [Aeneas] was buffeted on lands and deep sea') with an explanation that the Russian translation would have more force if the word *iactatus* were translated not as 'buffeted' but as 'suffering'. As a further confirmation of a necessity of such occasional 'innovations' by a translator, Petrov cites the famous lines uttered by Aeneas in the temple of Juno in Book 1 when he saw the murals with the scenes of Trojan War (1.461–2):

> En Priamus! sunt hic etiam sua praemia laudi;
> sunt lacrimae rerum et mentem mortalia tangunt.

> Behold Priam! Even here glory has its rewards;
> Tears are shed for the ways of the world and mortal affairs
>   touch hearts.

While overall Petrov renders these difficult lines into Russian rather precisely, he translates *En Priamus* as 'here is *our* Priam', explaining his choice of a possessive adjective *наш* ('our') is necessary because Aeneas was speaking to Achates, and both of them had a familial or personal relationship with Priam.[98] Such subjective interpretational additions are ubiquitous in the text and become apparent right from the opening lines of the translation, where it appears that Petrov took significant licence not only with the wording but also with the prosody in his work:

> Пою оружий звук и подвиги героя,
> Что первый, как легла вся в прах от Греков Троя
> Судьбой гоним достиг Италии брегов;
> Страдал под игом зол, средь суши и валов
> Несланным от руки злопамятной Юноны
> В кровавых бранях нес тяжайшие уроны;

Когда в Италии град новый возводил,
В латинскую страну богов своих вносил;
Откуду проистек Латинов род преславный,
Албанские цари и Рим возник державный.

I sing the sound of weapons and feats of the hero,
Who first, since the whole of Troy was laid to dust by
    the Greeks,
Chased by the fates reached the shores of Italy;
He suffered under the yoke of evils on land and on
    sea-waves,
Sent by the grudge-holding Juno;
In bloody battles he suffered most heavy losses;
When in Italy he was building a new city,
And was bringing into the Latin country his gods;
Whence the most famous Latin clan came,
Alban kings and the sovereign Rome has risen.

As an illustration of Petrov's careless translation techniques this passage is by no means unique. Apart from the distracting rhyming pattern and increased number of lines (ten instead of the Latin seven), it is easy to detect how far this excerpt steers from the original Latin text. Petrov in his zeal to make the translation accessible clarifies the circumstances of Aeneas' departure from Troy: 'since the whole of Troy was laid to dust by the Greeks'; he omits *Lavina . . . litora* of the original text, perhaps considering the expression redundant in conjunction with *Italiam*. Furthermore, Petrov, while oblivious to certain poetic devices such as the transferred epithet in the last line (*altae moenia Romae*), adds some adjectives to the translation that do not exist in the original, such as 'new' to modify 'city' or 'famous' to modify 'clan'. As much as he tries to justify it, this approach could have appalled his contemporaries who strove to make Russian translations accessible but also accurate for the public. In addition to such startling poetic 'innovations' throughout his translation Petrov also uses too many colloquial words and even coins some words himself («содетель», 'creator', «мятёт», 'vexes', 4.663–4; «приосеняющей», 'casting a shadow', 6.595). While the meaning of these words is clear from their cognates and the context, overall they make an impression of an overly artificial text that alienates the reader. The whole translation reads like a spoof of the *Aeneid*, a feature that clearly did not go unnoticed by Maikov, who with his parody of Petrov's translation aimed at drawing for the educated public a clear distinction between Vergil's style and Petrov's.

From a literary point of view we can understand why Petrov's achievement was seen as a failure. However, Catherine's open admiration of Petrov's translation supported by the newly established academy is deserving of further discussion. Catherine, who actively participated in Petrov's translation by correcting it and offering comments, appreciated its value from a perspective entirely different from the poet's literary peers.

Dux femina facti—Catherine as Dido?

Andrew Kahn in his seminal article on Russian readings of imperial Rome points out that for Catherine 'the *Aeneid* was a prestige poem' because it celebrated *imperium sine fine* and because of Vergil's emphasis in Books 1–4 on a female ruler.[99] Kahn writes:

> '*Dux femina facti*': Virgil's remark on the unusual phenomenon of a female warrior might well be applied to the *Aeneid* read as a celebration of a female monarch. The success of political allegory depends on development, usually brief and pointed, of parallel traits of character or circumstance. Emphasis falls on points of contiguity. Equally important is the tactful suspension of the parallel either when it is no longer decorous or when it becomes irrelevant.[100]

Dido's first appearance in Book 1 (496–504) depicts the queen as a proud founder of her own city and as a lawgiver. When she enters the temple of Juno she is surrounded by a throng of young men (*magna iuvenum stipante caterva*); she strides through the middle of the Tyrians happy with the toil of her kingdom being built (*se laeta ferebat per medios instans operi regnisque futuris*); she sits aloft on her throne (*solio alte . . . resedit*).

Here Petrov for the most part is faithful to the original but modernizes it in noticeable ways: Dido was surrounded by her 'courtiers' («по обоим ея вельможи сторонам»); she carried her head higher than everybody else («выше всех она главу свою несла»); she sat herself on 'an elevated and splendid throne' («возшед на блещущий и возвышенный трон»). The majesty and glamour of the queen's presence are emphasized by Petrov's addition of words that are not in the original text to give it a more pronounced comparison to Catherine.

The parallel that Petrov's contemporaries could have drawn between Catherine and Dido becomes especially apparent in Petrov's depiction of the new city that Dido was building. Since the times of Peter the Great the 'myth' of St Petersburg had become prevalent in literary and aristocratic circles. Vying with the 'retrograde' Moscow for the title of the 'Third Rome', St Petersburg stood for everything that was progressive, refined, and sophisticated. During Catherine's time the rhetorical meaning of 'the city' became especially strong. In Petrov's rendition the description of the rising city of Carthage acquires meaningful importance as a parallel to Peter's city and now that of his heir, Catherine. In the first book of the *Aeneid* Aeneas looks from the top of a hill at the Tyrians at work building the city of Carthage (1.421–9):

> Miratur molem Aeneas, magalia quondam,
> miratur portas strepitumque et strata viarum.
> Instant ardentes Tyrii: pars ducere muros
> molirique arcem et manibus subvolvere saxa,
> pars optare locum tecto et concludere sulco;
> iura magistratusque legunt sanctumque senatum.
> Hic portus alii effodiunt; hic alta theatris
> fundamenta locant alii immanisque columnas
> rupibus excidunt, scaenis decora alta futuris.

This is how Petrov renders this passage (1.536–50):

> Эней огромности чудится новых стен,
> Нестройность где была лишь шалашей презренных,
> Вратам и чистоте стогн камнем умощенных;
> Немолчный слышен крик, и шум, и стук везде,
> Всяк тщится преуспеть в предписанном труде.
> Ины над градскими ведут свою работу
> Стенами, не щадя телесных сил и поту;
> Согбеньшись, крепостью неутомленных рук,
> Каменья движут с мест, дают орудьми звук;
> Ины кладут размер, где кровам быть жилищным,
> Сенату и другим местам у них судищным;
> Там сооружают порт, там театральный дом
> Прилежным основать готовятся трудом;
> Изсечены из гор обильных камнем диким
> Влекут столбы красу театрам превеликим.

> Aeneas marvels at the immenseness of the new walls,
> Where there used to be only the disorder of despicable huts,
> He marvels at the gates and the streets paved with stones;

> The relentless shouts are heard, and the noise, and knocking
>   everywhere;
> Everyone tries to excel in the assigned task.
> Some carry on working on the city walls,
> Without sparing their body's strength and sweat;
> Bending over, with the might of their tireless hands,
> They move the stones, they make noise with their tools;
> Others measure the space, where the houses need to be,
> As well as the senate and other places for the law courts;
> There they are building the harbour, and there, with
>   diligent work,
> They prepare to lay the foundation of the theatre;
> Chiselled from the massive mountains of the crude stone
> They carry beautiful columns for the great theatres.

Petrov significantly embellishes the description of the rising new city, adding to it the sense of splendour, the overcoming of 'disorder' of the previous humble huts with the magnificence of chiselled and refined architecture. Catherine took great pride in continuing Peter's building programme of his city. Vera Proskurina points out that it was Catherine who replaced Peter's restrained designs and the baroque tastes of her predecessor Elizabeth, who was devoted to Rastrelli's designs, with more sophisticated and stylish classical forms represented by Falconet and Quarenghi.[101] Furthermore, Proskurina also notes that in the first (1779) edition of the translation Petrov emphasized the process of building the city, while in the later 1781 edition he changed the lines to focus on the city's splendour and perfection. The famous line uttered by Aeneas upon seeing Dido's teeming city—*o fortunati quorum iam moenia surgunt* (1.437)—was translated in the first edition as 'blessed are those whose city is close to fruition' («блаженны те . . . у коих спеет град», 1.560). In the 1781 edition Petrov changed that line to 'blessed are those whose city rises to the clouds' («блаженны, коих град до облак возницает»). This slight difference in the text between the editions represented a shift in Petrov's own perception of St Petersburg from a city of great hopes to the new and completed glamorous capital of a new European power.[102] Petrov undoubtedly wanted his contemporaries to 'read' Dido as Catherine and Carthage as St Petersburg, but, as I will demonstrate later, only to the point where he, as Kahn observes, tactfully suspended the parallel.

The biographical circumstances of Dido's ascent to power, upon which she ruminates in her introductory speech in Book 4, were similar to Catherine's own. Catherine was a foreigner whose initial hold on the Russian monarchy was under much threat; her willingness to defend and expand her frontiers against all internal and external enemies was impressive; and her involvement in all these affairs as well as the building of the state was profound. But it is tempting to ask if Petrov was even slightly aware of the fact that the comparison of the ill-fated Carthaginian queen to the great tsarina might be seen as not altogether auspicious. For now let us examine the reception of Dido in English.

Two examples will serve our purpose: one is Thomas Phaer's 1555 translation of Vergil's *Aeneid*, which invited the contemplation and eventually condemnation of the power of an authoritative female monarch; the other is John Dryden's 1697 translation in which he portrayed Dido sympathetically, but nevertheless justified Aeneas' abandonment of her.[103] In addition, Dryden painted Dido as an authoritative political figure, basing her character on both Mary I and Elizabeth I, who ruled England some hundred years earlier. Dido had already become an ambivalent and contradictory metaphor for Queen Elizabeth in Christopher Marlowe's and John Nashe's 1594 work, *Dido, Queen of Carthage*. P. Bono and M. V. Tessitore in their study of this parallel between Dido and Elizabeth point out any absence of an explicit analogy between the two, but note the possibility that most readers of the play could have easily inferred it. What Marlowe's and Nashe's *Dido* emphasized specifically was the negative effect of love in terms of Dido's hold on her power as a queen. The scene in the play when Dido showed Aeneas the portraits of all of her rejected suitors foreshadowed her undoing by her inability to resist Aeneas.[104] William Gager's *Dido* (1583), which preceded Marlowe's, also carefully approached the parallel with Elizabeth while juxtaposing Dido's queenly responsibility with her private emotions.[105] Dryden, who began his translation during the reign of Mary II, drew on the model of previous female monarchs and revised the portrayal of Dido in his translation through 'female glamorization' in the context of controlled political authority, and as an empowered and sympathetic political figure.[106] Even though Dryden, faithful to the original text, had to portray a pained Dido, he always maintained her sense of authority.[107] It would be hard to believe that Petrov, widely read and broadly educated, who from 1771 to 1774 travelled extensively in England and in 1777 undertook the translation (although in prose) of Milton's *Paradise Lost*, would have been unfamiliar with Dryden's and Phaer's translations, at least when he was producing the final edition of his *Enei*.[108]

We initially saw Dido in the *Aeneid* as the great queen in the full glory of her power. As she falls in love with Aeneas, she forgets about her most important legacy, the city of Carthage. She is partly the casualty of divine providence and partly a victim of her own femininity that longs for a husband and a child. She is also the undoing, ultimately a tragically mad one, of her own civilization. Vergil's words about her demise move us to tears, but nonetheless we witness a defeat of *dux femina facti*, and are disheartened by her inability to overcome her passion as she falls victim to divinely ordained fate.

It may be useful to look at how Petrov tackled the Dido of the fourth book in order to understand how and to what extent he wanted Dido to be read by his contemporaries as a parallel to Catherine. In Vergil's tragic tale of Dido's love and demise there is a great emphasis on Dido's gradual descent into madness. But Petrov almost never refers to that madness in the same explicit terms as Vergil. Where Vergil describes Dido's initial suspicions of Aeneas' pending departure as the beginning of her downward spiral into insanity, he employs '*inops animi*' ('bereft of her mind'), '*incensa*' ('inflamed'), and '*bacchatur*' ('she raves') (4.300–1). Petrov replaces these words with 'carrying despair and annoyance in her heart' («нося отчаянье внутрь сердца, и досаду») and 'she raves, and frenzied she runs around the city' («лютует, бегает неистова по граду», 4.417–18»). Petrov's emphasis is on the anger and on Dido's pain rather than on the loss of control, although we do get a glimpse of madness in the simile describing a Bacchante in the ensuing lines. In the confrontation scene (4.371–2) where Dido accusingly scrutinizes Aeneas ('*totumque pererrat*') after his attempt at justifying his actions ('*Italiam non sponte sequor*'), Petrov yet again mitigates the impression of Dido as a woman in the grip of madness ('*volvens oculos*'). Instead he shifts the focus to her disdain for Aeneas and the wrath rising in her heart («презор к нему и бунт души своей являла», 4.505), which is not explicitly present in the Latin original. Elsewhere in the text Petrov elaborates on Dido's torment from love and anger at being abandoned by presenting her mostly as a woman unjustly wronged rather than an obstacle in the way of the hero's divine mission. When Dido before her suicide is engulfed in the final contemplation of her suffering and sadness, Vergil concludes her complaint with one simple line: '*tantos illa suo rumpebat pectore questus*' ('such complaints she was bursting forth from her heart'). Petrov, however, takes it upon himself to translate this one line with two: 'such was the groan Dido poured out in the darkness of the night / from her heart, which was torn apart between anger, love and sadness' («таков Дидона стон во мгле ночной лила / из сердца, кое гнев, любовь и грусть рвала», 4.786). Petrov, at times blatantly, glosses over the devolution of Dido's love into madness, sensing Vergil's own sympathy for his tragic heroine and enhancing it. In Petrov's rendition Dido emerges as a great queen who succumbed to her even greater passion. The parallel to Catherine, which could have appeared to some inappropriate, considering Catherine's numerous amorous liaisons, is turned by Petrov into a flattering (for Catherine) juxtaposition between the doomed and passion-driven Carthaginian queen and the Russian tsarina.

The key elements of Vergil's composition are manipulated to that very end. Even Aeneas' stature is diminished to accommodate the comparison. The famous epithet *pius* is rephrased by Petrov as 'renowned for his piety Aeneas' («благочестием прославленный Эней», 1.484). Thus Aeneas' most recognizable character trait is presented merely as a part of his reputation, something that he was famous for but did not necessarily possess. Furthermore in Book 4, after the fateful confrontation, when Dido, having fainted, has been carried away by her servants and the Latin narrative resumes with '*at pius Aeneas*' (4.393), Petrov removes the epithet completely, thus expressing his disapproval of it, given the context.[109]

Aeneas' Eastern (Trojan) origins, from which educated Russians such as Petrov, aware of Russia's peculiar geopolitical status between 'East' and 'West', tried to distance themselves, also contributed to his diminished stature. To achieve this diminution Petrov even freely improvised in translating the famous complaint of Iarbas to Jupiter in which Iarbas described Aeneas and his companions (4.215–17):

> Et nunc ille Paris cum semiviro comitatu,
> Maeonia mentum mitra crinemque madentem
> subnexus, rapto potitur.

Here is Petrov's treatment of these lines (4.301–4):

> И сей второй Парид со слабыми скопцами
> С блудящими за ним по свету беглецами,
> Под митрой подвязной, что кажет к неге страсть,
> В кудрях, отколь течет благоуханна масть,

Едва ступить успел на брег наш робким шагом,
Отъятым у меня днесь пользуется благом!

And this second Paris with his weak eunuchs,
Wandering[110] with him as fugitives all over the world,
With his mitre tied underneath his chin, spelling his passion
   for pleasure,
With his curls oozing the fragrant ointment,
Barely he stepped off on our shores with his timid step,
And already he takes possession of the goods taken away from me!

While Iarbas' depiction of Aeneas in Vergil's text also presented Aeneas as an effeminate, Eastern man (perhaps bringing to mind the modern Turks, Russia's enemy at the time), Petrov's elaboration on these points reflects his own desire to undermine Aeneas' heroic appeal even more. Even in the final encounter between Aeneas and Dido in the underworld, Petrov makes Aeneas appear almost as a suppliant when faced with Dido's shadow, as a remorseful lover who came too late to an understanding of his guilt. He replaces Aeneas' bewildered question '*funeris heu tibi causa fui?*' ('alas, was I the cause of your death?', 6.458) with the significantly more expressive and assertive statement 'But woe to me, it was I, I who drove you to your grave' («и я, О горе, я во гроб вогнал тебя», 6.616). This admission of guilt then culminates in Aeneas' ardent confession, not present in the Latin original, that he never meant to reject Dido's love («любови я твоей отнюдь не пренебрег», 6.619) and he left the 'beloved shore' of Carthage under duress («по принуждению оставил милый брег», 6.620). Petrov's Aeneas, for all his 'fatal attraction of heroism',[111] was reduced by Petrov to Dido's cruel, ungrateful, and eventually remorseful lover, whose role as the founder of the great Roman civilization has been completely marginalized and who failed to match the strength of the queen's passion and drove her into an isolating anger and eventual suicide. And that is where the parallel between Dido and Catharine became carefully suspended.

The similarities of Catherine's succession to the Russian crown to Dido's rule of Carthage were perhaps many, but Catherine was not by any means prone to reckless emotional upheavals. Although she was brought to Russia at the age of fifteen from Prussia, she succeeded her deposed husband Peter III and became an empress regnant. She ruled the country from 1762 to 1796,[112] despite the fact that she was 'the only Russian ruler since Riurik to have no Russian parent'.[113]

Her many lovers came and went, but she unwaveringly remained a monarch at the height of her powers. Was Petrov teaching Russian readers a lesson, speaking through this mythological allegory of Dido? The task of translation turned then into a discourse of pride in enlightened absolutism and patriotism.

Dido served as a mythological predecessor of the eighteenth-century enlightened Russian monarch. But she also became an inferior point of comparison to that monarch and reflected the attitudes characteristic of her age and the men of letters surrounding her. Petrov's method of approaching Dido as a means of mythological allegory takes us back again to Lomonosov's rhetoric and the poetics of empire and its ruler. In his second New Year's ode written in 1763 and addressed to Catherine, Lomonosov hailed her as an enlightened European monarch and compared her rule with that of the Chinese emperor whose model of oriental despotism he found abhorrent. Harsha Ram points out that in this juxtaposition 'European Russia is associated with the spread of knowledge and law-based governance,' while 'Asia emerges not merely as a rival force but as a politically alien system.'[114] Could it be then that comparison with Dido accomplished for Petrov what the comparison with the Chinese emperor did for Lomonosov?

By any standards Dido was an oriental queen, as she was considered in Roman times. Although Petrov expressed sympathy for Dido and downplayed her emerging madness, he by no means marginalized her Eastern roots, because for him Dido, despite many similarities to Catherine, represented Eastern excess, and the inability to control emotions that stand in the way of civilized ('Western') behaviour. By comparing Catherine with Dido, Petrov was then extolling his sovereign as a type of European monarch, an ideal that Dido could never actualize. Catherine, however, could and did.

It should also be noted that Petrov was most famous, and to some of his literary rivals infamous, for odes celebrating Russian victories in the First Turkish War (1768–74). These odes employed the traditional rhetoric of Russia as the Christian Orthodox Empire saving Europe from the infidels. This rhetoric, as Irina Reyfman notes, was 'fine tuned' by Catherine's correspondence with Voltaire, which shows concerns not with the old Orthodox Byzantine Empire, but with classical Greece, whose liberator Catherine was supposed to become.[115] In one of his poems celebrating the Russian capture of the Turkish fortress Khotin, Voltaire called the tsarina a 'Minerva' and 'sister of Apollo', and beseeched her to join him on the fields of Marathon so that she could 'avenge Greece by chasing out those reprobates, / Those enemies of the arts and jailors of women.'[116] Catherine enthusiastically incorporated these ancient Greek comparisons into her ideological rhetoric, and showed significant zeal for Voltaire's proposed 'Greek project', as it came to be called, by naming her two older grandsons Alexander and Konstantin. The latter was groomed by Catherine to be placed on the throne over the restored empire of Constantinople. As Asen Kirin observes, although this project 'was often deemed illusionary, or at the very least unrealistic ... its greatest contribution was to show the possibility of reconciliation between Russia's newly acquired sense of Western identity and its own medieval past'.[117] This project, especially its Roman part, also contributed to the theme of *translatio imperii*, because 'making Russia the semblance of the Roman Empire elevated the monarch and the serf-holding elite as heirs to the highest values of the classical West'.[118]

It is also important to remember that in 1771 Eugenios Voulgaris (1716–1806), a leading figure of the Greek Enlightenment, came to Russia at Catherine's invitation and remained there till the end of his life. Voulgaris became especially fond of Grigorii Potemkin, then Catherine's favourite, who distinguished himself in the Russo-Turkish wars, built a powerful navy, and achieved the peaceful annexation of Crimea. In the 76-line-long dedicatory letter that preceded his translation of Vergil's *Georgics* into Greek and was addressed to Potemkin as Prince of the Holy Roman Empire, Voulgaris compared Russia to Rome, extolled Catherine above Octavian Augustus, and identified Potemkin with Maecenas, 'to whom the translator offered his services posing as another Vergil'. In this dedication Voulgaris also 'summarizes the hopes he placed in Potemkin as the agent of a regenerated Hellenism:

> Where once was a colony of Miletus
> And a prosperous city named Olvios
> Here to see again Greece reborn
> May, glorious Potemkin, be your labour to achieve!'[119]

Petrov in one of his Turkish odes also sang in tune with Voltaire and Voulgaris by calling Catherine the Athena (Pallas) who will be able to be the lawgiver and liberator of Greece and make Russia no longer a mere disciple of European nations but their equal, the *par inter pares*.

Stephen Batalden in his study of Eugenios Voulgaris' career observes that Voulgaris' presence at Catherine's court had a great impact upon classical studies in Russia and may even have influenced Nikolai Gnedich (1784–1833), whose translation of Homer's *Iliad* into literary Russian remains canonical to this day.[120]

The translation of the Roman national epic by Petrov became then the extension of 'the Greek project' so ardently supported by Voltaire and embraced by Catherine. The expression of the 'Russian' through the 'Roman' (Rome being an heir to the Greek legacy) became a part of this project that was designed to cast Russia and her monarch Catherine as a 'civilizing' power. Furthermore, the first translation of the *Aeneid* into Russian may have reminded Russian readers of the 'Third Rome' doctrine initiated by Filofei in the sixteenth century and perpetuated in later writings with less eschatological and more secular sensibility. The parallels to Rome, as Boris Kagarlitsky points out, were meant 'to affirm the symbolic importance of Russia as a leading European power'.[121] The *Aeneid* in Russian was turned into state-sponsored discourse and, although it did not earn Petrov literary accolades, showed how even the work of translation can serve ideological purposes. But more importantly, for Catherine and for Petrov himself the translation claimed the Russian tsarina's rightful place in the family of European, not Eastern, monarchs. For Catherine this was an important distinction since Western Europe considered Russia an Eastern country.

Petrov's translation undoubtedly did not accomplish its literary claim of being the first adequate translation of the Roman epic into Russian. However, its role in developing Russian translation practices should not be underestimated. Toporov points out that for a receiving culture sometimes 'the quality of the translation and even the translated text are to a certain degree secondary in comparison with the mere occurrence of a demand for translation and its actualization in producing the text that is "your own"'.[122] The primary goal set by Petrov for his translation was misunderstood by his literary peers, who were looking for literary accuracy and refinement that would at least approximate the Roman original. Although in that respect the translation turned out to be unsatisfactory, it initiated, as we will see in the last chapter, an impressive chain of Russian translations of the *Aeneid*, which claimed literary longevity not merely for their accuracy but for their poetic value and ideological agenda independent from that of the original.[123]

NOTES

1. N. Karamzin, *Polnoe sobranie sochinenii*, 18 vols (St Petersburg: S. Selivanovsky, 1803–4), 4.288. Cited in Greenfeld (1992), 233.
2. Wortman (1995), 42–3.
3. Braund (2010), 451.
4. Griffiths and Rabinowitz (2011), 177.
5. Bakhtin (1981), 13.
6. Bakhtin (1981), 13.
7. Segel (1973), 54–5. This opinion clearly contradicts Gasparov's statement cited in the introduction that in Russia 'the romantic nineteenth century, dreaming about natural and spontaneous poetry, did not like the civilized Roman classics and preferred the Greek'. In the eighteenth century, however, Vergil, not Homer, became the focus of attention of national aspirations, which served the more practical purpose of bringing Russia into the world of European nations. This turn to Rome and away from Greece in eighteenth-century Russia was remarkable considering that, as Andrew Kahn points out, in the rest of Europe and even in Italy at that time 'Rome's afterlife had gone into decline' and 'operatic reform of the 1750s advocated a return directly to Greek rather than Roman antiquity' (Kahn, 1993, 750).
8. For more on the shift from Rome to Greece in Russian culture during the nineteenth century, see Maguire (1994), 296–301. It is during that time, as Maguire observes, that 'the *Aeneid* came to be perceived as markedly inferior to Homeric poems' (300). The shift also had much to do with an interest in philosophy to which ancient Rome contributed little. We will also see later in this study Nikolai Gogol's unbridled enthusiasm for Homeric poems.
9. Kahn (1993), 750.
10. Kallendorf (2005), 577.
11. Clark (2011), 23.
12. Quint (1992), 7.
13. Clark (2011), 24, also makes an interesting observation describing how the message of the *Aeneid* became relevant during Stalin's terror. She cites the speech of Nikolai Bukharin delivered to the First Congress of the Writers' Union in 1934. Bukharin emphasized the pedagogical impact of the epic because 'society and its social upper echelons [thereby] reproduced themselves ideologically, in an idealized version, and inculcated their ideas, thoughts, conceptions, feelings, characters, aims, ideals and virtues'. For the proponents of 'socialist realism' these were invaluable qualities for a literary artefact.
14. The representatives of Russian classicism, however, did not call it such. The term 'classicism' came into use only later, during the war of the Romantics against eighteenth-century literary traditions. See Serman

(1989), 63. See also Lotman (1996), 123–47, on the controversy surrounding the application of this term in Russian culture.

15. This characterization belongs to Gavrila Derzhavin, quoted in Rogger (1960), 259.
16. Lomonosov (1959), 7.589.
17. Lednicki (1978), 44.
18. Lomonosov (1959), 8.1125.
19. Galinsky (1996), 244–5.
20. Zetzel (1982), 101.
21. Conington (1898).
22. For example by Sforza (1935).
23. See especially Brooks (1953), Parry (1963), Clausen (1964), Putnam (1965), and most recently Thomas (2001). Thomas's book shows that 'pessimistic' readings of the *Aeneid* already existed in antiquity. The proponents of the more 'pessimistic' readings of the *Aeneid* came to be called the 'Harvard school', but, as noted later by both Richard Thomas and Craig Kallendorf, the Harvard connection was rather tenuous. See Kallendorf (2007), vii n. 3.
24. Galinsky (1996), 245.
25. Lomonosov (1959), 8.696. *Петр Великий* is also available online: <http://www.rvb.ru/18vek/lomonosov/01text/01text/07petr/110.htm> [last visited 15 April 2013].
26. Lomonosov (1959), 7.589.
27. 'In order to really know epic, it's not enough to have read Virgil and Homer.' Voltaire, *The Complete Works* (Geneva: Institut et Musée Voltaire; Toronto: University of Toronto Press, 1968–), 13.443. See Jones (1976), 106.
28. He studied with Gottsched in Marburg on the Lahn in 1736–9. See Wes (1992), 33. See also Segel (1973), 50–1.
29. Jones (1976), 103. Lotman (1996), 123ff., also takes issue with the term 'classicism' in Russia.
30. Lomonosov (1959), 698.
31. Lomonosov (1959), 8.1129.
32. Segel (1973), 50.
33. See Lomonosov (1959), 6.89–96, 359–64, 563–8, 592–4. Also Lomonosov's letter: 10.53, 55, 62, 67.
34. For more information see Mackiw (1983) and Tairova-Iakovleva (2007). See also Hughes (1998), 35–7. According to legend, Mazepa in his youth was tied to the back of a wild horse and sent into the steppes by a jealous husband. This was described in Lord Byron's poem *Mazeppa*.
35. Lomonosov (1959), 8.1137.
36. Wortman (2003), 99.
37. Wortman (2003), 99.

38. See Lomonosov 8.1127, commentary Vinogradov, Andreev, Blok.
39. Cited in Lomonosov (1959), 8.1127.
40. The epigram is «Терентий здесь живет Облаевич Цербер» ('Terence Cerberus, son of Barker, lives here'). The name is a reference to Sumarokov's biting attack on Lomonosov.
41. Karamzin (1848), 1.591.
42. Belinskii (1955), 7.110.
43. Belinskii (1953), 1.164.
44. Kheraskov's *Rossiada* is available online: <http://az.lib.ru/h/heraskow_m_m/text_0010oldorfo.shtml> [last accessed 11 October 2012].
45. Serman (1989), 81.
46. Allworth (2003), 141.
47. During Catherine's reign Russia was victorious in two Turkish wars of 1768–74 and 1787–92.
48. Pypin (1902–13), 4.105.
49. Serman (1989), 82.
50. Terras (1985), 406.
51. Allworth (2003), 159.
52. Other examples of such 'Byronic' poems are Konstantin Ryleev's historical poem 'Voinarovskii' (1824), approved by Pushkin also, and Evgenii Baratynskii's 'Edda' (1825). The latter, however, visibly toned down the romantic tendencies. For more examples see Terras (1985), 345.
53. A version of the following discussion of Petrov's translation of the *Aeneid* first appeared in print in Torlone (2011).
54. Sumarokov (1957), 114, 'Epistola I'.
55. Friedberg (1997), 20.
56. For a more detailed account of translations of religious texts, see Friedberg (1997), 20. Friedberg details (22–4) the translations of the Bible into Church Slavonic and the activity of Maksim the Greek, who in 1552 made the first adequate translation of the Psalms from Greek. However, the Holy Synod's Russian-language Bible did not appear until 1824.
57. See Burrow (1997), 23.
58. See Hughes (1998), 324, who cites a letter Musin-Pushkin wrote to F. Polikarpov, translator of Varenius' *Geographia generalis*, 'forwarding Peter's complaint that he had done it "very badly" and demanding that he "make thorough corrections not in high-flown Slavonic words but in simple Russian language"'.
59. *Zakonodatel'nye akty* (1945), 139 (23 January 1724). See also Hughes (1998), 324.
60. *Materialy* (1885), 1.79–80. See also Friedberg (1997), 28.
61. Toporov (1996), 593.
62. Lomonosov (1959), 8.391–2. Almost a century and a half later, in 1918 Alexander Blok, one of the leading Russian Symbolists, in his famous

Scythians (*Скифы*) echoed these words: 'We render with comprehension everything—the sharp Gallic meaning and gloomy German genius' («Нам внятно все — и острый галльский смысл, и сумрачный германский гений»). See Blok (1958), 21. *Скифы* is available online: <http://www.world-art.ru/lyric/lyric.php?id=10518> [last visited 6 September 2013]. It is worth noting that the context of Blok's statement is different from Lomonosov's since the poem *Scythians* contemplates Russia's Eastern roots.

63. Sumarokov (1957), 125: «прекрасный наш язык способен ко всему».
64. Greenfeld (1992), 244–5.
65. Frolov (1999), 89: «Переводчик от творца только что именем рознится».
66. Frolov (1999), 89. On the controversy around *Tilemakhida*, see Reyfman (1990), 44–5, 177–90.
67. Friedberg (1997), 30.
68. The first book that specifically and comprehensively addressed Russian translation techniques for poetry did not appear until 1811. It was written in French by Prince B. V. Golitsyn and titled *Réflexions sur les traducteurs russes*. See Brower (1959), 275, and Friedberg (1997), 21. At the time when Petrov was embarking on his translation of the *Aeneid* French was rapidly gaining ground as the language of the educated aristocracy, but English writers, as I will try to demonstrate, might have been significantly more important in Petrov's approach to the translation of the *Aeneid*.
69. Armstrong (2008), 169.
70. Cited and translated by Griffiths and Rabinowitz (1990), 7.
71. Griffiths and Rabinowitz (1990), 9.
72. Kalb (2008), 3. Kalb (15–18) also offers a concise discussion of the Russian 'Third Rome' doctrine closely connected with Russian interest in ancient Rome. The most detailed discussion of the doctrine can be found in Sinitsyna (1998).
73. Frolov (1999), 102–3.
74. Frolov (1999), 102.
75. Frolov cites here Egunov (1964), 40–9. Frolov (1999), 103.
76. Cited in Frolov (1999), 103.
77. Frolov (1999), 104.
78. Burrow (1997), 21 and 24.
79. The nineteenth-century Russian translators also supported this view. A Russian poet of that time, Vasilii Zhukovskii (1783–1852), for example, whose translation of the *Odyssey*, first published in 1849, became canonical, stated in his letter to Nikolai Gnedich: 'almost everything I have is someone else's or because of someone else,—but it is, nonetheless, mine' («у меня всё чужое или по поводу чужого, и всё, однако, моё»). Cited in Russian in Etkind (1973), 3.

80. Reyfman (1990), 35.
81. Friedberg (1997), 30.
82. Friedberg (1997), 31.
83. This approach was by no means uniquely Russian. In 1656 John Denham wrote in his preface to a London edition of *The Destruction of Troy*, an English rendition of Book 2 of the *Aeneid*: 'If Virgil must needs speak English, it were fit that he should speak it not only as a man of this Nation, but as a man of this age' (Brower, 1959, 274, and Friedberg, 1997, 25).
84. The most comprehensive biography of Petrov can be found in Shliapkin (1885).
85. Gukovskii (1927), 45–6. Translated in Kahn (1993), 752.
86. Reyfman (2003), 63.
87. Frolov (1999), 104.
88. See Shliapkin (1885), 386, and Frolov (1999), 105.
89. Ekaterina II (1901), 7.256.
90. This quip was especially offensive because Petrov had been known to stutter.
91. This poem, entitled 'Eliseus, or Bacchus Enraged' («Елисей, или раздраженный Вакх»), published in 1771, narrated the cynical and rather outrageous adventures of the hero Eliseus, who served as Bacchus' tool of revenge to punish the wine merchants for the high prices of wine.
92. For a review of the controversy see Serman and Kochetkova (1973), 1.325.
93. See Grigorii Gukovskii's 1947 article on Petrov at: <http://feb-web.ru/feb/irl/il0/il4/il4-3532.htm> [last visited 31 January 2013].
94. Petrov (1781), 3.
95. Petrov (1781), 6.
96. Petrov (1781), 6.
97. Petrov (1781), 11–12.
98. Petrov (1781), 14.
99. Kahn (1993), 754–5.
100. Kahn (1993), 755. Petrov was not the first writer in the Russian literary landscape who took a special interest in Dido. Iakov Kniazhnin wrote *Dido* (*Didona*) in 1767 and also presented Dido as a strong queen (see Chapter 2).
101. Proskurina (2005).
102. Proskurina (2005).
103. Thomas (2001), 172.
104. See Marlowe and Nashe (1968). The play tells the story of Dido's failed attempt to persuade Aeneas to stay in Carthage and Dido's consequent suicide. Bono and Tessitore (1998), 151, note: 'tema dell'effeto negativo dell'amore in termini di potere'.

105. Bono and Tessitore (1998), 168.
106. See Capern (2008), 170. See also Thomas's analysis on the influence of 'royalist French theory' on Dryden's translation.
107. See Thomas (2001), 171–2, who observes: 'Dido in his [Dryden's] version has been the active force in the affair, and it is Dido who pays.' See also Hammond (1999), 265–6, who discusses Aeneas' *pietas* as Dryden's main focus in his rendering of Book 4 of the *Aeneid*.
108. While I have little doubt that English translation practices had significant influence on Petrov, I have found no references to any French influence on his translation despite the fact that by the eighteenth century French was gaining more popularity and more literary clout among the Russian nobility.
109. Kahn (1993), 756.
110. Here Petrov uses the word «блудящий», which in Russian is a double entendre and can be translated as 'wandering' or as 'fornicating'.
111. Ross (2007), 34.
112. Greenfeld (1992), 200, aptly observes that in actuality Catherine's ascent to power 'was a usurpation of the Russian throne'.
113. Wortman (1995), 136.
114. See Ram (2003), 81.
115. Reyfman (2003), 64.
116. Cited in Reyfman (2003), 64.
117. Kirin (2010), 144.
118. Wortman (1995), 137.
119. I am thankful to Michael Paschalis for allowing me to use his paper written for the 'Vergil's Translators' workshop which took place in Vancouver in September 2012 (p. 5). See also Pappaioannou (2009).
120. Batalden (1982), 80–1.
121. Kagarlitsky (2008), 75.
122. Toporov (1996), 591.
123. While there is still no canonical translation of the *Aeneid* into Russian, the most commonly read translations will be discussed in the last chapter of this study.

2

Subversion and Mockery

IAKOV KNIAZHNIN'S TRAGEDY *DIDO*

> Волшебный край! Там в стары годы,
> Сатиры смелый властелин,
> Блистал Фонвизин, друг свободы,
> И переимчивый Княжнин.

> Miraculous realm! There in olden times,
> A bold master of satire,
> Fonvizin shone, freedom's friend,
> And also imitative Kniazhnin.
>
> Alexander Pushkin, *Evgenii Onegin*

Epic was only one of the 'high' genres with which Russian writers attempted to assert their place within the European literary canon and build literary bridges to classical antiquity. While efforts toward the Russian national epic in the eighteenth century failed and Petrov's translation endured a lukewarm reception, the 'Vergilian' text was successfully remapped by the tragic pen of Iakov Kniazhnin (1742–93).

Philip Hardie observes that '[s]ince antiquity Virgil the epicist has also been viewed as Virgil the tragedian' and that 'the definitive Roman epic' included 'many elements from the distinct . . . genre of tragedy'.[1] Book 4 of the *Aeneid* is traditionally considered the most tragic in the Roman epic, since the essence of tragedy is a conflict that requires the reader to take sides. But the consequence of reading the *Aeneid*, and especially the story of Dido and Aeneas, in the tragic light, offers deeper understanding of Vergil's intent. Hardie notes:

> The paradigm shift in much recent criticism of Attic tragedy has been away from a focus on individual psychology and morality to a concern

with political, social, and cultural relationships. The tragic self is understood not so much as the heroic individual struggling for self-determination, but as the *locus* of contesting roles within the structures of gender, household, and city.[2]

In the same vein the tragic plot and pathos of the fourth book of the *Aeneid* attracts so much attention in its reception because it offers every receiving culture the opportunity to search for solutions to moral or social dilemmas of the time, within their own historical and the political contexts. The first Russian attempt at mythological tragedy should be viewed from the same angle. Just as Vergil's use of tragedy needs to be assessed against the background of the cultural and ideological contexts of Augustan Rome, Kniazhnin's drama must be considered as part of the larger picture of Catherine's ideological practices as she continued Petrine initiatives to shape Russian national identity.

Iakov Kniazhnin's literary reputation has been mostly conditioned by Alexander Pushkin's dismissive labelling of him in *Evgenii Onegin* (XVIII) as 'imitative Kniazhnin' («переимчивый Княжнин»), an opinion that led to the literary obscurity of the playwright. As we can see from the epigraph, while Pushkin in his praise of stage performances appreciated the acerbic wit of Denis Fonvizin (1745–91) and his freedom of expression, Kniazhnin received one scathing adjective for his numerous tragedies and comedies. However, he deserves some consideration if only because with him, as Simon Karlinsky points out, started 'the inauguration of a full-fledged censorship over Russian drama', and we might say over all of Russian literature.[3] The 1760s in Russia, when Kniazhnin began his literary career, were a time when social and patriotic ideas took root. These ideas sometimes inadvertently found a reflection in Kniazhnin's literary output, which resulted in his depiction as a subversive figure, the object of Catherine's fear and her persecution.[4]

It would certainly be an exaggeration to call Kniazhnin intentionally subversive. But the ideas that he persistently chose to develop in his works showed his preoccupation with the humanistic ideals of dignity, civic identity, and, ubiquitously, the duty of a ruler towards his citizenry. Contemporary accounts speak highly about the enormous success Kniazhnin's tragedies enjoyed with the public. The imitative quality of his work, which Pushkin condescendingly held against him, was, as we have seen before, a part of eighteenth-century literary development and was organically necessary in the social evolution of

Russian literature.[5] The imitation of Western literary genres had its role in the Russian Enlightenment, compensating for the belatedness and absence of a firmly established literary canon and literary language. Russian readers introduced to these new literary genres and diction began to find their novelty applicable to their own emerging literary aesthetics and in tune with their own sentiments. Russian literature of that era became replete with odes, satires, tragedies, and comedies; the core contents of these genres brought to the fore the centuries-old European humanistic thoughts on virtue, citizenship, individual integrity, and justice. When Belinskii, a harsh judge of early Russian literature, categorically stated that 'true' Russian literature did not start until Pushkin and Gogol,[6] he was unfair to their eighteenth-century predecessors. Russian literature during the time of Kniazhnin acquired the most important features of any independent national literature: a genuine feeling of self-importance and an awareness of its mission. The timid 'imitative' steps were as unavoidable as they were for the Romans moving into the literary landscape after the Greeks had dominated and excelled in almost every literary genre. Themes that during Pushkin's time became commonplace were fresh and new in the literary expression of the eighteenth century.

Kniazhnin's most famous tragedy, *Vadim of Novgorod* (*Вадим Новгородский*, 1789), which so frightened and enraged Catherine that she dismissed from her graces her old friend and confidante Princess Dashkova, who sanctioned its posthumous publication, offers little evidence for the romantic revolutionary reputation that has surrounded it for years. That reputation resulted in a perception of some historical coincidences that had little to do with Kniazhnin's original intention for the play. Following Alexander Sumarokov's example in selecting the tragic protagonists from the medieval Russian chronicles, Kniazhnin chose as his plot the unsuccessful uprising in the ninth century of the native Novgorod leader Vadim against the Scandinavian prince Riurik, the progenitor of the most powerful dynasty, one that ruled Russia from the ninth to the seventeenth century, that very Riurik whose mythological ancestor Prusus was proclaimed Octavian Augustus' 'brother'. Novgorod in Russian lore was, of course, shrouded in the romanticized reputation of republicanism, which might have sounded to Catherine like a homage to the events of the recent French Revolution.

At the beginning of her rule Catherine enjoyed playing the role of a liberal monarch, even entrusting Nikolai Novikov (1744–1818) with 'establishing satirical journalism's right to treat such social phenomena as had formerly been within the sole jurisdiction of the bureaucracy in Tsarist Russia, which could be considered only in secret and then only with the knowledge and approval of the authorities'.[7] Catherine herself started publishing a satirical journal, *Всякая всячина* (*Miscellany*), which was chiefly concerned with 'the problem of Russia's cultural independence and the discovery of native values'.[8] Novikov followed suit by publishing several satirical journals such as *Трутень* (*The Drone*) and *Живописец* (*The Painter*) directed against Russian nobility, 'which refused to adopt the ideas of the Enlightenment or yield even a fraction of its privileges'.[9] However, Catherine, despite her original liberal tendencies, became displeased with Novikov's aggressive satire. Emel'ian Pugachev's rebellion (1773) exacerbated her reactionary tendencies. Pugachev was one of the impostors that declared himself to be Emperor Peter III, who was in fact deceased. However, Pugachev, unlike the other impostors, was able to ignite an organized revolt and head the so-called Peasant War from 1773 until his capture in 1775. Catherine had no patience for disobedience of her subjects and she ordered his execution. The rebellion, however, clearly left her frightened.

Novikov subsequently ceased to publish his satirical journals, and busied himself instead with several educational enterprises. These also met with suspicion from Catherine, who in 1792 ordered Novikov's arrest and imprisoned him for fifteen years.[10] The relationship between Catherine and Novikov, however, demonstrated the changing nature of the Russian literary landscape against which we can better understand the tsarina's reaction to Kniazhnin's work and his later reception as some sort of a 'revolutionary'. As Serman points out, 'the very fact that the ruler was participating directly in literary life was an astounding novelty in Russia'.[11] Secondly, the fact that the ruler actually feared the impact and influence of literature on her subjects is most certainly noteworthy and a phenomenon to which we will return repeatedly in this study.

Catherine declared Kniazhnin's *Vadim of Novgorod* dangerous and ordered the entire edition destroyed. This was because of her overreaction to the bloody events of 1789, which brought Louis XVI and Marie Antoinette to the guillotine, a terrifying reality which only contributed to her growing fear of unruly subjects such as Pugachev. If before the events of the French Revolution Catherine charmingly declared 'Chez moi, tout le monde a son franc-parler,'[12] she clearly had not been so tolerant after the frightening events on her own soil, which almost grew out of control. The showdown in France, the repetition of which she feared in Russia, also contributed to the tsarina's fears. What became clear from her extreme reaction to the play was that Russian literary history had achieved its hallmark milestone: the government began to perceive literature as a rival authority and the entrenched powers started to suspect subversion in literary works.

This change raises the question whether or not Kniazhnin in fact meant anything subversive by his play. It is hard to disagree with Karlinsky, who persuasively argues that as soon as Kniazhnin realized the 'unexpected contemporary relevance' of the play, he 'requested that the projected production of his play be abandoned'. It would have also been somewhat illogical if his widow petitioned the Princess Dashkova for help in the publication if the play was meant to be subversive.[13] Kniazhnin, perhaps, did not intend to be the defender of republican freedoms against tyrannical absolutism, but it was not the first time that he displayed a tendency to convey in his writings ideas that may be interpreted as subversive. It also has to be noted that if Catherine perceived the play as subversive, that reaction was perhaps more telling that the author's intent.

Furthermore, *Vadim of Novgorod* was one of Kniazhnin's late works and was preceded by several other dramatic works, which are now largely forgotten. One of these, particularly relevant to the purposes of this study, was staged in 1769 in St Petersburg with Sumarokov's blessing and at Catherine's command. The play was Kniazhnin's first tragedy, *Dido* (*Дидона*, *Didona*), and was initially read to the tsarina privately by the author.[14] The first performance was overwhelmingly successful and afterwards it became his most widely performed play, although it was the only one of his plays that was based in a foreign locale and did not select its protagonists from medieval Russian chronicles. Although it garnered noticeable theatrical success, it received, however, very little attention in literary criticism. Since this tragedy has never been translated into English, I offer here a detailed summary of the plot, along with translations of the passages most relevant to my analysis of the play in the context of the reception of the Vergilian *Aeneid*.

The tragedy consists of five acts with six dramatis personae: Dido, Aeneas, Iarbas, Antenor (Aeneas' comrade), Gias (Iarbas' confidant), and Timar (Dido's courtier). The action takes place entirely in Dido's palace in Carthage. The first act opens with a dialogue between Aeneas and Antenor during which the former confesses to the latter that he is agonizing about his impending marriage to Dido. He admits that his passion (страсть) for Dido distracts him from his primary duty, loyalty to his legacy, as the last Trojan royal destined to restore the former glory of Troy:

> Всё, всё Энееву к Дидоне страсть винит:
> Родителева тень, Троянская держава,
> Мой долг, Зевес, сама моя бессмертна слава.[15]

> Everything, everything blames my passion for Dido:
> My father's ghost, the commonwealth of Troy,
> My duty, Zeus, and my immortal glory itself.

Aeneas' moral dilemma at the beginning of the play is reminiscent of his Vergilian counterpart's. Vergil's Aeneas also expresses his desire to have died near the walls of Troy along with his peers and bewails his destiny as a survivor (*Aen.* 1.94–6: *O terque quaterque beati, / quis ante ora patrum Troiae sub moenibus altis / contigit oppetere!*—'Oh you, blessed three and four times, to whom it befell to meet their end in front of their fathers under the walls of Troy'). Unlike Vergil's Aeneas, however, Kniazhnin's hero experiences an emotional upheaval, the pangs of love and inability at first to overcome Dido's erotic appeal. His dialogue with Antenor in the first act evokes Dido's confession to Anna at the beginning of Book 4, displaying a power of emotion uncharacteristic of the *pius Aeneas*. Antenor himself is puzzled by the strong passion in his friend:[16]

> Эней, которого судьбина избирает
> За Трою умереть, от страсти умирает.

> Aeneas, whom fate chooses
> To die for Troy, is dying of passion.

He prompts Aeneas to be stronger in his resistance to Dido's unquestionable charms:[17]

> Тот счастлив, кто любви отравы не вкушает;
> Но тот велик, ее кто узы разрушает:
> И, оставляючи, Эней, страну сию,
> Любовью славу днесь величишь ты свою.

> That man is happy who has not tasted love's poison;
> But that one is great, who severs its ties:
> And by leaving, Aeneas, this country,
> With your love you will increase your glory.

Aeneas seems persuaded, as Vergil's Dido was by Anna, by the power of his friend's argument. He resolves to leave Dido. When Dido enters the stage she mistakenly interprets his agony of indecision as the fading of his love until he persuades her that his passion remains unchanged, but he must pursue his heroic destiny. To which she replies: «Будь меньше ты герой, люби меня лишь боле» ('Be less of a hero, but only love me more'). The scene ends with Dido leaving under the impression that Aeneas is jealous of Iarbas, her royal neighbour and suitor, and thus he still loves her.

In the second act, which begins with a dialogue between Iarbas and Gias and evokes Iarbas' famous monologue in Book 4, Iarbas expresses his fury over the love between Dido and Aeneas and reveals that many nobles at Dido's own court are waiting for a chance to overthrow her. Hopeful that Dido will come to her senses and marry him, he praises her talent for governing and city building and puts at her feet his kingship and his love. He also appeals to her sense of duty as a queen:[18]

> Склонись к сему царю: желание его
> Есть польза важная престола твоего.

> Yield to this king: his desire
> Is an important benefit for your throne.

Dido rejects her powerful suitor firmly but politely, offering him instead her friendship and support in military exploits. 'But we cannot order our heart' («Но сердцем нам своим нельзя повелевать»), she asserts, insisting on her love for Aeneas. Infuriated, Iarbas exclaims then: 'Queen, be ashamed of your passion!' («Царица![19] постыдись ты страсти своея»). Dido then openly confesses that her passion for Aeneas consumes her, and Iarbas warns her that such a union would belittle her crown («Но знай, что брак твой с ним унизит твой венец»). Dido leaves and Iarbas promises to Gias that now with all hope for Dido's affection gone he will have his revenge.

In the third act Dido, replete with foreshadowing abandonment by Aeneas, confronts him. Her reproaches, to which we will return, echo almost verbatim the Vergilian Dido. Aeneas, employing a similar argument to that of Book 4 of the *Aeneid*, tells her that it is by the will of the gods that he leaves Carthage and seeks the shores destined for him. The emotions of Kniazhnin's Aeneas, however, are unbridled, his passion for Dido full of unrestrained abandon as he presents to her his difficult choice (89):[20]

> Я стражду, рвуся;
> И как не рваться мне? — с Дидоной расстаюся!
> Днесь гибнет весь мой свет, теряю всё, что есть;
> Тебя теряю, жизнь . . . но остается честь.

> I suffer, I am torn;
> And how could I not?—I am parting with Dido!
> Thus all my light is gone, I lose everything that there is;
> I lose you, my life . . . but my honour remains.

The main conflict of the play is for the first time articulated clearly in these lines: the choice for both Aeneas and Dido is duty or love. And each of them makes a choice by the end of the play. Dido's response to this candid plea by Aeneas is the exact replica of her scolding of Aeneas in Book 4 of the *Aeneid*, when in her hour of despair she exclaims (*Aen.* 4.365–7):

> Nec tibi diva parens generis nec Dardanus auctor,
> perfide, sed duris genuit te cautibus horrens
> Caucasus Hyrcanaeque admorunt ubera tigres.

> Neither a goddess is your mother nor the Dardanian founder,
> faithless one, but under rough rocks Caucasus begot you
> And the Hyrcanian tigers suckled you.

Kniazhnin's Dido reiterates these sentiments:[21]

> Вещают, что в тебе бессмертных кровь течет;
> Неправда, — лютый тигр тебе дал видеть свет;
> В утробе ты зачат свирепейшия львицы!

> They say that blood of the immortals flows in your veins;
> This is a lie,—a savage tiger let you into the light;
> You were conceived in the womb of the fiercest lioness.

However, after this familiar attack on Aeneas, in an unexpected plot twist, Dido threatens him with a union with Iarbas in case Aeneas abandons her. Aeneas in an uncharacteristic fit of jealousy decides to stay and Dido gives orders to prepare everything for the wedding.

As Iarbas in the fourth act contemplates his revenge against the two lovers and addresses his father, Jupiter, in words evocative of Vergil, he receives the news of Dido's and Aeneas' impending nuptials. After attacking Aeneas, Iarbas is defeated and brought in chains before Dido and Aeneas, who have to decide their enemy's fate. Aeneas sets him free, but Iarbas, who now owes Aeneas his life, begins to hate him even more. In the next scene Antenor confronts Aeneas and encourages him to spurn the kingdom which will be handed to him by his future wife (101, «Ступай и презри скиптр, вручаемый женой!»), which brings to mind Mercury calling Aeneas in Book 4 (line 266) of the *Aeneid 'uxorius'* ('under his wife's control'). With a heavy heart Aeneas accepts Antenor's arguments, but orders his friend to prepare furtively the ships for sailing. Aeneas intends to leave without saying goodbye.

The fifth and final act finds Dido and the ladies of her court learning that Aeneas has sailed away. Dido, fully understanding the extent of Aeneas' betrayal, declares that she cannot go on living without him. Threatened by Iarbas, who now besieges Carthage and revels in the bloodshed, Dido pleads with him, asking him to kill her but to spare her people. The merciless Iarbas offers her a choice either to marry him or perish with her city. Faced with the same choice as Aeneas earlier between love and duty, Dido predictably chooses to die, throwing herself into the bonfire that has already engulfed her city: 'Let Carthage be Dido's tomb' («Да будет Карфаген Дидониной гробницей»). The play ends with Iarbas' words (116):

> Дидона!.. нет ее!.. Я злобой омрачен,
> Бросая гром, своим сам громом поражен.
>
> Dido! She is gone! I am sombre with spite,
> And hurling thunder, I am smitten by thunder myself.

Kniazhnin's first tragedy is especially captivating considering that it is one of the first examples of Russian mythological tragedy. It is worthwhile addressing here Kniazhnin's sources. It is clear from the tragedy's text that Kniazhnin was very familiar with the Vergilian text, which he quotes, as we have seen, sometimes almost verbatim. Educated at the gymnasium of the Academy of Russian Sciences, Kniazhnin probably knew some Latin. He would have read Vergil, however, most likely in a French translation, since French was the language that later helped him to earn his living by translating Corneille and Voltaire, when he was in disfavour with the court.

There were at least two other sources that appear to have had a significant influence on Kniazhnin's reception of the Vergilian love story: *Didone abbandonata* (*Dido Abandoned*, 1724), the Italian opera with a text by Pietro Metastasio, and the *Didon* (*Dido*, 1734) of Lefranc de Pompignan. It is beneficial to look briefly at these two *Dido*s and separate their influence on Kniazhnin from that of Vergil.[22]

Didone abbandonata was the first opera by Metastasio; though largely forgotten today, it made him famous in his lifetime. It was Metastasio who in his departure from Vergil added to the plot Iarbas as an active participant in the dramatic events. In the *Aeneid* Iarbas appears only once, enraged at Dido's rejection of him and her affair with Aeneas, as he addresses his father Jupiter Hammon and calls for his vengeance upon the two lovers. Vergil's Dido builds herself a funeral pyre and kills herself with Aeneas' sword, cursing him and his descendants and invoking the 'avenging spirit', ultimately Hanni- bal, to wage endless war against Aeneas' progeny. Justin, a late antiquity author, relates another version of the story in which Iarbas, relentlessly pursuing Dido with an offer of marriage, threatens to destroy Carthage; Dido, hating him, decides to kill herself and ascends the funeral pyre, in this way saving her citizens from Iarbas' persecu- tion. In both Vergil's and Justin's renditions of the myth the most important theme that emerges is one of aetiology: in Vergil's case the origins of enmity between Rome and Carthage, and in Justin's, the foundation story of Carthage, at the core of which is the story of human sacrifice and martyrdom for the sake of the common good. Metastasio, however, despite borrowing Justin's active participation of Iarbas in Dido's demise, is not interested in any problems of historiosophy. His interests are primarily emotional and psychological. Unruly passion dominates the events of Metastasio's play, but the characters are linear and their struggles all directed towards the culmination of the play in Dido's *Flammentod*, as Dido and her city perish in the fire. Metasta- sio's Aeneas is purely heroic: from the first scene to the last he remains steadfast in his decision to leave Carthage and is completely free of any of the hesitations apparent in Aeneas' dialogues with his attendant in Kniazhnin's play. Aeneas' sparing of Iarbas is also a manifestation of his noble heroic nature, which is juxtaposed with Dido's somewhat irrational and reckless passion. In essence Metastasio's work is a baroque drama full of intrigue, recognitions, confessions, and emo- tional upheavals which are directed towards the development of the plot, but do not affect the behaviour of the characters. What was important for Kniazhnin in Metastasio's rendition was the morally significant differentiation between the steadfastness of Aeneas' heroic character and Dido's self-absorbed blind passion. For Metastasio it was a marginal concern, but for Kniazhnin it became the focus.

In Lefranc de Pompignan's *Didon* the historical and philosophical aspects play a large role, and they contributed to Kniazhnin's interest in the myth's historiosophical aspects. Both Aeneas and Dido are royal heroes—he, the last survivor and hope of the House of Priam; she, the fugitive from Tyre and the founder of Carthage. Both heroes carry the burden of responsibility for their own mission and those who depend on them. Dido's words 'L'amour a ses moments, l'Etat a ses besoins' ('Love has its moments, the State has its needs,' 24) are at the centre of the play's conflict. However, the theme that was to become crucial for Kniazhnin, the story of the restoration of Troy and state building, was still marginalized. Aeneas justifies his abandonment of Dido not by his mission as a founder of a future civilization, but by abstract ideas of heroism: 'Non, ce n'est point l'amour, c'est la guerre, seigneur, / Qui seul d'un héros doit payer la valeur' ('No, it is not love but war, my Lord, that is the only thing that can prove a hero's virtue,' 25). In addition to such ruminations, Pompignan's Aeneas, like Vergil's, feels responsible for the fates of his comrades, who complain about being exiles in a land ruled by someone else. Like Metastasio's Dido, Pompignan's also admits the destructive force of her passion for Aeneas: 'Je devrois te haïr, ingrat, et je t'adore' ('I should hate you, ungrateful one, and I love you passionately,' 29). Both plays in effect present a similar type of conflict: the choice between heroic duty and indulgence in emotion. In the case of Metastasio we are dealing with a baroque drama which absorbed some precepts of classical tragedy. Pompignan follows the main conventions of the eighteenth-century drama conditioned by Corneille and Racine, but without their metaphysical perspectives.

What, then, was the idea behind Kniazhnin's Dido, who, like both his ancient model and these two European influences, also contemplated the conflict between love and duty?

Kniazhnin's play appeared at about the same time as Vasilii Petrov's first translated books of the *Aeneid*.[23] It is hard not to notice the parallels in their shared interest in the figure of Dido as a female monarch. We have seen in the previous chapter how Petrov used the Dido of the *Aeneid* as a point of comparison with Catherine, a comparison beneficial for the Russian tsarina, but damaging to the queen of Carthage. Kniazhnin's contemplations in his tragedy about the nature of female rule seem to hinge upon the same issue. Dido again emerges as an inferior Eastern queen, noble, indeed, but unable to resist her human passions. In the minds of Kniazhnin's contemporaries the comparison was perhaps obvious and flattering to the tsarina in the same way Petrov's translation was. While Dido was unable to put her duty before her love, Catherine ruled Russia with never faltering confidence, despite her many 'passions'. However, is it reasonable to assume that Kniazhnin meant anything negative by Dido's submission to her love and was judgemental of Catherine's numerous affairs, which undermined the dignity of her position? This conjecture seems possible. However, his contemporaries at least viewed the play in a very innocuous light, as one of the letters of Mikhail Murav'ev (1757–1807), an important source for our understanding of eighteenth-century Russian culture, testifies:[24]

Я был вчерась на преставлении «Дидоны» Якова Борисовича Княжнина, сего столь тихого и любви достойного человека, который заставляет ждать в себе трагика, может быть, превосходнейшего чем его тесть.

Yesterday I was at the performance of 'Dido' by Iakov Borisovich Kniazhnin, such a quiet man and so worthy of love, who forces us to anticipate in him a tragic writer, perhaps even better than his father-in-law [Alexander Sumarokov].

While admiring the performance, where the role of indomitable Iarbas was played by the legendary actor Ivan Dmitrievskii, Murav'ev offers an interesting evaluation of Kniazhnin as a 'quiet man' and 'worthy of love', a characterization which does not invite any conjecture of subversive activity. Murav'ev was a remarkable figure in the cultural milieu of eighteenth-century St Petersburg, himself a writer of both poetry and prose. Among his many acquaintances were Kheraskov and Petrov, and he closely followed all the events related to music, theatre, and literature. His letters present, in fact, an invaluable account of the cultural life in Russia of his time. However, he saw no hidden message in Kniazhnin's mythological play. Perhaps there was none, and this drama was merely a prelude to Kniazhnin's career as a playwright who would tackle more indigenous Russian themes which, as with *Vadim of Novgorod*, hit closer to home and made the tsarina nervous.

NIKOLAI OSIPOV'S *AENEID TURNED*
UPSIDE DOWN

The reception of Vergil in the eighteenth century was not all as serious as it might seem from the failed attempts at the national epic, Petrov's translation, and Kniazhnin's treatment of Dido's story as a theme for tragedy. In his 'Epistle II' Sumarokov predicted the appearance of mock *Aeneid*s as an inevitable step in the development of versification in Russian in imitation of classical genres:

> Он в подлу женщину Дидону превращает,
> Или нам бурлака Энеем представляет,
> Являя рыцарьми буянов, забияк . . . .
> Стихи, владеющи высокими делами,
> В сем складе пишутся пренизкими словами.[25]

> He will turn Dido into a base woman,
> And will present Aeneas as a *burlak*,[26]
> While the knights will become scoundrels and bullies . . . .
> The verses that were concerned with lofty ideals,
> In this rendition will be written by base words.

These lines were composed in 1747, more than forty years before the appearance of Nikolai Osipov's mock epic, his travesty-masterwork *Вергилиева Энеида, вывороченная наизнанку* (*Vergil's Aeneid Turned Upside Down*, 1791–96), which signified a new stage in the development of the comic genre in Russian literature. Little is known of the life and career of Nikolai Osipov (1751–99). Most of what we do know is contained in a dictionary of Russian writers compiled by Evgenii Bolkhovitinov.[27] He was educated initially at home and then in various boarding schools. His education was sufficient, but his knowledge of foreign languages was limited to French and German. He did not produce any other significant writings and the travestied *Aeneid* remains his only original poetic work. Osipov started publishing it in 1791 (the first two parts), and after a major success, he published the third and fourth parts in 1796. The combined parts contained seven songs and saw a second edition in 1800.[28]

The idea for a mock epic was, of course, not original and owed much to the European travestied *Aeneid*s, namely, the classic of the genre by Paul Scarron, *Le Virgile travesti en vers burlesques* (1648–52), and especially Aloys Blumauer's *Die Abenteuer des* *frommen Helden Aeneas* (1782–8). Scarron's burlesque poems were not created for mere entertainment but showed a defined political intent. An active participant in the Fronde, Scarron wrote several poignant poems directed against Cardinal Mazarin. As Scarron mocked the style of the high epic, he also pointedly derided inconsistencies in Vergil's plot and Aeneas' piety and tendency to whine.[29]

Although Scarron is often cited as the most salient example of the travestied epics, he himself most likely imported this genre to France from Italy, where Giovanni Battista Lalli composed *L'Eneide travestita* in 1633–5.[30] In fact Lalli was the first to apply the term 'travesty' (from Latin *transvestire*, to present a subject in a dress intended for someone else) to his parody. The *Aeneid* was an easy target for mockery for Lalli and Scarron alike. Both in Italy and in France it was still a 'classical age', and after Dante's *Divine Comedy* the *Aeneid* was still seen as the most sublime of any literary achievements. In the period from 1603 to 1639 alone the *Aeneid* was translated into French at least twelve times. Osipov's *Aeneid* followed for the most part the technique established by Scarron in the creation of his mock epic. The debasement of both the form and content was important. The lofty language typically associated with epic was also abandoned in favour of a street vernacular, following the example of Scarron, who commenced his mock epic in this way:

> Je chante cet homme pieux,
> Qui vint, chargé de tous ses dieux
> Et de monsieur son père Anchise,
> Beau vieillard à la barbe grise,
> Depuis la ville où les Grégeois
> Occirent tant de bons bourgeois.[31]

> I sing of this pious man,
> Who came weighed down with all his gods
> And with Monsieur Anchises, his father,
> A handsome old man with a vile beard
> From the town where the Greeks
> Killed so many good bourgeois.

While Scarron's direct influence on Osipov's *Aeneid* has often been questioned, there was another influence on the Russian mock epic which by consensus had a greater impact.[32] Although not widely read today, Aloys Blumauer's satiric and philosophic poetry, especially his

Abenteuer des frommen Helden Aeneas, made him extremely popular with the reading public in Austria and Germany.[33] His travesty of the *Aeneid* was begun in 1782, shortly after Pope Pius VI's visit to Vienna, and was understood as a satire on the Pope and the Catholic Church. Blumauer started his satire eagerly, and the first instalment, *Das zweyte Buch von Virgils Aeneis. Travestirt von A. Blumauer* (1782), was full of wit and humour that even today retains much of its original appeal.[34] Blumauer himself denied any influence of Scarron on his work. While Scarron for the most part recognized the literary value of Vergil's epic and even showed a certain admiration for some parts of the *Aeneid* by creatively interpreting them, Blumauer used the Latin epic merely as a skeleton, which his satirical intuition then endowed with flesh. Blumauer also had a clear agenda that went beyond mere entertainment of the public: to attack the Catholic Church, not its doctrine but its clericalism, and juxtapose it with the enlightened atmosphere that came to Austria under Joseph II.[35] Like Scarron, who introduced the mundane life of Paris into his parody, Blumauer made references to Vienna and all aspects of contemporary life ubiquitous in his parody. However, unlike Scarron, he was rather fond of double entendres and vulgarisms, which he generously inserted into his narrative. In his anti-clerical sentiments he did not strive to present himself as a leader of an intellectual movement, but rather as an astute observer of his country's mores.

A. I. Sobolevskii once observed that Osipov's *Aeneid* 'could be called a remake or even a free translation of Blumauer's *Aeneid*'. Osipov indeed follows Blumauer rather closely, replacing his stanzas of seven lines with stanzas of ten lines, but mainly substituting the details of everyday German life with those of Russian: if in Blumauer Aeneas while in Carthage enters a *Kaffeehaus* and asks for *Milchkaffee*, Osipov makes him go to a *kabak* ('Russian pub') and drink vodka.[36] Although Osipov's *Aeneid* closely followed in Blumauer's steps, it is much harder to pinpoint its broader ideological agenda. Boris Tomashevskii noted:

> while writing the travestied *Aeneid* Osipov was thinking neither about a literary parody on Vergil nor about political satire. His main goal was the piling up of comical situations. Following Blumauer, Osipov blurred the former's narrative, which featured relative briefness . . . Aiming at making the poem as hilarious as possible, Osipov reached for the limits when debasing the language and description of his characters.[37]

While the poem's hidden agenda is not as obvious as that of Scarron and Blumauer, it would be altogether unfair to treat it merely as a source of entertainment, although undoubtedly Osipov wanted to please his readers.

In terms of Russian literary development, the travestied *Aeneid* was a reaction against the stultified and impersonal attempts at imitating the ancients. It also, unlike Blumauer, but very much like Scarron, parodies Vergil's work in a refined way revealing a great understanding and closer familiarity with the Vergilian text, even if Osipov did read it in translation.

The Russian mock epic appearing almost simultaneously with Vasilii Petrov's translation of the *Aeneid* served as a counterbalance for writers and readers alike as it helped them descend from the lofty plane of Greco-Roman Parnassus into the reality of everyday life, in which the heroic became intertwined with the base, and the court poetry took on the form of everyday speech.

Osipov for the first time used for his poem the tetrameter (four iambic feet), which in 1820 was canonized by Alexander Pushkin's famous and brilliant poem *Ruslan and Liudmila*. Here is how Osipov begins his poem:

> Еней был удалой детина.
> И самой хватской молодец;
> Герои все пред ним скотина;
> Душил их так, как волк овец.
> Но после свального как бою
> Сожгли обманом греки Трою,
> Он, взяв котомку, ну бежать;
> Бродягой принужден скитаться,
> Как нищий по миру шататься,
> От бабьей злости пропадать.

> Aeneas was a daring fellow,
> And by all means a crafty lad;
> All heroes are cattle before him;
> He strangled them like a wolf does sheep.
> But after a rather messy battle
> The Greek burned Troy through deceit;
> And he took off with a little knapsack,
> Like a vagabond he was forced to wander
> To roam the world like a beggar,
> And be destroyed by a wench's anger.

Just like in Scarron, Juno, the main cause of Aeneas' wanderings, is ridiculed for her feminine pettiness:

> Но знать, что на Олимпе бабы
> По нашему ж бывают слабы,
> И так же трудно их унять.

> But be it known, that on Olympus,
> The wenches are as weak as ours,
> And as difficult to control.

This snippet from the beginning of Osipov's poem presents an interesting linguistic study. It is most certainly a far cry from Lomonosov's, Petrov's, and Kheraskov's высокий стиль, the lofty form of verse. It is also completely removed from Kniazhnin's more accessible but nevertheless extremely stylized language of mythological tragedy. Osipov's language is debased to the point of ridicule, which in effect was the whole point of the travestied *Aeneid*s. Unfortunately, the English translation cannot adequately render words such as «детина» ('daring fellow'), «скотина» ('cattle'), «шататься» ('wander'), or «бабы» ('wenches') as they present a type of vulgar Russian vernacular that Lomonosov and Petrov tried to avoid. Educated Russians would not have used this language in their everyday speech and that was precisely Osipov's point in employing it. However, it was also not quite the language of the people, for it was too stylized and contrived in its effort to be base.

A closer comparative look at the texts of Osipov, Vergil, Scarron, and Blumauer better reveals the peculiarly Russian nature of Osipov's parody. In the first book of Vergil's *Aeneid*, Jupiter predicts the future of Aeneas and the Roman race to Venus, who comes to him in tears over her son's plight (*Aen.* 1.257–90):

> Parce metu, Cytherea, manet immota tuorum
> fata tibi; cernes urbem et promissa Lavini
> moenia sublimem feres ad sidera caeli
> magnanimum Aenean; neque me sententia vertit. . . .
> At puer Ascanius, cui nunc cognomen Iulo
> additur (Ilus erat, dum res stetit Ilia regno),
> triginta magnos volvendis mensibus orbis
> imperio explebit, regnum ab sede Lavini
> transferet, et Longam multa vi muniet Albam.
> Hic iam ter centum totos regnabitur annos
> gente sub Hectorea, donec regina sacerdos
> Marte gravis geminam partu dabit Ilia prolem.

Inde lupae fulvo nutrice tegmine laetus
Romulus excipiet gentem et Mavortia condet
moenia Romanosque suo de nomine dicet.
His ego nec metas rerum nec tempora pono:
imperium sine fine dedi. . . .
Nascetur pulchra Troianus origine Caesar,
imperium Oceano, famam qui terminet astris,
Iulius, a magno demissum nomen Iulo.
Hunc tu olim caelo spoliis Orientis onustum
accipies secura; vocabitur hic quoque votis.

Spare your fear, Venus, the fate of your kin
remains unchanged for your benefit; you will behold a city
and the promised Lavinian walls and you will carry high
towards the stars of the sky the great-hearted Aeneas;
I have not changed my mind. . . .
But the boy Ascanius, to whose name the surname Iulus
is now added (it was Ilus, while the Trojan kingdom stood),
he will fulfil three hundred circles of years
with their swift passing months and he will transfer
the kingdom from the seat of Lavinium
and he will fortify with great force Alba Longa.
Here the race of Hector will rule three hundred
whole years, until the queen priestess
Ilia, pregnant by Mars, will give birth to twin progeny.
Then Romulus rejoicing in the tawny hide
of his nurse, a she-wolf, will receive the race
and will establish the walls of Mars
and call the Romans after his own name.
For these prophecies I establish neither the limit nor
    the timeline:
I have given power without end. . . .
From this beautiful origin Trojan Caesar will be born,
Who will limit his power with the Ocean and his glory
    with the stars,
Iulius, a name descended from great Iulus.
At some point you will accept him free from care
into the sky burdened with the spoils of the Orient.

This is one of the most programmatic and ideological passages of the
Vergilian epic. All three travesties try to reflect the importance of this
passage, taking from this very long speech of Jupiter only a small

fraction relevant to their concerns. All three writers undoubtedly understood the central nature of this prophecy for the ideology of the *Aeneid* and they tried to reflect it. They also knew that it would be the theme most familiar to their educated reader. Scarron's imitation is:

> Ne pleurez plus, la Cythérée,
> Et tenez pour chose assurée
> Tout ce qu'a prédit le Destin
> D'Enée et du pays latin.
> Vous le verrez bâtir muraille
> De brique et de pierre de taille.[38]

> Don't cry any more, Cytherea,
> And take as a sure thing
> Everything that destiny has predicted
> Of Aeneas and the Latin country.
> You will see him build a wall
> Of brick and whittled stone.

The lofty style of Vergil's divine prophecy is parodied here with refinement and sophistication but it is significantly shortened. Blumauer in turn used this prophecy to state clearly the main agenda of his mock epic (253–9):

> Ja einer soll einmal
> Ein Kindlein prokreieren!
> Das soll von unserm Feldmarschall,
> Herrn Mars, den Namen führen.
> Es lässt mich zwar Vergilius
> Das prohezei'n: allein man muss
> Dem Narrn nich alles glauben.

> Yes, one should for once
> Procreate a little child!
> It should bear the name
> Of Mr Mars, our general.
> Vergil lets me, to be sure,
> Prophesize that: still, one does
> Not need to believe everything from a fool.

The prophecy then is turned into a satire against the future popes, who were to rule the world. The prophecy, however, is questioned and so is Vergil's credibility.

Osipov uses all three of his predecessors:[39]

Старик Зевес оскаля зубы
Улыбку нежну оказал;
Усы разгладивши и губы,
С усмешкой дочь поцеловал:
Сказал: «Об нем ты не пекися;
Но на меня в том положися
Всегда я в слове господин.
Эней во всем себя прославит,
Потомство сильное возставит;
Или я не Сатурнов сын . . . .
Потом явится сильно племя
Одних мущин всех холостых;
С себя те сбросят светско бремя;
Не будет вовсе жен у них.
Все будут петь по их погудке,
Плясать по их все будут дудке,
Весь свет под власть свою возьмут;
Везде пошлют свои законы,
Везде свои поставят троны,
И всех под ноготь свой прижмут.
Их власть дотоле продолжится

И будут все их почитать;
Доколе слепота продлится,
И будут ноги целовать.
Начальник их, старик не промах,
Воздвигнет трон на царских тронах,
Возьмет под власть свою Царей;
Ему все будут поклоняться,
Его все будут устрашаться
И чтить во слепоте своей.»

The old man Zeus baring his teeth
Showed a gentle smile;
Smoothing his moustache and his lips,
He kissed his daughter, laughing:
And said: 'Do not worry about him;
But rely in everything on me;
I am always a man of my word.
Aeneas will make himself famous in everything;
And will leave behind a strong race of descendants;
Or I am not the son of Saturn. . . .

Then the strong tribe will come
Of only unmarried men;
They will get rid of societal burdens;
And won't have wives at all.

Everybody will sing their tune,
Everybody will dance to their flute,
And they will take the whole world under their sway;
They will send their laws everywhere,
And put their thrones everywhere,
And get everyone under their thumb.

'Their rule will last, and everybody will respect them
As long as the blindness lasts,
And they will kiss their feet.
Their leader, a savvy fellow,
Will build a throne over other tsars' thrones,
And will take other tsars under his sway.
Everybody will bow to him,
Everybody will fear him
And revere him in their blindness.'

Osipov's prophecy of Jove is almost as long as Vergil's. The gentle irony of the relationship between Venus and Jupiter so palpable in Vergil is also apparent in Osipov. So is the imperial rhetoric of expansion and domination. But then the tone changes. The grand prophecy turns into its antithesis. The observation 'everybody will respect them / As long as the blindness lasts' is repeated at the end of the excerpt: 'Everybody will fear him / And revere him in their blindness.' These lines smack of subversion and political criticism rather than the light-hearted laughter that is pervasive in the poem. Overall, however, Osipov's subversion, if there was any, can barely be detected, and it is most certainly significantly less focused than that of his European predecessors.

In general, however, Osipov's poem is remarkably close to Vergil's *Aeneid* in imagery, poetic tropes, and plot development. Since this study repeatedly focuses upon the Dido and Aeneas episode, I have chosen Osipov's rendition of Book 4 as a case study of his diction.

Like every 'song' of the poem, the 'fourth song' is preceded by a short summary of what the book narrates: 'The way in which the Libyan queen fell headlong in love; their trip to hunt and the events that transpired there. How then Aeneas left that queen, and she killed herself with her own hands' («Каким образом Ливийская царица влюбилась чрезвычайно; езда их на охоту, и бывшие там происшествия. Как потом Эней царицу ту оставил, и она умертвила себя собственными своими руками»). The song itself begins in Vergilian mode with a thorough description of Dido's emotional state, which then manifests itself in her physical illness:[40]

Дидоны тлело все сердечко
Енеем больно непутем;
И каждое его словечко
Как будто врезывалось в нем.
Всю ночь о нем лишь помышляла,
Из памяти не выпускала,
Не могши вовсе глаз сомкнуть.
В постелю легши лишь металась;
Как угорелая бросалась,
И не могла никак заснуть.

На все бока она вертелась,
Лежала будто на иглах;
И чуть от вздохов не надселась
В любовных мучась хлопотах;
Кусала ногти, грызла губы;
Едва от скрежета все зубы
Не стерла вплоть и с корнем вон.

Dido's whole heart was smouldering
Awfully sick with Aeneas;
His every little word
Was as if etched in it.
She was thinking about him all night long,
Did not let him leave her memory
And could not shut her eyes.
Lying in bed she only turned over;
As if burning she tossed,
And could not fall asleep.

She was turning on each side
As if lying on needles;
And her sighing almost did her in
As she was suffering from her cares;
She was biting her nails, gnawing her lips;
She almost ground all her teeth
To dust and to the very root.

The influence of Vergil's description of Dido's suffering in the opening lines of Book 4 is obvious in this rendition of Osipov, regardless of the somewhat 'unqueenly' grinding of teeth and gnawing of lips. The first stanza, despite its comic diction and use of colloquialisms, could have belonged to a more serious poem. Especially interesting is the use of Vergil in details: the heart of Dido smoulders, evocative of Vergil's '*caeco carpitur igni*' (4.2); the words etched in her heart reflect quite closely the Vergilian '*haerent infixi pectore vultus verbaque*' (3–4); and the word «хлопоты» ('cares') serves as a very close translation of the repeated word '*cura*' in Vergil (1 and 5). The same faithfulness to Vergil is observed in most of the fourth song which, it seems, Osipov, just like Petrov, wrote with special care and attention to the intricacies of the dialogues and striking poetic devices. Dido's conversation with Anna, for example, is rendered with dramatic force and little parody, except for occasional slips into vulgarisms. Dido's suicide is also described with perceptible sympathy and is even followed by a general rumination on the destructive force of love rather unusual for a comic poem (74):

Вот был какой конец несчастный
Дидоны бедной от любви;
За то, что не могла жар страстный
Ничем залить в своей крови.
Огнем она и в жизни тлела
И от огня ж в костре сгорела;
Жила и умерла огнем.
В любви хоть мало кто потрется,
Тот очень больно обожжется,
И все как трут сотлеет в нем.

This was the end of
Poor Dido because of love;
Since she was not able to quench
The passionate heat in her blood.
She was smouldering during her life
And she burned to death in the bonfire;
She lived and died by fire.
Anybody who rubbed even a bit against love,
Will be very painfully burned,
And everything in him will burn to ashes.

Despite the overuse of the fire imagery, this passage has a remarkable poetic quality in Russian and is evocative of Vergil's line: '*Improbe Amor, quid non mortalia pectora cogis!*' (412: 'Wicked love, to what do you not drive the mortal hearts!'). Vergil's tragic pathos was clearly appreciated by Osipov and used extensively, and not necessarily for comic effect. The Dido in Osipov's rendition surprisingly enough remains a tragic heroine worthy of sympathy and is ironically compared with modern women in the final stanza:

> Ни в чем никак не уступают
> Дидоне бабы и у нас;
> И в том ей верно подражают
> Все взапуски как на заказ.
> Вся разность в том у наших с нею:
> Рассталась с жизнью та своею,
> Сгоревши вся одним огнем.
> У нас огнем не умирают,
> Хоть часто свой огонь меняют;
> Но смерти не находят в нем.

> Our own wenches in no way
> Are second to Dido;
> And all of them as if competing
> Imitate her.
> But here is the main difference between her and them:
> She parted with her life
> Having burned in a single fire.
> Ours do not die by fire;
> Although they do change their fires quite often;
> But they find their death in none of them.

The reference to 'our wenches' in this passage is a clear example of how the borrowing from Vergil was aimed to be fashioned into a work of literature that can have local, national appeal. In light of the previous discussions of Petrov's translation and Kniazhnin's play, we can ask again if these lines also have anything to do with Catherine and her many 'fires'. If that is indeed the case, can we detect some subversion in this passage? While that is certainly possible, these lines can also be read again as a laudation of Catherine, in the same vein as Petrov's and Kniazhnin's comparisons to Dido. Osipov states that Russian 'wenches' (presumably the tsarina among them) are comparable to Dido except that they manage to stay alive through all the emotional upheavals. Is this a sarcastic observation? Unquestionably. But it is also quite consistent with contemporary literary allusions to Catherine which cast her as superior to the erratic Carthaginian queen.

Furthermore this passage is also one of the few poetic highlights in the whole poem. If all of Osipov's travesty were written in this way, which skilfully combines a close rendition of Vergil's imagery with acerbic wit and subtle irony, perhaps the poem would have undergone several reprints instead of lapsing into complete obscurity. But the poem is extremely uneven, sometimes contrived and often simply tedious. Osipov also displays a tendency to overuse vulgar language and an inability to walk the fine line that separates everyday language from outright slang, which the reader might find disconcerting. In this context seeing these lines as any intentional and pointed criticism of the Russian tsarina would be a conjecture unworthy of the poem's compelling wit.

Osipov died before finishing his mock poem. He published only seven books of it, but more importantly he inspired the creation of yet another travestied *Aeneid*, this time in Ukrainian, by Ivan Kotliarevskii (1769–1838), a native of Poltava.

This travestied *Aeneid*, the full version of which was published only in 1842, after the author's death, was significantly more influential and enduring than Osipov's mock poem, and it merits a brief mention in this study. In its 1839 issue the leading Russian literary journal *Notes of the Fatherland* (*Otechestvennye zapiski*) gave the following review of Kotliarevskii's poem: 'The native Russians who read Kotliarevskii's *Aeneid*, although they only half understood it, were nevertheless in awe of its wondrous language and author's wit; at the same time Osipov's remaking of the *Aeneid* in Russian, which was completely accessible to them, made them fall into a deep sleep. Such is the power of talent!'[41] It is clear from this comment that Russian readers acknowledged the superiority of the Ukrainian mock *Aeneid* to its Russian predecessor, and with good reason. While Osipov was intentionally debasing the language, at times he made the tone of his poem almost repulsively flippant: it was not a language spoken by any part of society, high or low. Kotliarevskii, on the other hand, wrote in the language of the Ukrainian people, namely, their folk songs and their fairy tales.

As W. T. Zyla observes, this 'travesty of Vergil's *Aeneid* surpassed those of his predecessors, because in his poem, he made an attempt to transform the ancient heroes into Ukrainian Cossacks in yet another attempt at national refashioning. His Italian, French, German and

Russian forerunners were parodying the individual situations and portrayals of Trojans, but never attempted any extensive organic transformations.'[42] Kotliarevskii's travesty is deeply rooted in Ukraine; his Trojans sing Cossack songs, eat local meals, and smoke local tobacco. While undoubtedly influenced by Osipov's travestied *Aeneid*, it nonetheless surpassed it and in one critic's words 'resembles it as much as a fresh flower resembles a cloth one'.[43] What is, however, the most important fact of the Ukrainian *Aeneid* is that this poem, for all its frivolous nature, was the most formative work for the foundation of Ukrainian national literature. It provided Ukrainian writers with a new literary language and 'with a combination of that sentimentality and comedy which later became an integral part of [Nikolai] Gogol's works'.[44] The detractors of Kotliarevskii's achievement were worried that his popularity would be detrimental to Ukrainian literature as a whole because nothing written in Ukrainian could be read seriously after the wildly popular poem.[45]

Osipov's poem, although it did not enjoy equal popularity in Russia, was finished by one Alexander Kotel'nitskii, about whom even less is known than about Osipov. He co-authored with Lutsenko the 'Abduction of Proserpine' («Похищение Прозерпины», 1791), another comic poem on mythological themes. The last part of the *Aeneid* by Kotel'nitskii was published in 1808. By his own admission Kotel'nitskii undertook the project unwillingly and under the pressure of contractual obligations.[46] His completion of Osipov's work, however, did not interfere with his sympathy for and adherence to Horace's poetry, whose many odes he translated into Russian and whose metre he studied zealously.

Kotel'nitskii finished the epic on a note of complete revelry that ensued after Turnus' death and Aeneas' marriage to Lavinia. As the Latins and Trojans discover their newly found fondness for each other amplified by celebratory wine and food, Kotel'nitskii bids goodbye to this last scene with an amusing conclusion, happy to move away from the long and tedious project:

> Но пусть в восторгах утопает
> Воспетый нами, Муза, род;
> Пускай он римлян добывает,
> Что сильной мышцей потрясет
> Оружием своим полсвета.
> Теперь уж песенка допета,

Пора завесу опустить:
Откланявшись, с своей гуднею
Пойдем-ка мы домой с тобою
Свои тож силы подкрепить.

И так трудились мы не мало,
Виргилий вывернут совсем,
Работы более не стало,
Мы дело сделали с концом:
Как надо Турна умертвили,
Энея мирно воцарили,
Друзьями сделались враги.
А дальше знать коль что желает,
Исторью римску пусть читает,
А мы покорные слуги!

But let the race sung by us be drowned,
Oh Muse, in its own exhilaration;
Let it stretch as far as the Romans
Who will shake with their muscle and
Their arms half of the world.
But the little song is now finished,
It is time for the curtain to fall:
Bowing out, with our own noise
Let us go together home
And fortify our strengths with sustenance.

Thus we worked enough,
Vergil is completely inverted,
There is no more work left
We have done the job to the end:
Put Turnus to death appropriately,
Put Aeneas on the throne peacefully,
Enemies became friends.
And if someone wants to know more,
Let him read Roman history,
But we wash our hands of the task.

The poem had come full circle. The whole point of this 'little song' was to entertain the reader who was not interested in reading Roman history or the true epic. But Kotel'nitskii dismissed his readers by encouraging them to turn their attention to more precise and less frivolous literary accounts.

In conclusion one more point needs to be made in relation to mockery and subversion of Vergil in Russia. Vergil's popularity made him the subject of important parodies in almost every major European language, as we have seen from some examples above. Yet most if not all of the European parodies are much more pronounced in their mockery and subversion. The Russian versions seem significantly gentler in their criticism of current mores and less focused on delivering any precise moral message. In fact, Osipov's work, like Kniazhnin's play, can barely be attributed to the genre of subversive literary works. Both writers were perhaps more concerned with defining the place for their works not in social or political but in literary terms: as a departure from the stilted and artificial tenets of classicism. The nineteenth century with its new cultural agenda loomed on the horizon, and it was time for Vergil to turn a new page in Russian literature. Enter Alexander Sergeevich Pushkin.

NOTES

1. Hardie (1997), 312.
2. Hardie (1997), 314.
3. Karlinsky (1985), 137.
4. In the Soviet Union, Kniazhnin was studied by Liubov' Kulakova, who, with an admirable but misguided determination, ascribed to him revolutionary tendencies. Kulakova (1951, 1959).
5. See Pypin (1902–13), 3.82.
6. Pypin (1902–13), 3.69.
7. Serman (1989), 71.
8. Rogger (1960), 71.
9. Serman (1989), 72.
10. Serman (1989), 73. Novikov was freed by Catherine's successor, Paul, in 1796.
11. Serman (1989), 72.
12. 'At my house everyone speaks their mind.' Pypin (1902–13), 3.68.
13. Karlinsky (1985), 138. Karlinsky, 141, is also persuasive in asserting that a legend claiming Kniazhnin died from flogging during an interrogation connected with the banning of the play has no foundation.
14. Karlinsky (1985), 133.
15. Kniazhnin (1961), 64.
16. Kniazhnin (1961), 66.
17. Kniazhnin (1961), 68.

18. Kniazhnin (1961), 79.
19. It is noteworthy that for the word 'queen' Kniazhnin uses the word 'tsaritsa', usually applied to the Russian tsarina, instead of the word 'koroleva', which also means 'queen' and is applied to all other female monarchs except the Russian ones.
20. Kniazhnin (1961), 89.
21. Kniazhnin (1961), 89.
22. For detailed analysis of these plays, see E. Vilk, *Problem of Tragedy and Tragic Consciousness in Russia at the Turn of the 19th Century* [in Russian], 1999, <http://rss.archives.ceu.hu/archive/00001056/01/56.pdf> [last visited 11 March 2013].
23. The widely accepted date of publication for Kniazhnin's *Dido* is 1769. Petrov published his first instalment in 1770.
24. Dated 8 February 1778. See M. Murav'ev's letters at: <http://imwerden.de/pdf/muravjev_pisma_1777-78.pdf> [last visited 31 January 2013], p. 71.
25. Sumarokov (1957), 123.
26. *Burlaks* were hired workers from the seventeenth century to the beginning of the twentieth century who manually hauled river barges. Their work was hard and often debilitating.
27. The information from Bolkhovitinov is given by Tomashevskii in Osipov (1933), 263.
28. Tomashevskii in Osipov (1933), 265.
29. While Scarron's *Virgile travesti* was regarded by his contemporaries as the poet's major work, it is all but forgotten today. Rather his *Typhon* is seen as the example of the burlesque, while the never finished *Aeneid* is extremely long and full of tedious details which the reader, looking for easy entertainment, may find exceedingly tiresome.
30. De Armas (1972), 142.
31. Scarron (1858), 53.
32. Titunik argues against the assertion that Scarron had little influence on Osipov. He presents numerous parallels between the two texts that show Scarron played a vital role in the composition of Osipov's *Aeneid*. See I. R. Titunik, 'A Note about Paul Scarron's Virgile Travesti and N. P. Osipov's Eneida', *Study Group on Eighteenth-Century Russia Newsletter* 21 (1993), <http://www.sgecr.co.uk/1993-titunik.html> [last visited 15 January 2013].
33. For more on Blumauer, see Becker-Cantarino (1973).
34. Blumauer, however, like Scarron before him, had energy only for the completion of nine books and the last instalment, books 5 to 9, was nothing more than an imitation of his witty and entertaining former self.
35. Blumauer turned Aeneas' companions into 'Klerisei' ('clerics') who were 'voll Mist bis an die Ohren' ('up to their ears in shit', 373), and the 'pius

Aeneas' himself into a ridiculously superstitious pious knight who aimlessly wanders from one adventure to the next without any goal. Dido is nothing more than a vain lust-driven princess who in distress reads *Die Leiden des jungen Werter*.

36. Sobolevskii (1889), 190. See also Aizenshtok in Kotliarevskii (1969), 19.
37. Tomashevskii in Osipov (1933), 254. See also Aizenshtok's introduction in Kotliarevskii (1969), 19.
38. Scarron (1858), 4.
39. Osipov (1933), 26–8.
40. Osipov (1933), 293.
41. See Aizenshtok's introduction in Kotliarevskii (1969), 6.
42. Zyla (1972), 194.
43. The comparison is that of O. I. Efimenko, 'Kotliarevskii in Historical Surroundings', cited in an essay by Mikola Zerov, a leading Ukrainian critic: 'Kotliarevs'kii i Osipov' <http://www.ukrlib.com.ua/krstat/printout.php?id=19> [last visited 3 September 2012].
44. Zyla (1972), 194–5.
45. I am grateful to Vitaly Chernetsky for this insight. See also Aizenshtok's introduction in Kotliarevskii (1969), 7. The Belorussian version, *Энеида навыворот* (*Aeneid Turned Upside Down*), written by one Vikentii Rovinksii around the 1820s, lacked the same influence.
46. Tomashevskii in Osipov (1933), 467.

3

Appropriation

Pushkin and Vergil

The poet must be very conscious of the most distinguished reputations. He must be quite aware of the obvious fact that art never improves, but that the material of art is never quite the same . . . That this development, refinement perhaps, complication certainly, is not, from the point of view of the artist, any improvement . . . But the difference between the present and the past is that the conscious present is an awareness of the past in a way and to an extent which the past's awareness of itself cannot show.

T. S. Eliot, 'Tradition and the Individual Talent'

The love for Pushkin, which is incomprehensible to foreigners, is the true sign of a person born of Russian culture. You can like or dislike any other Russian writer, that's a matter of taste. But Pushkin as a phenomenon is obligatory for us. Pushkin is the pivot on which Russian culture turns, he connects the past to the future. Take away the pivot and the connections will disintegrate.

Lidiia Ginzburg[1]

No discussion of any aspect of Russian literature can avoid Alexander Sergeevich Pushkin (Figure 4). 'Pushkin is the pivot', and although his allusions to Vergil prove to be rather elusive, it is important to consider the greatest Russian poet's attitude towards the greatest Roman poet.

Pushkin is the *fons et origo* of Russian poetic language. As Stephanie Sandler pithily observes, 'the example of his life and work is perceived as giving meaning to the nation's identity', especially its literary one, because he stands in the minds of Russians for all that poetry is meant to be.[2]

А. С. Пушкин
Портрет работы художника В. Тропинина, 1827 г.

Figure 4. Portrait of Alexander Pushkin by V. Tropinin (1827).

Pushkin was extremely well-read. The study in his apartment at 12 Moika Embankment in St Petersburg contains one of Russia's best private libraries. Empowered by his erudition to expand the boundaries of genres in Russian literature, he composed lyric poems, elegies, verse narratives, a novel-in-verse, prose fiction, historiography—a variety that earned Pushkin the title of the 'Russian Proteus'. Every Russian poet who came after Pushkin viewed him (sometimes reluctantly so) with a deeply ingrained sense of debt and an understandable sense of inferiority. Pushkin himself, however, did not experience any insecurity as far as the preceding literary tradition was concerned. He handled the obligatory confrontation with his literary predecessors soberly, as *the* Russian poet par excellence, manipulating their texts and theories to accommodate the metapoetic narrative of his personal evolution and of his evolving views about the nature and function of poetry. He keenly understood and at times boastfully asserted his unique importance in the Russian literary landscape. With Pushkin, poetry in Russia confidently took on the burden of cultural leadership. At the heart of that leadership was the dissatisfaction that he and his contemporaries felt at merely 'catching up' to the West and their desire that the Russian literary tradition rival those of France, Germany, and England. Also with Pushkin, Russian literature started acquiring the subtlety of its intertext. Pushkin's allusions to Vergil, like most of his allusions to his literary predecessors, are not obvious and require attentive unwrapping.

Perhaps it should come as no surprise that the first Russian poet with the true *Naturgenie* was more interested in the travestied *Aeneid*s than he was in the real one. A close analytical reading of Vergil in Latin was not taught at Pushkin's educational institution, the Tsarskosel'skii Lycée, until his fifth year of instruction.[3] Pushkin, a student there of Nikolai Koshanskii, most certainly studied Latin but was not fond of it.[4] The book that he used to study Vergil and then passed on to the subsequent generations of students at the Lycée was *Publius Vergilius Maro: Bucolica, Georgica et Aeneis*, editio stereotypa (Parisiis: P. Didot et F. Didot, 1814).[5] From his overall attitude towards Latin and his repeatedly expressed boredom with the subject, it is more credible that Pushkin read and knew Vergil from his early youth but mostly in French, although he was most likely familiar with Petrov's Russian translation.[6] Raised on the precepts of Russian classicism, the young Pushkin for the most part inherited the opinion that in bucolic poetry Vergil ranked higher than Theocritus and in epic higher than Homer. This opinion, however, changed as Pushkin discovered the Romantics. In one of his early poems, 'Bova' (1814), he admitted that for all his immense admiration for the great Roman poet, he would never imitate him if it came to expressing deep emotions:

> Несравненного Вергилия
> Я читал и перечитывал,
> Не стараясь подражать ему
> В нежных чувствах и гармонии.

> I have read and reread
> The unrivalled Vergil,
> Not trying to imitate him
> In tender feelings and harmony.

The youthful Pushkin of these lines, while calling the Roman poet 'unrivalled', nonetheless found Vergilian epic unsuitable for his poetic pursuits concerned mainly with amatory discourse. He clearly also perceived Vergil's 'harmony' to be understood as metre here, a classical element not worthy of imitation. His reaction to the Roman poet is consistent with his overall reception of antiquity early in his career when

Pushkin saw classical references mainly as a background decoration, somewhat formal and definitely foreign to his poetic passions.

Although Pushkin shows awareness of Vergil in his writing and even familiarity with the Vergilian texts, it would be an exaggeration to say that Vergil had any direct influence or impact on his writings. There is a certain obsession in Pushkin's works with the motif of the underworld which is evocative of Book 6 of the *Aeneid*, as for example in 'The Shade of Von Vizin' («Тень Фон-Визина»), 'Vadim (A Fragment)' («Вадим (Отрывок)»), 'A Dagger' («Кинжал»), 'Cleopatra' («Клеопатра»), and some others. However, that interest cannot be solely attributed to Vergil's influence but rather has a long European tradition including the mock epics of Paul Scarron and Osipov, which most likely were more formative for Pushkin than any of the archetypal elements of formal classicism. Although Pushkin on several occasions quoted Vergil, these quotations demonstrate the casual acquaintance with the most clichéd phrases that any educated European would use, rather than a profound knowledge of Vergilian text. In fact, the feeling of boredom induced by his readings of Vergil was expressed by Pushkin several times. In his poem 'Scene from *Faust*' («Сцена из *Фауста*») Mephistopheles in his conversation with Faust questions his state of perpetual ennui in the following words:

> Скажи, когда ты не скучал?
> Подумай, поищи. Тогда ли,
> как над Вергилием дремал,
> А розги ум твой возбуждали?

> Tell me, when were you not bored?
> Think, search. Was it when you
> Where slumbering over Vergil,
> or when whipping excited your mind?

The years of boring and even torturous classical education that Mephistopheles is referring to in these lines were also echoed in the draft of *Evgenii Onegin* 8.1, dated 24 December 1829, in which Pushkin mentions that while at the Lyceum he 'yawned over Vergil' («над Вергилием зевал»). Perhaps, like many men of his education and noble upbringing, he admired Vergil, but by Pushkin's time Vergil had become such a predictable part of the school curriculum that Pushkin could, without any qualms, express boredom at a required text, like so many students before and since. The only time when

Pushkin actually mentioned any feeling of pleasure upon reading Vergil was in his youthful poem 'A Little Town' («Городок»):

> Люблю с моим Мароном
> Под ясным небосклоном
> Близ озера сидеть.

> I like with my Maro
> To sit by the lake
> Under a clear sky.

In these lines describing idyllic surroundings he most likely recalls the *Eclogues* or the *Georgics* while he muses about the countryside. Pushkin hardly ever explicitly alludes to the *Aeneid* in his poetry. Furthermore, the poet expressed reluctance to be measured against the masterpieces of ancient epic, as is evident in his foreword to the second edition of his youthful masterpiece *Ruslan and Liudmila* (*Руслан и Людмила*), a poem which he started while still at the Lyceum. When the poem was first published in 1820, when Pushkin was barely twenty-one years old, the reviews exploded with criticism in which the speeches of the main heroes in the poem were compared with those in the *Iliad* and the *Aeneid*. In his foreword to the 1828 edition, Pushkin expressed his disdain for such comparisons:[7]

> Зачем, разбирая «Руслана и Людмилу», говорить об «Илиаде» и «Энеиде»? Что есть общего между ними? Как писать (и, кажется серьезно) что речи Владимира, Руслана, Финна и проч. не идут в сравнение с Омеровыми? Вот вещи, которых я не понимаю и которых многие также не понимают.

> Why, when analysing *Ruslan and Liudmila*, talk about the *Iliad* and the *Aeneid*? What do they have in common? How can one write (and it seems, in all seriousness) that the speeches of Vladimir, Ruslan, Finn, and the others cannot be compared with Homer's? These are the things I do not understand and many also do not understand.

It is clear from this remark that Pushkin did not strive to emulate the poets whom his conservative critics wanted him to emulate because the Greco-Roman canon became at this point completely normalized in Russian literature.[8] Pushkin acknowledged their importance, as he did for example in his *A Journey from Moscow to Petersburg* (*Путешествие из Москвы в Петербург*), where he lists all the poets who in his opinion will be read 'as long as the human race is alive' («пока не истребится род человеческий»): Homer, Vergil,

Milton, Racine, Voltaire, Shakespeare, and Tasso.[9] While he declares them his poetic predecessors, they should not be seen as his models.

Pushkin never positioned himself as a humble pupil of any of the great poets who came before. It is not only Vergil in Pushkin's poetry who became a keenly felt absence, but many of the other poets whom he read and most likely admired but never imitated. However, the absence of direct allusion or imitation can be as meaningful as the ubiquitous presence and persistent acknowledgement of influence. It is from this point of view that this study dwells on Pushkin's relationship to Vergil. Before I meditate further on how Pushkin and Vergil connect, I would like to dwell briefly on Vergil's relationship to Homer, discussed so often in almost every work on the *Aeneid*. C. M. Bowra once observed:

> It is wrong to treat them [the characters in the *Aeneid*] as if they were dramatic characters like Homer's. They are more and they are less. They are more, because they stand for something outside themselves, for something typically and essentially Roman; they are types, examples, symbols. And they are less, because any typical character will lack the lineaments and idiosyncrasies, the personal appeal and the intimate claims, of a character who is created for his own sake and for the poet's pleasure of him.[10]

What animated Vergil's epic was a specifically Roman experience, the problems that Rome faced as a nation and an emerging empire, and in the end a significantly human dilemma faced by Aeneas when Vergil challenged us, the readers, to validate Aeneas' behaviour. Pushkin's subtle allusions to Vergil, and especially the parallels to the *Aeneid* in *The Bronze Horseman* must be viewed in the same light.

While my analysis of the relationship between Vergil and Pushkin by no means implies the latter's intentional evocation of Vergil (unlike Vergil's allusions to Homer), it nonetheless informs several of the main concerns of this book, namely, as described by Sandler, 'what it means to be Russian, what role the poet is fated to play in the drama of national self-definition, and how all who lived after Pushkin's death can comprehend themselves as Russians through and against his experience'.[11] Like the *Aeneid* for the Romans, *The Bronze Horseman* offered Russians the fulfilment of their national craving by both filling the gap the epic should have occupied and appealing to human emotions with poetry that endured. Karl Galinsky points out that '[t]he interaction between its historicity and its transcendence is an important part of the *Aeneid*'s special dynamic' because the poem is 'a combination of tradition with new departures'.[12] As we will see, this is also an important part of Pushkin's poem.

In these pages I would like to analyse *The Bronze Horseman*, which, although not in any way an explicit imitation of Vergil, treats in a strikingly Vergilian manner a very Vergilian theme: the state versus the individual, a theme summed up by D. S. Mirsky's representative quote that the poem presents the 'irreconcilable conflict of the rights of the community, as incarnate in the Bronze Statue of Peter the Great . . . and those of the individual as represented by Evgeny'.[13] Because of such a monumental theme this poem was also seen by some influential critics, such as Vasilii Rudich and J. K. Newman, as Pushkin's version of a Russian national epic, this time a successful one.

The Bronze Horseman was composed in 1833, only four years before Pushkin's death and by all accounts one of Pushkin's unquestionable masterpieces. The poem was inspired by Étienne Maurice Falconet's equestrian statue of Peter the Great, completed in 1782, which stands on Senate Square in St Petersburg (Figure 5). Orlando Figes writes:

> The statue symbolized the dangerous underpinning of the capital's imperial grandeur—on the one hand trumpeting Peter's dazzling achievements in surpassing nature and, on the other, leaving it unclear to what extent he actually controlled the horse . . . The horseman seemed to teeter on the edge of an abyss, held back only by the taut reins of his steed.[14]

As we will see later, this ambivalent interpretation of the statue was transferred also onto Pushkin's poem as well. An important question about *The Bronze Horseman* concerns the literary tradition to which Pushkin perceived his poem to belong. J. K. Newman asks: 'When Pushkin wrote this poem, was he breaking entirely fresh ground, or did he stand in some kind of tradition, which could throw light on his achievement, and thus help to resolve the many diverse speculations about its precise significance?'[15] Pushkin himself calls his work a 'tale' («повесть», «рассказ»), a word that usually implies a work in prose. Newman further asks, if in fact *The Bronze Horseman* qualifies as an epic, wouldn't that 'demand a larger scale of treatment' and characters 'who are conceived on a heroic scale'?[16] He continues by comparing Pushkin's poem with the Alexandrian Callimachus' *Hecale*, a different kind of epic, one that 'pay[s] attention to the

Figure 5. Peter's statue by Falconet (*The Bronze Horseman*) with the Latin inscription *Petro Primo Catharina Secunda*. Photograph by Sergio Sanabria.

humble as well as ostensibly great', an epic also exemplified in the Renaissance by Ariosto's *Orlando*.[17]

Vasilii Rudich in his ground-breaking article on the subject, which will be addressed below in greater detail, analyses the main conflict of the poem and also considers the possibility that in *The Bronze Horseman* that truly national epic may indeed have been achieved at which Pushkin's esteemed predecessors Kantemir, Lomonosov, and Kheraskov failed. At the centre of both Newman's and Rudich's analysis is a conflict between a humble man and a higher power, exemplified both by the city of St Petersburg and by its builder, Peter. Similarly the *Aeneid* juxtaposes the private life of Aeneas with the public duty that was preordained for him and, despite his personal passions, a duty he must submit to. My remarks here are not concerned with traditional analysis of intertextuality between *The Bronze Horseman* and the *Aeneid* but rather the idea of 'literary filiation', a concept which does not necessarily imply any conscious or intentional allusion to any text or texts previously read. Indeed, Gian Biagio Conte emphasizes the role of 'poetic memory' on the part of both author and reader as a possible intertextual discourse that can function independently of subjective intentionality.[18] Thomas Hubbard also uses the idea of 'literary filiation' in the sense of 'the author's choice of specific precursors or precursor with whose work he stands in a special and significant relation'.[19] This concept, by Hubbard's own admission, owes much to Harold Bloom's emphasis on the importance of the creative subject and his intentionality. That intentionality does not necessarily have to be conscious, since any poet is himself or herself a compilation of the texts previously read. Poets can recall unintentionally a text of their precursors and can even 'creatively "misread"' it as a way of drawing from the 'poetic memory' while appropriating it for their individual poetic expression.[20] It is this, perhaps unintentional, evocation of the *Aeneid* that I would like to explore as part of Pushkin's *The Bronze Horseman*.

The poem was written by a mature Pushkin in Boldino during one of the most prolific periods in his life, known as the 'Boldino autumn' («Болдинская осень»). During his lifetime only a small excerpt, entitled 'Petersburg: A Fragment from a Poem' («Петербург. Отрывок из поэмы»), was published. The poem could not be published in full because Nicholas I demanded from Pushkin that he change the poem in several places, and the poet refused. The complete poem was not published until 1837, after Pushkin's tragic and untimely death in a duel, and even then the publication contained many corrections made by the censors, among them Vasilii Zhukovskii, the translator of the *Odyssey*. It is clear that the poem was considered by Tsar Nicholas to be subversive.

In the following pages I have divided my discussion into three parts: first, I present briefly a summary of the plot; second, I analyse Rudich's argument about the main conflict of the poem as it relates to Vergil's *Aeneid*; and, finally, I offer an analysis of the poem in the context of previous Russian epics and Nicholas's negative reaction to *The Bronze Horseman*.

G. Vinokur in his commentary on *The Bronze Horseman* pointed out that to some degree *The Bronze Horseman* was written in response to the third part of *Dziady* by Adam Mickiewicz (1798–1855), which came to Pushkin's attention in the summer of 1833 and contained a cycle of poems dedicated to Russia and specifically to the monument of Peter on Senate Square and to the flood of 1824. In the prologue to his poem Pushkin enters into a polemic with Mickiewicz and offers a panegyric to the city of St Petersburg, since the city appeared in a more satirical depiction in Mickiewicz.[21] However, the plot and the main idea for the poem were formed by Pushkin without Mickiewicz's influence and resulted most likely from Pushkin's overall interests in Russian statehood, especially in the figure of Peter the Great, whom he appears initially to idealize in a similar way to Vergil's treatment of Augustus.[22]

The poem opens with a laudatory prologue to the city of St Petersburg and its creator, Peter:

> На берегу пустынных волн
> Стоял *он*, дум великих полн,
> И вдаль глядел. Пред ним широко
> Река неслася; бедный челн
> По ней стремился одиноко....
>   И думал он:
> Отсель грозить мы будем шведу.
> Здесь будет город заложен
> На зло надменному соседу.
> Природой здесь нам суждено
> В Европу прорубить окно;
> Ногою твердой стать при море....
>   Прошло сто лет, и юный град,
> Полнощных стран краса и диво,
> Из тьмы лесов, из топи блат
> Вознесся пышно, горделиво....
>   Люблю тебя, Петра творенье,
> Люблю твой строгий, стройный вид,
> Невы державное теченье,
> Береговой ее гранит....
>   Красуйся, град Петров, и стой
> Неколебимо, как Россия,
> Да умирится же с тобой
> И побежденная стихия.[23]

> Upon the bank by barren waves
> *He* stood and pondered mighty thoughts
> While gazing outward to the sea.
> The river broadly flowed before Him.
> Alone, a poor boat raced along....
>   Thought he:
> From here our might will menace Sweden;
> For here a city will be built
> To spite our neighbor's arrogance;

> Here nature has decreed that we
> Will hack a window into Europe
> And stand on strong legs near the sea. . . .
>   A hundred years went by, and out
> Of forests dark and marshes dank
> A city rose, a noble beauty,
> The wonder of all northern lands. . . .
>   I love you, Peter's proud creation.
> I love your profile's austere grace,
> The mighty current of the Neva,
> Between her granite covered banks. . . .
>   Display your splendor, Peter's city,
> And stand, unshakeable, like Russia;
> Let even conquered elements
> Now make their peace with you.[24]

Richard Gregg writes that the prologue is 'built on the unbalanced opposition of a raw, inchoate, and primitive world with the ordered, progressive, and dynamic state which supplants it'.[25] This panegyric to St Petersburg seems also to follow the trend started by Gavriil Buzhinskii, who wrote the first formal ode to the city in 1718, and eagerly continued by Gavrila Derzhavin's famous 'Felitsa'. Sidney Monas observes that 'such poems [as Buzhinskii's and Derzhavin's] became quite standard, very much in the spirit of the *laudes Romae* of the Latin poets'.[26] Indeed, Averintsev notes the striking parallel between Pushkin's prologue and a scene in the *Aeneid* (7.29–34) where Aeneas for the first time beholds the bank of the river Tiber still unknown to him:

> atque hic Aeneas ingentem ex aequore lucum
> prospicit. Hunc inter fluvio Tiberinus amoeno
> verticibus rapidis et multa flavus harena
> in mare prorumpit.

> And here Aeneas sees from sea a large forest.
> Running through it with its beautiful course
> The Tiber golden with sand and fast whirlpools
> Bursts into the sea.

Averintsev observes that both Vergil and Pushkin here effectively use the fact that the unknown landscape which both Aeneas and Peter respectively behold is very familiar to the readers of the poems:[27]

Увидеть в уме те места, которые сейчас насыщены историей и человеческой жизнью, еще пустыми, но ожидающими уготованного им наполнения, — патетично. Берега Тибра, берега Невы, привычны, до мелочей знакомые и совсем иные; подразумеваемый подтекст — вот как история меняет лик земли. И Вергилий и Пушкин апеллируют к пафосу истории.

To see in one's mind those places which now are saturated with history and human life, to see them still empty but in anticipation of their destined fulfilment,—that is full of pathos. The banks of the Tiber, the banks of the Neva, so habitual, so familiar down to the minor details, and yet so different; the intended subtext here is that this is how history changes the face of the earth. Both Pushkin and Vergil appeal to the pathos of history.

The effect of this poetic device, in Averintsev's opinion, is to create 'the theme of proximity of the remote and distance of the near' («тема близости дальнего и удаленности близкого»), an extremely powerful device in both poems as it allows the reader to feel empowered and to participate in major historical events.

The Peter of Pushkin's prologue is the harbinger of the new order, of civilization where there was once none. In Monas's words, '[w]here once there had stood an empty wilderness, now half the world came to pay tribute. Where once there had been an empty swamp, now proud places greeted the eye.'[28] Only the last line of this excerpt hints that the poem in fact is not a grand foundation story or merely a panegyric to Peter's unrivalled achievements, as Lomonosov's poem was intended to be. The story that follows this prologue is, in Pushkin's own words, 'a sad narration' («печален будет мой рассказ»).

The narrative of the poem is concerned with a well-known and indeed extremely devastating episode from St Petersburg's history—the flood of 1824, when the Neva burst its banks and claimed many lives and buildings. It is against the story of this flood that Pushkin tells his tale about a lowly government clerk, Evgenii, whose main concern is to secure happy domesticity with his fiancée, Parasha. Caught up in the middle of the devastating flood, he loses his beloved Parasha, the only driving force of any ambition he might have harboured. In a 'ludicrous and wholly pathetic scene'[29] Evgenii, after his vain attempt to rescue Parasha, is found trapped on a stone lion, a helpless victim of the elements. 'Poor Evgenii', as Pushkin immediately addresses him («но бедный, бедный мой Евгений»—'but my poor, poor Evgenii'), showing that he has little hope for his protagonist, upon discovering that Parasha's house has been swept off by the flood, lets go of his senses and becomes a vagabond aimlessly roaming the streets of the city. During his wanderings he stumbles again into Senate Square, where he sees Falconet's famous horseman, Peter's statue, 'the idol with extended hand / sat astride his proud bronze steed' («Кумир с простертою рукою / Сидел на бронзовом коне»). Evgenii, completely mad at this point, lashes out at the statue:

> Добро, строитель чудотворный! —
> Шепнул он, злобно задрожав, —
> Ужо тебе!

> 'Just wait, proud miracle creator,'
> Evgenii whispered angrily
> And in his fear began to tremble,
> 'I'll get revenge!'[30]

After his threat to the statue of the great tsar, Evgenii hastily takes off, as he envisions that the statue comes alive and pursues him. Following this hallucinatory incident, Evgenii becomes even more withdrawn and eventually dies forgotten and abandoned by all. At the end of the poem his corpse turns up on a small island in the Neva river, further emphasizing his isolation from his city and its citizenry and Pushkin's message that 'human destiny stems from human character'.[31] This is the protagonist of *The Bronze Horseman*, a man sympathetic because of his suffering but largely insignificant because of his daunting passivity. The ordinary clerk with small dreams and little ambition is pitted against the elemental forces of nature on the one hand and the 'historical spirit of Russia on the other'.[32]

Rudich observed that 'Virgil's *Aeneid* and Pushkin's *The Bronze Horseman*—separated by almost two millennia in time—exhibit striking similarities, even coincidences, as regards their authors' creative concerns and responses to several major, historical, moral, and philosophical issues.'[33] At the centre of Rudich's argument is the debate surrounding the elusive main messages of both poems manifested especially in the later reception of them. 'Until relatively recent times,' Rudich observes, 'the scholarship on Vergil, over the course of several centuries, proceeded from the assumption that his unequivocal intention had been precisely to celebrate in the *Aeneid*, within the larger frame of Rome's history, the political achievement of Augustus and thus contribute to the latter's imperial propaganda.'[34] It was not until the seminal studies of Victor Pöschl and subsequently Michael Putnam and W. R. Johnson that 'a dark and powerful undercurrent which militates against any overly optimistic reading of the epic'[35] was recognized in Vergil's narrative. The story of the critical response to Pushkin's great poem was exactly the opposite. The dominant view supported by Dmitrii Mirsky, Wacław Lednicki, and Roman Jacobson asserted that the poem's main idea was the destruction of an individual life by an autocratic state, represented by the statue of Peter. The poem read in the context of the 'Petersburg texts' of Gogol's 'Nevskii Prospekt' and Dostoevskii's *Double* (in which the protagonist also goes mad) and *Crime and Punishment* became a part of a dominant theme in Russian literature: the devouring city and cruel state that crushes private happiness.[36] However, in recent criticism another view has emerged. The hapless Evgenii in his simple desire for individual happiness came to be seen as incapable of understanding the importance of the communal good. As the city returns to its daily life, recovering, rebuilding, renewing, from the devastation of the flood, he becomes a derelict completely overwhelmed by his personal grief and refuses to contribute to the city's reconstruction. He is unable to absorb the shock of his loss and the adversity that faces his city, whose collective citizenry becomes resilient and self-reliant. Evgenii's 'revolt' against Peter's autocracy is nothing but a hallucination engendered by the sorrow he in his weakness cannot overcome. Rudich's concluding argument is that 'both Virgil and Pushkin profoundly appreciated necessities and complexities inherent in the historical process', and that they were both 'étatistes, supporters of strong statehood'.[37] Both poets were preoccupied with what Rudich terms 'historiodicy', a justification of history, when the sacrifice of an individual's happiness and maybe even life becomes a necessary condition of the historical process and progress.[38] Newman also sees the conflict of the poem along the same lines, only he slightly shifts his argument by comparing not only Evgenii to Peter but also Peter to the random acts of nature:

> The thought that such heroes [as Peter] can only win their victories by crushing lesser men, and perhaps their own humanity, is common to Pushkin and Virgil.

> Where Pushkin has his deepest contact with Virgil, however, is in his combination of irony and seriousness. The Augustan poets were haunted by the thought of transience, and Virgil, Horace, and

Propertius gave expression to the idea that cities wax and wane. When Peter stands on the banks of the Neva, we feel again in European poetry one of its characteristic themes: nature as the eternal, sentient witness to humanity's ephemeral grandeur. The river, brought down to the level of a petitioner knocking on some indifferent judge's door, is the ironical counterpart to Peter's imperial dreams.[39]

The confrontation between Peter's ambitious designs and nature is emphasized in the prologue, as we saw earlier. But unlike Evgenii, Peter is not to be deterred in his single-minded purpose to overcome the obstacles in his way, despite the enormous toll it exacts. The poem then does not provide us with a clearly defined and resolved epic conflict, but rather suggests ambivalence in authorial intent and ambiguity in its message.

Now let us focus in greater detail upon the text of Pushkin's poem, analysing it not only against the text of the *Aeneid*, but also in the context of the Russian national epic and more specifically Lomonosov's *Petriad*. Furthermore, I would like to pose and hopefully answer two questions. The first is whether or not Pushkin successfully 'corrected' Lomonosov's attempt at the national epic with the great tsar-reformer as his hero. The second is concerned with Nicholas's somewhat violent reaction to the poem as a subversive work, reminiscent of Catherine's reaction to Kniazhnin's *Vadim of Novgorod* as discussed in the previous chapter. Why did the tsar not read in the poem a strong support for statehood but instead suspect an attempt at subversion? This question must be discussed in the larger context of the relationship between a poet and his sovereign.

As the description of the flood progresses in the poem, Pushkin calls our attention to the Russian monarch, who looks out upon the devastation from the balcony of his palace:

> В тот грозный год
> Покойный царь еще Россией
> Со славой правил. На балкон
> Печален, смутен вышел он
> И молвил: «С божией стихией
> Царям не совладеть». Он сел
> И в думе скорбными очами
> на злое бедствие глядел.

> The late tsar in that dreadful year
> In glory governed Russia still.

He strode out on the balcony
And spoke in sorrow and confusion:
'Not even tsars can overcome
The anger of God's elements.'
And thoughtfully through mournful eyes
He looked upon the tragedy.[40]

The late tsar referred to in these lines is Alexander I, who ruled Russia from 1801 to December of 1825 and then was succeeded by Nicholas I. The strange contradictions of Alexander's character made him one of the most interesting Russian monarchs. At the beginning of his reign he became a supporter of several liberal reforms and then later on revoked them. He also ruled Russia during the difficult time of the war with Napoleon, and his general Kutuzov guided the Russian army to victory in 1812. Furthermore, Alexander had succeeded in the foreign policy of expansion by acquiring Finland and parts of Poland. But Pushkin, while briefly acknowledging that the tsar ruled 'with glory', chose nonetheless a rather curious representation of the late monarch. Alexander is rendered contemplative but powerless even as he dispatches his generals to offer some help to his drowning subjects. The words the tsar mutters as he looks upon his drowning city are especially bizarre: 'Not even tsars can overcome / The anger of God's elements.' The only act Alexander is capable of as in despair he views the flooded city is to dispatch his generals to rescue the marooned, but overall he is a man 'out of his element—literally—in the fight to control and master nature'.[41]

The irony of Alexander's predicament cannot escape any reader familiar with the history of St Petersburg's foundation. The location that Peter chose for his 'window into Europe' was the most unsuitable, miserable place for the foundation of any settlement, much less the new imperial capital. The fact that Pushkin was keenly aware of that follows from the prologue in which the rise of the new city occurs 'out of forests dark and marshes dank' («из тьмы лесов, из топи блат») and from the scene where 'poor Evgenii' confronts the statue of Peter:

Кто неподвижно возвышался
Во мраке медною главой,
Того, чьей волей роковой
Под морем город основался . . .

And he whose towering head of bronze
Unmoving loomed in evening's gloom,
The tsar whose fatal will had built
His capital so near the sea.[42]

While Pushkin's assessment of Peter's impossible endeavour is full of awe, the hero of his poem feels differently. Evgenii's perception of Peter and his city is manifest in the sarcastic remark thrown at Peter's statue: 'Just wait, proud miracle creator!' («Добро, строитель чудотворный!»). Although Pushkin marvels at the fact that Peter succeeded in building his city against all odds, Evgenii cannot hide his bitterness at the tsar's lack of foresight that a city built in such an inclement location will be flooded and devastated.

St Petersburg, the 'Venice of the North', the new 'Third Rome', was built on the bones of thousands of anonymous serfs who perished from the draining of the swamps, consumption, hunger, and cold. The city was willed into existence by the sheer power of the tsar-reformer. The new tsar, Alexander, however, unlike his predecessor, is portrayed in the poem as someone who is unable to fight against the elements. From the height of his balcony he observes the devastation as a philosopher almost detached from the physicality of the losses experienced by his people. If Pushkin's poem were to be interpreted as subversive it would be in this portrayal of Alexander as an impotent ruler. In a sense he is as forgetful of the past history of the city and his own ancestry as 'poor Evgenii', who shows no interest in the past, whether that of his own family or his country:

> Живет в Коломне, где-то служит,
> Дичится знатных и не тужит
> Ни о почиющей родне,
> Ни о забытой старине.

> Our hero lives in Kolomna.
> He works, is shy, and does not grieve
> For his departed ancestors
> Or for the unremembered past.[43]

Significantly enough Evgenii is described as living not in the great capital itself but in its outlying suburb, Kolomna, a detail which further emphasizes his marginalization. Rudich observes that Evgenii's 'lack of genealogical knowledge is equated with the ignorance of history in general which is responsible for his failure to undergo successfully the rite of passage in order to achieve socialization'.[44] But in this respect Tsar Alexander and his humble subject are alike. The tsar forgot who built the city which he now has to save. For him his genealogical forgetfulness is as much of a shortcoming as is Evgenii's ignorance of Russian history.

For Pushkin's poetics the importance of memory, especially the memory of one's roots, loomed large. Indeed the poet could boast of aristocratic ancestors who figured prominently in Nikolai Karamzin's twelve-volume *History of the Russian State*. But it is the memory of one's actions in a time of national crisis that proves even more important in *The Bronze Horseman*. In his 'imitation' of Horace's *Monument*, his own 'testament' poem—'I built myself a monument not made by human hands'—Pushkin shows yet again his attitude towards Tsar Alexander, this time in the context of his own legacy (a physical monument to the poet is shown in Figure 6). While alluding to Horace, Pushkin asserts that the poetic monument that he built for himself will soar over the Alexander Column erected on Palace Square and unveiled in 1834 to celebrate Russia's victory over Napoleon. In *The Bronze Horseman* the dissatisfaction with Alexander as an inadequate leader is obvious and stands in stark contrast to Vergil's perception of a capable leader. This concern with the role of a leader in shaping the events of history and with his ability to lead others is certainly a familiar theme of any epic.

In Book 1 of the *Aeneid* (198–209), Aeneas, caught in the devastating storm, famously addresses his frightened compatriots:

'O socii (neque enim ignari sumus ante malorum),
O passi graviora, dabit deus his quoque finem.
Vos et Scyllaeam rabiem, penitusque sonantis
accestis scopulos, vos et Cyclopia saxa
experti; revocate animos maestumque timorem
mittite; forsan et haec olim meminisse iuvabit.
Per varios casus, per tot discrimina rerum
tendimus in Latium, sedes ubi fata quietas
ostendunt; illic fas regna resurgere Troiae.
Durate, et vosmet rebus servate secundis.'
Talia voce refert curisque ingentibus aeger
spem vultu simulat, premit arte corde dolorem.

'Comrades (for indeed you are not unfamiliar with misfortunes),
You who suffered worse things, to these ones also god will
    grant an end.
You approached the rage of Scylla and the deep sounding cliffs,
You experienced the Cyclopean rocks:
Restore your souls and dismiss sad fear;
Perhaps at some point even these things will be a pleasure
    to recall.

Figure 6. Statue of Alexander Pushkin by Alexander Opekushin on Pushkin Square in Moscow (1880). Photograph by Sergio Sanabria.

We are headed towards Latium, where the fates promise
Restful settlements; there it is allowed for the kingdom of Troy
   to rise again.
Endure, and save yourselves for the happy events.'
He says these words aloud but vexed with great sorrows
He feigns hope on his face, and suppresses with skill sadness in
   his heart.

Whatever we may think of Aeneas as a hero, in these lines at least he faces the tempest, the 'acts of god', in his case, Juno, with the stoicism expected of a Roman leader. He feigns hope when all hope is lost, despite his knowledge that a man is powerless when faced with divine vengeance. And yet his words of support and encouragement inspire his comrades. In fact, throughout the *Aeneid* Vergil, as Christine Perkell observes, 'suggests a troubled vision of moral experience, for he depicts a universe continually menaced by irrational evil on the divine, human, and natural levels'.[45] But Aeneas withstands these trials. Although often ignorant of their meaning and the greater purpose of his own destiny, he nonetheless displays the qualities of steadfast faith and endurance. In the context of new beginnings, whether a foundation of a new city or a new nation, these are the required qualities. In this speech addressed to his loyal friends Aeneas is 'generous and reflective' but also selfless, 'on behalf of the cause larger than himself'.[46] Throughout the poem his memory of his genealogy both past and future never fades. The penates as much as Anchises and Ascanius guide him on his journey, and, although in some parts of the poem his weakness and his lack of loyalty to his human ties shock the reader, his devotion to the cause never wavers.

Is this the kind of hero Pushkin had in mind, a hero who did not materialize either in the contemplative but defeated tsar or in his besotted and wretched subject Evgenii? Did this type of hero, however, found its fulfilment in Peter? Is it fair to say, as Newman phrases it, that '[b]etween poor, mad Evgenii, whose only ambition was to marry or save his Parasha, and the proud bronze Czar, preoccupied with his struggle against the elements (his only gesture is one of threat), and reacting with angry annoyance to any protest against his preoccupation, there is no common ground?'[47] And if so, does Pushkin unconditionally sympathize with Tsar Peter? The poem starts as a panegyric to the great tsar and his achievements and remains faithful to this inaugural theme in the prologue. However, it would be unfair to conclude that Pushkin is not fully empathetic when it comes to human frailty. In fact, as Evgenii looks with horror at the shore, where Parasha's modest house used to stand, being swept by the waves of the flood, it is Pushkin who steps in and remarks:

> Иль во сне
> Он это видит — иль вся наша
> и жизнь ничто, как сон пустой,
> Насмешка неба над землей?

> His dream . . . or is he dreaming this?
> Or can it be that all our lives
> Are nothing but an empty dream,
> The heavens' sneering at the earth?[48]

There is little doubt that Pushkin read Lomonosov's *Peter the Great.* Thus the allusion to Lomonosov's pessimistic passage about the unpredictability and frailty of the human condition discussed earlier is unmistakable. But Pushkin's remark is not placed amid the pompous epic; his contemplations are timely, tactful, and appropriate. In case the reader wonders about the poet's feelings, they are right here. Amid the storm, the devastation, the criticisms of the current tsar's and Evgenii's inertness, the poet also mourns the loss of human life. Furthermore, Pushkin was well aware of the sinister side of Russian despotism: the events of 14 December 1825, when the best of Russia's army elite and aristocratic families came into Senate Square to protest against Nicholas I's assumption of the throne and advocate for democratic changes to Russia, events which caused the death and exile of many of his dear friends, were never far from the poet's mind.

The Bronze Horseman, like the *Aeneid,* is ambivalent about the price of nation-building and about unwavering dedication to one's duty. W. R. Johnson pithily describes Vergil's own ambivalence towards the greatness of Rome and Italy:

> The powerful idealism that shapes, for example, the *laudes Italiae* in *Georgics* I more than balances the anxiety of nostalgia that pervades the *Eclogues* (and much of the *Georgics* itself). As for the *Aeneid*, the great set pieces of Books VI and VIII alone, those wonderfully baroque patriotic tableaux, testify to a desire for the hybridity to become reality. Nevertheless, like many (most?) of his 'naturalized' (ex-non-Roman, Italian) contemporaries, poets and non-poets alike, he may well have been deeply conflicted; may have hailed the fusion, and yet, so strong was the pull of birthplace and homeland, so bitter too were the memories of recent slaughter and oppression and humiliation, he may also have experienced confusion and grief, an ugly sense of a wrong ending, of annihilation of something dead and fragile and unrecoverable . . . Roman Italy was something both to be loved and hated.[49]

These lines are also applicable to Pushkin's feelings towards Russia. The much-repeated and usually misquoted phrase 'It must have been the devil who propelled me to be born in Russia with soul and talent' («Черт догадал меня родиться в России с душой и талантом»)[50] indeed expresses the depth of Pushkin's frustration with his homeland. Prohibited from travelling abroad, humiliated by the demeaning government posts assigned to him, plagued by financial troubles and rumours of his wife's infidelity, Pushkin nonetheless was perceived even by his contemporaries as an unsurpassed Russian poetic genius. His relationship to his land and his pride and love for Russia went hand in hand with his resentment of it. In 1836 Pushkin wrote in a letter to Peter Chaadaev (1794–1856):

> Of course the schism separated us from the rest of Europe and we took no part in any of the great events that stirred her; but we have had our own mission. It was Russia who contained the Mongol conquest with her vast expanses . . . The Tatar invasion is a sad and impressive history . . . Do you not discern something imposing in the situation of Russia, something that will strike future historians? Do you think they will put us outside Europe? . . . I do not by any means admire all that I see around me . . . but I swear to you that not for anything in the world would I change my country for another, nor have any history other than that of our ancestors, such as it has been given us by God.[51]

As Figes observes, Pushkin was almost unique among Russian intellectuals of that time in embracing wholeheartedly the dual nature of the legacy handed to Russia: East and West intertwined. It is also important to consider the addressee of this letter: the Russian Europhile Chaadaev would hardly have found the Mongol legacy impressive—indeed he probably considered it abhorrent. Chaadaev was an example of a Russian intellectual who (at least earlier in his life) welcomed Western influences into Russian culture at the expense of undermining the Eastern ones.

In 1836 Chaadaev published the first of his *Philosophical Letters* (*Философские письма*), which, in Alexander Herzen's words, had 'the effect of a pistol shot in the dead of night'. The anger provoked by this letter went as high as Nicholas I, who felt that Chaadaev had insulted Russia and the emperor himself. Even a short excerpt from this letter demonstrates why there was such a violent reaction from the Russian public:

> We do not belong to any of the great families of the human race; we are neither of the West nor of the East, and we have not the traditions of either. Placed, as it were, outside of time, we have not been touched by the universal education of the human race . . . What is the life of man, says Cicero, if memory of earlier events does not relate the present to

the past? But we [Russians], who have come into the world like illegit-
imate children, without a heritage, without any ties binding us to the
men who came before us on this earth, carry in our hearts none of the
lessons preceding our own existence.[52]

Chaadaev is often cited as an example of Russian cultural consciousness
and even insecurity in the face of European intellectual achievement.[53]
After the publication of this letter, morbidly signed 'Necropolis, 1
December 1829', Chaadaev was declared insane, put under house
arrest, and essentially made an internal emigrant in his homeland. He
composed eight other letters between 1827 and 1831 (not printed in his
lifetime) in which he predominantly contemplated religious questions,
but the first letter sharply delineated the complexity of Russia's relationship with the West. It is clear from his somewhat bitter and perhaps
not altogether fair dismissal of Russian national heritage that, like
most Russian intellectuals, Chaadaev wanted Russia to have ties to
the Western tradition, which he saw as a progressive movement of
ideas. He characterized these Western ideas as ones 'of duty, justice,
right, and order' and juxtaposed them with the 'frivolity' of even the
most enlightened Russian minds.[54]

It is also noteworthy that Chaadaev started his discussion of Russia's relationship with the West with the citation from Cicero, quoting
the Roman author almost as a sage whose single opinion would
outweigh years of national history. If Russia were not connected to
that past to which Cicero was referring (to Greek and early Roman
history), then Russia would need to change its ways. Chaadaev then
went on to lament that 'fundamentally, we Russians have nothing in
common with Homer, the Greeks, the Romans, and the Germans; all
that is completely foreign to us'.[55] In 1837 he wrote a 'palinode' to his
unfair assessment of Russia's place in the family of nations. In his
'Apologie d'un fou' ('Apology of a madman') he still lamented and
assertively stated that Russia's topographic location to the east of
Europe does not mean that it has 'ever been part of the East'.[56] In
the same work Chaadaev also declared a deep love of his country and
praised Russia's ability to 'perfect most of the ideas which have come
up in the old societies', warning at the same time against the blind
patriotism that led to such a violent reaction to his first letter.[57]

Pushkin anticipated Chaadaev's palinode, not only by his response
to the first letter, but also in his poetry: pride in Russia and resentment of its disregard for the life of its citizens go hand in hand in

The Bronze Horseman. The poem is in effect the first true Russian epic, not in terms of monumentality, but certainly in a sense of poetic accomplishment. It dwarfs the eighteenth century's sincere but ill-conceived attempts at grandeur similar to that of the ancient epics. Pushkin had his finger on the poetic pulse of his time. He was fascinated by Russian history and Peter was for him, unlike Lomonosov, not a historical figure, but a manifestation of Russian identity full of appalling contrasts. Furthermore, Pushkin also had the benefit of that necessary distance from Peter's era, the lack of which Shuvalov saw as the main reason for Lomonosov's failure at his epic. Like the *Aeneid*, *The Bronze Horseman* was never intended solely as a panegyric, in the latter case for the tsar-reformer and the city built on swamps. The poem had to convey both sadness and triumph. It 'has the unusual quality of simultaneously lauding the vision and the will of Peter while treating his victim compassionately'.[58] But from the standpoint of the juxtaposition between human will and order and the random anarchy that threatens it, *The Bronze Horseman* became a true Russian epic because, like Vergil's *Aeneid*, it spoke 'for a moral order in society if civilization is to be worthy of its name'.[59]

The Bronze Horseman is not the only narrative work by Pushkin focused on a tension between random, anarchic forces and the power of civilized order. In the *Gypsies* (*Цыганы*) he presents a 'civilized' hero who enters into conflict with the people whose way of life is lawlessness; in *Poltava* (*Полтава*) Peter the Great again defends the state against the treacherous uprising of Mazepa, that very Ukrainian hetman whom we also saw in Lomonosov's epic; in the *Stone Guest* (*Каменный гость*) the anarchy of the dissipated Don is stopped by a vengeful statue. Even in his prose work 'The Captain's Daughter' («Капитанская дочка») the state forces ordered by Catherine fight against Emel'ian Pugachev's unruly throngs.[60] But it is in *The Bronze Horseman* that the struggle between civilized order and the random violence of nature becomes explicit and reaches epic proportions, swallowing with it also the considerations of individual happiness. But is the poet explicitly a partisan in his sympathies? And that brings us to the next question I sought to explore in this chapter, namely Nicholas's excessive reaction to the poem and his refusal to publish it during the poet's lifetime.

Nicholas, like his ancestor Catherine and her predecessor Peter, deemed himself to be an enlightened monarch. However, the first day of his reign was etched forever in the collective Russian memory.

As I have mentioned before, the events of December 1825 weighed heavily on Pushkin's mind. He indicated several times that if he had been in St Petersburg on that fateful day, he would have walked out on Senate Square with his friends who ended up in Siberian exile. And yet Pushkin's relationship with Nicholas was not always full of ill humour, although it was also never like that which Vergil enjoyed with Augustus. Nicholas understood the enormous significance of Pushkin for Russian letters. He also could have misinterpreted the poem, since at the time it was written Pushkin was in a tense relationship with the court. What could Nicholas have expected from a self-proclaimed Decembrist and a man who came to despise the court's intrigues, as became especially apparent in the year preceding the poet's death? If not the tsar's collusion, at least his acceptance of Pushkin's fatal duel is indicated by the fact that the victor, the arrogant but ignorant Georges d'Anthès, was never punished to the extent expected by the Russian public. It is not altogether impossible that, as John Mersereau suggests, Pushkin's ambivalent attitude to the power of the state represented by Peter and simultaneous sympathy for Evgenii crushed by the state's grand designs 'reflected Pushkin's own frustrations in his relationship with Nicholas I, who for personal and state reasons kept the poet in physical and economic bondage'.[61] In the last years of his life Pushkin 'was a man under permanent special surveillance'[62], but Serena Vitale observes that 'Poet and Tsar were truly an odd couple, one testier than the other.'[63] Although Nicholas frequently expressed his benevolence in the form of financial subsidies to the poet, he nonetheless expected him to become less proud and more obsequious, which was incompatible with Pushkin's character. Pushkin, despite humiliating positions forced upon him at court, never saw himself as a 'poor Evgenii' and his poetic output showed that, although we, as his later readers, may find Nicholas's relentless suspicions somewhat unreasonable. Perhaps Nicholas considered Pushkin almost a rival authority, although Pushkin was neither a politician nor a public figure, but simply a poet whose word had such an important impact on the hearts and minds of Nicholas's subjects that, from the perspective of the absolute sovereign, it simply had to be controlled. Even in the aftermath of his tragic death, the tsar's anxiety about Pushkin's possible subversive writings did not subside. The tsar entrusted the chief of his secret police, General Alexander von Benckendorff, to make sure that all of Pushkin's papers were examined, 'not with any intent whatsoever to harm the deceased, but solely for the exceptionally just necessity of hiding nothing from the surveillance of the government, whose vigilance must extend to all possible materials'.[64] Thankfully, Benckendorff entrusted this unpleasant task to an extremely reluctant Vasilii Zhukovskii (the translator of the *Odyssey*), who, repulsed by the way the tsar handled the whole situation with the greatest Russian poet, precluded any efforts at censoring his posthumous legacy. In the apt words of Vitale, 'in death Pushkin inspired words and thoughts worthy of a *frondeur* in this most devoted Russian subject [i.e. Zhukovskii]',[65] an outcome that Nicholas perhaps did not anticipate.

With Pushkin, Russian literature acquired its utmost relevance to society as writers began marrying their literary aspirations to dreams of freedom, and their poetry to political rights and initiation of social reforms. As subtle as Pushkin's response to Vergil (even if unintentional) was, it also showed that Russian literature had matured and now had a poet who, like Vergil in Rome, became the pivot in the national literary landscape. However, after Pushkin, Vergilian reception also underwent a dramatic change as Russia approached the end of the nineteenth century and stepped into the twentieth, marked by the unspeakable political cataclysms and suffering that crystallized this time not the political or courtly Vergil, but Vergil the philosopher, spiritual messiah, and lonely artist.

NOTES

1. Ginzburg (1987), 331.
2. Sandler (2004), 197.
3. Seleznev (1861), 87.
4. For more on Pushkin's education at the Lyceum and Koshanskii, see Torlone (2009), 40–1.
5. Torlone (2009), 52.
6. For more on Pushkin's Latin, see Torlone (2009), 36–43.
7. Pushkin (1949), 882.
8. It is interesting to compare Pushkin's reluctance to promote the emulation of ancient poets with Nikolai Gogol's ecstatic letter on Zhukovskii's translation of Homer's *Odyssey*: «Появление *Одиссеи* произведет эпоху. *Одиссея* есть решительно совершеннейшее произведение всех веков ... Теперь перевод первейшего поэтического творения производится на языке, полнейшем и богатейшем всех европейских языков. Вся литературная жизнь Жуковского была как бы приготовлением к этому делу. Нужно было его стиху выработаться на сочинениях и переводах с поэтов всех

наций и языков, чтобы сделаться потом способным передать вечный стих Гомера ... Зато вышло что-то чудное. Это не перевод, но скорей воссоздание, восстановленье, воскресенье Гомера. Перевод как бы еще более вводит в древнюю жизнь, чем сам оригинал.» ('The appearance of the *Odyssey* will be an epoch. The *Odyssey* is definitely a perfect work for all ages ... Now the translation of the very first poetic creation is occurring in the language, which is fuller and richer than all the European languages. Zhukovskii's whole literary life was a preparation for this work. His verses had to acquire experience in his own works and translations from the poets of all nations and languages in order to be able to convey the eternal Homeric verse ... But something miraculous happened. It is not a translation, it is a re-creation, rebuilding, resurrection of Homer. The translation leads us even more into the ancient life than the original.') N. V. Gogol', 'Ob Odissee, perevodimoi Zhukovskim (pis'mo k N. M. Ya ... vu)', *Polnoe sobranie sochinenii*, [Moscow and Leningrad], AN SSSR, 1952, 8.236–44. Available at: <http://feb-web.ru/feb/gogol/texts/ps0/ps8/ps8-236-.htm> [last visited 31 January 2013].

This overly enthusiastic endorsement by Gogol of Zhukovskii's translation stands in stark contrast to Pushkin's bewilderment about what his own work has to do with the ancient epics. Unlike Pushkin, Gogol clearly saw Homer's relevance to Russian letters. We will return to this letter in the last chapter in connection with Russian translations of the *Aeneid*.

9. In a letter to Alexander Bestuzhev (May–June 1825) Pushkin again expressed a positive assessment of Vergil, calling him a 'genius', but in a somewhat contradictory manner immediately thereafter called him an 'imitator'. See Rudich (2002a), 36. It is clear from all these mentions of Vergil that Pushkin did not have as strong a feeling about him as he did about Horace and especially Ovid.

10. Bowra (1945), 37.

11. Sandler (2004), 199.

12. Galinsky (1996), 250.

13. Cited in Gregg (1977), 173.

14. Figes (2002), 158.

15. Newman (1972), 175.

16. Newman (1972), 175.

17. Newman (1972), 176.

18. Conte (1986), 32–40.

19. Hubbard (1998), 11. See also Forrester (2004), 2–3, on the distinction between the terms 'affiliation' and 'filiation' and their use in scholarship on modernist authors.

20. Hubbard (1998), 11.

21. Vinokur, in Pushkin (1949), 889. For a detailed discussion of Pushkin and Mickiewicz, see Lednicki (1978), *passim*.

22. Rudich (2002a), 40.
23. Pushkin (1949), 303–4 (the complete poem in Russian is on pp. 303–8). The translations of all the excerpts from *The Bronze Horseman* are by Catharine Nepomnyaschy, in Rydel (1984).
24. Nepomnyaschy, in Rydel (1984), 151–2.
25. Gregg (1977), 168.
26. Monas (1983), 37.
27. Averintsev (1996), 38.
28. Monas (1983), 37.
29. Gregg (1977), 170.
30. Pushkin (1949), 307; Nepomnyaschy, in Rydel (1984), 155.
31. Gregg (1977), 175.
32. Gregg (1977), 169.
33. Rudich (2002a), 38.
34. Rudich (2002a), 45.
35. Rudich (2002a), 45.
36. For comparison of *The Bronze Horseman* and Dostoevskii, see Rosenshield (1996).
37. Rudich (2002a), 47.
38. Rudich (2002a), 50.
39. Newman (1972), 187.
40. Pushkin (1949), 305; Nepomnyaschy, in Rydel (1984), 153.
41. Newman (1972), 174.
42. Pushkin (1949), 307; Nepomnyaschy, in Rydel (1984), 155.
43. Pushkin (1949), 304; Nepomnyaschy, in Rydel (1984), 152.
44. Rudich (2002a), 46.
45. Perkell (1999), 31.
46. Rudich (2002a), 42.
47. Newman (1972), 190.
48. Pushkin (1949), 305; Nepomnyaschy, in Rydel (1984), 153.
49. Johnson (2001), 15.
50. The misquote is: «Черт догадал меня родиться в России с *умом* и *талантом*» ('It must have been the devil who propelled me to be born in Russia with *wit* and talent'). The confusion is most likely due to A. Griboedov's verse comedy *Woe from Wit* (*Горе от ума*).
51. Letter (in French) to Chaadaev, 19 October 1836, in A. Pushkin, *Sochineniia: Perepiska*, 3 vols (St Petersburg: Imp. Akademii nauk, 1906–11), 3.388. Translated in Figes (2002), 368.
52. Raeff (1999), 162, 164.
53. Rzhevsky (1998), 5. Riasanovsky (1952), 3, correctly observes that the defeat of Napoleon in 1812 became 'a great landmark in Russian thought' as far as the attitude to the West was concerned. The sense of inferiority was greatly diminished because 'Russia had faced the West,

and Russia had defeated the West.' So Chaadaev's negative remarks about Russia were offensive to many precisely because after 1812 there was a newly acquired sense of Russia's importance and power in the world.

54. Raeff (1999), 165.
55. See Riha (1969), 2.307–8. This statement again contrasts with Gogol's exalted praise of Zhukovskii's *Odyssey* as something extremely appropriate and timely for Russian letters, as discussed earlier.
56. Riha (1969), 2.313. As we saw in the first chapter, Russian culture had a complicated history of changing definitions of East and West.
57. Riha (1969), 2.313–14.
58. Mersereau (1999), 178.
59. Newman (1972), 190.
60. Gregg (1977), 168.
61. Mersereau (1999), 178.
62. Vitale (2000), 84.
63. Vitale (2000), 85.
64. From a letter of Benckendorff to Vasilii Zhukovskii, 6 February 1837. In Vitale (2000), 269.
65. Vitale (2000), 274.

4

The Messianic and Prophetic Vergil

Имя Братства и Свободы
Чтут начертано народы:
Галл—на храмах и дворцах,
Бритт—в законах, мы—в сердцах.

The name of Brotherhood and Liberty,
Peoples worship in a predestined way:
The Gaul—at the shrines and palaces,
The Briton—according to laws, and we—in our hearts.

Viacheslav Ivanov 'Suum cuique'[1]

The idea of Moscow as the Third Rome originated, as we have seen, in the early sixteenth century in the letters of a Pskovian monk, Filofei, who based this concept 'on the predominantly religious premise that Russia had assumed the Orthodox Christian mantle that the Byzantines had lost when conquered in 1453 by the Moslem Turks'.[2] Although the doctrine largely lost its appeal in the seventeenth and eighteenth centuries, interest in it became revived in the middle of the nineteenth century and intensified after the events of 1917, especially in the writings of the Silver Age.[3] The reception of Vergil during that time reflected the preoccupation of Russian intellectuals with the destiny and mission of Russia, as they turned away from political and cultural contemplations of Russia's status vis-à-vis Europe to Russia's ecclesiastical and spiritual role.

VLADIMIR SOLOV'EV

Не три свечи горели, а три встречи, —
Одну из них сам Бог благословил,
Четвертой не бывать, а Рим далече, —
И никогда он Рима не любил.

Not three candles were burning but three meetings,
One of them was blessed by God himself,
The fourth will never be, but Rome is far away—
And he never really loved Rome.

O. Mandel'shtam[4]

This stanza taken from Osip Mandel'shtam's 1916 poem 'On a Sled Covered with Hay' («На розвальнях, уложенных соломой») alludes to the Third Rome doctrine. More likely, however, it alludes to the use of that doctrine by one of the most prominent Russian religious philosophers, Vladimir Solov'ev, and his poem 'Three Meetings' («Три свидания», 1899) dedicated to the divine Sophia and extremely popular at the beginning of the twentieth century.[5] Vladimir Solov'ev's works and his interpretation of the role of Roman and Byzantine legacy for Russian national destiny became formative for the twentieth-century 'messianic' reception of Vergil by Viacheslav Ivanov and, to a more limited degree, Georgii Fedotov.

The poem 'Three Meetings' so ambivalently alluded to by Mandel'shtam (I will return to that later) is of utmost importance for an understanding of Solov'ev's interpretation of Vergil, and it needs to be put in the broader context of Solov'ev's life and work. In 1877 Solov'ev met and fell in love with Sophia Petrovna Khitrovo, who, although never reciprocating his romantic feelings, nevertheless opened her estate, Pustyn'ka, to him. Pustyn'ka then became for the philosopher 'the closest thing to a permanent residence'.[6] 'Three Meetings' was in fact written in Pustyn'ka, and Solov'ev, despite calling the poem 'humorous verses', also acknowledged that the poem reflected the most significant moments of his life. One of those moments was undoubtedly his friendship with Khitrovo, whose first name, Sophia, can perhaps be considered a partial inspiration for Solov'ev's divine female.[7]

In this poem Solov'ev states that three times in his life he had the revelation of the glory and unity of the world, and that this revelation was given to him by the visions of divine Sophia, who appeared to him in a female form of ethereal beauty. While he never actually refers to the beautiful vision as Sophia or Wisdom, the identity of the beautiful apparition is obvious and harks back to lecture 7 of Solov'ev's popular presentations, where he for the first time introduces Sophia by that name:

> In the divine organism of Christ, the acting, unifying principle, the principle that expresses the unity of that which absolutely is, is obviously the Word, or Logos. The second kind of unity, *the produced unity, is called Sophia* in Christian theosophy.[8]

As Judith Kornblatt notes, Solov'ev's concept of Divine Sophia or Holy Wisdom (Hagia Sophia of Eastern Orthodoxy), while 'a verbal incarnation of his personal visions', was also 'informed by a host of earlier religious and literary traditions, including the biblical ones . . . as well as Neoplatonism, early Christian Gnosticism, Russian and Byzantine iconography and liturgy, the Jewish Kabbalah', and most importantly by the Russian fascination with her 'as a manifestation of the Eternal Feminine'.[9]

His visions of Sophia Solov'ev interpreted, as N. Zernov observes, not 'as the illusions of a distorted mind nor poetic objectifications of emotional state; these were cardinal facts, on which he built his entire outlook'.[10] At the centre of that outlook was Solov'ev's concept of «всеединство» ('the whole of things', 'pan-oneness'), of which Sophia appears to be a component part.[11] Influenced by the writings of the Slavophiles, an intellectual movement in Russia which propagated values different from those in Western Europe, especially Ivan Kireevskii (1806–56), Solov'ev furthered their ideas that European culture had exhausted its creative strength and that the further progress of humanity rested now with the Christian East, and especially Russia. Solov'ev believed that Russia had a special mission to give back to Europe the sense of the Divine, because Russian monarchs were the successors of the Byzantine emperors and because Eastern and Western churches were inextricably connected.[12] In his study *La Russie et l'Eglise universelle* (*Russia and the Universal Church*, 1889; Russian translation, 1911) Solov'ev advocated an alliance between the pope and the Russian emperor,[13] whom he saw as the consecrated power destined to fulfil Russia's Christian mission. Some of Solov'ev's poems, such as '*Ex Oriente Lux*' (1890) and 'Panmongolism' («Панмонголизм», 1894) reflected his lifelong preoccupation with Russia's purpose in the world. Both poems deserve some discussion since in them Solov'ev 'touched upon Russia's national destiny and the future of humanity at large'.[14] These poems also crystallize the ideas that influenced the Vergilian reception of Ivanov and Fedotov.[15]

Solov'ev starts the first poem, '*Ex Oriente Lux*', with the declaration 'Light comes from the East, strength comes from the East!' («С Востока свет, с Востока силы!»), which then unexpectedly turns into recounting the history of confrontation between the East and the West starting with the battle at Thermopylae (480 BCE), in which the outnumbered Greek army defeated the Persian Empire of Xerxes. Solov'ev ascribes the victory to the fact that the Greeks were free citizens fighting against Persian slaves: the Western love of democratic rule is juxtaposed to the despotism of the Eastern empire that, for all its claims to greatness, cannot achieve victory because its citizens do not fight for liberty. Solov'ev reinforces this premise with the victories of Alexander the Great and then of Rome, which gave the world unity and reason. It is only with the advent of Christ, in Solov'ev's opinion, that the East and the West had the possibility of becoming united in the spirit of love and faith. The last three stanzas of the poem proceed to clarifying the opening line's glorification of the East:

> И слово вещее — не ложно,
> И свет с Востока засиял,
> И то, что было невозможно,
> Он возместил и обещал.
>
> И, разливаяся широко,
> Исполнен знамений и сил,
> Тот скот, исшедший от Востока,
> С Востоком Запад примирил.
>
> О Русь! в предвиденье высоком
> Ты мыслью гордой занята;
> Каким ты хочешь быть Востоком:
> Востоком Ксеркса иль Христа?
>
> And the prophetic word was not false,
> And a light from the East shone,
> Heralding and promising
> What had been impossible.
>
> And, spilling wide,
> Full of portents and might,

> That light from the East
> Made peace between East and West.
>
> O Rus! In lofty premonition
> You ponder a proud thought;
> Which East do you want to be:
> The East of Xerxes or of Christ?

In these lines Solov'ev connects with Russia the future of civilization and the ability to unite East and West in the name of Christ if Russia chooses to do so. The barbaric Eastern legacy associated with Xerxes would be forgotten, replaced by the 'light' brought from the East by Christ. It is interesting that in this poem Solov'ev allows Russia to be an Eastern country, which will finally fulfil the prophecy of all-powerful East declared in the first line.

The poem 'Panmongolism', however, is far less optimistic about Russian destiny. The poem starts with a misleading stanza:

> Панмонголизм! Хоть имя дико,
> Но мне ласкает слух оно,
> Как бы предвестием великой
> Судьбины Божией полно.
>
> Panmongolism! Although the name is monstrous,
> Yet it caresses my ear
> As if filled with the premonition
> Of a grand divine fate.

That fate, however, does not materialize in the poem. Rather, Solov'ev envisions Western civilization being overwhelmed by the people from the East, 'countless as locusts' («как саранча неисчислимы»), who destroy the last hope of Russia's ideal unifying mission:

> О Русь! забудь былую славу:
> Орел двуглавый сокрушен,
> И желтым детям на забаву
> Даны клочки твоих знамен.
>
> Смирится в трепете и страхе,
> Кто мог завет любви забыть . . .
> И третий Рим лежит во прахе,
>   А уж четвертому не быть.
>
> O Rus! Forget your former glory:
> The two-headed eagle is ravaged,

> And your tattered banners passed
> Like toys among yellow children.
>
> He who neglects love's precepts,
> Will be overcome by dread and fear . . .
> And the third Rome falls to dust,
>   Nor will there ever be a fourth.

In this poem, as well as in his essay 'Byzantinism and Russia', Solov'ev questions the idea of Moscow as the Third Rome. Jonathan Sutton notes that for Solov'ev 'the ideal of the Third Rome was becoming increasingly remote and deceptive—one that only Russia's flatterers wish to perpetuate'.[16] These writings display Solov'ev's extreme concern about Russia's reduced commitment to spiritual practice, and Christian ideals replaced by the distractions of secular life and intellectual trends.[17]

At the same time, as Greg Gaut observes, 'Solov'ev tended to an arrogant Eurocentrism when speaking of non-Christian people outside Europe.'[18] However, for the subsequent thinkers and writers of the Russian Silver Age, such as Ivanov and Andrei Belyi (1880–1934), Solov'ev, as Susanna Lim points out, 'was above all the great prophet of reconciliation and unity'.[19] Pamela Davidson is right in emphasizing in Russian literature 'the image of writer as a divinely inspired prophet, responsible for shaping the spiritual and moral destiny of the nation'.[20] While this tendency is not unique to Solov'ev and its rise goes back to the time of Derzhavin and later Pushkin,[21] Solov'ev (along with Tolstoi and Dostoevskii) greatly contributed to the future development of this inherited tradition and allowed the writings of Ivanov and Fedotov to assume the same tone of prophetic declarations.

Solov'ev's famous and influential work *The History and Future of Theocracy* (*История и будущность теократии*, 1885–7) contains a zealous plea for restoration of unity between the Latin and the Orthodox churches.[22] While his work had little appeal to Catholicism, Solov'ev did offer an entirely novel interpretation of the 'Third Rome' doctrine. He suggested that Moscow had a mission to reconcile two ancient rivals, Rome and Constantinople, and be the place where the Latin world and the Christian East would unite in the perfect symbiosis.

Between 1881 and 1891 Solov'ev developed friendships with Nikolai Fedorov (1828–1903) and Afanasii Fet (1820–92). These years also coincided with Solov'ev's intense interest in the unity of East and West through Christendom. In 1887 Solov'ev and Fet embarked on a Russian translation of the *Aeneid*, which we will discuss in detail in the last chapter of this study. Fet was attracted to the project because it presented him as a poet with a challenge. For Solov'ev, however, the *Aeneid* represented 'the perfect embodiment of the Roman principle of universalism'.[23] In a letter to Nikolai Strakhov, Solov'ev stated:

> [П]еревожу с Афанасием Афанасьевичем «Энеиду». Я считаю «отца Энея» вместе с «отцом верующих» Авраамом настоящими родоначальниками Христианства, которое (исторически говоря) явилось лишь синтезом этих двух parentali'й.

> Afanasii Afanas'evich [Fet] and I are now translating the *Aeneid*. I consider 'Father Aeneas' along with Abraham, the 'father of believers,' to be the true ancestors of Christianity, which was (historically speaking) only a synthesis of these two forefathers.[24]

There had certainly been centuries of Christianizing interpretation that viewed Aeneas 'as a good proto-Christian or at least Stoic'.[25] But for Solov'ev the historical necessity inherent in Aeneas' divinely ordained missions represented the confirmation of the idea of Rome's pre-eminence as the spiritual guide of the world. In another of his letters, this time to the Jesuit Paul Perling, he elaborated on this idea:

> Переводя теперь в часы досуга «Энеиду» русскими стихами, я с особенною живостью ощущаю в иные минуты ту таинственную и вместе естественную необходимость, которая сделала из Рима центр Вселенской Церкви.

> Dum domus Aeneae Capitoli immobili Saxum (*petra*)

> Accolet imperiumque pater Romanus habebit.

> Чем это не пророчество?

> Now that I am spending my leisure time translating the *Aeneid* into Russian verse, I occasionally sense with a special acuity that mysterious and simultaneously natural necessity which made Rome the center of the Universal Church.

> Dum domus Aeneae Capitoli immobili Saxum (*petra*)

> Accolet imperiumque pater Romanus habebit.

> Is this not a prophecy?[26]

These lines taken out of their context are cited by Solov'ev from the *Aeneid* (9.448–9) and refer to a famous episode about Nisus and

Euryalus, two Trojan lovers who die together during a brave foray among the enemy. Vergil glorifies Euryalus as he describes his untimely death:

> Fortunati ambo! Si quid mea carmina possunt,
> nulla dies umquam memori vos eximet aevo
> dum domus Aeneae Capitoli immobili saxum
> accolet imperiumque pater Romanus habebit.

> Both of you fortunate! If my songs have any power,
> No day will ever come that wipes you from the memory
>   of the ages,
> not while the house of Aeneas stands by the Capitol's rock
>   unshaken,
> not while the Roman Father rules the world.

The story of the homoerotic love and death on behalf of that love becomes in Solov'ev's rendition a Christian prophecy. The Greek word *petra*, which he adds parenthetically as a translation of Latin *saxum* is meant to suggest a parallel to the biblical passage Matthew 16:18 in which Christ founds his Church upon Peter (the Greek word, as David Matual points out, 'is an ad hoc creation based on *petra*, rock'[27]). This passage, as we will see later, will also attract Ivanov, who following his mentor would interpret it in the light of Christian love.

While Solov'ev tried to apply his beliefs to the *Aeneid*, the ultimate culmination of his 'messianic' interpretation of Vergil manifested itself in his translation of the Fourth Eclogue, in which the birth of a mysterious child is predicted.[28] In his commentary on the *Eclogues* Wendell Clausen observes that 'the Christian, or Messianic, interpretation prevailed unchallenged for centuries, supported by, and supporting, Virgil's reputation as a seer, a Christian before Christ'.[29]

It is hard to imagine that Solov'ev was not aware of the secular interpretation of the poem and scepticism in classical scholarship about the parallels between Vergil's text and the Bible.[30] After all, such interpretations were dismissed as early as 1858 by John Conington, the most important nineteenth-century commentator on Vergil. However, both Solov'ev and Ivanov, as we will see, preferred the medieval view of the Fourth Eclogue as a prophecy of the birth of Christ. In order to understand their choice we need to put it in the broader perspective of what the Fourth Eclogue meant for Russian thinkers, a perspective best explained by Averintsev in his formative essay on Vergil, familiar from our earlier discussion. Here is what he writes about Vergil's 'messianic' eclogue:

Ученые Нового времени, в отличие от наивных людей Средневековья, исходили из того что истинный смысл эклоги — это смысл происходящий, злободневно-актуальный, и потратили немало усилий в безрезультатных поисках выяснить, в каком именно из важных семейств Рима — у самого Августа, у Поллиона или у кого иного — должен был родиться чудесный отпрыск. Если бы эклога значила не больше этого, она устарела бы через год. Но средневековое перетолкование при всей своей наивности, по крайней мере, воздает должное двум первостепенным фактам: во-первых, центральный смысл стихотворения Вергилия, рядом с которым должны отступить все прочие его смысловые аспекты,—это пророчество о наступлении нового цикла жизни человечества, об обновлении времен; во-вторых, Вергилий оказался прав. Он чувствовал время. Что касается перетолкований, таков уж объективный характер Вергилиевой поэзии, что она не просто для них открыта, но несет в себе их необходимость, *эстетически их предвосхищает*. Голос поэта сам летит в будущее и, можно сказать, акустически рассчитан на отзвук в сердцах тех кто придет позднее.[31]

The scholars of the New time, unlike the naive people of the Middle Ages, were keen on interpreting the meaning of the eclogue as it related to the current events, to burning issues of the day, and they spent considerable efforts on futile attempts to find out in exactly which prominent Roman family—perhaps Augustus', or Pollio's, or someone else's—a miraculous child was supposed to be born. If the eclogue meant nothing more than that, it would have been outdated in a year. But the medieval interpretation, despite all its naivety, at least took into consideration two most important facts: first, the central meaning of Vergil's poem to which all other semantic aspects must yield,—namely that this poem is a prophecy about the arrival of a new cycle of life, the renewal of times; secondly, Vergil was right. He felt time. As for the interpretations, such is the objective nature of Vergil's poetry that it is not just open to them, but carries in itself a necessity for such interpretations, *anticipates them aesthetically*.[32] The poet's voice flies into the future and, one can say, it anticipates acoustically the echo in the hearts of those who will come later.

This statement by Averintsev reflects a similar tendency in modern scholarship to steer away from too close political readings of the poem.[33] Bruce Arnold observes that the Fourth Eclogue 'cannot even at this early date be disassociated from Vergil's own lifelong struggle with the complex problem of moral and political regeneration that informs all of his work'.[34] Following the same lines of argument, Solov'ev's and Ivanov's preoccupation with the proleptic message of the eclogue was not some misguided proselytizing of Christian zealots. The poem for them presented an opportunity to contemplate the destiny of humankind in general and Russia in particular. They were exactly those 'hearts' whose echo, in Averintsev's words, Vergil's poetry 'aesthetically anticipated'.

For Solov'ev the poem was a ready poetic expression for most of his persistent ideas. Matual discusses in detail the parallels between Solov'ev writings and the Vergilian text. I would like to outline here only a few ideas crucial for Solov'ev's interpretation of the poem and reflected in his Russian translation.

Solov'ev (and later Ivanov) found Vergil's historiosophy in tune with his own. He especially favoured Vergil's association of the new Golden Age with the arrival of a saviour, a miraculous child. The inherent difference between Vergil's view of history and Solov'ev's is, as Matual aptly points out, that for the former the age of Saturn was not a blissful closure to the succession of ages, but only a link in a historical cycle and might be followed by yet another age of human deterioration.[35] For Solov'ev, however, 'the God-man is the fulfillment of history'.[36] Solov'ev's preoccupation with the divine Sophia also found its reflection in his interpretation of the Fourth Eclogue. Vergil's *iam redit et Virgo* ('already the Virgin returns') in line 6 of the poem was interpreted by Solov'ev not only as the mother of the coming saviour, but also the feminine ideal, which the divine Sophia also represented. Solov'ev accepted the medieval Christian understanding of the Fourth Eclogue, the messianic message of which both St Jerome and St Augustine found doubtful.[37] Furthermore, Solov'ev took some liberties in translating the Vergilian text in order to emphasize his messianic interpretation of the poem. For example, lines 38–9 of the eclogue read:

> nec nautica pinus
> mutabit merces; omnis feret omnia tellus.
> The pine ship
> will no longer exchange wares; the whole earth will bear everything.

Solov'ev translated this as: 'And the pine ship / will no longer exchange wares; the whole earth will give equally to everyone' («И сосне корабельной / товаров уж не менять: вся земля давать всем поровну будет»). The word 'equally' not even hinted at in Vergil's text is added to the translation by Solov'ev as a way to emphasize Christian equality and love in the predicted new order of things.

As becomes clear from Solov'ev's letters to his brother Mikhail, there existed two versions of the translation: one was loose and adapted to reflect Solov'ev's main religious beliefs; the other, favoured by Afanasii Fet, stayed faithful to the original.[38] Solov'ev stated in one of the letters that he tore up the loose translation and preserved only the one that closely followed the Vergilian text. Solov'ev's rejection of the freer version is puzzling, but allows for a conjecture that in the end he decided that Russian readers must infer from Vergil's eclogue their own conclusions without being pushed into a certain direction by the poetic licence of the translator. Vergil, the pagan Roman poet, must speak to Russian readers on his own terms. The translation of the poem by Solov'ev that we have now is sometimes exceedingly literal and goes against the natural Russian word order, as if Solov'ev were overly conscious of his tendency to distort the Vergilian text for his own philosophical purposes. He even imitates Vergil's hexameter as much as Russian prosody allows, following the same goal of staying close to the original.

Even Solov'ev's translation practices proved to be influential, especially for the Russian Symbolists, who became saturated with his ideas.[39] One of the most prominent Russian Symbolists, Valerii Briusov (1873–1924), accused, as we will see in Chapter 6, of 'literalism' («буквализм»), seems to have taken Solov'ev's approach very much to heart and reproduced the *Aeneid* in the same vein of sometimes 'foreignizing' translation practice. However, the reaction to Solov'ev's teachings among Russian intellectuals was not always positive, as one can infer from Mandel'shtam's vague mention of Solov'ev's 'Three Meetings' cited at the beginning of this chapter. If the pronoun 'he' in the line 'and he never really loved Rome' does refer to Solov'ev's reception of Roman legacy, Mandel'shtam's assessment might seem somewhat unfair, because Solov'ev strove to synthesize East and West and in fact did 'love' Rome. However, Mandel'shtam, an erudite Russian poet of Jewish descent, once proverbially defined Acmeism, the literary movement he belonged to, as 'yearning for world culture' («тоска по мировой культуре»).[40] Rome for him, but especially ancient Rome, held universal significance: it existed as an idealized entity, an unbroken focal point of human existence, but most importantly as an unchanging civiliz-ation of perfect harmony between nature and humanity.[41] Although, as Kalb notes, for Solov'ev 'Russia represented a "third principle", one that could overcome the differences between the East's "God-man," focused on religious faith, and the West's "Mangod," intent on human, worldly potential,'[42] the religious messianic underpinnings of Solov'ev's vision of Rome did not fit into Mandel'shtam's concept of the eternal city as a cultural landscape open for all. Mandel'sh-tam's reception of Rome throughout his poetry (with a strong preference for Ovid) remained largely secular and distanced from any religious revelations pursued by Solov'ev.[43] The religious prin-ciples of the latter, however, deeply influenced Viacheslav Ivanov, who was, as Alexei Losev points out, 'the most consistent pupil of Solov'ev'.[44]

Kalb observes that 'the story of Aeneas, along with Virgil's model of literary nation-building, held deep resonance for Russian Symbolist writers at the turn of the twentieth century, as they put Virgil's myth and example to work in their own nationally based writings'.[45] In order to better appreciate Ivanov's deep engagement with Vergil, explored in the following pages, we need to briefly place it in the context of Russian Symbolism, the most prominent movement of the 1890s and the first decade of the twentieth century, since Ivanov is considered one of its leading figures. Michael Wachtel emphasizes that the 'Russian Symbolists' creativity was based on a type of reception diametrically opposed to that posited by [Harold] Bloom,' at the basis of whose theory is the poet's continuous struggle with his 'belatedness' and wilful 'repression' of the tradition. Wachtel continues:

> The Symbolists, an erudite group of poets and thinkers, shared a reverence for past accomplishment. If the English Romantics strove to escape the burden of the past, the Russian Symbolists sought with equal fervor to integrate themselves with it. Rather than exemplifying Bloom's notorious 'anxiety of influence,' the works of the Symbolists evince what might be termed an 'anxious desire to be influenced.' Rarely has a creative movement so eagerly and energetically looked backwards. . . . Reception, in short, was not simply an aspect of Russian Symbolism; it was one of its guiding principles and lifelong pursuits.[46]

It is in this light that we have to consider Ivanov's reception of Vergil, in whose writings he found answers as he contemplated the crisis of Russian national identity after the Revolution of 1917. As Ivanov took Solov'ev's Roman text to heart and fell under the spell of his reception of Vergil, he gave the Roman poet perhaps the most messianic rendition in the whole history of the Russian reception of Vergil.

VERGIL IN EXILE

> А я уже стою в саду иной земли,
> Среди кровавых роз и влажных лилий,
> И повествует мне гекзаметром Виргилий
> О высшей радости земли.

> But I am already standing in a garden of a foreign land,
> Amid the bloody roses and moist lilies,
> And Vergil with his hexameter relates to me
> The lofty joy of earth.

> Nikolai Gumilev[47]

Russian emigration circles in Europe after the Revolution offered a unique cultural environment since it caused a massive exodus from Russia, mostly of the intellectual and political elite.[48] These exiles to a large degree conditioned and influenced the direction of Russian thought abroad, and within only a couple of decades provided important and long-lasting contributions to the literary and philosophical landscape. To name only a few, the prose and poetry of Bunin, Nabokov, Merezhkovskii, Tsvetaeva, and Georgii Ivanov; music by Rakhmaninov and Stravinskii; the theatre of Mikhail Chekhov and ballet of Fokin and Nizhinskii; the paintings of Korovin, Kandinskii, and Rerikh; the philosophy of Berdiaev and Stepun; the historical works of Rostovtsev and Vernadskii—this was the intellectual environment where Viacheslav Ivanov and Georgii Fedotov left their valuable input.[49] As A. Kiselev correctly points out, what emerged in these culturally thriving surroundings was the enduring history of debates about the history and mission of Russia in the world.[50] Most of Ivanov's and Fedotov's works written abroad inevitably return to these discussions, as do their works on Vergil. However, in order to engage more deeply with the works on Vergil written after they left Russia, it is important to consider the broader intellectual and philosophical context of these thinkers' writings.

Viacheslav Ivanov

Русь! на тебя дух мести мечной
Восстал и первенцев сразил;
И скорой казнию конечной
Тебе, дрожащей, угрозил:
За то, что ты стоишь, немея,
У перепутного креста, —
Ни Зверя скиптр нести не смея,
Ни иго легкое Христа.

Russia! The sword-bearing spirit against you
Has risen in revenge and crushed your firstborns;
And threatened you while you have trembled
With imminent and final execution.
Because you stand confused,
Before the cross on the crossroads—
Neither daring to carry the sceptre of the Beast,
Nor the light yoke of Christ.

V. Ivanov, *Cor Ardens*[51]

These lines written by Ivanov (Figure 7) as he contemplated Russian defeats in the Russo-Japanese War of 1904–5 and the future of Russia are cited by him again in his essay 'On the Russian Idea' («О русской идее», 1909) and further explained:

Не было ни конечной казни, ни в следующие годы — конечного освобождения. Развязка, казавшаяся близкой, была отсрочена. Но поистине, хоть и глухо, сознала Россия, что в то время, как душевное тело вражеской державы было во внутренней ему свойственной гармонии и в величайшем напряжении всех ему присущих сил, наше собирательное душевное тело было в дисгармонии, внутреннем разладе и крайнем расслаблении, ибо не слышало над своими хаотическими темными водами веющего Духа, и не умела русская душа решиться и выбрать путь на перекрестке дорог, — не смела ни сесть на Зверя и высоко поднять его скиптр, ни цельно понести легкое иго Христово. Мы не хотели цельно ни владычества над океаном, который будет средоточием всех жизненных сил земли, ни смиренного служения Свету в своих пределах; и воевали ни во чье имя.[52]

There was neither the final execution, nor in the following years the final liberation. The closure, which seemed so close, was postponed. But indeed, perhaps in a muffled way, Russia understood, that at the time

Иванов Вячеслав
Иванович

Figure 7. Portrait of Viacheslav Ivanov by Konstantin Somov (1906).

when the spiritual body of the enemy state was full of its inner self-renewing harmony and replete with the great tension of its powers, our collective spiritual body was in disharmony, in inner disarray and extreme weakness, because it did not hear over its dark chaotic waters the fluttering Spirit, and the Russian soul did not know how to choose decisively its path at the crossroads. It neither dared to mount the Beast and lift up high its sceptre, nor did it dare to carry the light yoke of Christ with determination. We did not want with any determination either to have sway over the ocean that will be the centre of all forces of life, nor to take on the humble service to the Light within our own boundaries. And we waged the war in the name of nothing.

Ivanov's ruminations certainly reflect the influence of Solov'ev's 'response to concrete historical and cultural changes originating from China and Japan at the point when the modernization and westernization of these nations were challenging the existing relationship between and indeed the very categories of, east and west', the response we have seen in his poems '*Ex Oriente Lux*' and

'Panmongolism'.[53] However, most importantly, this very pessimistic excerpt crystallizes Ivanov's lifelong preoccupation with Russian national destiny in the context of his two main interests: the classical world and Christianity. As he contemplated the first losses in the Russo-Japanese War and then the events of the Russian Revolution of 1917, he once again brought to the fore the two main discourses that characterize also the Russian reception of Vergil in the context of Russian identity: the imperial and the religious. Russia, in his opinion, needed direction. Unable to achieve its imperial aspirations and most importantly having been defeated now by an Asian country, Russia needed to reposition itself towards its spirituality, more specifically Christ. This idea persists in most of Ivanov's writings about Vergil. While Ivanov's allusions to Vergil are scattered throughout his works, from early poetry to the later 'Roman Diary' of 1944, in the following pages I address only texts that contribute to a consistent theme in Ivanov's reception of Vergil, that of spiritual awakening and inspiration. Before we closely consider these works, it is necessary to say a few words about Ivanov's education and background.

As Vasilii Rudich aptly observes, Ivanov 'was regarded by many, with a mixture of bewilderment and admiration, as the Hellenic spirit incarnate'.[54] Ivanov began his study of ancient Greek and Latin on his own at the age of twelve. After graduating from a classical gymnasium in Moscow with the highest honours, he immediately attracted the attention of his professors as he pursued the study of history and philosophy at Moscow University, where he made an impression with his impeccable knowledge of ancient languages. Recognizing his great promise as a scholar, in 1886 Ivanov's teachers arranged for him to study at the University of Berlin at the seminar of the famous Theodor Mommsen.[55] Under the tutelage of Mommsen and Otto Hirschfeld, Ivanov wrote a Latin dissertation, *On the Tax-Farming Companies of the Roman People* (*De societatibus vectigalium publicorum populi Romani*), which he completed in 1895 but only published fifteen years later. Although the thesis was undertaken in the spirit of Mommsen's *Römisches Staatsrecht* (*Roman Constitutional Law*) and in accordance with his teacher's methodology, Ivanov's conclusions ran counter to Mommsen's own theory.[56] Ivanov's thesis was, however, well received by Mommsen and highly praised by Hirschfield, who both acknowledged their young student's outstanding achievements.[57] Ivanov, however, chose not to pursue the academic career open to him in Germany.

Perhaps Ivanov's disinclination to study Roman history further was largely due to his inability 'to identify himself with the Roman spirit' because of its imperial ideals and aspirations.[58] During his dissertation years Ivanov immersed himself at first in the study of the origins of Roman belief in Rome's high historical mission. That study, as we will see, is directly connected to his reception of Vergil. At that time, however, under the influence of Nietzsche, Ivanov's interests shifted from Rome to the study of Dionysiac religion, which became his main interest. His *The Hellenic Religion of the Suffering God* (*Эллинская религия страдающего бога*, 1903–5) and his second book, *Dionysus and Predionysianism* (*Дионис и прадионисийство*, 1923), are both sophisticated and complex works in which Ivanov displays his lifelong drive to reconcile the disparate elements of his world view, mainly Classics and Christianity. Ivanov's drive to construct a syncretic view of paganism and Christianity was by no means a new one. As Pamela Davidson observes, 'in post-Renaissance humanist culture' the tension that existed for St Jerome and St Augustine and 'the line of demarcation, drawn by Dante, who firmly excluded pagans from the sphere of Christian revelation,' became considerably blurred. Russia at the turn of the century was also characterized by 'an all-embracing tendency towards cultural syncretism'.[59]

The Hellenic Religion of the Suffering God was not strictly speaking a scholarly book, but rather a course of lectures Ivanov developed and delivered in Paris in 1903. In these lectures he argued that Dionysus must be seen as 'prototype or forerunner of Christ' and that the cult of the pagan god 'offered a certain method of psychological parallel to that of Jesus'.[60] These ideas found their deeper development in Ivanov's *Dionysus and Predionysianism*, which reflects in more detail Ivanov's religious and philosophical quest and contains traces of such influences as Nietzsche, Erwin Rohde, Ulrich von Wilamowitz-Moellendorff, Gilbert Murray, and E. R. Dodds.[61]

The core and starting concept for understanding Ivanov's reception of Vergil is Ivanov's view of ancient Rome not as a phenomenon of 'natural' impromptu culture, but as a historical and cultural context for Christianity, just as in the case of his approach to Hellenism in general and the Dionysiac cult in particular. Ivanov's move to Rome in 1924 and conversion to Catholicism in 1926 contributed to and even enforced this tendency to assimilate the most influential pagan legacy in his Christian world view.[62] Rome and *Latinitas* existed for Ivanov as an embodiment of what he termed the 'Hellenic principle' («эллинство») identified with Mediterranean and European culture and rooted in 'the blood and language of the Latin tribes'.[63] Rome for Ivanov was a perfect locale that housed two of his spiritual passions, not as a utopian fantasy, but as a geographical city in which pagan shrines and the Hellenic spirit existed side by side with Christian churches, and the pagan past was neither disturbed nor annihilated by the advent of a new religion. For Ivanov there existed a miraculous, uninterrupted continuity that stretched from Dionysiac mysticism through Vergil and on to Christian Dante.

It is also necessary to consider Ivanov's view on Vergil in the context of his other 'Roman' texts.[64] During his first trip to Rome in 1892 Ivanov wrote a poem entitled 'Laeta' ('Joys') in which he exclaimed with exhilaration: 'Having reached my sacred goal, I, a pilgrim, have attained bliss.'[65] Ivanov declared Rome 'a new homeland', the place where finally the 'homeless traveller' could 'establish the altar for his penates'. The poem, 156 lines of elegiac distichs (in imitation of the ancient elegiac metre), was written in response to Ovidian exilic poetry. It echoes and juxtaposes Ovid's *Tristia* with the title of the poem 'Laeta' in order to emphasize Ivanov's exhilaration at being in Rome and contrast it with Ovid's devastation at being banished from his beloved city.[66]

Apart from his personal experiences that were so inextricably connected to Rome, Rome is central to Ivanov's poetics as the focus of the world culture in which the Russian artist could assert his place. Influenced by the writings of Vladimir Solov'ev, Ivanov saw the task of a Russian artist as twofold. On the one hand, a Russian poet living in the First Rome had a duty to contemplate thoroughly and to understand Russia's role as the Third Rome and its 'selfless ability to synthesize East and West'.[67] On the other hand, the merging of East and West would be fully realized by joining in the creation of a Kingdom of God, in which the Eastern and Western churches could enter the long-awaited union.[68] Cultural unity would lead to a religious one, human culture would merge with religious faith, and the Christian *Civitas Domini* could be understood through Rome's ancient past as the *Caput Mundi*, the centre of the world. Thus Ivanov claimed kinship in his vision of Rome not only with Vergil and Aeneas, but also with the Augustine of the *Confessions* and Dante of the *Divine Comedy*.

By 1924, the year of his final move to Rome, Ivanov had lived through the deaths of his two beloved wives, Lydia Zinovieva-Annibal (1907) and Vera Shvarsalon (1920), and the havoc of the first post-revolutionary years in Moscow and Baku.[69] He found in Rome once more his promised land and expressed his exultation in the *Roman Sonnets*. The first sonnet, written a few days after his arrival, relates his feelings of Phoenix-like rebirth, a resurrection from the cleansing fire:

> Вновь, арок древних верный пилигрим,
> В мой поздний час вечерним 'Ave, Roma'
> Приветствую, как свод родного дома,
> Тебя, скитаний пристань, вечный Рим.
>
> Мы Трою предков пламени дарим;
> Дробятся оси колесниц меж грома
> И фурий мирового ипподрома:
> Ты, царь путей, глядишь, как мы горим.
>
> И ты пылал и восставал из пепла,
> И памятливая голубизна
> Твоих небес глубоких не ослепла.
>
> И помнит, в ласке золотого сна,
> Твой вратарь кипарис, как Троя крепла,
> Когда лежала Троя сожжена.[70]

> Again, true pilgrim of your ancient arches,
> I greet you, as my own ancestral home,
> With evening 'Ave, Roma',
> You, wanderer's harbour, eternal Rome.
>
> The Troy of our forebears we give to fire;
> The chariots' axles crack between the thunder
> And furies of the world hippodrome:
> You, king of roads, see how we are burning.
>
> And you went down in flames and rose from the ashes;
> The mindful blueness
> Of your deep skies did not grow blind.
>
> Your cypress, standing sentinel, remembers
> In the caress of golden dream
> How strong grew Troy as she lay burned.

Ivanov's lyric protagonist greets his beloved city in Latin: 'Ave, Roma'. The introduction of Latin, as Kalb observes, 'into an otherwise Cyrillic text semantically links Russia to the Western world, thus echoing the poet's own journey from Russia to Rome'.[71] Just as Troy had metamorphosed into Rome, so the poet feels that he has been granted another life and has been raised from the ashes, as he emerges from Russia in turmoil into the eternal city, the 'wanderer's harbour'. The poem brings to mind Aeneas' address to his comrades amid the devastating shipwreck (*Aen.* 1.202–7):[72]

> revocate animos maestumque timorem
> mittite; forsan et haec olim meminisse iuvabit.
> Per varios casus, per tot discrimina rerum
> tendimus in Latium, sedes ubi fata quietas
> ostendunt; illic fas regna resurgere Troiae.
> Durate, et vosmet rebus servate secundis.

> Restore your souls and dismiss sad fear;
> Perhaps at some point even these things will be a pleasure
>   to recall.
> We are headed towards Latium, where the fates promise
> Restful settlements; there it is allowed for the kingdom
>   of Troy to rise again.
> Endure, and save yourselves for the happy events.

In contrast to Aeneas, who is terrified by the storm and uncertain of his future when he delivers these words (208–9: '*talia voce refert curisque ingentibus aeger* / *spem vultu simulat*'—'he says these words aloud but vexed with great sorrows / he feigns hope on his face'), Ivanov's triumph over fear and trying fate is unreserved. The identification with the Trojan hero en route to his new home was not new to Ivanov's poetry. In his first collection, *The Pilot Stars*, the poem 'Cumae' («Кумы»)[73] referred to Aeneas' plight again through the prophecy of the Cumaean Sibyl given to the hero during his descent to the underworld in Book 6 of the *Aeneid*. That descent had been necessary for Aeneas to abandon his past as a vanquished Trojan and prepare for his future as the victorious if ruthless Roman. Without the descent into the underworld the rebirth of Aeneas from the Trojan *Flammentod* would have been impossible.

In the *Roman Sonnets* Ivanov identifies himself even more with the plight of the hero Aeneas who had to undergo the transformation from a Trojan into a Roman. The poet envisions the rise of the new city from the Trojan fire and life from the destroyed civilization. The hope is not feigned; it is confident and exhilarating. The cypress tree, in Roman poetry a traditional symbol of death, becomes a symbol of resurrection, a new beginning that the poet anticipates in Rome, his new abode. Resurrection from the annihilating fire as a spiritual rebirth was one of Ivanov's persistent themes, and was especially prominent in his *Cor Ardens* collection (1911) and was even reflected in the title. Zelinskii explained Ivanov's interest in the theme of rebirth by means of fire with reference to the suffering and resurrected god Dionysus, Ivanov's main scholarly interest.[74] The poem not only evoked the burned Troy, but also the rebirth of Rome herself: «и ты пылал и восставал из пепла» ('and you burned and rose from the ashes'). Ivanov might have been alluding here to the numerous resurrections of the city: from destruction by the Gauls, from the great fire of Nero, from the barbarian attacks. Rome in a cyclical motion soared over time, and the sky of the city became 'mindful' («памятливая») of all its history; the word in Russian is derived from «память» ('memory'). The idea of memory was reiterated again in relation to the cypress tree, to which the ability to remember was also attributed.[75] Here Ivanov was following in the footsteps of his beloved Greeks, for whom loss of memory signified death: Lethe, the river of oblivion, was located in Hades; as long as memory persisted, however, resurrection was inevitable and death was kept at bay.

Rome for Ivanov acquired a universalism in which the Eastern Trojan Aeneas was transformed into the founder of the Western Roman nation, and the Russian poet into a harbinger of a renewed Christian ideal, a role that Ivanov assumed persistently. For Ivanov, furthermore, Vergil stood on the threshold of a new world, bridging the gap between the pagan past and the Christian present and future.[76] Therefore even Vergil's own doubts about the brutalizing price of building Rome did not enter Ivanov's perception of Rome and his interpretation of its greatest poet. This curious detail, however, in Ivanov's treatment of the Vergilian text is consistent with Ivanov's overall philosophical views.

In his essay 'Legion and Communality' («Легион и соборность», 1916) Ivanov juxtaposes the two terms: 'legion' represents the power of the community against which any individual within that community is powerless; *sobornost'* («соборность», 'communality') is the Orthodox concept of a unity of believers in the Church through Christ within which any individual is respected and valued.[77] That concept, in Olga Deschartes's words, 'unifies the living with the living and the living with the dead, it springs from *Memoria Aeterna* and creates the

Communio Sanctorum'.[78] While Ivanov associates ancient Rome and the new Communist Russia with the concept of the 'legion', *sobornost'* for him is a uniquely old Slavic concept which was closely linked both to Ivanov's 'metatemporal, or "panchronic", interpretation and representation of culture' and to his belief that Russia and the Russians had a 'Roman' unifying mission in the history of Christendom.[79] This interpretation yet again has to be put in a broader context upon which we briefly touched in the introduction to this study and to which it is necessary to return now. As Russian intellectuals from the eighteenth century on tried to align Russia with Western values, alongside the overall sense of inferiority to the West there lingered a continuous sentiment that 'Russia would contribute to the total renewal of world civilization, of which Russians would serve as both the prophets and the architects.'[80] Greenfeld writes:

> One final step had to be taken before the transvaluation of the Western canon could crystallize as the Russian national consciousness. The backwardness of Russia meant the immaturity and underachievement of its civilization by Western standards. The Russian patriots connected the abomination of reason to too much civilization—a curse they were spared—and interpreted the latter as separation from vital, primeval sources, of which they had to spare. (While in the course of the eighteenth century, it was many times emphasized that backwardness was not necessarily an obstacle on the road to greatness, this intellectual somersault, making virtue out of necessity, turned backwardness into a guarantee of greatness.) At this juncture the Russian nationalist elite discovered, or perhaps invented, the 'people,' which determined the criteria of membership in the nation and led to its definition as an ethnic collectivity. For they connected the spiritual virtues of the Russian soul: spontaneity and feeling, to these vital forces: blood and soil... The soul—the sign of Russianness—derived from blood and soil.[81]

We can see how Ivanov's interpretation of the Russian mission in the world fits into this construct of seeing the Russian soul as a stronghold of true spirituality, ready to assume leadership on the road to spiritual epiphany while also encompassing all the benefits of Western culture. Greenfeld suggests that for the most part this construct was '*ressentiment*... that fueled Russian national consciousness'. In the eighteenth century it proved to be especially important because it was 'the period of gestation' of Russian national identity.[82] But after the Revolution of 1917, reverting to that idea of the collective power of the pure Russian soul was bound to happen in order to recover whatever of that identity was left.[83] For Ivanov it became connected with the Russian spiritual mission. Ivanov also extended this syllogism into the realm of Christianity, where the idea of ethnic collectivity was supplanted by the concept of *sobornost'*, the Orthodox concept of religious unity. Vergil's work was not treated by Ivanov solely as a text of the emerging Roman Empire conquering the world with its imperial collective enforced by legions, but also as a religious text transfigured in the epiphanic light of unifying *sobornost'*.[84]

In the *Roman Sonnets* Ivanov saw himself as the new Aeneas, who would start his journey from the ancient gates of Rome and end it at the citadel of the Christian fate, St Peter's. This journey also showed Ivanov's persistent integration of Classics and Christianity, with a strong preference for the latter; like Dante he chose Vergil to be his guide and then abandoned him at the gates of St Peter's because, as a pagan, even Vergil must be barred from the Kingdom of God.

That spiritual journey through Rome also fits into Ivanov's perception of Russia as a Third Rome, which, unlike its Roman predecessor, would have different priorities. Ivanov thought of the Russian Revolution as he was writing his sixth sonnet, 'Fontana delle Tartarughe'.[85] The entry in his diary dated 3 December 1924 reads: 'The entire time I've been abroad, I've been maintaining "Hannibal *ad portas*".'[86] By interpreting Communism as Russia's Hannibal, and thus its undoing, Ivanov linked together Russian and Roman history.[87] While Russia, with Hannibal-Communism at its gates, was temporarily unable to fulfil its Christian mission, Ivanov, like a Russian Aeneas, took upon himself the task of being the mouthpiece of the Third Rome in the first one until Hannibal could be defeated.

In this respect Russia's designation as the spiritual Third Rome (although temporarily hindered in its mission) becomes particularly poignant. In the essay 'On the Russian Idea' with which I started my discussion of Ivanov, he finally reveals his expectations: 'You, Russian, must remember one thing: universal truth is your truth and if you want to preserve your soul, do not be afraid to lose it.'[88] Here Vergil's importance for Ivanov is disclosed by the author himself through his citation of the famous lines in *Aeneid* 6.788–853 alongside his injunction to Russians. When Aeneas descended into the underworld in Book 6 to hear the prophecy about his destiny from his father, Anchises, the latter showed him the 'Roman parade' populated by the future great figures of Roman history: following Augustus were the souls of heroes from earlier times—the kings of Rome, then the great men of the republic, ending with the two Scipios who had defeated the Carthaginians and Quintus Fabius Maximus Cunctator, who had saved Italy from Hannibal. Anchises broke off this pageant to prophesy Rome's mission (851–3):

> tu regere imperio populos, Romane, memento
> (hae tibi erunt artes), pacique imponere morem,
> parcere subiectis et debellare superbos.
> Roman, remember to rule the nations with your sway
> (these will be your arts), and to impose the custom of peace,
> to spare the vanquished and to bring down the haughty.

Ivanov construes these Vergilian lines not as an expression of 'national selfishness but the providential will and idea of sovereign Rome in the process of becoming the world' («не эгоизм народный, но провиденциальную волю и идею державного Рима, становящегося миром»).[89] Subsequently he borrowed the didactic tone for his message to his compatriots, but the imperial pride was gone, replaced by a spiritual quest. In this essay Ivanov makes it clear that Rome represented for him not just an image of empire but a spiritual entity with a spiritual mission, thus again linking classical antiquity to Christian values on the common basis of faith. Russia's loss of itself would culminate in a resurrection of the spirit, just as Troy in the *Roman Sonnets* rose from the ashes to become Rome. By understating Roman imperial aspirations and linking them to Russia's spiritual role in the world, Ivanov moved even further away from the world of classical antiquity into the world of Christian faith.

In 1931 Ivanov returned to Vergil one more time and wrote in German[90] his essay 'Vergils Historiosophie', which was published in the prestigious literary journal *Corona* edited and published at that time in Zurich and Munich by Martin Bodmer and Herbert Steiner.[91] In this essay Ivanov's continual allusions to Dante, whom he saw as the only poet who understood the essence of the 'Christian' Vergil, are, as Pamela Davidson observes, full of several 'intellectual inconsistencies'. Ivanov viewed Dante as a poet 'whose spiritual outlook exhibited Dionysiac traits' and as such can be used as yet another proof that the Dionysiac religion is a 'prefiguration of the ideal, primitive essence of Christianity'.[92] However, as in the case of Ivanov's reception of Vergil, we must not look for the reflection of the historical Dante and his attitudes to pagan antiquity in Ivanov's essay. Ivanov was interested in Dante 'as a vehicle which he could invest with his projected spiritual ideal of a synthesis of Greek and Christian mysticism'.[93] The same approach is at the core of his reception of Vergil, whom Ivanov in a very decisive way read through the lens of mysticism and Christian belief. Furthermore, as Rudich points out, Ivanov's reception of the *Aeneid* was connected with Ivanov's theory of *antiroia* (the reverse flow), the flow of causality, directed from future to past.[94] In Ivanov's view the Christian beliefs and texts illuminate the poetry of the pagan past. This later essay unequivocally presents Vergil in a messianic light in tune with his medieval reception, which Ivanov, despite his fine classical training, accepted as 'instinctual' when assessing Vergil. Does Vergil, asks Ivanov, 'no longer belong completely to antiquity, but also already to the "progenies" who in fact know themselves to be installed in Heaven?' Although Ivanov in this essay no longer directly addresses the question of Russian national destiny in the context of Vergil, it is clear that it is on his mind as he returns again to contemplation of Aeneas' mission and especially his dispute with Dido:

> The belief which for the Greeks is clearly characterized by the content of their ideas and the inherent dialectics of basic knowledge as the point of departure for a philosophy of history—verified, by the way, by Aristotle's concurrence—is especially Aeschylus' and Herodotus' magnificent view of the Persian Wars as the pinnacle of the age-old struggle between Europe, proud of the ethical make-up of the free ancient Greeks, and Asia, with its Libyan foothills, represented by the principle of theocratic despotism. Virgil remains true to this view, in his own, truly Roman way, as one for whom Hellas represents the transmitter of tradition and *Urbs Roma*, the universal city. This perspective provides him with a deeper justification for the dispute with Carthage over world rule, a struggle that was decisive for the development of national power, and helps to interpret the divine directive that dutifully burdened his hero with the painful dispute with Dido. To be sure, the poet must, in order to adapt the classical theory to his national point of view, undertake a colossal adjustment: he removes the Trojan War, where the Greeks perceive an important moment precisely in their struggle with the Orient, from the traditional connections, blames Ilion's fall only on Laomedon and the Priamides (*Laomedonteae luimus periuria Troiae*, *Georg.* 1.502;[95] *culpatus . . . Paris*,[96] *Aen.* 2.602; Aeneas, as we know, belongs by lineage to an auxiliary strand of the royal house),[97] and, highlighting this artificially, has the Trojan people, after emigrating to Hesperia, appear to be the true bearers and shapers of the civic ideal ('*Polisidee*') of the Occident. Yet even this very broad scope appears too

narrow for the lofty flight of the poet; proof of the historical necessity and the beneficial effects of this new world regime, supplied (most insistently via Polybius) by political historiography, is not enough for him: he strives to make the case for transcendental justification of the events in order to prove for everyone the religious consecration of Roman political power.[98]

In this passage Ivanov's earlier preoccupation with Russian national destiny shines through. He saw Roman political power as 'consecrated', 'divinely ordained'. More importantly, the age-old juxtaposition between East and West was brought forth by Ivanov again. Trojans, originally from the Orient, became true shapers of the fates of the Occident. It is hard not to recognize Ivanov's thoughts on Russia in these lines. Caught between Eastern despotism and Western secular imperialism, Russia had to shape its destiny by accepting Christ as the only source of power, both religious and secular. Ivanov perceived Vergil as the 'first poet to speak of national determination as mission' and cited here again the celebratory warning '*tu regere imperio populos, Romane, memento (hae tibi erunt artes)*' ('Roman, remember to rule the nations with your sway (these will be your arts)'), interpreting it as 'national self-determination on the one hand, universal on the other—within one harmonious single entity'. Ivanov ended his essay on the optimistic and proleptic note:

> Following the collapse of the ecumenical ideal that fades out in Dante's treatise *De monarchia*, the newly born national consciousness mines from the same quarry, fulfilling its needs in accordance with its capacity. The songs of praise of Italy in the *Aeneid* and in the second book of the *Georgics* inspire Petrarch to patriotic hymns. Virgil's vernacular becomes a holy relic, a spiritual palladium of nations proud of belonging to the *genus Latinum* by descent, language, moral stance.

Ivanov wanted to see Russia as a part of the 'genus Latinum' that he is describing. In 1931, however, it became clear that Russia was irrevocably consumed by the Communists, and all hope was lost. That is perhaps the reason why Ivanov's contemplation of the Russian national mission is suppressed here, hidden under his 'Vergilian' text.

Ivanov's essay on Vergil must be considered side by side with another contemporary contemplation of Vergil, by the famous Russian religious philosopher Georgii Fedotov.

Georgii Fedotov

Georgii Fedotov, like Ivanov, also voiced a reception of Vergil closely connected with his hopes of Russia's mission in the world, although his interpretation of the Roman poet in messianic light was less pronounced and less connected with Solov'ev's and Ivanov's ideas of Christian unity.

Born in 1886 in Saratov, Fedotov graduated from St Petersburg Technology Institute and was caught up in the sweep and excitement of the 1905 revolution, which found him at first supporting radical socialists. His subsequent arrest and exile to Germany, where he studied history in Berlin and Jena, brought him under the influence of humanist philosophy, the study of which he pursued upon his return to Russia, where he entered the University of St Petersburg. Under the tutelage of Ivan Grevs, Fedotov completely severed his links with any political movement and devoted himself entirely to the study of the European Middle Ages.[99] Persecution related to his politically active past, however, persisted and in 1911 forced him to leave for Italy, where he worked for a while in the libraries of Rome and Florence; he returned to Russia the following year. It was Italy, by Fedotov's admission, that shaped him as a historian of Russian culture: 'It was precisely the deep immersion into the sources of Western culture which opened up the magnificent beauty of Russian culture. Returning from Rome, we for the first time quivering with awe peered into the columns of Kazan Cathedral; the medieval Italy made Moscow more understandable.'[100] This approach also became palpable in Fedotov's reception of Vergil as he tried to connect the *Aeneid* with the trials of Russian emigration after the Bolshevik revolution.

Fedotov left Russia for good in September 1925. He lived for a short time in Berlin, but found his permanent residence in Paris. There he took a position at the St Sergii Theological Institute (Institut de Théologie Orthodoxe Saint-Serge) where such important figures as Sergii Bulgakov and G. V. Florovskii also taught. Until 1940 Fedotov taught there the history of Western Christianity, hagiology, and Latin. In the 1920s–30s he published a series of monographs on the history of the Russian Orthodox Church, which manifested his philosophical goal of seeing Christianity not in any narrowly defined denomination, but as a wholesome, unifying, not separating concept, which reflected Solov'ev's ideas of unity.[101] His last two major works were written in the United States, where he moved in 1941: *The Russian Religious Mind* (*Русская религиозность*) and *The Treasury of Russian Spirituality*. In 1943 Fedotov started teaching in St Vladimir's Seminary in New York, where he remained until his death in 1951.

As A. Kara-Murza points out in his essay on Fedotov's legacy, despite the many different interests manifested in Fedotov's numerous publications, his philosophical views are consistent and are primarily concerned with the philosophy of culture.[102] Iurii Ivask, an important figure in Russian émigré circles who knew Fedotov personally, wrote that Fedotov's whole legacy is centred on one thought, namely, that human freedom can be the result not of political coup, but cultural creativity: 'His task', wrote Ivask, 'is the justification of culture («оправдание культуры»), which in so many ways and so passionately was denied among us.'[103] This concentration on broad concepts, and a tendency to bring disparate ideas together, characterizes both the religious and historical teachings of Fedotov.

One of the main defining characteristics of Fedotov's philosophy was finding common ground between Slavophiles and Westernizers and absorbing national tendencies within a common striving for humanity and spirituality.[104] It is no surprise that Fedotov made his publishing debut in Paris in the journal *Версты* (*Miles*), characterized by its Eurasian tendencies, which embraced the intertwining of both Russia's European and Asiatic roots, but also its insistence on the uniqueness of Russian history and culture.[105]

In Paris, Fedotov became especially close to Nikolai Berdiaev (1874–1948), whose Christian existentialism influenced him. Like Berdiaev, Fedotov also became concerned with the ideas of freedom and uninhibited human creativity, which knows no national boundaries or political borders. A devout Christian, Fedotov remained, unlike Ivanov, with the Russian Orthodox Church, but, as for Ivanov, religion for him was inextricably connected with culture.[106] In *The Russian Religious Mind* Fedotov argues that history and culture are in essence human components of religion.[107]

Fedotov's concept of, in Dostoevskii's words, the 'Russian European' hinged on the idea of an individual whose intellectual interests would be deeply rooted in the European legacy, but who would not lose connection with the 'old Russia' that existed before Peter's reforms and was closely connected with Christian spirituality.

Although he never idealized Europe and knew thoroughly the dark pages of European history, he considered the Bolshevik victory the result of Russia's abandonment of the high humanistic European tradition, which took its beginnings from classical antiquity.[108] He himself, as Ioann Meiendorf points out in his introduction to Fedotov's work, liked 'to juxtapose his own point of view on Russian history with those of classical Russian historians—Sergei Solov'ev and Vasilii Kliuchevskii', who admired the Moscow kingdom, created in the fifteenth and sixteenth centuries as 'the pinnacle of Russian civilization'.[109] For the Slavophiles of the nineteenth century, who influenced such historiography, Peter's empire was a betrayal of Russian uniqueness and slavish imitation of the Western path that remained foreign to the Russian national spirit. Fedotov, on the contrary, admired Peter and the Western city he created, 'branding the period of Moscow's rule as the dark ages of Russian history', ages which brought about the 'distorted Byzantinism' that later manifested itself in the Soviet state. In Fedotov's opinion Peter's reforms and the new capital of St Petersburg partook of the virtues of Western civilization, which brought to Russia the ideals of liberty and human dignity.[110]

Fedotov's short essay on Vergil is a showcase of these beliefs. He chose to reflect on Vergil as the common denominator of everything that he valued about Western civilization, even more so because he found himself in exile in the West and away from Russia. Before we look closely at the text of this essay, it has to be noted that Fedotov's overall style of writing, as N. Zaitseva observes, is more emotional and exalted than what might be expected from a philosopher. His prose is often heavily marked by exclamation marks and outbursts, and his definitions and observations are most certainly biased and when it comes to Vergil sometimes inaccurate.[111] Furthermore, it has to be pointed out that, to this day, Fedotov's essay on Vergil remains a relatively unknown text. While it is written with the passion characteristic of many Fedotov's writings, the Russian thinker's reception of the great Roman poet is somewhat one-sided and lacks the depth and complexity of Ivanov's understanding of Vergil.

The following analysis does not aim at pinpointing the inconsistencies of Fedotov's Vergilian reception, but rather at emphasizing how this essay fits into the context of Russian Vergilian reception in general and Fedotov's overall philosophy in particular.[112]

'On Vergil' («О Виргилии») was first published in 1930 in Paris in the journal *Числа* (*Numbers*, 2–3). This essay, written on the 2000th anniversary of Vergil's birth, deals with the connection between Russia and Vergil in a much more pronounced way than Ivanov's essay published a year later. Fedotov starts with caution:

> Но нам-то что до Гекубы? Мы, скифы, званы ли сегодня на праздник? Кажется, Виргилий всегда был чужд русской душе.[113]

> But what is Hecuba to us? Are we, as Scythians, even invited today to the feast? It seems that Vergil was always foreign to the Russian soul.

What these lines reveal in Fedotov's contemplation of the relevance of Vergil to Russia is the ambivalence that we have not encountered in Ivanov's Vergilian texts, but which we have seen expressed by Mikhail Gasparov. By calling Russians the Scythians,[114] Fedotov returns to the old question that preoccupied, as we have seen, the Russian philosopher Peter Chaadaev: can Russia really lay claim to the Western heritage, to the classics, or does it have a Scythian, or more precisely Asiatic soul, alien to the cultural achievement of classical antiquity? Fedotov, it seems, like Ivanov, strove to find a place for the Vergilian legacy in Russia. Unlike Ivanov, however, he did not completely reconfigure Vergil's text to suit his own religious convictions. Fedotov's first thought is of the imperial connection:

> Тень Виргилия — может быть, незримо — стояла над Русской Империей. В классическую эпоху ее мощи латинский гений проявляется уже зримо. В холодных и пышных залах Эрмитажа, в помпейских фресках на стенах Николаевских дворцов, в мерной тяжести Истории Государства Российского — звучит Виргилиева медь. *Tu regere imperio populos, Romane, memento.*[115]

> The shadow of Vergil—perhaps even invisibly—stood over the Russian Empire. In the classical era of its might the Latin genius already palpably revealed itself. In the cold and lavish halls of the Hermitage, in the Pompeian frescos on the walls of Nicholas's palaces, in the measured weight of the *History of the Russian State*[116]—Vergilian copper resounds. *Tu regere imperio populos, Romane, memento.*

Here Fedotov cites the same words as Ivanov did in the admonition to his compatriots in his 'Vergils Historiosophie' when he contemplated Rome's universal mission. Thus Fedotov also sees the Russian mission as a guiding force in the family of nations. At first his view is purely secular, the context being that of the imperial aspirations: 'The mission of Peter-Nicholas I repeated the mission of Augustus: to unite a number of nations under the rule of a crown-bearing nation, enlightened by a foreign culture' («Дело Петра-Николая I повторяет дело Августа: соединить сонм народов под водительством народа-венценосца, просвещенного чужой культурой»).[117] It is the empire that Fedotov sees as Russia's main connection to Vergil, and he ruminates over the meaning of the Roman poet in post-revolutionary times: 'With the death of the Russian Empire has Vergil retained any meaning for us?' («С гибелью Русской Империи сохранился ли для нас какой-либо смысл Виргилия?»).[118] The answer to this question does not appear until the end of the essay, as Fedotov's discourse unexpectedly turns from contemplation of the national mission to that of exile, a theme poignant for writers of the Russian emigration, whose voice and hopes often become reflected in Fedotov's philosophical output. To that extent Fedotov approaches even Vergil's biography, calling him (incorrectly) a 'peasant's son' («крестьянский сын»), a 'plebeian' («плебей») and even a 'peasant poet' («крестьянский поэт»). He further elaborates:

> То, что не удалось его взысканным музами современникам, Ови-дию, Горацию: преодоление эпикурейства, беспечной эротики, бе-зответственного скептицизма, то совершил в себе крестьянский поэт, по иному чем Гораций, связанный с родной землей. Вот почему он мог стать воспитателем не только последних сыновей Рима, но и нового Израиля, поделившего Римскую землю.

> Не хочется быть назойливым, но как не сказать, что судьба Вирги-лия полна вещего значения для судеб русской культуры и именно ее сегодняшнего дня?[119]

His contemporaries Ovid and Horace, also summoned by the Muses, did not succeed in overcoming Epicureanism, careless eroticism, irresponsible scepticism.[120] That was done by a peasant poet connected with his native land in a different way than Horace was. That is why he could become an educator not only of the last sons of Rome, but also of the new Israel, which shared Roman land.

I do not want to appear annoying, but how can one avoid saying that Vergil's fate was full of prophetic meaning for the fate of Russian culture, and especially for its present state?

These assertions about Vergil's origins[121] and his poetic evolution from the *Eclogues* to the *Aeneid* are, to say the least, reductive. However, it is clear what is at the core of Fedotov's argument: Russia, unlike other 'frivolous' nations (paralleled to Ovid and Horace), has to be more like Vergil, it has to overcome carelessness and irresponsibility and devote itself completely to the spiritual and cultural 'education' of others. We have seen similar thoughts in Ivanov's approach to Russia's mission in the world. In émigré circles the contemplation of Russia's post-revolutionary fate became commonplace. The exiles found themselves isolated both linguistically and politically from Russia. As the years after the events of 1917 passed without any hope of return, the debates about the future and Russia's destiny continued unabated.

It is clear that Fedotov's reception of Vergil is completely different from that of Solov'ev and Ivanov on one key point: he does not use Vergil's text to stress Russia's universalizing mission in the Christian context, and is more concerned with reading Vergil as a means to find and offer consolation to himself and his compatriots in forced exile, contemplating and even predicting at the same time the future of Russia:

> Сейчас, в неизбывной тоске о потерянной отчизне, мы впервые слышим тоску Энея. Мы понимаем, что Энеида, как всякий великий эпос, песнь о гибели, вместе с обетованием спасения. «Потерянная и возвращенная родина». Можно ли теперь без глубокого волнения читать вторую песнь — о пожаре Трои, о последней, безнадежной борьбе Энея? *Vidi Hecubam centumque nurus Priamumque per aras / Sanguine foedantem quos ipse sacraverat ignes* [sic].
>
> Да, мы видели Приама, убитого на крови собственного сына. Да, мы бежали с пожарища со старцем Анхизом и святынями Пергама. Это мы дрались с гарпиями за скудные остатки пищи. Это мы съели наши «столы». Мы миновали счастливо циклопов и Сциллу, но сколько старцев мы схоронили, сколько товарищей не досчитались, унесенных волнами.[122]

Now, in inconsolable sorrow over our lost fatherland, we for the first time hear Aeneas' longing. We understand that the *Aeneid*, like any great epos, is a song about death, together with achieving the promise of salvation. 'Lost and regained homeland.' How can we without deep emotion read the second book—about the burning of Troy, about the last and hopeless battle of Aeneas? *Vidi Hecubam centumque nurus Priamumque per aras / sanguine foedantem quos ipse sacraverat ignis* ['I saw Hecuba and her hundred daughters and (I saw) Priam near the altars defiling with his blood the fires which he himself had consecrated'].[123]

Yes, we saw Priam, killed in the blood of his own son. Yes, we escaped the fire with the old man Anchises and the sacred treasures of Troy. It was we who fought with the Harpies for the meagre remnants of food. It was we who ate our 'tables'. We auspiciously passed by the Cyclopes and Scylla, but how many old men have we buried, how many friends are missing swept away in the waves.

In these lines the difference between Fedotov's and Ivanov's interpretations of Vergil becomes apparent. For Fedotov, Aeneas' plight and the story of toppled Troy represent a metaphor for the Russian Revolution and its numerous victims. Fedotov is aware of 'messianic' interpretations of Vergil, but approaches them with caution: 'Let's agree that for Orthodoxy the school of Vergil was indeed a strange and inappropriate garment—not so with the Russian Empire, which it fits perfectly' («Согласимся, что для православия школа Виргилия была, действительно, одеянием странным и неуместным, — не то что для Русской Империи, которой она почти адекватна»).[124] With the loss of the Russian Empire, Fedotov saw Vergil's future in Russia as bleak:

> Воскреснет ли когда-нибудь Виргилий для России? Боюсь, что нет. Наш путь иной—широкий, столбовой путь истории, с которого мы так непокорно свернули—еще в Московские времена. Наш путь ведет не через Трою-Рим, но через Грецию, которая дала нам слово, дала молитву и—в самый последний час нашей истории— открыла таинственную глубину своей вещей и вечно возрождающейся красоты.[125]

> Will Vergil ever be revived for Russia? I am afraid not. Our road is different—the broad, meted road of history from which ever since the time of Muscovy we have disobediently deviated. Our road does not go through Troy-Rome, but through Greece, which gave us the word, gave us the prayer, and, in the last hour of our history, opened a mysterious depth of prophetic and eternally self-renewing beauty.

While emphasizing the widening gap between the new Russia and the classical legacy, Fedotov, however, still tries to connect Russian identity with antiquity and Europe, this time Greece, illuminating again the shifting reinventions of that identity through a classical lens: 'Vergil will never replace Homer for us, whose delectable verses in Russian hexameter have lulled our hearing since childhood' («Виргилий не заменит нам Гомера, сладостные строфы которого, в русском гекзаметре, с детства баюкают наш слух»). Referring here most likely to Gnedich's translation of the *Iliad* and Zhukovskii's of the *Odyssey*, both of which were repeatedly mentioned earlier in this study, Fedotov denies Vergil any longevity and meaning in Russia. He sees Homer as a soothing, calming influence, juxtaposing his poetry with Vergil's, whose sound in Russian is still foreign. It is important to note that, unlike Ivanov, Fedotov essentially rejects Rome for Greece rather than integrating them into a whole. Only at the end of his essay does Fedotov proclaim the *Aeneid* as inspirational 'in the hour of a solemn feat, when we will be required to give up everything vital and dear, the beauty itself' («в час сурового подвига, когда от нас потребуется отречение от кровного и родного, от самой красоты»). Fedotov thus refuses to appreciate Vergil's poetry aesthetically, disregarding its poetic value as on a par with the Homeric poems. Vergil's epic is cast by him as a narrative of sacrifice and complete isolation as Fedotov becomes concerned with aligning Russia with Greece for reasons of religious and spiritual legacy.

After Ivanov and Fedotov, Russian artists and thinkers rarely returned to the messianic or prophetic readings of Vergil's poetry. As the Soviet state emerged from the Civil War and massive exodus, the national discourse in Russian literature also changed, turning away from imperialist and spiritual doctrines towards more individualistic personal contemplations. This change in the perception of Rome in general, and Vergil in particular, again reflected an effort to assign meaning to the present, but the sweeping political and religious interpretations receded into the background, yielding to the less grandiose Vergil. In the later twentieth century Vergil found a complex postmodern response in the poetry of Joseph Brodsky (1940–96), who initiated a new kind of Vergilian reception concerned neither with empire nor with Christianity, but with the place of an artist in his own country and in the world.

NOTES

1. Ivanov (1971–9), 1.628, 'To each his own.'
2. Kalb (2008), 15.
3. In some cases the Silver Age figures when attempting to interpret the new environment rejected the promise the doctrine conveyed. Later in the Soviet period (under Stalin) the doctrine came back into use yet again. See Clark (2011), 169–209.

4. Mandel'shtam (1974), 97–8.

5. The poem is multi-layered and, along with allusions to Solov'ev's poem, 'three meetings' also evokes Mandel'shtam's brief romance with Marina Tsvetaeva and their meetings. See Gasparov's commentary in Mandel'shtam (2001), 754. A. M. Ranchin points out several possible interpretations of the pronoun 'he' in Mandel'shtam's stanza. He singles out three most likely ones: one referring to Mandel'shtam himself and his 1917 essay 'Skriabin and Christianity', in which he doubted the benefits of Roman culture; the second pointing towards Vladimir Solov'ev and his poem 'Three Meetings'; and the third an allusion to Pseudo-Dimitri, who falsely declared himself an heir to the Russian throne, accepted Catholicism, and, after receiving support from Rome, refused to try to bring Russia under the Pope's control. See A. M. Ranchin, «Византия и «Третий Рим» в поэзии Осипа Мандельштама» ('Byzantium and the "Third Rome" in the poetry of Osip Mandel'shtam'), 8 December 2010. Available at: <http://www.portal-slovo.ru/phil ology/43764.php> [last visited 10 May 2013]. See also Freidin (1987), 114–15, who suggests that the pronoun might have referred to the unfortunate Tsarevich Aleksei, the 'scheming son of Peter the Great', and again perhaps to Mandel'shtam himself. While all these interpretations are plausible, I do not see them as mutually exclusive, and would like to address in more detail the allusion to Solov'ev as most relevant to this study. See also Sinitsyna (1998), 8, who believes that Mandel'shtam in these lines engages in polemic with Solov'ev and disagrees with his views on Rome.

6. Kornblatt (2009), 13.

7. Kornblatt (2009), 13.

8. Cited in Kornblatt (2009), 7.

9. Kornblatt (2009), 11. Kornblatt also points out that Sophia 'appears in Byzantine iconography as male (Christ the Wisdom of God)'.

10. Zernov (1944), 117.

11. See Gustafson (1996), 31. Marina Kostalevsky (1997), 3, observes that the idea of unity, 'from time immemorial, held a persistent fascination for minds reared against the geopolitical backdrop of the boundless, scattered lands called Russia'. Kostalevsky also traces this idea back to the 'Third Rome' doctrine.

12. On the teachings of Ivan Kireevskii, see Gleason (1972). On the Slavophiles in general, see Riasanovsky (1952).

13. This connection to Catholicism became as important for Ivanov later as it was for Solov'ev.

14. Connolly (1992), 384.

15. Both poems can be found at: <http://az.lib.ru/s/solowxew_wladimir_ sergeewich/text_0060.shtml#064> [last visited 1 March 2013]. The

poems were also influential for the writings of Alexander Blok, Valerii Briusov, Andrei Belyi, Georgii Chulkov, and Sergei Solov'ev.

16. Sutton (1988), 175.

17. One reason for Solov'ev's concern and disillusionment at the time was the tsar's refusal to pardon regicide.

18. Gaut (1998), 93.

19. Lim (2008), 321. Lim also points out significant contradictions in Solov'ev's universalism, as it pertains to his writings on China and Japan. See also Ram (2003), 225, on Solov'ev's uncertainty about the Orient and xenophobic tendencies regarding China.

20. Davidson (2000), 643.

21. See Davidson (2007).

22. Zernov (1944), 125.

23. Matual (1982), 276.

24. Solov'ev (1970), 1.36. Trans. in Matual (1982), 276. For 'forefathers', however, Solov'ev uses the word *parentalia*, declining it in Russian.

25. Galinsky (1996), 249.

26. Solov'ev (1970), 3.154–5. Matual (1982), 276.

27. Matual (1982), 276.

28. The most exhaustive review of all the identifications of who the child might have been can be found in Coleiro (1979), 219–54.

29. Clausen (1994), 127.

30. Several classical scholars have hinted at a religious interpretation of the eclogue. Brooks Otis (1964), 137, described the poem 'as prophetic and inspired—almost like a prayer that is answered'. Before him W. F. Jackson Knight (1944), 137, went so far as to suggest: 'Perhaps Virgil already reached his greatest poetic discovery, that the Holy Family, human and divine in one, is enough to unify the explorations of the spirit.' The most influential secular interpretations of the eclogue are (to name a few) those of Putnam (1970), Leach (1974), Alpers (1979), and the commentary by Clausen (1994). The influential study by Edward Norden (1924) made, as Clausen (1994), 128–9, points out, the Christian interpretation acceptable and connected the Fourth Eclogue with Eastern theology and ritual.

31. Averintsev (1996), 40.

32. The italics are omitted from the online version cited but appear in the 2004 edition (222).

33. Some important bibliography on those interpretations can be found in Briggs (1981), 1267–1357. For a shorter but comprehensive discussion see Clausen (1994), 121, who dates the 'blessed event' (the birth of the child) to the year 40 BCE. He suggests that 'Virgil is alluding to the Pact of Brundisium, a political settlement between Antony and Octavian', which was 'solemnized, in the high Roman fashion, with a dynastic marriage as

Antony took to wife Octavian's sister, the blameless Octavia'. The offspring of that union would be the 'expected son of Antony and Octavia and heir to Antony's greatness—the son that never was; a daughter was born instead.'

34. Arnold (1994), 160.

35. Matual (1982), 278.

36. Matual (1982), 278.

37. Clausen (1994), 127.

38. See Matual (1982).

39. For the detailed account of the Symbolist assessment of Solov'ev, see Cioran (1977), 89–104.

40. See the N. Ia. Mandel'shtam, *Vospominaniia* (*Memoirs*), <http://www.sakharov-center.ru/asfcd/auth/?t=page&num=11706>, p. 296 [last visited 12 May 2013].

41. For more on Mandel'shtam and Rome, see Torlone (2009), 132–52.

42. Kalb (2008), 17.

43. See Torlone (2009), 132–52.

44. Losev (2000), 585. Losev (575–94) also offers a comprehensive overview of Solov'ev's influence on the other leading Symbolists, such as Valerii Briusov.

45. Kalb (2008), 10. Clark (2011), 24, also points out that the story of Aeneas 'resurfaced periodically in works by Soviet writers, most notably in Boris Pasternak's *Doctor Zhivago*'. For the numerous parallels between *Doctor Zhivago* and the *Aeneid*, see Griffiths and Rabinowitz (2011), 176–94, who aptly observe that '[i]t was Virgil who set the pattern for focusing the history of a people through the myth of a single life' (180).

46. Wachtel (1994a), 4–5. Bloom (1976).

47. This fragment is cited in Ronen (2008), 107.

48. Kiselev (2004), 21.

49. Although some of these figures had already made their reputations in Russia, they were less successful abroad but undoubtedly contributed greatly to the creation of the impressive Russian cultural milieu.

50. Kiselev (2004), 22.

51. The collected works of Ivanov are available at: <http://www.rvb.ru/ivanov/> [last visited 3 March 2013].

52. Ivanov (1971–9), 3.323.

53. Lim (1998), 323.

54. Rudich (1986), 275.

55. Wachtel (1994b).

56. Rudich (1986), 276. Mommsen's theories later met with much criticism as well, especially his treatment of the institution of the principate, which he considered solely from the legal point of view, excluding its political and social aspects. The 'grand fallacy' of that approach was that

Mommsen wanted to 'describe and understand a social organism by studying only its formal law'. See Linderski (1990), 53.

57. Wachtel (1994b), 360, has convincingly demonstrated that Otto Hirschfeld was considerably more involved than Mommsen in Ivanov's academic career, since Hirschfeld was in charge of the progress of Ivanov's dissertation thesis. Later Ivanov downplayed Hirschfeld's role and exaggerated his own closeness to Mommsen, whom he admired immensely.

58. Rudich (1986), 278.

59. Davidson (1996a), 85–6.

60. Davidson (1996a), 86.

61. For further most recent discussion of these two works, see Westbroek (2007).

62. Ivanov did not officially emigrate to Rome, but went there in fact as a representative of the Soviet state with permission from Anatolii Lunacharskii, the first Soviet Commissar of Enlightenment, and with the assignment of establishing a Russian Academy in Rome. He took this task seriously, but nothing came of it. He never renounced his Russian citizenship explicitly, although in 1929 he was declared «невозвращенец» ('one who failed to return'), and his citizenship lapsed in 1936 (Kalb, 2003, 25 n. 7).

63. Myers (1992), 86.

64. A detailed analysis of these and other 'Roman' poems of Ivanov can be found in Torlone (2009).

65. Ivanov (1971–9), 1.636.

66. Frajlich (2007), 100 and 119 n. 24, cites Vladimir Toporov's suggestion that in 'Laeta': 'a vivid panoramic description of Rome, synthesized in its various spatial and temporal images, leads to the theme of returning again according to his circuits and faithfulness to Rome . . . and further to the theme of homeland'.

67. Kalb (2008), 17.

68. Ivanov's vision of Rome was also strongly linked to Solov'ev's advocacy of a unification of the Orthodox and Roman churches in his most famous theological work, *La Russie et l'Eglise universelle*. In this unified church, according to Solov'ev, East and West would be equal partners, but Russia would have a special role to play.

69. In 1920–4 Ivanov was professor of classical philology and poetics at the newly founded University of Baku.

70. Ivanov (1971–9), 3.578. I have followed the division of the lines in the English translation of the poem according to this edition.

71. Kalb (2008), 152.

72. We have already seen these lines in the discussion of *The Bronze Horseman* in Chapter 3.

73. Ivanov (1971–9), 1.574.

74. Zelinskii (1916), 3.103. Zelinskii emphasized Heraclitus as well as Dionysus as a source for Ivanov's interest in rebirth by fire.
75. Klimoff (1986), 131.
76. Kalb (2003), 32.
77. Rosenthal (1993) analyses the term «соборность» in works by Ivanov, Sergei Bulgakov, and Pavel Florenskii. This concept was influenced by Solov'ev's idea of universalism. See Losev (2000), 585. See also Cioran (1977), 246–51 and 252–73, for the influence of Solov'ev's concept of Sophia on Florenskii and Bulgakov respectively.
78. Trans. Kalb (2008), 147.
79. Meerson (1999), 719. Ivanov (1971–9), 3.259–60.
80. Raeff (2003), 136.
81. Greenfeld (1992), 258.
82. Greenfeld (1992), 259–60.
83. The Bolsheviks for the most part tried to do away with the discourse of national identity or 'Russianness', replacing it instead with the idea of the 'Soviet people', again a contrived construct that proved to be extremely feeble in the aftermath of the collapse of the Soviet Union.
84. See Kalb (2008), 151–2.
85. Kalb (2003), 37.
86. Ivanov (1971–9), 3.852.
87. Braginskaia (2004), 62, points out that the equation of the Russian Revolution with foreign attacks on the Roman state was customary at that time among Russian intellectuals.
88. Ivanov (1971–9), 3.326.
89. Ivanov (1971–9), 3.326. In the Russian version the play on the palindromic effect of the words «Рим» ('Rome') and «мир» ('world') gives the lines a special emphasis.
90. Ivanov wrote other works in German as well, among them poetry. His engagement with German poetry, philosophy, and music remained lifelong. See Wachtel (1994a), 9–14. Wachtel points out that Ivanov 'mastered ornate, literary German' (11), which manifested itself in his essay on Vergil.
91. Davidson (1996b), xxxix. The translation of Ivanov's 'Vergils Historiosophie' first appeared in print in 2009 in the work co-authored by me and my colleague John Jeep, whose expertise in German and unlimited patience made the translation of this very challenging text possible. See Jeep and Torlone (2009).
92. Davidson (1989), 43.
93. Davidson (1989), 46.
94. Rudich (2002a), 35. Ivanov worked out this concept in his commentary to the poem 'Melampus's Dream' («Сон Мелампа», 1907).

95. The full quote is '*satis iam pridem sanguine nostro / Laomedonteae luimus periuria Troiae*' ('long since we have paid with our blood for the sacrileges of Laomedon's Troy'). Instead of using the neutral 'Trojan' or 'Dardanian' here, Vergil chooses to remind his readers of King Laomedon, Priam's father, who tricked the gods twice by perjuring himself and caused the first destruction of Troy. See Mack (1999), 140.

96. This quote is taken from Venus' appeal to Aeneas when he amid burning Troy sees Helen and wants to kill her for Troy's destruction. Venus in fact says: '*Non tibi Tyndaridis facies invisa Lacaenae / Culpatusve Paris, divum inclementia, divum, / Has evertit opes sternitque a culmine Troiam*' ('It is not the hated face of the Spartan daughter of Tyndareus that you must blame, nor Paris, but the cruelty of the gods, the gods, destroys these riches and topples Troy from its height'). Ivanov's choice of the first quote supports his argument but this quote does not. Paris, according to Venus, his most eager supporter, should *not* be blamed for the Trojan disaster.

97. Aeneas was the son of Anchises, brother of Priam, king of Troy, father of Hector, the champion of the Trojans.

98. The full text of the translation of Ivanov's essay can be found in Appendix I.

99. For more on Grevs's influence on Fedotov, see S. S. Bychkov's biographical essay in G. P. Fedotov (1996–), 1.15–16.

100. Kara-Murza (2006), 90.

101. Fedotov most likely had become deeply engaged with Solov'ev's ideas in Russia, especially as a member of the religious-philosophical circle 'Voskresenie' founded in 1917 in St Petersburg by A. A. Meier and his wife, K. A. Polovtseva. This deep engagement is especially manifest in his much later essay published in 1926 in which he reflects on Solov'ev's major work «Три разговора» ('Three conversations').

102. Kara-Murza (2006), 92.

103. Cited in Russian in Kara-Murza (2006), 92.

104. Zaitseva (2001), 12.

105. Bychkov, in Fedotov (1996–), 1.25. For more on 'Eurasianism' and especially the philosophy of N. S. Trubetskoi, see Zaitseva (2001), 63–73. Fedotov later criticized 'Eurasianism' for militant nationalism and anti-European rhetoric (Zaitseva, 2001, 72–3).

106. This connection between religion and culture can be seen in Ivanov's and Gershenzon's *Correspondence from Two Corners* (*Переписка из двух углов*), <http://rvb.ru/ivanov/2_lifetime/perepiska_iz_dvuh_uglov/text.htm> [last visited 20 October 2013]. See also Davidson (1996b), 367.

107. Fedotov (1996–), 10.9 (2001: *The Russian Religious Mind*, vol. 1).

108. For more on Russia's place between East and West, see Zaitseva (2001), 117–32.

109. Fedotov (1996–), 11.7 (2004: *The Russian Religious Mind*, vol. 2).
110. Fedotov (1996–), 11.7 (2004: *The Russian Religious Mind*, vol. 2).
111. I point out the inaccuracies in Appendix II, which contains the whole essay with commentary.
112. Detailed notes about Fedotov's treatment of the Vergilian text can be found in Appendix II.
113. Fedotov (1952), 216.
114. Here we have again the identification of Russia with Scythia so defiantly invoked by Alexander Blok, as we have seen.
115. Fedotov (1952), 216.
116. Here Fedotov refers to Nikolai Karamzin's *History of the Russian State*.
117. Fedotov (1952), 217.
118. Fedotov (1952), 218.
119. Fedotov (1952), 220–1.
120. Fedotov's take on Roman poetry is of course rather subjective. While he finds both Ovid and Horace to be frivolous, in Vergil he sees, like Ivanov, the messianic tendency, which he then connects with Vergil's presence in Christianity despite his pagan origins.
121. Vergil's biography can be found in Levi (1998). Vergil was not born in a peasant family. He was a middle-class child and a Roman citizen by birth. His mother's and father's family held office as magistrates in Rome.
122. Fedotov (1952), 218.
123. Book 2, lines 501–2, taken from Aeneas' narration to Dido of the destruction of Troy.
124. Fedotov (1952), 218.
125. Fedotov (1952), 221–2.

5

Vergilian Episodes

Joseph Brodsky

> Like every human being, a poet has to deal with three questions:
> how, what for, and in the name of what to live. The *Bucolics*, the
> *Georgics* and the *Aeneid* answer all three, and these answers
> apply equally to the Emperor and to his subjects, to antiquity as
> well as to our times. The modern reader may use Vergil in the
> same way as Dante used him in his passage through Hell and
> Purgatory: as a guide.

The epigraph to this chapter is taken from Joseph Brodsky's essay
'Vergil: Older than Christianity, a Poet for the New Age'.[1] This essay
belongs to the mature Brodsky, a Russian poet in exile, and it is
written in English, the language of his new home. But Vergil has a
continuous presence in Brodsky's poetics from his early poems and
all the way into his last 'poems-testaments'.

Brodsky's interest in Vergil was of course not sudden and contains
traces of the influence of the Russian poets whom he perceived as
formative for his own poetics.[2] In the first decades of the twentieth
century, for example, representatives of Russian Acmeism alluded to
Vergil frequently, since they saw him 'as a harbinger of a universal
cultural and historic code when one system is transformed into
another, especially in extreme . . . circumstances' («носитель универ-
сального культурно-исторического кода при переходе из одной
системы в другую, а особенно в крайних . . . обстоятельствах»).[3]
The Revolution of 1917 most certainly presented the poets with such
'extreme circumstances' as they turned to Vergil. Osip Mandel'shtam,
perhaps the most 'classical' of the Acmeists, alludes most frequently
to Ovid, but evokes Vergil in his formative essay 'Conversation about

Dante', in which, true to the preoccupations of Acmeism, he sees Vergil as a mediator in 'the synchronism of events, names, and tales, torn apart by centuries' («синхронизм разорванных веками событий, имен и преданий»).[4] We find allusions to Vergil also in Nikolai Gumilev[5] and most importantly Anna Akhmatova, who, as we will see later, influenced to some degree Brodsky's reception of the story of Dido and Aeneas in the *Aeneid*.

With Brodsky, however, the Russian Vergil enters the postmodernist stage, an era of sceptical interpretation of previous conventions and self-irony. Brodsky is a poet keenly aware of all of the preceding tradition: European as well as Russian. Thus his Vergil is often self-conscious and extremely personalized as Brodsky responds to his literary heritage and carefully carves his own space within it.

In her introduction to *Poets and Critics Read Vergil*, Sarah Spence cites an excerpt of a debate that occurred in 1995 during a conference at the University of Georgia featuring six speakers, three of whom were poets[6] and three classical scholars.[7] What emerges from the debate is a major difference between the two groups in the way they approach the reading of an ancient text. For the scholars, Vergil's text appeared as a *fait accompli*, a finished masterpiece, one, however, that stands in need of interpretation. Christine Perkell even pointed out that 'it never crosses [her] mind that Vergil is deficient'.[8]

The poets, however, offered a different approach. Mark Strand emphasized: 'Poets read all poetry as contemporaneous with themselves.' Rosanna Warren further elaborated that the way poets read other poets could be seen as an act of violence by committing which a poet tries to 'conjure an ancient poetic energy to come among us'.[9] For the classical scholars Vergil's text was an object for explication and commentary, whereas the poets approached it 'in terms of process more than product'.[10]

Brodsky, one of the poets participating in this conference, had never been simply an admirer of ancient poetry. His 'Odyssean' poems undermine the uplifting lyricism of the Homeric hero's homecoming. His Odysseus is a bitter man lost in time and space, disoriented, betrayed, and largely forgotten by those who should have loved him most.[11] Brodsky's Vergilian readings are no less confusing in their reversal of classical pathos. Performed in the same melancholy and contemplative voice as his consideration of the *Odyssey*, his evocation of the *Aeneid* is full of doubt, foreboding, and uneasiness about the price of heroic achievement.[12]

ARCADIA OF THE NORTH: REMAPPING THE PASTORAL SPACE

I would like to start my reading of Brodsky (Figure 8) with the eclogues, not the Vergilian ones, but Brodsky's own, the first of which was written as early as 1963 and was called 'Field Eclogue' («Полевая эклога»).[13] Before I address the text of this eclogue I should say a few words about Brodsky's understanding of what he termed an 'eclogue'. In his essay entitled 'On Grief and Reason', Brodsky discussed Robert Frost's poem 'Home Burial':

> 'Home Burial' is not a narrative; it is an eclogue. Or, more exactly, it is a pastoral—except that it is a very dark one. Insofar as it tells a story, it is, of course, a narrative; the means of that story's transportation, though, is dialogue, and it is the means of transportation that defines a genre. Invented by Theocritus in his Idylls, refined by Vergil in the poems he called eclogues or bucolics, the pastoral is essentially an exchange

Figure 8. Previously unpublished photograph of Joseph Brodsky during a visit to Armenia in April 1972, in the bucolic surroundings of academic Artem Alikhanian's garden. Left to right: Joseph Brodsky, Samvelina Pogosova, Sergey Martirosov, Marina Alikhanian, Artem Alikhanian. Image from the author's family archive.

between two or more characters in a rural setting, returning often to that perennial subject, love.[14]

Brodsky further elaborates on the general nature of Vergilian poetry and calls his 'phlegmatic musings' contemplative, as opposed to Propertius' 'choleric intensity', Ovid's 'sanguine couplings', and Horace's 'melancholic equipoise'.[15] He attributes the same contemplative melancholy to Frost and to American poetry in general, but it seems to me that Brodsky in his reception of Vergil has also been extremely attracted to it.

Brodsky's earliest 'Field Eclogue' displayed only one of the generic characteristics of pastoral, according to his own schema. The poem is full of references to a generalized rural landscape, which is eerily uninhabited, abandoned:

> Пустота, ни избы, ни двора,
> шум листвы, ни избы, ни землянки.
>
> Emptiness, with no huts, no yards,
> Only the leaves rustling, but no huts, no shelters.[16]

The landscape is completely deprived of human presence. It lacks even the everyday 'utensils' of mundane life: plates, jars, and buckets. As the poet continues to depict the deserted landscape he imagines climbing into the bucket for the well and pulling himself down, eventually disappearing from sight, from the world of light and sunshine into complete darkness in which even the stars cannot be seen. He then somewhat sarcastically calls this descent down into the well a 'reflection of Russian swings' («отражение русских качелей»). But now at least we know where this pastoral landscape is geographically placed and why its features are so explicitly anti-Arcadian.

It is most certainly not the picturesque landscape of Tityrus' leisurely existence in Vergil's First Eclogue. But it is that of the dispossessed Meliboeus, who leaves his native farm. Meliboeus, the exile, deprived of his livelihood and his songs, encounters the felicitous Tityrus, who in a politically charged monologue recounts his good fortune received from some young 'god' at Rome (*Ecl.* 1.6–8). The countryside, which Tityrus inhabits, is filled with leisure, abundance, and song. Tityrus, in fact, as Wendell Clausen points out, 'has a purely poetic existence'.[17] Meliboeus' exilic plight is only a temporary intrusion into the Arcadia of Tityrus, which by and large is a land free of strife. But it is exactly the strife that captures Brodsky's attention.

I am reluctant to draw any precise biographical parallels, agreeing with David Bethea that 'Brodsky himself would take bitter issue with any outside attempt to place a causal connection ("because," "as a result of") between the facts of his life and, as he puts it in an English phrase that owes its birth to the Russian («изгибы стиля»), his "twists of language".'[18] The biographical connection I am pursuing is not causal but rather complementary to the literary interpretation. The year 1963 was difficult for the poet. On 29 November in *Evening Leningrad* (*Вечерний Ленинград*) an article appeared entitled 'Periliterary Drone' («Окололитературный трутень») in which Brodsky's poetry was condemned. His arrest was only a matter of time, and Brodsky spent two of the following winter months in the countryside hiding in the dachas of his friends. The 'Field Eclogue' indeed does not describe any particular locale but is rather a string of memory shots of the Russian countryside as if the person is on the move, wandering from one place to the next. The narrative of the poem finally culminates in the contemplation of what constitutes a true exile:

> Настоящий изгнанник с собой
> все уносит. И даже сомненью
> обладанья другою судьбой
> не оставит, как повод к волненью....
>
> Нет, не тот изгнанник, кого
> в спину ветер, несущий проклятья,
> подгоняет, толкая его,
> разрывая любые объятья,
> в бедный мозг, где сознанье мертво,
> проникая сквозь ветхое платье.
>
> Нет, не тот, кто виденьями полн,
> начинает тонуть в половодьях,
> как Назон возле сумрачных волн,
> ненавидящий душу и плоть их,
> словно бурей застигнутый челн,
> проклиная их ропот. Напротив.
>
> Это тот неуемный пловец,
> рассекающий грудью озёра,
> шум листвы, словно гомон овец

различающий скрытых от взора,
над которым пернатый певец
распускает все краски убора.

Нет, не тот. И не тот, кто везде
даже собственной тени несносен,
кто себя не встречает в воде
меж верхушек листвяных и сосен.
И не тот, кто рукой в пустоте
шарит так, что под кожею просинь.

Натоящий изгнанник — никто
в море света, а также средь мрака.
Тот, чья плоть, словно то решето:
мягче ветра и тверже чем влага.
Кто бредет по дороге в пальто,
меньше леса, но больше оврага . . . .

В близоруком величье своем,
с коим взгляд твой к пространству прикован,
скрыто чувство, что странный объем,
как залог тебе долгий, дарован,
что от всякой прогулки вдвоем
и от смерти вдвоем — застрахован.[19]

The true exile takes with him
everything. Without even leaving
any pretext for a doubt that other fate
is possible since that can be
a source for anxiety. . . .

No, that man is not an exile, on whose
back the wind blows, carrying curses,
urging him on, pushing him,
breaking any embraces,
penetrating through his worn-out clothes
and into his poor mind, where all cognition is dead.

No, neither is that one, who, full of visions,
begins to drown in floods,
like Naso near the gloomy waters,
hating their soul and flesh,
like a boat caught up in a storm,
cursing their murmur. On the contrary.

It is that tireless swimmer,
Cutting the lakes with his chest,
detecting the rustling of the leaves
like the noise of the sheep, hidden from sight,
over whom the feathery singer
lets loose all the colours of his decoration.

No, that is not an exile either. Nor that one,
who is unbearable even to his own shadow,
who never sees his reflection in the water
amid the tops of leafy trees and pines.
Nor it is that man, who in emptiness
searches with his hand so much that his skin gets blue.

A true exile is nobody
in the sea of light, and amid darkness.
That one whose flesh is like a sieve:
softer than wind and harder than moisture.
Who is shuffling down the road in a coat,
smaller than the forest, but bigger than a ravine. . . .

In its short-sighted greatness,
with which your glance is nailed to the horizon,
a feeling is hidden, that a strange space,
is given to you as a long-lasting pledge,
that you are insured from any walk together,
and from death also if it is with someone else.

What emerges from all the *praeteritio* («нет не тот»—'not that one')
is what the true exile really is: the figure of 'nobody' («никто»), an
idea extremely familiar to the reader of Brodsky from his poems on
the themes of the *Odyssey*.[20] An exile is always a lonely man; the idea
of togetherness, a dialogue, which Brodsky considers so crucial for the
pastoral genre, is notably absent in the 'Field Eclogue': the exile does
not travel comforted by the presence of other human beings or by the
sound of their conversation. Brodsky's exile, unlike the Vergilian
Meliboeus, does not even encounter a temporary respite in the figure
of the more fortunate Tityrus. He encounters only indifferent even
hostile nature.

While it is not certain that Brodsky had Vergil's First Eclogue in
mind while writing this poem, he clearly conceived of it as an eclogue,
thus alluding to Vergil. It is also clear that Brodsky had more than one
Roman poet on his mind: the other poet is Ovid, whose exilic plight

many Russian poets found inspirational.[21] However, in this poem Brodsky asserts that Ovid is not a true exile because he cursed the place of his banishment (Tomi) and because he was too caught up in his misery. The true exile is a 'tireless swimmer', someone who embraces his state of misplacement and its creative potential. The exile is endowed with almost heroic features, with the air of tragic loneliness as a chosen lot. The 'Field Eclogue' then becomes a tautly narrated look at a very Russian theme of displacement and isolation told, however, without excessive sentiment. In Brodsky's poem the countryside, the idealized landscape of ancient poets, is also completely devoid of its soothing features of languishing midday amid the cornucopia of a bounteous landscape. The exile from the politically charged and uncomfortable city feels even less comfortable in the desolate and abandoned countryside. This poem also appears to be written by a young poet, perhaps at the beginning of his poetic career, since Brodsky feels compelled to insert himself in the tradition of poetic exile, both Vergil's and Ovid's. However, in retrospect this view of the countryside was to remain unchanged in Brodsky's poetry.

His 1992 'Elegy' ('Sweetheart, losing your looks, go to live in a village')[22] is a bitter, almost cantankerous poem, advising an aging woman to retire to the country where the process of getting old is not as painful as in the city, because ultimately it is the place where life comes to a complete halt. The view of the countryside in this much later poem is even more depressing than in the 'Field Eclogue'. In unambiguous terms the poet explains to his imaginary female addressee why the countryside would be an ideal place for her to retire:

Подруга, дурнея лицом, поселись в деревне.
Зеркальце там не слыхало ни о какой царевне.
Речка тоже рябит; а земля в морщинах
И думать забыла, поди, о своих мужчинах. . . .

Езжай в деревню, подруга. В поле, тем паче в роще
в землю смотреть и одеваться проще.
Там у тебя одной на сто верст помада,
но вынимать ее все равно не надо.

Знаешь, лучше стареть там, где верста маячит,
где красота ничего не значит
или значит не молодость, титьку, семя,
потому что природа вообще все время.[23]

Sweetheart, losing your looks, go to live in a village.
Mirrors there crave mildew, no maiden's visage.
A river, too, comes with ripples; and fields, in furrows,
Clearly forgot for good about stocky fellows.

Move to a village, sweetheart. A grove or a glebe are where
It's simpler to ponder humus, or what to wear.
There for a hundred miles yours is the only lipstick,
Though its slug will do better with no ballistics.

You know, it's better to age where a milepost is nodding,
Where beauty means absolutely nothing,
Or it means not youthfulness, bosom, semen—
Since time, on the whole, is indeed all seasons.

This poem in a sense is an anti-pastoral. It depicts a place where youth, sexuality, and fertility are banned and where even nature is deprived of the change of seasons and thus revival. In the ancient pastoral the countryside means the spontaneous fertility of the land, and the beauty of the landscape is tantamount. It is also a creative landscape, the place where poetic contests are held and the song is born. Brodsky's countryside is barren in every sense. When he advises the woman past her prime to retire there, he himself teases her in the seventh stanza with the possibility of a visit: «И я приеду к тебе» ('And I will come to join you there') and then in the next stanza: «Или пусть не приеду» ('And even if I won't come'). The countryside remains for Brodsky the place of solitude and of forced exile where one goes only to end life, but not to contemplate and definitely not to enjoy it. This poem is also a good example of Brodsky's acerbic humour, a feature familiar to the critics of Vergil's *Eclogues* who acknowledge Vergil's 'pastoral humor'.[24]

The 'Russian pastoral', as conceived by Brodsky in both the 'Field Eclogue' and 'Elegy', is a joyless landscape very much in tune with the tradition of previous Russian pastoral depictions. Thomas Newlin observes:

[T]he Russian pastoral dream tends to veer easily into the realm of squalid and the mundane, or even into the realm of nightmare. Sometimes the shift is sudden, dramatic, and lurchingly unpleasant; more often it creeps up on us, as changes in dreams are wont to do, in a more subtle and almost imperceptible fashion, and leaves us feeling merely vaguely queasy or dreary, but unsure quite why.[25]

Rachel Platonov similarly notes:

> Examinations of Russian versions of pastoral are replete with observations about the vulnerability of the Russian Arcadia. It is argued that in Ivan Turgenev's *Sportsman's Sketches*, for example, 'Pastoral itself becomes fragile and at risk, always in danger of being lost.' In a similar vein, the pastoralism of Nikolai Gogol's 'Old-World Landowners' is described as aggravated by a 'discordant undertone', while the 'arcadian features' of Ivan Goncharov's Oblomovka are said to be shaded with a 'deathly pallor'. All too often, it seems, rural retreats à la russe are fraught not just with death but also with degradation and strife, being contaminated by the common, the grotesque, and even the sordid. To make matters worse, the sickness of the Russian pastoral seems to stem not from external contagion, but rather from qualities inherent in these (so-called) idylls themselves.[26]

We can see how observations such as these could lead to characterizations of Russian Arcadias as anti-pastorals, as inversions or perversions of the pastoral dream.

Brodsky's poems discussed above seem to follow this long-standing perception of Russian pastoral space as inhospitable terrain. However, in his much later (1980) 'Fourth' or 'Winter Eclogue' Brodsky returns to the Vergilian pastoral again, and this time offers his own version of a pastoral *locus amoenus*.[27] The number of the eclogue does not signify its place in any previous sequence of Brodsky's eclogues but is in fact a clear allusion to Vergil's 'messianic' eclogue, as the epigraph to the poem makes clear (*Ecl.* 4.4–5):

> Ultima Cumaei venit iam carminis aetas:
> Magnus ab integro saeclorum nascitur ordo.
> The last age of Cumaean prophecy is coming,
> A great succession of centuries is born anew.

As we have seen, Brodsky had several Russian literary predecessors who were preoccupied with the messianic meaning of the Fourth Eclogue. The most influential was Viacheslav Ivanov, who interpreted the poem in the light of Christian spiritual epiphany.[28] Brodsky himself in his 1981 essay 'Virgil: Older than Christianity, a Poet for the New Age' emphasizes such an interpretation of the Fourth Eclogue in the opening paragraph, accusing Pontius Pilate of not paying much attention to poetry, because if he had: 'Pilate might have recognized in the man brought before him somebody whose arrival was prophesied . . . by Vergil in the Fourth Eclogue of his

Bucolics.' Brodsky even goes as far as to suggest that 'Jesus, had he known the poem, could have built a better case for himself.'[29]

The 'Winter Eclogue', however, is not a poem about prophecy, or awaiting a Golden Age, political or spiritual, although Lev Losev suggested in his recent commentary that Brodsky's choice of the season is inextricably connected with the 'messianic' interpretation of Vergil's poem: Christmas after all is a winter holiday.[30] It is an extremely complex and puzzling poem, but in the following analysis I would like to suggest that it stands at the core of Brodsky's reception and 'rewriting' of Vergil's *Eclogues*.

First of all, the whole idea of 'winter' in the pastoral space is an oxymoron. Winter comes neither to the Theocritean pastoral landscape nor to Vergil's Arcadia. Like old age, winter is not appropriate for the classical pastoral. The shepherds' singing contests resound in the hazy suspended time of the hot summer midday. Even if Vergil's landscape is not as idealized as Theocritus', summer remains the only possible season there. Brodsky's poem introduces the season of choice in the first line, in fact in the first word, зимой ('in winter'): 'In winter darkness falls right after dinner' («Зимой смеркается сразу после обеда»). What follows then is a series of episodic ruminations about winter. As we move from stanza to stanza we encounter words that aim to remind us that we are firmly ensconced in this most unpastoral of the seasons. The sequence of words as the poem moves forward, 'blizzard' («вьюга»), 'freeze' («оледенение»), 'frost' («мороз»), which in the second stanza is called 'angry' («злой»), 'snowman' («снежная баба»), 'freezing cold' («стужа»), reminds us that the word 'eclogue' contained in the title of the poem is a false hope for the languid soothing landscape familiar from Vergil.

Brodsky was undoubtedly aware of the fact that the countryside of Vergil's shepherds is full of gifts of ripe harvest and is not a frozen, unwelcoming winter terrain. So why the peculiar choice of season? Before I explore the text of the poem more carefully I would like to return one more time to the 1981 essay since it was written about the same time as the poem, and sheds light on Brodsky's overall reception of Vergil. While analysing the *Bucolics* and *Georgics* Brodsky writes:

> True, in both the *Bucolics* and the *Georgics* Virgil has done a lot to describe nature. However, in his case, nature was concrete arable land, not simply a background for heroic deeds. His treatment of the surrounding world differs radically not only from Homer but also from

that of Theocritus, the great Alexandrian poet who invented idyllic poetry as an antithesis to both the epic and dramatic manner characteristic of Greek poetry of the classical period. The gentle shepherds and their nymphs who wandered with the help of Theocritus into world literature acquire in Virgil the mortal features of real Italian peasants. They still converse at length of love and poetry, but they are keen on property issues, too.[31]

In this excerpt Brodsky's interest in Vergil reveals more defined features. The Russian poet is interested in the 'mortal features' of Vergil's pastoral, its reflection of reality, and the language of the Roman economy, which is so prominent in the *Eclogues*.[32] One may argue of course that Vergilian shepherds have very little to do with real Italian peasants and that Brodsky's eager appellation of Vergil as 'the first gentleman-farmer' is way off the mark.[33] Vergil's pastoral is still more of a 'spiritual landscape' than any real Italian *ager*.[34] But for Brodsky these are details that bother only classical scholars. His focus is the 'rewriting' of the generic profile. If the pastoral ideal is indeed 'an act of imagination'[35] that also attempts to acknowledge the poet's reality, then Brodsky's eclogues must stand in the same relationship to Vergil's pastoral as Vergil's *Eclogues* stood to Theocritus' *Idylls*. Furthermore, as Brodsky's discussion of Frost's 'Home Burial' indicates, the poet was also aware of the way that the modern pastoral, especially William Wordsworth's, 'revised' the classical and Renaissance pastoral. We can apply to Brodsky's pastoral a phrase that Wordsworth's friend John Stoddart used in relation to 'The Brothers'—that it is 'a local eclogue, of a new, and original species'.[36] That local flavour becomes especially apparent in the tenth stanza of Brodsky's 'Winter Eclogue':

Я не способен к жизни в других широтах.
Я нанизан на холод, как гусь на вертел.
Слава голой березе, колючей ели,
лампочке желтой в пустых воротах,
— слава всему, что приводит в движенье ветер!
В зрелом возрасте это — вариант колыбели.
Север — честная вещь. Ибо одно и то же
он твердит вам всю жизнь — шепотом, в полный голос
в затянувшейся жизни — разными голосами.
Пальцы мерзнут в унтах из оленьей кожи,
напоминая забравшемуся на полюс
о любви, о стоянии под часами.[37]

For me, other latitudes have no usage,
I am skewered by cold like a grilled-goose portion.
Glory to naked birches, to the fir-tree needle,
to the yellow bulb in an empty passage —
glory to everything set by the wind in motion:
at a ripe age, it can replace the cradle.
The North is the honest thing. For it keeps repeating
all your life the same stuff — whispering in full volume,
in the life dragged on, in all kinds of voices;
and toes freeze numb in your deerskin creepers,[38]
reminding you, as you complete your polar
conquest, of love, of shivering under clock faces.

This poem was written in 1980, when Brodsky turned forty. The persisting refrain of the whole poem is 'My life has dragged on' («Жизнь моя затянулась»). For a Russian poet in exile, reaching forty may have seemed like a long life, at least longer than many of Brodsky's famous predecessors and even contemporaries had. But ultimately this, like the 'Field Eclogue', is a poem about the effect of exile and nostalgia, as indicated by the dedication to Derek Walcott, to whose nostalgic 1984 collection *Midsummer* Brodsky might have felt close affinity (Brodsky's own bitter take on nostalgia can also be detected in a short unpublished poem, 'Visit Russia'; see Figure 9).[39]

For a person born and raised in St Petersburg, winter unsurprisingly becomes the season of choice. Therefore the landscape in the poem (one of the required features, according to Brodsky, for the pastoral genre) is generously supplied with uniquely Russian features: it is a description of a wintry terrain, which escalates into a panegyric to winter, that appeals to the senses of any person who has experienced Russian winter:

Зима! Я люблю твою горечь клюквы
к чаю, блюдца с дольками мандарина,
твой миндаль с арахисом, граммов двести.
Ты раскрываешь цыплячьи клювы
именами «Ольга» или «Марина»,
произносимыми с нежностью только в детстве

и в тепле. Я пою синеву сугроба
в сумерках, шорох фольги, частоту бемоля —
точно 'чижика' где подбирает рука Господня.
И дрова, грохотавшие в гулких дворах сырого

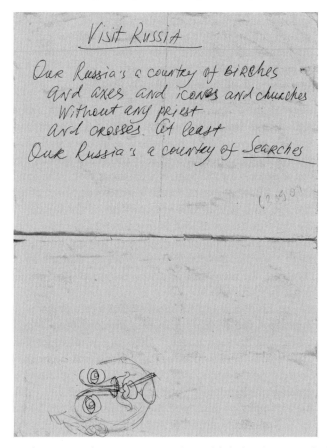

Figure 9. 'Visit Russia': a poem in Joseph Brodsky's handwriting which he left during his visit to Yerevan, Armenia, in April 1972, not long before his permanent exile to the West. Image from the author's family archive.

города, мерзнущего у моря,
меня согревают еще сегодня.

Winter! I cherish your bitter flavor
of cranberries, tangerine crescents on faience saucers,
the tea, sugar-frosted almonds (at best, two ounces).
You were opening our small beaks in favor
of names like Marina or Olga — morsels
of tenderness at that age that fancies
cousins.[40] I sing a snowpile's blue contours

> at dusk, rustling foil, clicking B-flat somewhere,
> as though 'Chopsticks' were tried by the Lord's own finger.
> And the logs, which rattled in stony courtyards
> of the gray, dank city that freezes bare
> by the sea, are still warming my every fiber.

The winter of these lines is soothing; it has flavours and smells familiar to anyone who has tasted the delicacies of a Russian New Year's holiday festive tables (cranberries, tangerines, and almonds). But the following lines spell out why only this landscape can suffice as a true pastoral locale for the poet. It is all about that 'gray, dank city', St Petersburg, whose perpetual freeze warms 'every fiber' of the poet exiled from it. And it is in this very context of the Russian winter landscape that the theme of love (singled out by Brodsky as a characteristic of the ancient pastoral) resurfaces: waiting for the beloved shivering in the cold, Russian female names as 'morsels of tenderness'. These are the memories of simple comforts. In fact these are memories of happiness.[41]

Brodsky, as his poems and essays show, was a careful reader of both the *Eclogues* and the *Georgics* and even grouped them together as poems addressing the same issues.[42] Therefore he might have noticed Vergil's description of two different types of pastoral landscape in the Third Georgic. At the end of this poem Vergil distinguishes between two shepherding experiences: one is 'the shepherd life in Africa', where the cattle always graze and the 'herdsman carries his chattels with him'; the opposite extreme of that landscape is in Scythia, 'where there is no grazing, and the cattle are always shut up'. Then the detailed description follows: 'Ice and snow are there all year long; day and night are similar; all liquids freeze; sudden snowstorms kill the cattle; deer are not hunted, but butchered in the ice; the natives live underground by fire, playing and drinking' (*Geo.* 3.339–83).

Brodsky, who explicitly identified his native country with ancient Scythia,[43] might have paid particularly close attention to this description and may be evoking it in his 'Winter Eclogue' as he contemplates the creation of his pastoral landscape. We now come to a full understanding of why 'the North is the honest thing' for a Russian poet, and why his attempts at describing the traditional pastoral landscape in the 'Field Eclogue' and the later 'Elegy' are unsuccessful. Northern man, whose poetry was nourished by and flourished on the banks of the river frozen half of the year in the wind-swept city, is at home in a more stringent climate. The hot, leisurely summers of the Mediterranean are attractive, but they are not *his* 'spiritual landscape'. To pretend otherwise would be paramount to pretending that Russian is not his mother tongue any longer.

I will return to the text of the 'Winter Eclogue' later in the following pages after I briefly turn to Brodsky's last attempt at a traditional pastoral landscape, in an eclogue which he wrote one year later, in 1981, entitled 'Eclogue 5th (Summer)'. The numbering of the eclogue is puzzling, since we are either to assume that it follows Brodsky's own fourth 'winter' eclogue or it is a subtle allusion to Vergil's fifth poem. Vergil's Fifth Eclogue contains perhaps the most pastoral theme, harking back to Theocritus' First Idyll: the death of Daphnis, the pastoral deity, a source of poetic inspiration whose untimely and mysterious death from love is lamented, in both the *Idylls* and the *Eclogues*, by the inhabitants of the idealized landscape. The song about the death of Daphnis, performed in a singing contest by the shepherd Mopsus, is followed by a song of another shepherd, Menalcas, who then sings about Daphnis' apotheosis. But the amoebaean exchange between two shepherds about the rural deity Daphnis is full of creative energy inspired by the summer landscape with the grazing flock and trees full of ripe fruit.

If Brodsky's 'Summer Eclogue' is indeed a subtle allusion to Vergil, then the Russian poet rewrites Arcadia again. The poem starts with a clear allusion to the slow motion of summer, its inertia:

> Вновь я слышу тебя, комариная песня лета!
> Потные муравьи спят в тени курослепа.

> I hear you again, mosquito hymn of summer!
> In the dogwood tepee, ants sweat in slumber.[44]

The lazy afternoon familiar from the ancient descriptions of slumbering nature on the hot summer midday then slips into a description of a short Russian summer:

> Душный июль! Избыток
> зелени и синевы избитых
> форм бытия.[45]

> Sultry July! The surplus
> of the green and the blue—of that threadbare surface
> of existence.

The Russian version of the poem is significantly more expressive. The colours of summer, green and blue, are literally to be translated as 'trite forms of existence' («избитых форм бытия»). Summer with its bright colours is a worn-out season, a sort of cliché. The summer landscape represents suspended life, almost unwelcome languor summed up in a phrase: 'Life is the sum of trifling motions' («Жизнь—сумма мелких движений»). This sentiment is even more eloquently expressed in an earlier poem from 1976:[46]

> Я не то что схожу с ума, но устал за лето.[47]
> За рубашкой в комод полезешь, и день потерян.
> Поскорей бы, что ли, пришла зима и занесла все это —
> города, человеков, но для начала зелень.

> It is not that I am going crazy but I am tired of summer.
> I reach for a shirt in the dresser, and the day is lost.
> I wish winter can come and blow it all over —
> cities, men, but definitely all the green to start with.

In this poem, as in the 'Summer Eclogue', summer reappears not as a season for contented contemplation but as a tedious state for both mind and body while they remain in the eager anticipation of winter. The same feeling fills Brodsky's last poem, 'August' (1996), where the summer in little (albeit American) towns invites ennui and resentment rather than a contented state of mind. Although many thorough critical readings of this poem already exist,[48] I would like to read it in the context of Brodsky's pastoral poems. Andrew Reynolds emphasizes Peter Vail's main preoccupation in this poem: 'Why, when snowed up in New York in January 1996, does Brodsky write of the heat of small towns in August?'[49] As Reynolds analyses Brodsky's last poem in the context of Brodsky's allusion to Pushkin, he states that 'to write about "January" would have seemed immodest', since in Russian poetry that month is directly associated with the death of *the* poet, i.e. Pushkin.[50] While this allusion is without doubt important, as well as the landscape describing some small provincial and most likely American towns, the season and month of choice are equally significant. If read in the context of Brodsky's eclogues, this poem shows that for him escape into the countryside, away from a big city, and during the month of August is the poetic equivalent of death. Reynolds interprets the presence of a bee in the first stanza of 'August' as an allusion to an idealized pastoral landscape and the poetic labour inspired by it. Then he concludes that 'death is always present in Arcadia too'.[51] The only problem with this argument is that while it is the Arcadia familiar to a Western reader since Theocritus, this is not Brodsky's Arcadia. He clearly spells out his own version of Arcadia in the 'Winter Eclogue'. The idealized landscape of the ancient pastoral is no longer placed in midsummer, when languor and mystical silence inspire poetic contests. In Brodsky's rendition it is the Russian wintery *city* of his youth which becomes the new metapoetic 'spiritual' pastoral landscape. The countryside in midsummer as the wondrous *locus amoenus* is far from Brodsky's pastoral terrain. His eerie description of the countryside in the 'Field Eclogue' coupled with the languid and uninspiring summer landscape in the 'Summer Eclogue' indicates his reluctance or perhaps even inability to pursue the traditional setting for the genre, the profile of which he himself so eloquently defined.

The 'Winter Eclogue', however, is an entirely different type of eclogue: despite its melancholy, it is uncharacteristically uplifting. The Russian seeker of pastoral peace realizes his potential as he finds a landscape appropriate for the language in which he sings. The north of the 'Winter Eclogue' is 'the honest thing' because it is true to the language in which the eclogue is written; Cyrillic naturally requires a winter landscape. There is no seduction by warmth, blooming trees, or shining sun. For any Russian the beauty of winter is in the constancy of cold, in its reliability. The poet also places love (an important feature of pastoral) in this very landscape as he thinks about his frozen toes when waiting for a date back at home, on the cold streets of his northern city. He finds strange satisfaction in that nostalgic memory because like the Russian winter it is real. As the description of the wintry landscape continues in the 'Winter Eclogue', Brodsky's challenge to Vergil becomes clearer in the last stanza of the poem:

> Так родится эклога. Взамен светила
> загорается лампа: кириллица, грешным делом,
> разбредясь по прописи вкривь ли, вкось ли,
> знает больше, чем та сивилла,
> о грядущем. О том, как чернеть на белом,
> покуда белое есть и после.

> That's the birth of an eclogue. Instead of the shepherd's signal
> a lamp's flaring up. Cyrillic, while running witless

on the pad as though to escape the captor,
knows more of the future than the famous sibyl:
of how to darken against the whiteness,
as long as the whiteness lasts. And after.

Vergil's Fourth Eclogue, to which the title and the epigraph of Brodsky's poem allude, was received by many generations of poets as a prediction of some universal importance, either political or spiritual. But in Brodsky there is no such universal meaning and he warns us about it by preceding this stanza with the sentence 'And the Muse's voice gains a reticent private timbre' («И голос Музы / звучит как сдержанный, частный голос»). This line is echoed in Brodsky's essay on Vergil in which he states: 'A poet, and indeed his content, are defined by the timbre of his voice, by his diction, by the way he chooses and uses his words.'[52] Brodsky's 'fourth' eclogue, most significant in terms of its title's allusiveness, does not convey any communal significance or spiritual epiphany. Instead it becomes a song inspired by a landscape and a season, which the poet cherishes in his memory. This is Vergil, using Richard Thomas's words, 'in a cold climate'.[53] It could not have been otherwise for a pastoral song composed in Russian. The breathtaking predictions of the divinely inspired Cumaean Sibyl (evoked in the epigraph to the poem) lose their importance when compared with a sheet of paper filled with new poetry in a new alphabet. The written word remains after everything else is gone. This idea seems to be one of Brodsky's favourites, and he reiterates it in several of his other poems. In his 'Roman Elegies',[54] a series of snapshots of Rome in August (!), he evokes Horace and his *Exegi monumentum* in order to juxtapose it with it his own:

и в горячей
полости горла холодным перлом
перекатывается Гораций.
Я не воздвиг уходящей к тучам
каменной вещи для их острастки.
О своем — и о любом — грядущем
я узнал у буквы, у черной краски.[55]

and a sultry porous
cavity of a mouth scatters around
cold pearls of Horace.

> I've never built that cloud-thrusting stony
> object that could explain clouds' pallor.
> I have learned about my own, and any
> fate, from a letter, from its black color.[56]

The juxtaposition of 'sultry' and 'cold' is prominent in this stanza. The poetic 'pearls' of Horace are cold, and they soothingly roll around in the 'sultry', still awkward mouth of the modern Russian poet, who learns to put them into the music of poetry in his own letters and in following his own calling.

By subtly alluding to their ancient counterpart, Brodsky's eclogues assertively claim their place within the genre of pastoral. For what is each new example of a known genre if not its reconfiguration? For this Russian poet the landscape becomes the focal point of generic innovation.[57] The only time when Brodsky's pastoral acquires that familiar feeling of *locus amoenus* is in the dead of Russian winter. It is amid the snow and blizzard that the Russian Tityrus begins to sing his song of love.[58]

Brodsky, unlike most of his predecessors, reads Vergil not as a harbinger of imperial grandeur or an oracle of sorts, but rather intimately. Such a reading of the *Eclogues* is hardly surprising, but Brodsky also transforms and alters Vergil's epic as well, and his reception of Vergilian heroics galvanizes yet again the preoccupations of his own poetics.

'DIDO AND AENEAS'

As early as 1969, when Brodsky was only twenty-nine, four years after his exile in the north of Russia and three years before his final departure to the West, he turned his attention to Vergil's *Aeneid*. In 'Dido and Aeneas' («Дидона и Эней»—'Didona i Enei') he offers an unusual take on Book 4 of the Roman epic:

> Великий человек смотрел в окно,
> а для нее весь мир кончался краем
> его широкой, греческой туники,
> обильем складок походившей на
> остановившееся море.
>
> Он же

смотрел в окно, и взор его сейчас
был так далек от этих мест, что губы
застыли, точно раковина, где
таился гул, и горизонт в бокале
был неподвижен.

          А ее любовь
была лишь рыбой — может и способной
пуститься в море вслед за кораблем
и, рассекая волны гибким телом,
возможно обогнать его . . . но он —
он мысленно уже ступил на сушу.
И море обернулось морем слез.
Но, как известно, именно в минуту
отчаянья и начинает дуть
попутный ветер. И великий муж
покинул Карфаген.

          Она стояла
Перед костром, который разожгли
под городской стеной ее солдаты,
и видела, как в мареве его,
дрожавшем между пламенем и дымом,
беззвучно рассыпался Карфаген
задолго до пророчества Катона.[59]

The great man stared through the window
but her entire world ended with the border
of his broad Greek tunic, whose abundant folds
resembled the sea on hold.

But he stared out through the window, and his gaze
was so far away from here, that his lips were immobile
like a seashell where the roar is hidden, and the horizon
in his goblet was still.

But her love
was just a fish—which might perhaps
plunge into the sea in the pursuit of the ship,
and knifing the waves with the supple body,
perhaps yet pass it—but he,
he in his thoughts already strode upon the land.
And the sea became a sea of tears.
But, as one knows, precisely at the moment
of despair, the auspicious wind begins to blow.

And the great man left Carthage.
She stood before the bonfire, which her soldiers
had kindled by the city walls,
and she envisioned looking at the mist,
trembling between the flame and smoke,
how Carthage silently crumbled
ages before Cato's prophecy.

In order to understand this poem we must put it first in the context of Joseph Brodsky's 'mythological' poems, specifically his allusions to the heroic myth. His ancient heroes, Odysseus, Hector, Ajax, Theseus, appear in his early poetry with remarkable frequency and are a large and enduring part of his 'masculine' poetics.[60] These heroic figures from Greco-Roman mythology almost always are seen as examples of the brutalizing price of any significant achievement, of the realization that with any heroic journey victory comes inseparable from defeat. Hector and Ajax are the tragic victims of the same irrational destiny of war in which there are no victors and no vanquished. Odysseus is a cynical man who lost his son and his wife and is disoriented in time and space, burdened by a fading desire for homecoming coupled with the loss of memory. In the poem 'On the Way to Scyros', Theseus, having emerged from Minos' cave with the hide of the beast, is betrayed by Ariadne, who loves not him but Bacchus. His reward is exile to Scyros, and he looks forward to facing his darkest hour at the hands of King Lycomedes. These heroes, whose main ancient narratives are represented by epos or tragedy (Catullus 64 is an epyllion relating Ariadne's abandonment by Theseus), are reconfigured by Brodsky through the prism of his lyric ego, which rejects epic glorification of male heroism as much as it abhors overly dramatized accounts of heroic predicament.

Brodsky's Aeneas therefore must be read in this very context of 'mythological inversions', the impossibility of rewarded heroic endeavour and the inevitability of significant emotional sacrifice inherent in man's quest for the meaning of life as he attempts to make deliberate, conscious, and often irrevocable choices. At the centre of Brodsky's mythological poetics is a figure of a lonely man, usually at the end or at the beginning of his heroic feat, tormented by doubt and resigned to his destiny. Brodsky's 'Dido and Aeneas', however, is a poem that requires careful unwrapping, a palimpsestic reading as Brodsky subtly moves between ancient and modern influences, between biographical allusions and fictional lyric personae. This poem is one of the most eloquent illustrations of Brodsky's 'making contemporary of myth', in the words of Michael Kreps.[61]

While Brodsky's overall Greco-Roman 'mythology' significantly contributes to the understanding of the poem, we must consider carefully all of his influences. Although there is little doubt that Brodsky had read Vergil's *Aeneid* (most likely in Russian translation), my argument in no way entails any definitive knowledge that Brodsky had any specific lines of Vergil in mind while writing his poem. However, upon closer reading of the poem I have come to the conclusion that Brodsky's poem contained such parallels to Vergil's text that they may constitute intertextuality in a broader sense, which we already encountered in Pushkin's *The Bronze Horseman* and termed as 'literary filiation'.

I would like to structure my argument in the following way: first, I will explore how Vergil depicts Dido's emotional state and Aeneas' response to it as she sinks deeper and deeper into the 'madness' of love; second, I will unravel how two other sources contributed to the 'gendered' reception of Dido and Aeneas by Brodsky; lastly, I will analyse Brodsky's poem in the light of all of his sources.

David Ross observes that Vergil's Dido is a composite of several Greek mythological heroines, Nausicaa of *Odyssey* 6, Apollonius' Medea, and Catullus' Ariadne, betrayed and abandoned by the hero.[62] The last two allusions evoke the inevitability of heroic betrayal and the 'fatal attraction of heroism'.[63] However, despite her vulnerability as a woman and notwithstanding her shortcomings as a queen, Vergil's Dido is never a shadow of Aeneas' greatness;[64] on the contrary, she is his rescuer, his only chance to recover from the devastating effects of the fall of Troy and to continue his search for a new one. Book 4 makes that distribution of power apparent from its first words, '*at regina*' ('but the queen'), thus introducing the dominant figure of the book. The contrasting particle *at*, as Austin suggests, 'points the antithesis' between Aeneas' past sufferings and Dido's that are about to be set into motion, 'between his composed silence and her agitation'.[65]

Initially, Aeneas is only a suppliant at Dido's mercy, nothing but a *hospes* (guest) later elevated to the status of a consort. She is the queen, one who has the power of choice, which she lives to regret: to succumb to Aeneas' charm and heroic past. She is also at the core of the love affair, whether she is confiding her feelings to Anna, confronting Aeneas, or ascending the funeral pyre she builds to make her final regal statement. In the fourth book of the *Aeneid*, for the first time Aeneas' claim to heroic greatness is called into question when juxtaposed with the character of Dido. Her only weakness is her destructive passion for Aeneas, which drives her to neglect her primary responsibility as a Carthaginian queen: the building of her city, her greatest aspiration and accomplishment ('*non coeptae adsurgunt turres*'—'the towers having been started no longer rise', *Aen.* 4.86). Even at the time of her suicide, she remains a powerful figure whom Vergil compares in her impassioned madness to the famous male tragic protagonists Pentheus and Orestes. Her role in the love affair is anything but that of a passive victim of unruly passion. Her love eventually becomes coupled with an even stronger emotion, anger, or, as R. G. Austin terms it in his commentary, 'a hissing rage',[66] that eventually escalates into the virtuous, even heroic, Ajax-like madness: 'Her pangs of love increase, and love rising up again rages and swirls in a great tide of anger' ('*ingeminant curae, rursus resurgens saevit amor magnoque irarum fluctuat aestu*', 4.530–1). However, as Christopher Gill aptly observes, Dido's madness 'is not the raving insanity of Pentheus and Orestes, because even in her final moments she reviews her life with 'rational lucidity' and '"cosmic" detachment', and sees 'that her state represents a negation of virtuous rationality that is fundamental to her nature as human being'.[67]

Dido's suicide is also not depicted as an irrational result of mad passion, but as the harbinger of Carthage's future threats to Rome. Although embittered and suicidal, Dido is nonetheless given the power of voicing her anguish and her desire for an avenger, indeed a historical one, Hannibal, of her trampled pride and destroyed regal ambitions ('*exoriare aliquis nostris ex ossibus ultor*'—'rise some avenger from our bones', 4.625). Thus her anger resulting from her betrayed love must continue even after her death and must have real and devastating ramifications. In her angry reaction to Aeneas' betrayal, Vergil's Dido reflects Aristotle's understanding of anger as a stimulant for 'the virtue of courage', because '"turning the other cheek" is to be despised as simple-minded, servile, and vulnerable to exploitation'.[68] The Vergilian Dido hardly fits into any of those categories, even at the point of her final beseeching of Aeneas to at least leave a child behind for her to love, which Austin interprets as her most overpowering emotion, which turns her fiercely begun accusation of Aeneas into a 'soliloquy, barely whispered'.[69]

It is also worth exploring what concerns Vergil and what he deems unimportant or suppressed in this very dramatic book of his epic: Dido's erotic 'madness' and suicide move the reader beyond words and elicit unconditional sympathy, but Aeneas' human emotions are entirely, or almost entirely, glossed over. That is, as Ross argues, 'Virgil's whole point—that the anguish felt by Dido's lover has to be suppressed and cannot be uttered to her or even admitted to himself.'[70] But in the final analysis this love story is about two people separated by divine destiny and led into madness, suicide, and most importantly, as we will see, for Brodsky's poetics, heroic isolation.

Brooks Otis observes that 'there could have been no Rome, as Vergil conceived it, without men like Aeneas, men of supreme *pietas*'.[71] E. L. Harrison echoes this opinion: 'Vergil makes it clear that when Aeneas deserts her he is thereby displaying his characteristic *pietas* at the highest level.'[72] Kenneth McLeish also emphasizes Vergil's focus on Aeneas' *pietas*, but pithily points out that to us, whose view of Dido is filtered through Purcell, Dryden, and Berlioz, she remains 'a three-dimensional character, a real person whose emotions and actions have a roundness, a wholeness, that often seems to be missing in Aeneas himself'.[73] There are several instances during the course of the *Aeneid* where Aeneas' human side becomes manifested, but every time it is dominated by his sense of duty that surpasses his vulnerability to love or pain. In Book 2, during the storm, Aeneas displays deep emotional upheaval and fear for his life and the lives of his companions. In Book 6 also he appears shaken and grief-stricken by Dido's refusal to talk to him. In Book 12 he once again shows his emotions when he sees the belt of Pallas on Turnus, but in that final episode of the poem, driven by a sense of revenge and duty, he proceeds to kill his vanquished enemy. In all of these instances, however, his torment is unspoken, suppressed to a degree that renders Aeneas almost ambivalent and earns him a title of a 'reluctant hero'. It also calls into question the strength of his character, which was attributed by Vergil, at least in Book 4, not to Aeneas, but to Dido, who 'by general consent . . . is the only truly great character to have emerged from Latin literature'.[74] Even Dido's Greek predecessors, similarly abandoned by their heroes, fade in comparison because 'the strength of Dido's personality towers above all the rhetoric' that was characteristic of Euripides' Medea, who commits unspeakable acts of filicide, or Catullus' Ariadne, 'a silly little thing for all her betrayal'.[75] In her darkest hour Vergil's Dido calls for and looks forward to an everlasting rivalry and hostility between Carthage and the future city of Rome as she struggles to regain her dignity as a Carthaginian queen. Dido and subsequently Carthage are defeated by destiny, and the failed love between Aeneas and Dido is only a casualty in the process. When measured against the intensity of Dido's character, the Aeneas of Book 4 emerges as less of a hero, despite his unwavering sense of duty.[76] Because of Vergil's own sensitivity towards his heroine, it is Dido with whom the reader identifies and who shows moral superiority and conscious (not divinely ordained) understanding of her legacy.[77]

Vergil is by no means the only source for Brodsky's take on Dido and Aeneas. In fact, in an interview with Ann-Marie Brumm, Brodsky clearly articulates what was on his mind when he was writing the poem:

> BRUMM: Who then are your Dido and Aeneas?
> BRODSKY: They are mythical personages.... I remember very well what influenced me. There were two things. The first was Anna Akhmatova's cycle about Dido and Aeneas. That was a sequence of love poems about her separation from her beloved. She embodied herself in Dido and the man was some kind of Aeneas.... The second thing which more or less moved me to write about that was Henry Purcell's opera, *Dido and Aeneas*. There was a certain aria which Dido sings that was so penetrating, so moving, so despairing. I remember this when Elizabeth Schwarzkopf sings, 'Remember Me.' It sounds absolutely incredible.
>
> There were a couple of reasons why I wrote this poem. Moreover, this is not a love poem. 'Aeneas and Dido' is a poem about destruction—the destruction of Carthage which happened before it happened in flesh. It's rather a historical poem in some sense. Aeneas left Dido. She didn't want him to leave her but he did. And, according to the myth, he created Rome, whose army in some centuries afterward came to destroy Carthage. So you see what love is and what betrayal in love is. The consequences are usually invisible, but I was trying to make them more or less visible.[78]

First of all Brodsky does not even mention Vergil as one of his sources, to avoid perhaps stating the obvious. He calls both Dido and Aeneas 'mythological personages', but the Russian poet was most likely unfamiliar with any other ancient sources that narrate the story of Dido's suicide. In Brodsky, Aeneas is clearly the culprit responsible for the undoing of 'a woman destroyed by her uncontrolled passion for a passing stranger'.[79] But most interesting are the contradictions in this statement. At first Brodsky states that this is a poem not about love but rather destruction. By the end of the statement, however, the two become inextricably linked, and the poem becomes then a manifestation of the destruction of love and by love. History becomes the consequence of love, and the historical poem becomes love lyric. In that light Brodsky's self-proclaimed influences on this poem merit further analysis. Anna Akhmatova's lyric cycle that Brodsky refers to here is the 1962 collection of poems 'A Wild Rose is Growing' («Шиповник растет»). The themes explored in this cycle are traditional for Akhmatova's poetics: the appearance of a mysterious guest from a faraway land, love, betrayal, abandonment, separation. The whole cycle was most likely inspired by Akhmatova's relationship with Isaiah Berlin, her meetings with him in 1945–6 and the later 'non-meeting' ten years later, in 1956, in Moscow, when he came to visit from Berlin. The fourteenth poem of that cycle was published in 1962 under the title 'Dido Speaks' («Говорит Дидона»), and it explicitly uses the self-identification of Akhmatova with the Carthaginian queen. The poem has two epigraphs: one is taken from the *Aeneid*, «Против воли я твой, царица, берег покинул» ('*Invitus, regina, tuo de litore cessi*'—'I left your shore, Queen, against my will', 6.460), and another is by Akhmatova herself, «Ромео не было, Эней, конечно был» ('Romeo never was, Aeneas was for sure'), which reflects the emotional and gender-specific point of the poem and the lyric cycle overall: men do not die for love, rather they leave women who love them. An earlier draft of the poem had another epigraph from the *Aeneid*, 'Anna, soror!' (4.9), which had a double meaning—as Dido's appeal to her sister, and as Akhmatova's own appeal to herself in the past while she reminisces about her separation from Berlin:

> Не пугайся, — я еще похожей
> Нас теперь изобразить могу.
> Призрак ты — иль человек прохожий,
> Тень твою зачем-то берегу.
>
> Был недолго ты моим Энеем, —
> Я тогда отделалась костром,
> Друг о друге мы молчать умеем.
> И забыл ты мой проклятый дом.
>
> Ты забыл те, в ужасе и муке,
> Сквозь огонь протянутые руки
> И надежды окаянной весть.

Ты не знаешь, что тебе простили . . .
Создан Рим, плывут стада флотилий,
И победу славословит лесть.[80]

Do not be scared, — I can with even more likeness
Depict us right now,
Although you either are a ghost or a passerby,
I, for some reason, keep your shadow.

You were not my Aeneas for long, —
Back then I got away with bonfire only.
We can keep silent about each other.
And you have forgotten my cursed house.

You have forgotten those hands,
Stretched across the fire in horror and agony,
And the news of the damned hope you have forgotten too.

You do not know, how much forgiveness has been granted
   to you . . .
Rome is built, the herds of fleets are passing,
And the flattery glorifies victory.

It is rather strange that Brodsky lists this poem as a source of inspiration for his poem, because it appears that he writes from the exact opposite gender perspective. Akhmatova's poem is an articulation of Dido's anguish over her abandonment, and Aeneas is only behind the scenes.[81] In Akhmatova the bonfire is not Dido's final moment, it is in fact a mild punishment for the forbidden passion ('I got away with bonfire only').[82] She clings to Aeneas' ghost and her memory of him, while he is presumed to have forgotten everything, even her agony on the pyre. But furthermore, the poem ends on the note of forgiveness still mixed with lingering attachment, certainly unimaginable for the Vergilian Dido, who categorically declares the end of love for centuries to come ('*nullus amor populis nec foedera sunto*'—'let there be neither any love nor truce between our people', *Aen.* 4.624). Akhmatova's Dido sees her house 'cursed' and her hope 'damned', but she does not curse or damn the beloved who betrayed her. And the last stanza explains why: Rome is built, the great fleet is sailing by, and the air resounds with the glory of a man's achievement. The high price for it was paid by a woman who is destined to fade into obscurity and insignificance. I will try to demonstrate that in these lines precisely lies Brodsky's inspiration for his own creative and gendered 'misreading' of the Vergilian Dido.

Before we move, however, to Brodsky's poem, I would like to take a closer look at his other self-proclaimed source: Dido's aria from Purcell's opera, with libretto by Nahum Tate. In his late 1995 essay 'In Memory of Stephen Spender', Brodsky mentions some precious items of his former Russian household, among others a recording of Purcell's *Dido and Aeneas*, sent to him by Spender himself, smuggled to the Soviet Union by Anna Akhmatova after she received an honorary doctorate from Oxford in 1965.[83] Two influences on his poem thus come together. The aria Brodsky refers to is 'When I Am Laid in Earth', also known as 'Dido's Lament', in Act 3 of the opera. The last lines of the aria, when Dido addresses her confidante Belinda, are similar to Akhmatova's tone of forgiving and forgetting:

> When I am laid in earth,
> May my wrongs create
> No trouble in thy breast;
> Remember me, but ah! forget my fate.[84]

In Purcell's opera as well as in Akhmatova's poem, Dido is resigned to her fate and departs from the stage with no words of reproach. In the opera Dido is also surprisingly passive, and in fact Aeneas is her pursuer and is given a strength of passion rather unimaginable for the Vergilian Aeneas:

> Aeneas has no fate but you!
> Let Dido smile and I'll defy
> The feeble stroke of Destiny. (Act 1)

His abandonment of Dido is full of torment and agony, two passions that the reader of Book 4 of the *Aeneid* expects in vain to be elicited from Aeneas by Dido's pleading and beseeching:

> But ah! what language can I try
> My injur'd Queen to Pacify:
> No sooner she resigns her heart,
> But from her arms I'm forc'd to part.
> How can so hard a fate be took?
> One night enjoy'd, the next forsook.
> Yours be the blame, ye gods! For I
> Obey your will, but with more ease could die. (Act 2)

It is clear from both Akhmatova's and Purcell's Didos that they set a stage for Brodsky's queen as a woman seduced and abandoned, but not powerful and most certainly not vengeful. Akhmatova's Dido has decisively and meekly forgiven all the wrongs done to her, and the response of Purcell's Dido to the news of abandonment evokes the Vergilian Dido's reproaches (*Aen.* 4.365–7) in an almost comical but not threatening way:

> Thus on the fatal Banks of Nile,
> Weeps the deceitful crocodile
> Thus hypocrites, that murder act,
> Make Heaven and Gods the authors of the Fact. (Act 3)

Brodsky's Dido, like Akhmatova's lyric heroine, is completely marginalized, and the focus is primarily on the man and his mission. Like Purcell's Dido, she expresses no anger and little bitterness as she becomes only a bleak shadow on his destiny, almost an annoying obstacle to his divinely inspired designs. While Dido is referred to only as 'she', Aeneas is twice described as a 'great man', and in a peculiar ironic twist his greatness is especially emphasized when he decisively leaves Carthage and Dido behind. Here Brodsky's classical metaphor evokes in a much more defined way Akhmatova's and Purcell's two radically different views of love: 'his' and 'hers'. These views alternate as the poet goes back and forth between the two contrasting perspectives («она же»—'but she', «а ее любовь»—'but her love', «но он»—'but he') described in terms of 'movement' and 'immobility'. The caesura in the poetic line that appears before the change in gender perspective serves as a symbolic line, which reflects two different psychological worlds, and two completely different approaches to emotion.[85] Furthermore, while his gaze wanders far into the horizon that beckons and awaits him, she cannot see beyond the folds of his tunic, where 'her world ends', as we see later in the poem, not only figuratively but literally. *Her* perspective is limited by the sight of *him*, and she cannot see anything beyond that. For her the whole world is the room in which the separation occurs; for him it is the sight of the sea where his future awaits and to which his longing gaze inevitably turns as he is about to leave her in the confining space of that room full of tension. The recurrent imagery of the sea, which in Brodsky often appears as a metaphor for freedom,[86] only intensifies the fact that Aeneas' immobility is merely temporary: his tunic is like a sea that has stopped its motion (his freedom thus is curtailed by his pause with Dido), his lips resemble a seashell, the horizon reflected in his goblet is a sea horizon, and he himself is a ship which Dido (the fish) is ready to follow. In contrast to this picture of his immobility stands the description of Dido's emotional state. That state completely locked inside is full of motion, speed, and impulsiveness. But as his plans are about to be set in motion, even her inside mobility would freeze. The phrase 'whole world ends with the border of his . . . tunic' acquires then both temporal and spatial meaning. The folds of his tunic on which her adoring eyes linger reflect his temporary halt in time and space contrary to his predestined duty, and predict Dido's limitations and future inability to follow Aeneas on his journey. At the moment of *her* ultimate despair, *his* 'auspicious wind begins to blow'.

The Vergilian Dido, *dux femina facti*, who angrily confronts Aeneas after his attempt to leave her secretly, is replaced by Brodsky's Dido, who only looks on as speechlessly as a fish.[87] Brodsky juxtaposes 'he already strode upon the land' with the comparison of Dido to a fish. Fish do not live on land; Aeneas belongs to a realm where Dido has no natural place. Furthermore the comparison to the fish has a deeper connotation in Russian, recalling the proverb «нем(а) как рыба» ('mute as a fish'). Not only is Dido banned from any land where he will settle, she is also deprived of the power to express her anguish, her anger, and her determination to retaliate even beyond her grave, the power so articulately and pointedly granted to her by Vergil in Book 6. By contrast, Brodsky's Dido is more evocative of the Dido Aeneas encounters in the underworld in Book 6, sullen and speechless. However, even in that last encounter of the two lovers in the *Aeneid* her superior strength of character is emphasized by Vergil, who describes her standing there 'like a stern rock crag or cliff of Marpesus' ('*quam si dura silex aut stet Marpesia cautes*', 471). This simile echoes Aeneas' earlier comparison (4.441–6), as he is besieged by Dido's pleas, to an oak tree that cannot be moved even by the gusty winds because it reaches high into the sky with its summit and deep into the earth with its roots. Dido's comparison to a cliff underlines her immobility, which is also picked up by Brodsky, but the Vergilian immobility displays her emotional steadfastness, her insistence on never forgiving Aeneas, even after his impassioned plea of regret. At the end of the episode, however, it is she who takes flight ('*tandem corripuit sese atque inimica refugit*', 472) away from *him*, thus answering his '*quem fugis?*' (466), which in turn echoes her earlier '*mene fugis?*' (314).

Brodsky's poem is explicitly and solely concerned with Aeneas' destiny and duty. The Vergilian hero's constant characteristic of *pius*, dedication to destiny and the divine will, enables him to endure the loss both of his homeland and of every meaningful human connection and to 'command our great respect'.[88] Although the sea of his journey turns out to be made of Dido's tears (in Russian the idiomatic phrase *more slez* is cleansed here by the poet of its clichéd meaning), Brodsky never questions the inevitability or moral virtue of Aeneas' choice. As outlined already in Akhmatova's poem, the theme of Aeneas betraying his saviour, Dido, is closely connected with his mission as founder of Rome. It was because of that mission that Brodsky's Dido foresees Carthage crumbling in the fire that is her own funeral pyre. If Dido has no place in the future of Rome, Aeneas must let her go, leave her defeated, predicting thus the defeat of her city by the race he is about to engender. The Vergilian bonfire upon which Dido throws herself in her final hour of despair becomes a conflagration that would eventually consume Carthage, her proud legacy. Unlike the Vergilian heroine, Brodsky's Dido in the departure of Aeneas does not predict Hannibal's attack on Italy during the Punic Wars; she foresees even further the undoing of her own Carthage, reduced to ashes at the end of those wars. Her vision foreshadowing Cato's *Carthago delenda est* is consistent with the Dido of the whole poem. Without Aeneas there is no Dido, and without Dido there is no Carthage.

The dramatic destruction of the woman anticipates the historical catastrophe of the city. In Purcell's opera the Chorus in the third act also connects the two events:

> Destruction's our delight
> Delight our greatest sorrow!
> Elissa dies tonight and Carthage flames tomorrow.

The theme of revenge is also completely excised by Brodsky: Dido's longing for Aeneas does not devolve into hatred or 'hissing rage'. In this brief poem Dido becomes the passive victim not even of divine ordinances but of the 'great man's' decisions. The tragic monumentality of her final suicidal act, the result of her excessive emotion, all but disappears in Brodsky's lyric rendition. The Vergilian grandiosity of epic design has no place in Brodsky's lyric, which, for its entire claim to be a poem about the historical destruction of the city, remains the contemplation of an irrevocable separation between a man and a woman. Brodsky in his 1981 essay on Vergil, mentioned at the beginning of this chapter, notes that 'Vergil was a realist; an epic realist to be precise, because speaking numerically, reality in itself is epic.'[89] It is clear from this comment that Brodsky did see the separation between Dido and Aeneas as a part of Vergil's grand design for creating an epic of national rebirth. He merely recasts the idea of epic in a different, more grounded and less politically charged light. For Brodsky the 'reality' of life replete with loss of attachments is an epic when viewed diachronically: two lovers on the verge of separation become but a small episode in an epic chain of life that in the final analysis must amount to some meaning. In this approach to Dido and Aeneas we can also hear Akhmatova's gendered interpretation of the unfortunate affair, both Dido's and her own: men always leave, forsaking love for the pursuit of a higher cause; women are always left behind bewailing their fate. This state of affairs becomes also a part of Brodsky's 'gendered' reality.

In conclusion I must say a few words about the diction of 'Dido and Aeneas', which is unusual for Brodsky's early poetics. Brodsky himself, as we have seen, put a special emphasis on the 'timbre' of the poet's voice, on the way 'he chooses and uses his words'.[90] First of all the poem is written without any rhyme, a form unusual for Brodsky's early poetry, and for Russian poetry of that time in general. Its syntax is lucid, with almost a colloquial flow, as if Brodsky tries to juxtapose the rhythm and cadence of Vergilian epic diction with the straightforwardness and mundane clarity (perhaps 'epic reality'?) of his lyric poem. The poem, then, for all its allusions to Vergil's epic, conveys to us in both its content and its diction that we are reading a love story in which the binary juxtaposition of genders is strictly observed: the man has to pay a price of personal loss and forsaken love in order to fulfil his destiny; the woman fails to understand the importance and consequences of that choice, which is never questioned. I am reluctant again to draw here any precise biographical parallels, mindful of Bethea's and Losev's warnings against them.[91] However, it is hard not to be aware that in 1969, two years before Brodsky's final exile to the West, the figure of Aeneas might have appeared to him as a suitable metaphor of his own plight and his own looming destiny. The truly Vergilian idea that, in Charles Segal's words, 'every conquest carries with it a vanquished human being whose suffering we are made to feel as keenly as the triumph of the victor' was relevant for Brodsky during his last years in Russia.[92]

In the poem the achievement of a meaningful goal becomes associated with the ultimate sacrifice of a genuine feeling. Furthermore, this sacrifice also entails the ideal that the hero (or the poet) must act alone, unburdened by any personal attachment—the same idea we have already seen in 'The Field Eclogue', where the idea of any companionship is also shunned.

The rewards for what the Russians call '*podvizhnichestvo*' (martyrdom achieved through a heroic feat, which is expressed in Russian with a word having the same root as that for a heroic feat itself—'*podvig*'), preclude any personal happiness. Brodsky identifies with Aeneas through the act of *podvizhnichestvo*, but there is a subtle feeling of uneasiness and self-contempt resulting from the hero's brutalized humanity and abandonment of his human ties.

Many years later Brodsky would return to Aeneas again, fleetingly and yet compellingly offering closure to the interpretation of the hero's longing gaze towards the sea in this poem. His poem «Иския в октябре» ('Ischia in October') (1993) describes an abandoned beach in the autumn, where the lyric protagonist accompanied by his wife and daughter contemplates the passage of time. The poem ends with the following stanza:

> Мы здесь втроем, и держу пари,
> то, что вместе мы видим, в три
> раза безадресней и синей,
> чем то, на что смотрел Эней.[93]

> We are threesome here and I bet
> what we together are looking at
> is three times more addressless and more blue
> than what Aeneas was sailing through.

In the earlier poem Aeneas was looking towards the sea where his destined land was waiting. That land had no name and no address yet. It was not even visible from the towers of Carthage lost in the blueness of the sea. The future back then did not have any recognizable features. In this later poem, it still does not. The sea still holds the mystery of the final destination, although the lyric protagonist is not embarking on it alone any more. It is his future times three, and in that the poet finds his consolation and his hope.

'DAEDALUS IN SICILY'

As we have seen from the above discussion of Brodsky's reception of the *Eclogues* and the *Aeneid*, most of his 'classical poetics' is closely intertwined with his contemplation of the poet's place, not on some monumental scale but in a sense of man's overall purpose in the world. Vergil is no exception. The epic or messianic Vergil is replaced with the individualistic reading of Vergilian poetry, be that the *Eclogues* or the *Aeneid*. Therefore it comes as no surprise that one of Brodsky's late poems, which contemplates an artist in exile and at the end of his life, is again a snapshot influenced by Vergil. This poem has received relatively little attention and yet in many respects it offers a perfect closure to many of the themes in Brodsky's classical and general poetics:[94]

«Дедал в Сицилии»
Всю жизнь он что-нибудь строил, что-нибудь изобретал.
То для критской царицы искуственную корову,
чтоб наставить рога царю, то — лабиринт (уже
для самого царя), чтобы скрыть от досужих взоров
скверный приплод; то — летательный аппарат,
когда наконец царь дознался, кто это у него
при дворе так сумел обеспечить себя работой.
Сын во время полета погиб, упав
в море, как Фаэтон, тоже некогда пренебрегший
наставленьем отца. Теперь на прибрежном камне
где-то в Сицилии, глядя перед собой,
сидит глубокий старик, способный премещаться
по воздуху, если нельзя по морю и по суше.
Всю жизнь он что-нибудь строил, что-нибудь изобретал.
Всю жизнь от этих построек, от этих изобретений
приходилось бежать, как будто изобретенья
и постройки стремятся отделаться от чертежей,
по-детски стыдясь родителей. Видимо, это — страх
повторимости. На песок набегают с журчаньем волны,
сзади синеют зубцы местных гор — но он
еще в молодости изобрел пилу,
использовав внешнее сходство статики и движенья.
Старик нагибается и, привязав к лодыжке
длинную нитку, чтобы не заблудиться,
направляется, крякнув, в сторону царства мертвых.[95]

'Daedalus in Sicily'
All his life he was building something, inventing something
Now for a Cretan queen, an artificial heifer,
  so as to cuckold the king. Then a labyrinth, this time for
the king himself, to hide from bewildered glances
an unbearable offspring. Or a flying contraption, when
the king figured out in the end who it was at his court
who was keeping himself so busy with new commissions.
The son on that journey perished falling into the sea,
like Phaeton, who, they say, also spurned his father's
orders. Here, in Sicily, stiff on its scorching sand;
sits a very old man, capable of transporting
himself through the air, if robbed of other means of passage.
All his life he was building something, inventing something.
All his life from those clever constructions, from those
   inventions
he had to flee. As though inventions
and constructions are anxious to get rid themselves of their
   blueprints
like children ashamed of their parents. Presumably, that's
   the fear
of replication. Waves are running onto the sand,
behind, shine the tusks of the local mountains.
Yet he had already invented when he was young, the seesaw,
using the strong resemblance between motion and stasis.
The old man bends down, ties to his brittle ankle
(so as not to get lost) a lengthy thread,
straightens up with a grunt, and heads out for Hades.[96]

It is not particularly surprising that the myth of Daedalus captured Brodsky's imagination; Bacchylides and Euripides, Vergil and Ovid, Shakespeare and Marlowe, Goethe and Swinburne: these are only a few predecessors of Brodsky for whom Daedalus had represented the figure of an artist par excellence, and his genius became closely intertwined with personal tragedy.

Even though the literary background to the myth of Daedalus is vast and deserves a more detailed discussion than it can receive in these pages, the only ancient text to which I intend to compare Brodsky's rendition is Vergil's *ecphrasis* in Book 6 of the *Aeneid*.[97] Although it is clear already from Brodsky's early poem 'Dido and Aeneas' that Brodsky had read Vergil's *Aeneid*, my argument does not entail any definitive knowledge that Brodsky was specifically alluding to Vergil's rendition of the Daedalus myth.

Book 6 is, briefly stated, the most perplexing book of the *Aeneid*. It contains a major *ecphrasis*, as well as the Golden Bough and the Gates of Sleep—hallmark conundrums of the poem. Structurally, it is at once integral and separate, retrospective and proleptic. It is in effect a 'pause' in the middle of the epic intended to contemplate the further meaning of Aeneas' mission. The key to this book and to the *Aeneid* as a whole is the Daedalus *ecphrasis* (6.14–33), which may be regarded as the book's true core.

I am providing the Latin version of the relevant passage in a note since Brodsky did not read Vergil in Latin and it will not play a significant role in my discussion.[98] The following translation from the *Aeneid* serves as a point of reference for discussion of Brodsky's poem:

> Daedalus, they say, when fleeing from Minos' kingdom
> dared to entrust himself to the sky on swift wings,
> he floated through the strange journey, up toward the frozen
>   North
> until he gently came to rest on the Chalcidian hill.
> Here he was returned to earth and he dedicated to you,
>   Phoebus,
> his oar-like wings and built a splendid temple.
> Upon the doors he carved Androgeos' death; then the
>   Athenians
> ordered to pay the penalty, alas! each year
> with lives of their seven sons; there stands the urn, the lots
>   are drawn.
> Opposite, rising from the sea, the Cretan land faces this:
> here is the cruel love of the bull, Pasiphae coupled in secret
> and the mongrel offspring, the two-formed progeny,
> Minotaur, a reminder of the unspeakable love;
> here that house of toil, the inextricable maze.
> Daedalus, pitying the princess's great love
> himself unwound the treachery and the duplicitous paths
>   of the palace,
> guiding blind steps with the thread. Icarus, you also
> would have had a large share in such work, had his grief
>   permitted;
> twice the father tried to carve your fall in gold,
> twice the father's hands fell down.

The metapoetry of this passage is obvious. According to Michael Putnam, it is 'the only occasion in ancient literature where an artist is described as constructing his literal, which in this case is also to say his spiritual, or psychic biography'. He further interprets it 'as a metaphor for the progress of any artist'.[99] The passage was indeed contrived as a *Bildungsroman* of the artist, yet I think that this carefully charted retrospective of self-realization was a very personal voyage. Daedalus is not Every Artist. Furthermore, he was an archetypal persecuted artist bound for exile.

Daedalus' panels within Vergil's *ecphrasis* constitute a triptych reflecting the tripartite divisions echoed throughout the *Aeneid*. Essentially, the first panel renders crime (Androgeos' death) and punishment (the annual sacrifice of seven Athenian youths); the second, the artist's own tale of artistic complicity (the construction of the artificial bull for Pasiphae) and a subsequent restitution of his product's pernicious consequences (the artist's help to Theseus); the third, emptiness, demarcating the limitations of art's capacities suggested in the previous panel. The conclusion conveyed by the empty frame that the image of his son Icarus would have occupied precluded the success of artistic representation in accomplishing its greatest desideratum. The artistic genius becomes a source of inconsolable sorrow, the only relief from which would be death.

Brodsky's Daedalus is the old artist in exile. In that respect the title of the poem is significant, just like the title of the previously discussed 'On the Way to Scyros'. Daedalus in Sicily, just like Theseus on Scyros, is at the end of his life's journey. According to the mythological tradition, unlike Scyros for Theseus, Sicily for Daedalus was a safe haven.[100] Protected by the Sicanian king Cocalus and released from Minos' persecution, he continued to create additional wonders.[101] Nevertheless, his most important 'creation' was lost on the way to that safe haven: Icarus perished during the journey there, and there is Brodsky's focus. Like Vergil, Brodsky lists many great artefacts of Daedalus: the artificial heifer, the Labyrinth, the wings. The 'building' and 'inventing', however, did not lead to rewards or glory, but to that most devastating loss—Icarus, whose death is mentioned only in passing and is accounted less a casualty of his father's genius than of filial disobedience.[102] The ability, then, to invent and to build in the safe environment in Sicily becomes for Daedalus not a final reward, but a prolonged artistic torment: he pays the highest price for his artistic freedom.

It would be trivial, perhaps, to elaborate here on all the obvious parallels with Brodsky's fate.[103] Furthermore, as Reynolds notes in his analysis of the poem, there is a conspicuous glossing of the story of Icarus through his comparison with Phaeton: 'to give someone else's son pride of place in what appears to be one's own son's narrative seems odd'.[104] Here, however, Vergil's *ecphrasis* is helpful again. Like the Vergilian Daedalus, Brodsky's artist is incapable of facing directly the artistic representation of his ineffable loss. The mythological mask assumes yet another mythological disguise: this time of Phaeton, who paralleled Icarus in filial arrogance and his own father's lack of foresight, as well as in the manner of his death, falling from a flight he could not sustain. Brodsky also edits the traditional myth of Daedalus in Sicily by omitting mention of any of his impressive Sicilian inventions: a reservoir for the river Alabon, a steam bath at Selinus, a fortress near Agrigentum, and a terrace for the temple of Aphrodite on Mt Eryx.[105] The Daedalus of the ancient tradition thus has not experienced artistic death, but perhaps even an artistic rebirth after the death of Icarus. So has the Vergilian Daedalus, who, despite his inability to depict Icarus, dedicated his wings to Apollo and built a splendid temple to the god. But Brodsky's Daedalus *runs away from* not *towards* his creations. The artistic rebirth is impossible for two reasons: the loss of Icarus is one, but the other, strangely enough, is the absence of Minos. The artistic decline is precipitated by the severing of the artist's most important human attachment and by the absence of tyranny. Brodsky's Daedalus in that respect is not very different from his Odysseus, Aeneas, or Theseus. Artistic as well as heroic success is fraught with and depends on the presence of suffering. For a Russian writer, even, in worldly terms, the most successful of them, this remained a constant in the early as well as the late poems.[106]

Brodsky brilliantly inverts one classical metaphor in this poem; he transforms the thread that Vergil's Daedalus, sympathetic to Ariadne's love, had once given her into a tool for the artist's own survival. Daedalus now is in need of the magic thread that he tied to his ankle as he heads towards his own Labyrinth, Hades. 'So as not to get lost'? What is the meaning of that line? Does it mean that Daedalus was destined for immortality and that he would find his way back to the living by the sheer power of his art? Or maybe, like the Icarus panel in Vergil, the image of the thread tied to Daedalus' ankle denotes the limitations of even the greatest artist to find his way around (not to mention back from) Hades. The artist by divine grace is on a par with the lowliest of the mortals when faced with artistic death.

NOTES

1. Brodsky (1981), 180.
2. Brodsky's reception of Vergil is also closely connected with the poet's 'love affair with Rome', as Thomas Venclova phrased it in his interview with Valentina Polukhina. He also pointed out: 'Rome is one with the world and at the same time its opposite . . . It is precisely that identity, that mirroring, that Brodsky's Roman poems are about.' See Polukhina (1992), 282. Brodsky continued the tradition of Ivanov's and Osip Mandel'shtam's Rome. See Torlone (2009), 174–85.
3. Ronen (2008), 104.
4. Cited in Ronen (2008), 111.
5. See Ronen (2008), 107–10.
6. Joseph Brodsky, Mark Strand, and Rosanna Warren.
7. Michael Putnam, Helen Bacon, and Christine Perkell.
8. Spence (2001), xvii.
9. Spence (2001), xvi–xvii.
10. Spence (2001), xviii.
11. Odysseus resurfaces in several of Brodsky's poems and essays. Especially noteworthy are 'Odysseus to Telemachus' («Одиссей Телемаку», 1972) and 'Ithaka' («Итака», 1993). For a detailed discussion of these poems see Torlone (2009), 158–65.
12. Torlone (2009), 166–9.
13. An earlier version of this analysis appeared in Z. M. Torlone, 'Russian Tityrus: Joseph Brodsky in Arcadia', *Classical Receptions Journal* 5.3 (2013): 285–98.
14. Brodsky (1995), 234.
15. Brodsky (1995), 235.
16. Brodsky (2001), 1.276.
17. Clausen (1994), 31.
18. See Bethea (1994), 8.34. See also Losev's literary biography of Brodsky (2006, 11–12); he observes that Brodsky considered 'his poems self-sufficient without any need of critical interpretation', especially if that included the circumstances of his biography.
19. Brodsky (2001), 1: 276–80.
20. For a detailed discussion of these themes, see Torlone (2009), 159–65.

21. For a detailed analysis of Ovid in the poetry of Pushkin, Ivanov, Mandel'shtam, and Ovid see Torlone (2009).

22. Brodsky (2000), 399. The translation is the poet's own.

23. Brodsky (2001), 1.123. The Russian version of the poem does not have the title 'Elegy'.

24. See Elder (1961).

25. Newlin (1996), 449. I also want to thank Thomas Newlin for his incredibly helpful remarks on the first version of this study delivered at the American Association for Slavic, East European, and Eurasian Studies Convention in Los Angeles in 2010.

26. Platonov (2007), 1105, citing A. Durkin, 'The Generic Context of Rural Prose: Turgenev and the Pastoral Tradition', in R. A. Maguire and A. Timberlake (eds) *American Contributions to the Eleventh International Congress of Slavists* (Columbus, OH: Slavica, 1993), 43–50 (49); C. Putney, *Russian Devils and Diabolic Continuity in Nikolai Gogol's 'Evening on a Farm near Dikanka'* (New York: Peter Lang, 1999), 216; A. C. Singleton, *Noplace like Home: The Literary Artists and Russia's Search for Cultural Identity* (Albany, NY: State University of New York Press, 1997), 7; and T. Newlin, 'The Return of the Russian Odysseus: Pastoral Dreams and Rude Awakenings', *Russian Review* 55 (1996): 448–74 (449).

27. The Russian text can be found in Brodsky (2001), 3.197–201.

28. See Jeep and Torlone (2009).

29. Brodsky (1981), 178. Valentina Polukhina (1989), 53, notes that here Brodsky's emphasis is not so much on the 'messianic' nature of the Fourth Eclogue as it is on the power and responsibility of poetry.

30. Brodsky (2011), 382.

31. Brodsky (1981), 178.

32. See Perkell (2001).

33. Brodsky (1981), 178.

34. Snell (1953). As a side note to this discussion I would like to mention Leo Tolstoy's attitude towards Vergil's agricultural pursuits as described in the memoirs of Alfons Vorms. The great Russian novelist was displeased by Vorms's assertion that Vergil knew little about agricultural reality but was rather following certain literary conventions. Tolstoy objected that 'Vergil's attitude towards agricultural reality was serious; his agricultural poems are deeply artistic and that is why they are independent works' («Отношение Вергилия к сельскому быту было серьезное; его сельские поэмы глубоко художественные, и как таковые—самостоятельные произведения»). It seems that Brodsky shared Tolstoy's conviction. See Vorms (2003), 1. Also available at: <http://ru.wikisource.org/wiki/Беседа_с_Л._Н._Толстым_о_Вергилии_%28Вормс%29> [last visited 1 March 2013].

35. Perkell (2001), 31.
36. Alpers (1996), 260.
37. Brodsky (2001), 3.200–1. The translation is the poet's own. See Brodsky (2000), 292–3.
38. In Russian, Brodsky uses *unty*, which is a word for winter boots used by the people who live in the extreme cold climate near the North Pole. This choice of word emphasizes even more Brodsky's focus on winter in the poem.
39. On nostalgia in Walcott, see Hardwick (2006), 212.
40. This translation is rather puzzling since it does not reflect the Russian original literally: 'You were opening chicken beaks with the names "Olga" and "Marina", pronounced with tenderness only in childhood and in warmth.' The English translation is much more Freudian, while Russian is replete with a disarming innocence and nostalgia.
41. The same idea of happiness in winter is expressed in the 1964 poem «Песни счастливой зимы» ('Songs of happy winter'). See Brodsky (2001), 2.13.
42. Brodsky (1981), 180.
43. Brodsky (1995), 429, in 'Letter to Horace'.
44. Brodsky (2001), 3.219. This translation is by George L. Kline with the author: Brodsky (2000), 295.
45. Brodsky (2001), 3.221.
46. Brodsky (2001), 3.144.
47. The line of course brings to mind Pushkin's famous 'God forbid I go crazy' («Не дай мне Бог сойти с ума»; Pushkin, 1949, 178–9).
48. See Reynolds (2005), 315.
49. Reynolds (2005), 315.
50. Reynolds (2005), 317. Reynolds explores also other significant allusions of the title connected with Boris Pasternak, Alexander Blok, Nikolai Gumilev, and Marina Tsvetaeva.
51. Reynolds (2005), 322.
52. Brodsky (1981), 180.
53. Thomas (2001), 222.
54. It is not clear what Brodsky meant by this title because the poems are not written in elegiac distich and they rhyme. The title might also have been influenced by Brodsky's interest in Propertius and Ovid.
55. Brodsky (2001), 3.229.
56. Brodsky's own translation (2000), 276. The same rejection of his predecessors' 'monumental' legacies was reflected in the 1987 poem 'The thought of you departs . . .' («Мысль о тебе удаляется . . .») in the line 'It seems that none of us will become a monument' («Видимо, никому из нас не сделаться памятником»). See Brodsky (2001), 4.26.

57. See Saunders (2008), 102, who points out that although the concept of 'landscape' has 'too many post-classical connotations', it, nonetheless, 'remains an appropriate term to bring to a discussion of the configuration and role of nature in the *Eclogues*' (111).

58. In his commentary on Brodsky's eclogues Lev Losev provides for the first time a full text of yet another of Brodsky's eclogues, one that had never made it into any of his previous collections of poems (Brodsky, 2011, 386–95). 'Eclogue VI: Spring' in its form most closely resembles ancient pastoral with its amoebaean exchanges, in Brodsky's case represented by the male voice (A) and female (B), with the exception of the last four stanzas. Losev wonders why Brodsky never included this poem in the number of his printed works although it was almost finished. In its structure, with the frequent repetition of the word 'spring' and elaboration on what spring represents, this poem is strongly evocative of the 'Winter Eclogue' but it lacks the latter's poetic quality, and unmistakable inspiration and elation from the season. I think that it is perhaps for that reason that Brodsky did not include it in the main collection. The number of the eclogue is somewhat puzzling, since Vergil's Sixth Eclogue contains the song of Silenus, who relates along with other things the initiation of Gallus as a poet. Brodsky perhaps thought of spring as poetic initiation, but the sentiment did not come through strongly in the actual poem.

59. Brodsky (2001), 2.313. Translation from Torlone (2009), 166–7.

60. A detailed and most recent analysis of Brodsky's mythological poetics is offered in Torlone (2009).

61. Kreps (1984), 147–8.

62. Ross (2007), 32–3.

63. Ross (2007), 34.

64. For the history of scholarship on the juxtaposition between the characters of Dido and Aeneas, see Spence (1999), 80–2.

65. Austin (1955), 25.

66. Austin (1955), 98.

67. Gill (1997), 229.

68. Wright (1997), 177.

69. Austin (1955), 98.

70. Ross (2007), 34.

71. Otis (1964), 220.

72. Harrison (1989), 21.

73. McLeish (1990), 134.

74. Harrison (1989), 21. See also Covi (1964) and Spence (1999), 80–95.

75. Austin (1955), 98.

76. See Perkell (1981), 221, who, in an implicit response to Otis, argues that Aeneas, unlike Dido, demonstrated 'incomplete humanity'. See also

Monti (1981), 76, who interprets Aeneas' behaviour in Book 4 as his fall from *pietas*.

77. See Otis (1964), 236, who points out that Dido could be understood as 'Aeneas' alter ego—one who has foiled the crime of the past by founding a city of the future, one who likewise has an object of *pietas* (in the dead Sychaeus and in her own mission of empire)—and a tragic figure'.

78. Brumm (2002), 15.

79. For other sources of the story about Dido, see Harrison (1989), 1–3.

80. Akhmatova (1990), 421. Translation from Z. Torlone, 'Engendering Reception: Joseph Brodsky's "Dido and Aeneas"', in D. L. Munteanu (ed.), *Emotion, Genre and Gender in Classical Antiquity* (London: Bloomsbury, 2011), 250.

81. Omry Ronen (2008), 107, observes that in the last stanza of this poem there is a hidden allusion to Vergil by Akhmatova: «В конце этого сонета, как бывает в стихах Ахматовой, по-видимому, подавлена напрашивающаяся—в связи с темой лести и репутацией любимого поэта Августа — рифма «Вергилий»» ('At the end of this sonnet, as happens in Akhmatova's verses, it seems, there is a rhyme that invites itself but is repressed in connection with the theme of flattery and the reputation of Augustus' favourite poet: "Vergil"'). In Russian 'Vergil' («Вергилий») rhymes with 'fleet' («флотилий»).

82. Akhmatova alludes perhaps here to a decree of 1946 issued by Andrei Zhdanov in which her poetry was condemned as decadent and civically inappropriate.

83. Brodsky (1995), 460.

84. *Dido and Aeneas* (1689). Music composed by Henry Purcell. Libretto by Nahum Tate. Available at: <http://opera.stanford.edu/iu/libretti/dido.html> [last visited 23 March 2014].

85. See Verheul (1973), n. 3.

86. Loseff (1990), 38.

87. These lines were also evocative of the Nisus and Scylla episode in Ovid's *Metamorphoses* 8.

88. See McLeish (1990), 141.

89. Brodsky (1981), 180.

90. Brodsky (1981), 180.

91. See Bethea (1994), 8, 34, and Losev (2006), 11–12.

92. Segal (1990), 12.

93. Brodsky (2001), 135; translation, 431.

94. Several critics have pointed out the importance of the poem. See Smith (2005), 401; Reynolds (2007).

95. Brodsky (2001), 4.137.

96. Brodsky's own translation (2000), 404. This translation first appeared in *The New York Review of Books*, 7 October 1993.

97. There was also an obvious allusion in the poem to Ovid's *Metamorphoses* 8.183–235, especially in the lines 'capable of transporting himself through the air, if robbed of other means of passage'. Cf. Ovid's *'Terras licet'* inquit *'et undas obstruat: at caelum certe patet, ibimus illac'* ('he [Minos] may hinder us on land and on sea: but the sky is surely open, we will go that way').

98.   Daedalus, ut fama est, fugiens Minoia regna,
      praepetibus pinnis ausus se credere caelo,
      insuetum per iter gelidas enavit ad Arctos
      Chalcidicaque levis tandem super adstitit arce.
      redditus his primum terris tibi, Phoebe, sacravit
      remigium alarum posuitque immania templa.
      in foribus letum Androgeo; tum pendere poenas
      Cecropidae iussi, miserum! septena quotannis
      corpora natorum; stat ductis sortibus urna.
      contra elata mari respondet Gnosia tellus:
      his crudelis amor tauri suppostaque furto
      Pasiphae mixtumque genus prolesque biformis
      Minotaurus inest, veneris monumenta nefandae;
      his labor ille domus et inextricabilis error;
      magnum reginae sed enim miseratus amorem
      Daedalus ipse dolos tecti ambagesque resolvit,
      caeca regens filo vestigia. tu quoque magnam
      partem opere in tanto, sineret dolor, Icare, haberes;
      bis conatus erat casus effingere in auro,
      bis patriae cecidere manus.

99. See Putnam (1987), 174.

100. One place where the English translation differs from the Russian original is the reiteration in English of 'here, in Sicily', whereas in Russian that line contains only a word meaning 'now' (теперь).

101. See N. G. L. Hammond and H. H. Scullard (eds), *Oxford Classical Dictionary*, 2nd edn (Oxford: Clarendon, 1970), Daedalus, 309.

102. The idea of mentioning Icarus only in passing recalls also W. H. Auden's famous 1938 poem 'Musée des Beaux Arts', in which there is the *ecphrasis* of Pieter Breughel's *Fall of Icarus*. For more on the issue of Auden's profound influence on Brodsky, see Losev (2006), 178–82, and Reynolds (2007). Among other influences on this poem of Brodsky, Reynolds also mentions Shakespeare's Prospero and Tennyson's 'Ulysses' (576).

103. Gillespie (2004), 37, observes that 'Brodsky's portrait of the ancient inventor in old age is also a trenchant self-portrait.'

104. Reynolds (2007), 560.

105. See note 101.
106. Reynolds (2007), 578, has a less pessimistic reading of this poem, arguing that 'one may perhaps consider Daedalus happy'. I agree in the sense that Brodsky's Daedalus, as an old man, was free from the yearnings and pitfalls of his youthful ambitions.

6

Vergil in Russian

Lost in Translation?

Nec verbo verbum curabis reddere fidus
interpres.
As a true translator you will take care not to translate word for
word.

Horace, *Ars poetica*

Vasilii Petrov's monumental attempt at canonizing the *Aeneid* on
Russian soil was unsuccessful, and his peers ridiculed his commendable attempt as a caricature of the great Roman epic. The eighteenth
century, when Petrov embarked on his task, was still a time when the
translation of Vergil was not possible because the necessary vernacular and the linguistic idiom were only taking shape. However, that
translation accomplished one important thing: it demonstrated to
future translators how even the text of the translation can be inscribed
with meaning that is relevant to the receiving culture and does not
just mimic or slavishly imitate the source text.

In the pages below I would like to discuss Russian translations of
the *Aeneid* mostly, but a few words need to be said about two other
Vergilian works translated into Russian. The *Georgics*, with an alter-
native title, 'Four Books on Agriculture', was translated by V. G. Ruban
in 1777 and published in St Petersburg. The first translation of
the *Eclogues* did not appear until 1807 in Moscow, translated by
A. Merzliakov. In 1821 the *Georgics* was retranslated by A. Raich and
published again in Moscow. I. Sosnetskii undertook another translation of both the *Eclogues* and the *Georgics* in 1873. Vladimir Solov'ev
translated the Fourth Eclogue in 1891, choosing this poem, as we have
seen, because it reflected his belief in the 'messianic' message of Vergil's

poetry. A. V. Rudzianskii published his own translation of the *Eclogues* in 1897. The most widely read translation, however, of both the *Eclogues* and the *Georgics* belongs to Sergei Shervinskii and appeared in 1933 in the 'Treasures of World Literature' («Сокровища мировой литературы») series published by the Russian Academy. This last edition was reprinted many times and I would like to look briefly at an example of that translation, specifically an excerpt from the Fourth Eclogue, since this study has already addressed Vladimir Solov'ev's translation of it. Shervinskii's translation is impressively close to the original in both form and content. He stayed away from any attempt at attaching any 'messianic' interpretation to his rendering of the Fourth Eclogue and took great pains to stay faithful to the flow, metre, and word order of the Vergilian line. The only criticism that a Russian reader might have about Shervinskii's translation is his overzealous faithfulness.[1] For example, lines 18–20 of the Vergilian poem read:

> At tibi prima, puer, nullo munuscula cultu
> errantis hederas passim cum baccare tellus
> mixtaque ridenti colocasia fundet acantho.

This is how Shervinskii translates these lines:

> Мальчик, в подарок тебе земля, не возделана вовсе,
> Лучших первин принесет, с плющом блуждающий баккар
> Перемешав и цветы колокассий с аканфом веселым.

> Little boy, the earth without being tilled, as a gift to you,
> Will bring its first gifts, the wandering baccaris with ivy,
> Mixing the flowers, colocasia with merry acanthus.

It has to be said that in general the translation of the names of numerous plants in Vergil presents a significant challenge for a translator in any language, but for a Russian reader the «колокассий с аканфом» ('colocasia with acanthus') and «баккар» ('baccaris') mean very little if anything at all. Shervinskii did render '*hederas*' as «плющ», a name for ivy that is completely accessible both verbally and visually to a Russian reader. But Shervinskii also translates '*munuscula*' as «первин», a word rather archaic and most certainly unusual. This tendency to retain in the Russian text certain words that do not have the precise equivalent in the receiving language is certainly not unique to the Russian translation practice displayed here by Shervinskii. The English translation of the Fourth Eclogue by Guy Lee renders the names of these plants in exactly the same way, also translating only '*hederas*' as 'ivy' into the more familiar vernacular. While I will refrain from making any judgement concerning the effect of such translation on the ordinary English reader, for the Russian non-specialist reader the outlandishly unfamiliar words produce a distinctively alienating effect. We might attribute this effect to intentional 'foreignizing' on the part of the translator, a translation practice we will discuss in more detail in connection with Valerii Briusov's translation of the *Aeneid*.

THE *AENEID* IN RUSSIAN

As has been noted, there is still no canonical translation of the *Aeneid* into Russian with a reputation similar to Gnedich's *Iliad* or Zhukov-skii's *Odyssey*. The question of the canonical translation perhaps is a tricky one because it involves a question of what should be the main register for the translation of a work such as the *Aeneid*. Matthew Arnold thought that nobility was one of the main qualities that translators of Homer should convey.[2] The same quality should per-haps apply to translations of Vergil, since the reader of the receiving culture expects the presence of 'epic grandeur'[3] characteristic of the original. But should the translator also keep in mind that the work in translation must become a masterpiece in its own right, which can be read and enjoyed without constant comparison with the original, and satisfy the current cultural expectations? In more theoretical terms the 'battles of translations' often degenerate 'into conflict between the "scholarly" and the "poetic"' approach to the target text, a conflict 'that loses sight of the main function of a translation from classical poetry, which is to provide a contemporary means of understanding and responding to the ancient work'.[4] Russian translators struggled with these issues as they took different paths to 'universalizing' meaning and trying to remove or appropriate cultural differences that separated the Vergilian text from its Russian audience.

The absence of a unanimously accepted Russian translation of the *Aeneid* is rather surprising because, in Carlo Testa's words, 'Latin-to-Russian translators are, of course, lucky people.'[5] The reasons for such a statement are numerous: Russian is an inflected language with six cases that roughly correspond to the functions of cases in Latin. Latin syntax and Russian syntax are also very similar, and Russian, like Latin, allows tremendous flexibility in a sentence's word order.

Russian, unlike English, does not have to deal with articles, which thus eliminates extra syllables that may hinder the metre. Furthermore, as Testa also observes,

> Russian has plenty of monosyllabic or bi-syllabic pronoun, noun and verb forms, which can be combined with great effectiveness to match almost any desired metric pattern; besides Russian accents frequently shift from case to case, so that in order to obtain the desired tonic accent on a given word we sometimes need no more than trigger the circumstances for that word to appear in what is, for our purposes, its optimal case.[6]

With all these enormous conveniences that enabled Gnedich to successfully translate the *Iliad* into Russian, the *Aeneid* for some reason remained out of reach even after the formation of the stable poetic vernacular. In the following pages I aim to examine the most widely known Russian translations of the *Aeneid* which reflect the broader cultural shifts in approaching the Vergilian text. Recent works in translation studies point out 'the pitfalls of cultural approaches to translation that tend to ignore various participants in the translation enterprise'.[7] Anthony Pym observes that it is no longer enough to focus only on 'the sociocultural dimensions of source and target texts. We would like to know more about who is doing the mediating, for whom, within what networks and with what social effects.'[8] With that in mind this chapter, while describing the main milestones and sociocultural trends that have conditioned Russian translation practices, also aims to look closely at some individual translators who best reflect the cultural and aesthetic changes that underpin the struggle of Russian poets and scholars to bring the *Aeneid* to the Russian reader.

After Petrov a Russian translation of the *Aeneid* was obviously still very much needed, and that need was keenly understood by the Russian literary milieu that felt that it was important to discover Vergil through a translation in the way that the *Iliad* and the *Odyssey* had been discovered. We have already seen what high expectations Nikolai Gogol placed on the task of a translator in his exalted praise of Zhukovskii's *Odyssey*. While Gogol considered Russian a language that is 'fuller and richer than all the European languages' («полнейшем и богатейшем всех европейских языков»), he also expected that a translator, in this case Zhukovskii, 'becomes invisible as if an interpreter of Homer' («переводчик незримо стал как бы истолкователем Гомера»), and his translation will influence the purification of the Russian language («может подействовать значительно на очищение языка»).[9]

Lomonosov and Sumarokov expressed their 'linguistic nationalism'[10] by hailing Russian as more capable than any European language for any form of literary expression.[11] By the time Gogol was writing his panegyric to Zhukovskii's *Odyssey*, the Russian literary language was no longer a 'newcomer', and 'when Russian patriots' of Gogol's and later generations 'worshipped the "great Russian Word", it was no more a dream, but reality they worshipped'.[12]

It is clear from Gogol's remarks that the translation of the classics from the nineteenth century on acquired a much more important and broader goal than merely conveying the plot and the poetic devices to the reading public in the receiving culture. Julie Hayes in her study of translations in England and France observes:

> Translation is one of the key means by which the singularity of the literary event becomes absorbed into cultural practice. Translation makes language visible, reminding us that the bridges between cultures can never be taken for granted, but instead require patient probing and an openness to otherness and difference.[13]

The Russian translations of the *Aeneid* that followed Petrov's were significantly less concerned with ideology and more with poetics. Among the questions confronted by the translators were shifting attitudes towards the classical heritage and reconsiderations of national identity and its representation in the literary language. Lawrence Venuti points out that '[t]he selection of foreign texts and the development of translation strategies can establish peculiarly domestic canons for foreign literatures, canons that conform to domestic aesthetic values and therefore reveal exclusions and admissions, centers and peripheries that deviate from those current in the foreign language.'[14] In this respect the choice to translate the great Roman epic in Russia, despite numerous failures, proved to be remarkably enduring because it revealed the striving of Russian writers to make epic the centre of the Russian literary identity in order to provide Russian literature with more authority and canonicity.

Richard Armstrong in his study of retranslation of ancient epics notes that 'changing conceptions of epic in the target culture alter the translational horizon. Creative emulation, in other words, helps to shape the textual horizon of the original inspiring epic by reshaping the target culture's expectations of epic within the burgeoning literary tradition.' He further asserts that the act of retranslation 'is itself a realignment of literary genealogy, a desire to connect the newest literary norms to the numinous source and origin of epic discourse, to reappropriate an authoritative "classic" of the genre under the sign of *difference* from the previous translation(s) and literary norms'.[15] In Russia the *Aeneid* after Petrov belonged to the canon by which the Russian literary milieu allied itself with the European tradition, while inscribing the national literary history and its changing norms onto translation. The translations of the *Iliad* and the *Odyssey* proved to be enormously formative for the development of Russian literary self-positioning. The adequate translation of the *Aeneid* promised even more, because since Peter's time the Roman comparison had grown to be crucial for the Russian political and cultural identity.

Before I compare some specific translation techniques that were applied to Vergil's text by the translators that came after Petrov, it seems helpful to present in broad terms the chronological history of Russian translation practices from foreign languages, especially its different stages, informed largely by Mikhail Gasparov's essay 'Briusov, the Translator' («Брюсов-переводчик»).[16] Gasparov distinguishes five most prominent eras in the history of Russian translations. The first, dating from the eighteenth century, was characterized by a 'free' style of translation which tried to adjust the plots and forms of the foreign text to the tastes of the Russian reader barely familiar with the foreign cultures from which the source texts came. We might add to Gasparov's observation that such an approach to translation practices was not a Russian invention. In Europe, as Hayes notes, 'translations from the Greek and Latin classics afforded sources of inspiration and emulation that enabled the vernacular literature to develop its own voice'. Sometimes that voice was developed through the translation practice that in France was dubbed *les belles infidèles* for their tendency to 'localize' the translation, to make the original author 'speak French'.[17] Vasilii Petrov's translation, as we can see, might be attributed to that category. Though commendable as the first effort at such a monumental task, his translation was more concerned with contemporary politics than the source text. However, it initiated some awareness about different translation practices and subsequently triggered a debate involving discussions of freedom versus fidelity, the relation of the receiving culture to the source text, and the capacity of the Russian language to render adequately Roman cultural realities and the epic metre and diction.

Gasparov further notes that the romanticism of the early nineteenth century, best represented by Nikolai Gnedich's *Iliad* and Vasilii Zhukovskii's *Odyssey*, was an epoch of a precise translation, which attempted to make the reader understand and eventually like the unfamiliar plots and forms. The realism of the late nineteenth century became again the time of the 'free', 'adjustable' translation represented by Vasilii Kurochkin's Pierre-Jean de Béranger. The modernism of the beginning of the twentieth century returned to the aspirations of the precise translations: the original text should not be impoverished because of readers' demands or poor tastes; on the contrary, these tastes must be enriched by the complexity and 'foreignness' of the original. Not only Valerii Briusov, whom we will discuss later, fell into that category but also his contemporaries from Konstantin Bal'mont to Mikhail Lozinskii. In the Soviet era we can see a reaction against 'literalism' («буквализм») and demand for clarity, for lightness, exemplified by the extremely readable translations of Samuil Marshak. Now we can turn to the existing Russian translations of the *Aeneid* in an attempt to understand how they fit into Gasparov's helpful summary.

There were several unfinished attempts at translating the *Aeneid*, such as that by Vasilii Zhukovskii, who in 1822 published his translation in hexameters of Book 2 entitled 'The Destruction of Troy'. The choice of hexameter as the only appropriate form for translation of the *Aeneid* also informed the subsequent translation by I. Shershenevich, only the second complete translation after Petrov, which was published in instalments in the influential literary periodical *Sovremennik* (*The Contemporary*), starting from 1851. Like Petrov's, Shershenevich's translation was considered a failure for its contrived attempt at clarity, which resulted in phrasing unnatural to the Russian ear and eye. Towards the end of the nineteenth century there were several other failed attempts at translating Vergil's epic. In 1878 I. Sosnetskii tried to translate the *Aeneid* into anapaests, again unsuccessfully. Afanasii Fet's translation came in 1888 and N. Kvashnin-Samarin's in 1893. The former deserves a more detailed look. Fet was a major poetic figure of the 1840s–50s, a period when prose was paramount.[18] Fet was a meticulous craftsman of Russian verse. His verse abounds in imagery and he has an ear keenly attuned to the musicality of the verse (not surprisingly many of his poems were set to music by Peter Tchaikovsky and Nikolai Rimskii-Korsakov among others). Furthermore, even in his early poetry the interest in the classical theme becomes apparent. It seems that he would have been the most natural choice for the translation of the *Aeneid*.

In the introduction to his translation Fet offers the main reason for his ambitious undertaking. He observes that classical philologists in

Russia are attempting to make significant contributions to classical scholarship. However, he notes that 'it is strange to see a detailed analysis of a famous classical author, while Russian literature does not even have a translation of this author' («но не странно ли видеть на русском языке подробный разбор известного класcика в то время, когда русская литература не представляет даже перевода этого класcика»). What is interesting in this observation is that Fet refuses to acknowledge any previous attempts at translating Vergil, except for a brief mention at the end of his introduction that every time when he consulted his predecessors hoping to solve some of his difficulties, he was always left disappointed.[19] The only translation he actually acknowledges and considers acceptable is that by Zhukovskii, who, as was mentioned, translated only the second book under the title 'Destruction of Troy' («Разрушение Трои»). His own work he jubilantly declares to be very close to Zhukovskii's because both are 'close to the original'.[20] However, he also finds an insurmountable flaw with Zhukovskii's translation because it does not follow the line numbering of the original. He considers such licence unacceptable, especially in light of Zhukovskii's own canonical translation of the *Odyssey*, where the numbering of the lines is preserved as it is in the Greek text.

Fet outlines the main method and advantages of his own translation, although he initially falls into ornate poetic metaphor:

> Подобно тому, как у истинного, хотя бы и пожилого, охотника сердце радостно и пугливо вздрагивает каждый раз при взлете птицы, всегда новом и требующем особого приема при выстреле, внушаемого не правилами а чутьем, приходится и переводчику охотиться за каждым возникающим словом оригинала.[21]

> Just as the heart of the true even if aged hunter trembles joyfully and fearfully every time a bird takes off in flight, always a new one and demanding a special trick upon shooting, which is inspired not by the rules but by intuition, so does the translator have to hunt after every emerging word of the original.

He especially praises the ability of the Russian language to render with precision Vergilian hexameter, thus enabling the translator to 'preserve intact the verse of the original', even if sometimes a Vergilian dactyl is replaced with a Russian spondee.[22]

Fet did not finish his translation. While the sixth book was translated together with Vladimir Solov'ev, the seventh, ninth, and tenth books were translated by Vladimir Solov'ev alone.[23] However, despite there being two different translators, it was not a translation but a paraphrase of the great epic in hexameters, the characteristic with which later Valerii Briusov took issue.[24] Fet often disregarded Vergilian metaphors, and dismissed the intricacies of poetic diction, sacrificing poetry to a single-minded pursuit of the plot. While the translation by Kvashnin-Samarin is guilty of the same flaws, the Russian reading public expected more from Fet, whose original poetry was impeccably elegant and refined.

In the twentieth century poets searching for new forms of poetic expression started to turn away from classical forms or homage to classical tradition. The next full translation of the *Aeneid* did not happen until Valerii Briusov (Figure 10), one of the founders of Russian Symbolism and an extremely authoritative figure in the Russian literary landscape at the turn of the nineteenth century, undertook again the difficult task. His translational practices and theory of translation are the focus of the following pages. In addition I aim to compare his attempt at rendering the *Aeneid* with those of Afanasii Fet and Sergei Osherov, and to contemplate why none of these translations achieved canonical status.

In order to understand Briusov's valiant but misguided attempt at translating the *Aeneid*, we have to view it as an integral part of his whole literary career. He made his debut as a translator as early as the 1890s, when he produced translations of French Symbolist poetry (Paul Verlaine, Arthur Rimbaud, Stéphane Mallarmé, and Maurice Maeterlinck). His further publications included translations from Edgar Allan Poe, Hugo, Racine, Molière, Byron, Goethe, and Wilde. However, he saw the *Aeneid* as one of the most attractive challenges for his poetic talent.

Briusov's translations from Latin started early and were his first attempts to make a literary name. Under the tutelage of the renowned philologist V. G. Appelrot, Briusov began his work on the *Aeneid* as early as in the gymnasium, and from 1895 worked steadily on it.[25] In 1899 he translated *in toto* the second and fourth books, and in 1913 prepared more (as many as three books, according to some testimonies) which, after some comments from specialists such as F. F. Zelinskii and V. I. Ivanov, he destroyed, only to begin translating all over again.[26] Briusov loved Vergil and translation of the *Aeneid* became one of his life's tasks. He worked on his translation until his death in 1924, but he completed only the first seven books. We have as many as seven versions of the different translations that belong to

Figure 10. Portrait of Valerii Briusov.

different phases of his career as a translator. Gasparov analysed in detail all the different phases that finally led Briusov to the final version of his translation, which acquired such a bad reputation because of its 'literalism' («буквализм»—'bukvalism'; 'bukva' in Russian means letter of the alphabet). What interests me most in the context of this study is why Briusov, a man of flawless poetic taste, a seasoned translator, whose translations of French Symbolists and of Armenian poetry remain canonical to this day, could have so completely failed at translating Vergil.[27] Barry Scherr observes: 'Briusov ... strove so hard to convey every word, every syntactical structure, and every formal device with absolute faithfulness to the original that the Russian text is virtually unreadable—and this despite his extensive experience as a translator.'[28]

The final translation that we have today (with Sergei Solov'ev, the nephew of Vladimir Solov'ev) was in fact preceded by one completely free of such 'literalism' and the contrived and somewhat puzzling phrasing. Briusov, having started with free translation, moved towards trying to be more precise in his phrasing and imagery and finally to imitating the original precisely, even in his use of grammatical forms, word order, and at times confusing Latinisms. By slavishly copying every feature of the original, Briusov made a conscious choice that responded to some aesthetic and social preoccupations of the cultural environment and the poet's overall poetics. As Scherr notes, 'during the modernist period of the early twentieth century the predominant tendency was toward literalism, and Briusov moved in this direction further than the rest'.[29]

Briusov had explained his approach to the translation of ancient authors already in his 1913 essay «Овидий по-русски» ('Ovid in Russian'), in which he mercilessly criticizes Zelinskii's recently published translation of the *Heroides*.[30] Although Briusov acknowledges Zelinskii's competence in Latin and for the most part finds his translation precise, his main objection is Zelinskii's poetic licence and his tendency to render Ovid's verse sometimes in a more ornate way not present in the original. As an example he cites Penelope's last words to Ulysses from the first poem:

> Certe ego, quae fueram te discedente puella,
> Protinus ut venias, facta videbor anus.

> Indeed I, who had been a young girl on your departure,
> If you were to come now, I will seem to you an old woman.

Zelinskii renders these lines:

> Я же, красотка твоя . . . приезжай хоть сейчас, и ты скажешь,
> Что моей юности все уж облетели цветы.

> But I, once your beauty . . . if you come back now, you will say,
> That all the flowers of my youth have withered.[31]

What especially bothers Briusov in this rendition is Zelinskii's 'invention' of metaphors that were not in fact in Ovid. Ezra Pound once paid an ambivalent compliment to Gavin Douglas's translation of Vergil, saying that 'he gets more out of Vergil than any other translator'.[32] In the same vein Zelinskii's 'modernization' of Ovid's verse Briusov sees as unacceptable because then the translation ceases 'to render adequately Ovid's manner of writing and . . . changes the spirit of the epoch' («далеко не адекватно передает манеру письма Овидия и, на наш взгляд, видоизменяет дух эпохи»).[33]

Furthermore, Briusov sheds some light on his approach to the translation of the *Aeneid* in the introduction to the unpublished translation of the *Aeneid* (1920) cited by Gasparov from the archival materials. Briusov extols the merits of ancient literature and greatly admires the 'perfection' of form achieved by the ancient authors, especially Vergil. However, he appears adamant that the time of rigorous training in classical languages has passed and that the time of translations as the only educational tool has arrived. He then defines very concisely the task of the translator in this new cultural context:

> Переходя именно к переводам, можно кратко определить задачу переводчиков, сказав, что их труд должен будет для русского читателя *заменять подлинник*. Из этого следует прежде всего, что этот перевод не может ограничиваться пересказом — хотя бы в общем верным — содержания. Нигде форма не связана так тесно с содержанием, как в произведениях античных писателей, особенно поэтов.[34]

> As for the translations, one can briefly define the task of the translators by saying that their work will *replace the original* for the readers. What follows from this is that such a translation cannot be limited to a *paraphrase*—even if a correct one—of the plot. Nowhere else is the form as closely connected to the content as it is in the writings of the ancient writers, especially poets.

It is clear from this excerpt that Briusov's approach to the translation of the *Aeneid* was extremely ambitious. What emerges from his theory is that the work of translation must become an integral part of the literature in whose language the foreign text is translated. Thus the work of the original fades, replaced by the translation that now in form and content becomes part of a new literary canon. It is also clear why Briusov considered all the previous translations, including that by Fet, inadequate. In the introduction to his finally published translation of the *Aeneid* Briusov emphasizes the poetic value of the *Aeneid*, calling Vergil a 'great master of penning the sound, "of verbal instrumentation"' («величайший мастер звукописи «словесной инструментовки»»). Extremely preoccupied with the adequate rendition of Vergilian 'sound technique', Briusov succinctly phrases his dissatisfaction with the previous attempts at translating Vergil:

> Для поэта чтение «Энеиды» в подлиннике, помимо художественного наслаждения, есть сплошной ряд изумлений перед великим мастерством художника и перед властью человека над стихией слов.

Что сделали со всем этим русские переводчики? Они, так сказать, опростили Вергилия: раскрыли метафоры, которые им показались слишком смелыми, заменили намеки прямыми выражениями, расставили слова в их правильно грамматическом порядке, и на звукопись прямо не обратили внимания.[35]

For a poet the reading of the *Aeneid* in the original, apart from the aesthetic pleasure, is a constant feeling of wonder before the mastery of an artist and before the power of a human being over the natural force of words.

What did the Russian translators do with all of that? They, so to speak, dumbed down Vergil: spelled out the metaphors, which seemed to them too daring, replaced the hints with direct expressions, placed the words in the correct grammatical order, but they did not pay any attention to the way Vergil penned the sound.

Briusov follows this statement with numerous examples from the translations by Fet, Shershenevich, and Kvashnin-Samarin, which, in his opinion, illustrate their insufficient attention to the superb Vergilian verse composition because they tried to erase the foreignness, which of course invited the act of translation in the first place. He then claims that his translation would correct these inadequacies by reproducing all the 'specific features of the Vergilian verse form' («все особенности формы стихов Вергилия»). Following his desire to stay true to the verse 'music' of the original, Briusov even retains the original spelling of the Latin names, rejecting the accepted Russian rendition of them. Gasparov observes that 'in striving to translate for the Russian person the Latin worldview, Briusov . . . transfers into the Russian language the traits of the Latin language'.[36] This extreme attention to the purely formal features of the original unfortunately resulted in an adverse effect on the quality of the translation.

It appears that despite his ambition to 'replace' the original with his translation, Briusov achieved the exact opposite result by reminding his readers that what they were reading is in fact a translation, not an original work of poetry in Russian. The result of that approach was again, as we have seen with Shervinskii's *Eclogues*, the intentional 'foreignizing' of the translation, because in fact Briusov wanted his *Aeneid* to sound alien to his readers. While the desire to retain certain features of the original is appropriate, because these features would demarcate differences between the foreign and the receiving cultures, Briusov failed to assimilate the text to any values or vernacular of the Russian reader. The question is, why? Briusov it seems 'was not translating poetry, he was translating poetics'.[37] However, this practice clearly did not help him with the *Aeneid*, the translation of which Gasparov calls 'ill-begotten' («злополучная»), and that opinion is in tune with the general assessment of Briusov's translation.[38]

Lorna Hardwick notes that 'critical debate now stresses the importance of looking at a version or imitation of an ancient text in the context of the modern writer's whole work, and this applies equally whether the translator is a professional scholar, a poet or a hybrid figure'.[39] Briusov's predilection for immersing himself completely in the world of the source text was exacerbated by the eschatological feelings intensified in the years following the Revolution, the event perceived as near apocalyptic by many Russian writers. As Briusov's biographer V. E. Molodiakov observes, Briusov's attitude towards the Bolshevik revolution 'remains the question of questions' («вопросом вопросов было и оставалось отношение к большевистской революции»).[40] He adds that Briusov's 'acceptance of Bolshevism was not as rapid and unconditional as it was believed until recently' («принятие большевизма было вовсе не таким быстрым и безусловным, как принято было считать до недавнего времени»).[41] A series of anti-Bolshevik verses which he wrote in January 1918 reveal that Briusov was in no way delusional about the nature of the new regime, but he chose to compromise because, as Molodiakov also suggests, he perceived in the Bolsheviks the only possible 'saviours' of the empire, which he thought Russia should remain.[42] Briusov's approach was perhaps practical, as he joined the Communist Party in 1920 and organized the People's Commissariat of Public Education, but Briusov's compromise with the Bolsheviks was as tragic as many of his peers'.

In a literary atmosphere heavy with the tendency to do away with the past, as some rhetoric of the day required, and begin the future on a clean slate, Briusov felt, as Gasparov observes, that the most precious aspect of any literary legacy was what made it unique, nationally specific, not what appealed to the reader in the receiving culture.[43] Hence, the work of a translator of the texts of the past must be limited to conveying as precisely as possible the idiosyncratic quality, the national specific of the original text, not its universal appeal. The attention to culturally specific details is manifest already in Briusov's pre-revolutionary Roman novels *The Altar of Victory* (*Алтарь победы*, 1911–12) and *Jupiter Overthrown* (*Юпитер поверженный*, 1912–13), which he oversaturated with details aimed at producing the exotic and foreign quality of the life and events portrayed. Sometimes the effect bordered on the absurd, when a lamp was called «луцерна» ('lutserna', Lat. *lucerna*), a pool of water «писцина» ('pist-sina', Lat. *piscina*), and a dagger «пугион» ('pugion', Lat. *pugio*). The irony of such devotion to the lexical Latinization of the text is that the reader eventually becomes completely lost and cannot even visualize the verbal descriptions on the page. The goal, however, is not to make the text more comprehensible, but to make it actually less so.[44]

The same tendency is evident in Briusov's translations. Gasparov calls it «эффект отдаленности» ('the effect of distancing'), aimed at producing a distinct feeling of not belonging to the cultural context of the work, but rather looking at it from a distance, as an outsider, almost a voyeuristic effect. When translating French Symbolists, Briusov did not have to use the 'foreignizing' tendency because he tried to approximate one modern culture to another.[45] But with Roman literature the situation was different: Briusov had to make sure that the reader understood that the text in front of him was a thing of the past culture.[46]

The last translation of the *Aeneid* I would like to single out is by a Soviet scholar, Sergei Osherov (1931–83). Osherov's translation, published in 1971, helps us to draw some conclusions about Vergil in Russian. Osherov, although he did compose some original poetry, certainly did not have the poetic standing of Fet and Briusov. A classicist by training, Osherov became an important name in Soviet academia and one of the long-standing translation editors in the publishing house *Khudozhestvennaia literatura*—an important enterprise during the Soviet era which allowed Soviet citizens to enjoy great books from all over the world in outstanding translations.

I would like to look specifically at three examples of Russian translations done by Fet, Briusov, and Osherov and analyse them in terms of their accessibility for a Russian reader. Since this whole study has repeatedly returned to the theme of Dido, I take as my example the first eleven lines of Book 4 of the *Aeneid*:

1   At regina gravi iamdudum saucia cura
2   vulnus alit venis et caeco carpitur igni.
3   multa viri virtus animo multusque recursat
4   gentis honos: haerent infixi pectore vultus
5   verbaque, nec placidam membris dat cura quietem.
6   postera Phoebea lustrabat lampade terras
7   umentemque Aurora polo dimoverat umbram,
8   cum sic unanimam adloquitur male sana sororem:
9   'Anna soror, quae me suspensam insomnia terrent!
10 quis novus hic nostris successit sedibus hospes,
11 quem sese ore ferens, quam forti pectore et armis!'

This short excerpt of the most dramatic book of the *Aeneid* is challenging in Latin since it contains some idiomatic phraseology that does not necessary fall into any grammatical patterns and clearly presents a difficulty for a translator.

Here is Fet's rendition, with my interlinear and word-by-word English translation, in which, following Braund's method,[47] I use a hyphen where a single Russian word needs more words in English:

1 Но царица давно уж затронута сильной кручиной,
   But the-queen for-a-long-time already touched by-a-strong sorrow,

2 Рану питает внутри и огнем снедаема тайным.
   A-wound is-nourishing inside and by-fire is-consumed secret.

3 Доблесть мужа у ней и рода великая слава
   The-virtue of-a-man within her and race's great glory

4 Все возникает в душе; в груди его врезались взоры
   Everything arises in the-soul; in her-chest his are-engraved glances

5 И слова, и тоска не дает ея членам покоя.
   And words, and longing does-not give her limbs rest.

6 Светочем Феба опять озаряла землю Аврора
   With-the-torch of-Phoebus again illuminated the-earth Aurora

7 И росистую тень от полюса прочь отгоняла,
   And dewy shadow from the-pole away she-pushed,

8 Как безумная, так к любимой сестре обратилась:
   Like a-madwoman thusly to her-beloved sister she-spoke:

9 «Анна сестра, что за сны меня в раздумьи пугают!
   Anna sister, what dreams me in my-thoughts terrify!

10 Что за неведомый гость здесь к нашим прибыл жилищам,
   What unknown guest here to our has-arrived dwellings,

11 Что за вид у него, как он мощен плечами и грудью!
   What is his appearance, how he is-powerful in-his-shoulders and chest!

Fet tried to follow as much as possible Vergil's word order and case arrangement, for example in line 1 rendering the ablative of '*cura*' with the same case function of the word 'sorrow' in Russian («кручиной», instrumental case), and in line 2 '*caeco carpitur igni*', where the adjective is separated from its modifying noun by a verb. In and of itself the Russian language can accommodate these since it is also inflected, but the effect of such rendition is extremely awkward, as is the postponement of the main verb «возникает» ('arises') in line 4. The use of archaisms such as «ея» and «какия» instead of «ее» and «какие» also creates the effect of an archaic text. Some of the Vergilian adjectives, such as '*placidam*' (l. 5), are completely omitted from the translation, which thus reduces the poetic effect of the Vergilian text.

Here is Briusov's translation of the same passage:

1 Но беспощадной царица уже уязвленная страстью,
   But by-merciless queen already wounded passion

2 В жилах рану питает, сжигаема пламенем тайным,
   In veins her-wound nourishes, burned by-fire secret,

3 Доблесть великую мужа в душе вспоминает и рода
   Virtue great of-a-man in her-soul recalls and of-race

4 Славу великую; в сердце, врезаны, облик и речи
   Great glory; in her-heart, engraved, appearance and speeches

5 Держатся; страсть не дает отрадного членам покоя.
   Keep; passion does-not give joyous to-the-limbs rest.

6 Нового дня озаряла Фебейской лампадою земли
   Of-a-new day illuminated with-Phoebean torch the-lands

7 И содвигала Аврора влажную тень с небосвода,
   And pushing-together Aurora the dewy shadow from the-sky

8 Та же, объята недугом, любимой сестре говорила:
   She the-same possessed with-disease, to-the-beloved sister
       was-telling:

9 «Анна, сестра, что меня беспокойно бессонница мучит!
   'Anna, sister, why me relentlessly insomnia vexes!

10 Кто чужестранец сей новый, в наши прибывший владенья?
    Who is-foreigner this new, in our having-arrived abodes?

11 Что за лицо у него! Как мощны плечи и руки! . .
    What face has he! How powerful his-shoulders and arms! . . .

Briusov's rendition of these lines is undoubtedly more precise. He translates Latin '*venis*' with 'in veins' («в жилах») instead of Fet's generalizing 'inside', and 'Phoebean' as an adjective agreeing with 'torch' rather than as the genitive case of Phoebus in Fet. Line 8 clearly presented a problem for both translators, especially the phrase '*male sana*', which Fet renders as 'like a mad woman' and Briusov as 'possessed with-disease'. It is also rather puzzling why Briusov would change the Vergilian text and translate '*pectore et armis*' as 'shoulders and arms (hands)' although Fet stayed closer to the original ('shoulders and chest').

All these details might be completely irrelevant to the experience of the everyday reader and my goal here is not to nitpick, but to consider

why these translations of the *Aeneid* failed to achieve their main
desideratum: to become widely read by the general public. While
adequate in terms of their lexical accuracy and faithfulness to the
original, these two translations failed to meet the standards of a fine
and influential translation. At this point it would help to look at our
last example.

Here is Osherov's translation of the same passage:

1 Злая забота меж тем язвит царицу, и мучит
   An-evil care in-the-meanwhile vexes the-queen and tortures

2 Рана, и тайный огонь, разливаясь по жилам, снедает.
   the-wound, and secret fire, spilling through the-veins, consumes.

3 Мужество мужа она вспоминает и древнюю славу
   The-courage of-the-man she remembers and ancient glory

4 Рода его; лицо и слова ей врезались в сердце,
   of-his race; his-face and words are-etched in her heart,

5 И благодатный покой от нее прогоняет забота.
   and the-blissful rest from her chases-away sorrow.

6 Утром, едва лишь земля озарилась светочем Феба,
   In-the-morning, when barely the-earth lit-up with-the-torch
      of Phoebus

7 Только лишь влажную тень прогнала с небосвода Аврора,
   Just when the-humid shadow chased from the-sky Aurora,

8 Верной подруге своей, сестре, больная царица
   To-her faithful confidante, sister, the-ill queen

9 Так говорит: «О Анна, меня сновиденья пугают!
   Thusly spoke: 'O Anna, me the-dreams terrify!

10 Гость необычный вчера приплыл к нам в город нежданно!
   The-guest unusual yesterday sailed to us into the-city
      unexpectedly!

11 Как он прекрасен лицом, как могуч и сердцем отважен!
   How he is-beautiful in-his-face, how powerful and
      with-his-heart brave!

It perhaps would not take long to decide that the most accessible and the
least accurate translation of these three is that of Osherov. Not only is he
not faithful to the 'sound of music' of the original so valued by Briusov,
his rendition of meaning also remains unsatisfactory. Lines 2–3 have
subjects different from Vergil's and '*quam forti pectore et armis*' is
mistranslated, almost 'dumbed down', and does not convey the Vergilian Dido's admiration for Aeneas' physical appearance, her attraction to
him, which the other two translations do. Osherov's translation was

completed under the editorial tutelage of F. A. Petrovskii, an important classical scholar, a translator of Lucretius and Martial, and editor of Vergil's complete works (published in 1971 in a prestigious series, *Biblioteka vsemirnoi literatury* (*Library of world literature*), with an initial print run of 300,000). This edition contains Osherov's translation of the *Aeneid*, which was reissued in 1979 in the series *Biblioteka antichnoi literatury* (*Library of ancient literature*) with an introductory essay by Mikhail Gasparov. Petrovskii clearly tried to incorporate in Osherov's translation some of the principles he outlined in his early 1966 essay 'Russian Translations of the *Aeneid* and the Goals of Its New Translation'. First he criticized all the previous translations of the *Aeneid*, especially Briusov's, whose knowledge of Latin he considered insufficient for such a monumental task. He writes:

> Но главным несчастьем Брюсова было то, что он не отличал образов и словесных фигур, принадлежащих самому Вергилию, от образов и фигур, свойственных вообще латинскому языку и потерявших свою оригинальность; иными словами, Брюсов не делал различия в своем переводе между *идиомами латинского языка и идиомами Вергилия.*[48]

> But Briusov's main misfortune was the fact that he did not distinguish between imagery and poetic devices that were characteristic only of Vergil and those that belonged in general to the Latin language and had lost their originality; in other words, Briusov did not differentiate in his translation between *Latin idioms* and *Vergilian idioms*.

As a result, Petrovskii claims, Briusov's translation turned out to be contrived and bizarre, and did not convey the natural language flow of the original. Petrovskii elaborates on what he considers to be the main task of any translator of the *Aeneid*, which is 'to convey precisely the contents, trying not to miss any of its crucial nuances' («надо первым делом точно передать ее содержание, стараясь не упустить никаких существенных его оттенков»).[49]

   Petrovskii defines then several aspects of such a translation: Vergilian epithets should not be omitted, the translator must add nothing from himself but, if necessary, he can change the text of Vergil while maintaining the integrity of the development of the narrative and general Vergilian poetics. He points out the necessity for studying the ancient commentators in order to understand better the synchronic details of the text which have been lost in time. What is especially peculiar, however, is that Petrovskii calls the poetic ornamentation of the *Aeneid* 'stingy' («скуповатой») rather than 'opulent' («богатой»), thus warning translators against excessive poetic flourishes that Vergil himself would have abhorred.

These comments by Petrovskii should be interpreted in the context of the official aesthetic dogma of the Soviet period when the essay was written.[50] Braund pithily points out that Briusov's 'formalism' was frowned upon since 'socialist realism', an enforced aesthetic template during the time when Petrovskii was writing, dominated artistic expression of any kind, including translation practices.[51] Briusov's excessive attention to the 'music' of the verse, the form of the poem, the cadence of the verse had to give way to the 'realistic', down-to-earth translation of the epic. Furthermore, Petrovskii also could not have found appealing his theory of 'foreignization', although he did not specifically address it. In the context of 'socialist realism' the main requirements of any literary output were «народность» ('adherence to people') and «партийность» ('adherence to the party'). Fet's translation certainly did not fit the bill, because its language was hopelessly outdated and its verse cumbersome. But neither did that of Briusov, who, having died in 1924, did not anticipate these absurd developments of literary aesthetics. 'Foreignization' could not have been interpreted as a positive development in translation practices. The idea was to bring the foreign aspects of the source text closer to people, not to establish more distance from it. The subject matter of the *Aeneid* was foreign enough, without making it even more so by using the Latinized version of names or verse enjambment, an awkward device for Russian prosody.

The question then remains whether or not Osherov under Petrovskii's auspices finally completed the desired canonical translation of the *Aeneid* accessible to any Russian reader. My opinion certainly does not entail a definitive answer to this question, but in order to illuminate it, I need to step briefly down memory lane.

In 1985–90, when I was a student of Classics at the Moscow State University (MGU), Osherov's translation of the *Aeneid* was not circulated widely. In fact, we were urged to use no translation at all as we made our first steps in translating ancient authors. However, the demands of the rigorous and often overwhelming translation assignments were such that students sought out existing Russian translations to at least find out if they were on the right track in their translating efforts. What we had in our possession at the university library back then was mainly Afanasii Fet's version. Although archaic, cumbersome, and often inaccurate it, however, accomplished the difficult task of leading us through the intricacies of the Vergilian textual fabric almost as successfully as did Gnedich's *Iliad*. Briusov was in fact the second in line to Fet because his overuse of Latinisms annoyed more than helped. Fet's translation strove to be faithful, if not to the form, most certainly to the content of the original, and the students of Latin needed some reassurance that their own renditions were not completely off the mark. Fet's translation in that respect was helpful. However, my peers in the language departments other than Classics disliked Vergil, because both Fet's and Briusov's translations of the *Aeneid* sent them to sleep. These were not students who lacked a passion for literature. Moscow University was, and as far as I know remains, home to ambitious and intellectually curious students. They read the *Iliad* and the *Divine Comedy* with delight, they devoured Shakespeare and could not have enough of Victor Hugo, but Vergil in Russian remained elusive. And in that respect Osherov's translation accomplished the main goal. Vergil can be read with ease, the verse has an easy flow, the imagery and metaphors are not outlandish and obscure. Of course a stern Latin purist might find many a fault with translations such as those pointed out above. The truth, however, is that faults can be and are found with any translation of the *Aeneid*, or any poetic text, for that matter. I remember reading Shakespeare as a student in Boris Pasternak's translation and thinking that Shakespeare was superb. Years later I read him in English and realized that Pasternak's translation has little to do with Shakespeare except for the plot. We loved it because we were reading Pasternak's poetry, a familiar, sublime, frequently quoted text. The 'real' Shakespeare was all of these things too, but Pasternak made him truly a Russian poet.

It is ironic that two wonderful Russian poets, Fet and Briusov, whose original poetry is read with pleasure and imitated to this day, failed at translating Vergil, and that Osherov, not a poet of such standing, succeeded, although in a limited way. After all, the history of Russian translations of ancient epics showed that it was mostly the poets who felt up to the task. So why was the situation different with Vergil? Venuti observes in his discussion of the formation of translation practices:

> The cultural power of translation is uniquely revealed when we consider its role in the canonization of a foreign text in the receiving situation.

A translation contributes to this canonizing process by inscribing the foreign text with an interpretation that has achieved currency and in most cases dominance in academic or other powerful cultural institutions ... At the same time, however, the interpretation that the translator inscribes will also revise the foreign comprehension and evaluation of the text in so far as the translator inevitably puts to work patterns of linguistic usage, literary traditions and effects, and cultural values in the receiving situation, possibly in an effort to address specific readerships. In contributing to the canonicity of a foreign text, the translation leaves neither that text nor the receiving situation unaltered. The foreign text undergoes a radical transformation in which it comes to support a range of meanings and values that may have little or nothing to do with those it supported in the foreign culture.[52]

Let us see now if the Russian translations of Vergil achieved this degree of symbiosis with the receiving culture and if they adequately performed the work of domestication. Petrov's translation clearly failed in that, although it was the most attuned to 'inscribing' the foreign text with contemporary interpretation. However, it did not empower the Russian reader with the ability to interpret and assimilate the foreign aspects of the source text. The awkward linguistic usage was also at fault as the Russian poetic language was barely coming into its own. Fet's translation failed at making any contemporary connection. Here was Vergil's text in its most honest and well-intentioned Russian rendition, but it was 'dead' on arrival because poetically it was artificial. Briusov's text, on the other hand, while trying to convey the foreign nature of the Roman epic, became so carried away by form and outlandish linguistic usage that it alienated a very poetically attuned Russian eye and ear by trying to render the beauty and power of Vergilian masterpiece with unnatural and bizarre poetic devices. Osherov's translation most certainly did not achieve canonicity in the way it is described by Venuti. But it achieved one goal: it did address wider readerships, those who did not have professional interest in Latin, but had curiosity about why Vergil's poem was a part of the Western literary canon. In other words, Osherov's translation performed the best in terms of intercultural collaboration. It achieved the goal of 'demystifying' the foreign text and conveying 'in its own language the foreignness of the foreign text' without alienating the reader.[53] While Osherov's work never received the acknowledgement that Gnedich's *Iliad* did, nevertheless it made the reading of the Roman foundation story not an alien experience, but one that partook of the European legacy by now completely absorbed and assimilated by the Russian reading public.

NOTES

1. Among more recent translations of the *Eclogues* I would like to mention that of G. G. Starikovsky (2012). The edition is bilingual and the translation stays remarkably faithful to Latin and Vergilian prosody but may also create a 'foreignizing' effect. To be fair to all the translators of the *Eclogues*, the text because of the use of numerous plant names and agricultural details, not to mention the allusions to contemporary events, does not offer an easy reading experience in any translation.
2. Arnold (1905), 102.
3. I want to thank Stephen Harrison for asking the question about 'epic grandeur' in his discussion of English translations of the *Aeneid* at the 'Vergil's Translators' workshop in Vancouver in September 2012.
4. Hardwick (2004), 11–12.
5. I am thankful to Carlo Testa for allowing me to cite here '*Arma Virumque Cantaverunt*: A Gamut of Rhythmical Patterns in Italian, German and Russian Translations of Aeneid I 1–33 from the Renaissance to the 20th Century', presented at the 'Vergil's Translators' workshop, Vancouver, September 2012 (p. 7).
6. Testa, '*Arma Virumque Cantaverunt*'.
7. McElduff and Sciarrino (2011), 2.
8. Pym (2003), 4.
9. N. V. Gogol', 'Ob Odissee, perevodimoi Zhukovskim (pis'mo k N. M. Ya . . . vu)', *Polnoe sobranie sochinenii*, [Moscow and Leningrad], AN SSSR, 1952, 8.236–44. Available at: <http://feb-web.ru/feb/gogol/texts/ps0/ps8/ps8-236-.htm> [last visited 31 January 2013].
10. Greenfeld (1992), 244.
11. This 'linguistic nationalism' was not, however, embraced by everybody. Konstantin Batiushkov (1787–1855), a Russian poet of the Romantic era who identified mostly with the poetry of France, called 'his native tongue a foul sounding Mandarin, reeking of Asia and utterly deficient in music and beauty'. See Manning (1923), 477.
12. Greenfeld (1992), 245.
13. Hayes (2009), 2.
14. Venuti (1998), 67.
15. Armstrong (2008), 170. His italics.
16. Gasparov (1997), 128.

17. Hayes (2009), 2–3.
18. Peace (1989).
19. Fet (1888), x.
20. Fet (1888), vi.
21. Fet (1888), iii.
22. Fet (1888), vi.
23. See Fet (1888) ix.
24. See Petrovskii (1966), 295.
25. Gasparov (1971).
26. Gasparov (1971), 92. For more on translating of the *Aeneid* by Briusov see Vasilii Molodiakov's (2010) recent biography of the poet (pp. 487–8).
27. It is noteworthy that in 1944 Dmitri Mikhalchi published a short note on ancient literature in Russian translation in which he stated: 'The approximate rendition of Vergil in pre-revolutionary editions has been replaced by the new excellent translation of the *Aeneid* by that refined and exacting poet Valeri Briusov, with the co-operation of Sergei Solovyov' (Mikhalchi, 1944, 63). Briusov's translation unfortunately did not live up to expectations.
28. Scherr (2008), 244.
29. Scherr (2008), 244.
30. Briusov (1955), 253.
31. Briusov (1955), 253.
32. Cited in Hardwick (2004), 11.
33. Briusov (1955), 252.
34. Cited in Gasparov (1971), 122. The italics are Briusov's.
35. Briusov (1933), 40.
36. Gasparov (1971), 107–8.
37. Gasparov (1997), 122.
38. Gasparov (1997), 122.
39. Hardwick (2004), 17.
40. Molodiakov (1994), 266.
41. Molodiakov (1994), 266.
42. Molodiakov (1994), 267.
43. Gasparov (1971), 105.
44. Gasparov (1971), 105.
45. This 'foreignizing' tendency, as Braund has illustrated, was not characteristic solely of Briusov's translation. The translations of the *Aeneid* in French by Pierre Klossowski (1964) and in English by William Morris (1876) and Frederick Ahl as late as 2007 were also examples of 'foreignizing', or 'defamiliarization', as Ahl phrases it. See Braund (2010). I am thankful to Susanna Braund for kindly sending me the early version of her article.
46. Briusov's 'foreignizing' practices, however, despite their glaring shortcomings, had famous followers. One of them was Vladimir Nabokov

and his translation of *Evgenii Onegin* into English. In his commentary to *Onegin* Nabokov claims: 'The only concern has to be textual precision, while the music is allowed only to the degree that it does not weaken the clarity of the meaning' («Единственной заботой должна быть текстуальная точность, а музыка допустима лишь в той мере, насколько она не ослабляет ясности смысла», cited in Zverev, 2001, 378–9). Although Nabokov never directly named Briusov as his role model, except that he (ironically) calls Briusov's Vergil 'withered' («вялый»), his translation of Onegin is clearly an unfortunate product of Briusov's method where the rhythm, 'the music' of the original poem, is sacrificed to the most tediously followed 'letter' of the text. Nabokov's *Onegin* with its heavy and awkward English phrasing is as much a challenge for the reader as is Briusov's barely readable *Aeneid*.

47. Braund (2010).
48. Petrovskii (1966), 297. His italics.
49. Petrovskii (1966), 297.
50. For more information on the state of Classics in the Soviet period, see the section on Soviet Russia in Karsai et al. (2013), 3–42.
51. Braund (2010), 455.
52. Venuti (2008), 29–30.
53. Venuti (1998), 11.

Postscript

In his essay 'Eurasian Mystery' («Евразийская Мистерия») Pavel Kuznetsov writes:[1]

> Европа — роковой континент для России, Европа — роковая тема отечественной историософии: трудно отыскать русского мыслителя, у которого отсутствовало бы сочинение на эту сакраментальную тему. «Россия и Европа» — словосочетание из двенадцати букв, скрепленное союзом «и», за более чем двести лет своего литературно-философского существования превратилось в нечто особое, самостоятельное, в метафизическую дихотомию, подобную «свободе и необходимости», «причине и следствию», заняв почетное место в пантеоне парных философских категорий. Но сегодня, похоже, «роковая тема» во многом исчерпала себя: открывая очередной текст, уже заранее знаешь, что там прочтешь.

> Europe is a fateful continent for Russia, Europe is a fateful theme of our native historiosophy: it is hard to find a Russian thinker who would not have written on this sacramental theme. 'Russia and Europe'—a phrase of twelve letters, united by a conjunction 'and', for more than two hundred years of its existence in literature and philosophy, turned into something unique, independent, into a metaphysical dichotomy similar to 'freedom and necessity', 'cause and effect', and it occupies now an honoured place in the pantheon of twin philosophical categories. But today, it seems, the 'fateful theme' in many ways has exhausted itself: opening yet another text, you already know what you will read.

Vergil in Russia, at least at the beginning, was the extension of a Russian European identity. The thinkers and writers of the eighteenth and nineteenth centuries looked to Vergil as their gateway to the European continent which they perceived as the place of most progressive and forward ideas. While in the twentieth century the Russian Vergil became introverted and concerned with spiritual and personal identities, the interest in him still undoubtedly was Eurocentric.

That is why, perhaps, despite all the optimistic predictions of the twentieth-century writers we encountered in the preceding pages, the twenty-first century has not seen a significant revival of interest in Vergil. Although Greek and Latin are experiencing a renaissance of sorts and are now taught in secondary schools (which was not the case in the Soviet era), Vergil's glory has faded. That of course does not mean that the questions of identity lost their relevance. But their focus changed. There is a strong realization in Russia today that the country both geopolitically and culturally belongs as much to Asia as it does to Europe.[2] Part of that realization stems from the fact that since Peter's time Russia's identity was developed and interpreted through Western eyes, which resulted in strong resentment of Russia's marginalization. The turn to the East became then a means to cast Russia not as an epigone country, but as the dominant political and cultural power. In recent years leading Russian political figures have begun to stress a geopolitics that casts Russia in terms of Eurasianism[3] and promotes an ideology of Russian-Asian greatness away from a Western-dominated political and economic system.[4]

While the interest in the East always existed in Russia, Russia's artists and writers of the nineteenth century only visualized in their imaginations the sumptuous imaginary Asia, creating an aura, in Pushkin's words, of 'Eastern romance'.[5] By contrast, contemporary Russia's oriental connection is real and it is important. The essence of being Russian, the content of Russian patriotism, and the nature of Russian national identity no longer hinge on Russians' position in relation to the West. In a sense Europeanness became a problem for the Russian national identity, and the long anxiety about 'belonging' to the West has been replaced with the shift to 'unlearning' the West and embracing a unique Russian identity conditioned by Russia's peculiar geopolitical situation. With that shift Vergil lost his relevance. However, the history of thought is sometimes cyclical in nature. The author of this book dares to hope that Vergil will again return to the Russian literary landscape and offer with his texts an opportunity for new explorations that will satisfy the new cultural framing and craving of the modern Russia. *Pro captu lectoris, habent sua fata libelli.*[6]

NOTES

1. In *Novyi mir* no. 2 (1996). Available at: <http://magazines.russ.ru/novyi_mi/1996/2/kuzn.html> [last visited 3 March 2013].
2. Kuznetsov offers a detailed chronological survey of changing Russian attitudes towards the East and the current state of that attitude today. For a concise and detailed treatment of 'Russian orientalism', see Schimmelpenninck van der Oye (2010).
3. The term 'Eurasianism' is certainly extremely complicated and, as Marlène Laruelle observes, 'refers to historical and contemporary currents that are often difficult to identify' (Laruelle, 2008, 2).
4. Vladimir Putin, for example, emphasized that 'the greatest part of Russian territory is in Asia' and that the time has come 'to mate words with deeds together with the country of the Asia-pacific region'. See Laruelle (2008), 7–8, who also points out that neither Putin nor Boris Yeltsin before him ever used the term 'Eurasian' in the sense of a 'culturalist terminology to argue that Russia has an Asian *essence*'.
5. Allworth (2003), 158.
6. 'Books have their destinies according to the interest of the reader' (Terentianus Maurus, *De litteris, de syllabis, de metris*, verse 1286.

Viacheslav Ivanov's 'Vergils Historiosophie': Background, Translation, and Commentary

Jam nova progenies ['already a new generation'].
(Quote from Vergil, on Rafael's Sibyl frescos in
S. Maria della Pace.)

Probably due to its roots in the mythological and magical realms, the medieval age possessed a refined, reliable, and instinctual feeling for all kinds of affinities, congruencies, analogies, and elective affinities[1] that rule over the nature and the spiritual realm.

This instinctual feeling characteristic of the medieval age lends the charm of persuasive spontaneity to its universal symbolism in thought and creativity. Such a divination of essential relationships then also became obvious in the medieval assessment of Vergil: 'the greatest of the poets' ('*poetarum maximo*'). In this formulation, the apostle Paul was said to have mourned the pre-Christian poet as he was spreading tidings of Christ among the heathens, according to a hymn, 'Ad Maronis Mausoleum', that was still performed on Paul's feast day in fifteenth-century Mantua.[2] The darkly foreboding belief and superstition of the medieval era attributed to the Roman poet Vergil a deeper grasp of his final role, namely as a mediator between two cultural realms. That grasp went deeper than some of the humanist judgements about his fine-sounding verse, the lovely natural truth of his '*rura*' ['countryside'], and the lack of success in a contest with Homer inflicted upon him.[3] It was not only because of the Fourth Eclogue, whose apparent miracle converts Dante's Statius to Christianity ('per te poeta fui, per te cristiano,' *Purg.* 22.73) ['Through you I was a poet, and through you, a Christian'], that the medieval soul selected the son of Magia Polla[4] to be the ideal portrait of the theurgic poet, with the Muses' power of memory and at the same time with the Sibyl's divinatory power: the medieval soul had by necessity to be pleased by the prevailing tone of all of his creations. Characteristic in this regard is the praise of the *Aeneid* that Dante places in Statius' pronouncement (*Purg.* 21.88–92).[5] The *Aeneid* was of course for 'thousands and thousands' truly 'mother and wet nurse' ('mamma e nutrice'); above all, it was their poet's [Vergil's] special focus on the teleological and the eschatological that appealed to the spiritual constitution of the age to the same degree as antiquity looking to the past was foreign to them.

Whatever temporal position Vergil may assume—whether he, with the *Aeneid*, is striving towards the chosen promised land, or whether he sees Daphnis' resurrection mythically reflected in the world affairs of the present,[6] or even in proclaiming with holy impatience a greeting to the first rays of sunlight of the then just beginning '*novus saeclorum ordo*'[7] ['a great succession of ages is born anew'] with unprecedented hymns, '*o mihi tam longae maneat pars ultima vitae*' ['O, let the last part of a long life still linger for me'] (*Ecl.* 4.53)—Vergil, moved by a deeply felt longing, always practises that virtue [hope] undervalued by ancient wisdom that, according to the Christian 're-evaluation of all values', counts 'Hope', *Spes*, among the three cardinal virtues, as siblings of *Caritas* and *Fides*. As far as the last virtue [*Fides*] is concerned, does the *Aeneid*, in conflict with the Bible, not praise loyalty as the source of everything that is proven to be truly great and fruitful in human activity? It is amazing that this outwardly so robust age needed such an anachronistic spirituality to provide in a lasting fashion the memory of humanity with the puzzling news that it had arrived at a turning point. It seems, in fact, that the innermost strands and cell structure of this sensitive soul—one who is immediately conscious of the secret fact of standing on the threshold of a universal Transcensus[8]—will somehow transform themselves and change towards the waft of the approaching new world, so that this taciturn and shy man, the voice of his epoch, appears to even his closest friends and intellectual peers as a miraculous stranger. Do the shadows preceding the coming events reach so far back that the medieval age had already begun when great Pan, according to Plutarch's tale, had just died?[9] Does Vergil no longer belong completely to antiquity, but also already to the 'progenies' ['offspring'] who in fact know themselves to be installed in Heaven—announced by him even if not having come down from Heaven ('*caelo demittiur alto*', ['sent from the high heaven',] *Ecl.* 4.7)—and whose [offspring's] historical millennium began only after the final victories of the new religion?

'Anima cortese' (*Inf.* 2.58), 'ombra gentil' (*Purg.* 8.82)—with these words Vergil's noble and gentle nature is praised by the one who said, 'amor e il cor gentil sono una cosa' ['love and a gentle heart are but one thing'] (*Vita Nuova* 20), and one will easily agree with the disciple [Dante] that these ornate adjectives ['cortese' and 'gentil'] suit his 'dolce maestro' well—these linguistic symbols of values that quite accurately mark the high point of medieval civilization. Vergil's classical virtues are, in the light of his innate 'morbidezza' [morbidity], in the process of what Nietzsche would call the 'degeneration' or what we would call the refinement and transfiguration of Christian virtues. In his piety, based in ritual tradition, a deeper and more spiritual devotion to God shines through, one that brings him a deep trust in divine providence and direction, '*o passi graviora, dabit deus his quoque finem*' ['Oh you, who have suffered greater evils, god will put an end to these [sorrows] as well'] (*Aen.* 1.199).[10] A line from the messianic eclogue, '*incipe, parve puer, risu cognoscere matrem*' ['Little boy, begin to acknowledge your mother by smiling'],[11] reveals that the poet views the picture of pure motherliness—one can confidently say: the ideal of the Madonna—with the eyes of a Rafael.[12] His contemporaries—even those among them who were only joking—spoke of, were surprised and moved by, his '*castitas*' ['chastity']. The only amorous adventure to occur during Aeneas' wanderings, an adventure that imitates that of Odysseus[13] and is indispensable in the context of Dido's tragedy, one that would have provided Ariosto with a welcome opportunity for an elaborately decorated representation—the encounter with the royal huntress in a forest cave during a thunderstorm that interrupts the hunt—is not only dispensed with in modest and restrained manner, but is also accompanied with a harsh reprimand: '*ille dies primus leti primusque malorum causa fuit*' ['this day was the first one of destruction and the first cause of evils'].[14] Even if Vergil's Dido is as closely related to Medea of the Hellenistic 'Argonautica' [*Argonautenfahrt*] of Apollonius[15] as Camilla[16] is to the classical Penthesilea of *Aethiopis*,[17] the romanticism of Vergil's female figures contains a sense of sentimentality and chivalry that was, with good reason, taken up eagerly by Renaissance art both verbally and visually.

The horrific deeds of war, whose cruelty increases, with a nod to the Homeric canon, by the feeding of Pallas' men with the blood of sacrificed prisoners of war (*Aen.* 10.517ff.), are not carried out by Aeneas in a gruesome craze, such as was the case with Achilles drunk with anger inspired by Ares. Instead Aeneas carries out these deeds as an impersonal executor of a cruel priestly duty. For otherwise his compassion far exceeds the measure of humanity corresponding to cultural standards, be they of the Homeric age, or of the era of the gladiatorial games. The hero [Aeneas] '*ingemuit miserans graviter*' ['groans heavily as he pities'] while looking at the youthful Lausus, who as a loyal son is just as '*pius*' ['duty-bound'] as he himself and who nonetheless is to be slain by his own hand (*Aen.* 10.823).[18] At the last moment he wants to spare Turnus (*Aen.* 12.940): the gods do not allow him to do so.[19] While self-sacrifice by virtue of the love for a friend, a moving example of which we have before us in the story of Euryalus and Nisus, is classical—not, however, the expression that the entire guilt of the heroic boy consists of his '*nimium dilexit*' ['loved too much'] (*Aen.* 9.430), a strange coincidence with the '*quoniam dilexit multum*' ['because she loved a lot'] of the Gospel of Luke (7:47)[20]—and the post-mortem call of the poet to the fallen: 'the two of you are most fortunate' ('*fortunati ambo*', *Aen.* 9.446),[21] rings paradoxical in spite of the assurance of eternal fame that is to motivate him, not until Christian ecstasy, which Rome was to witness a century later, did the martyr's death seem to be similarly enviable.

So much for the poet's spiritual constitution that distances itself from that of his environment, as the first yellowish autumnal leaves contrast with the green of high summer. You can best grasp his way of thinking, however, when you look more precisely at his treatment of the philosophical historical problem in his heroic poem.

The belief which for the Greeks is clearly characterized by the content of their ideas and the inherent dialectics of basic knowledge as the point of departure for a philosophy of history—verified, by the way, by Aristotle's concurrence—is especially Aeschylus' and Herodotus' magnificent view of the Persian Wars as the pinnacle of the age-old struggle between Europe, proud of the ethical make-up of the free ancient Greeks, and Asia, with its Libyan foothills, represented by the principle of theocratic despotism. Vergil remains true to this view, in his own, truly Roman way, as one for whom Hellas represents the transmitter of tradition, *Urbs Roma*, the universal city. This perspective provides him with a deeper justification for the dispute with Carthage over world rule, a struggle that was decisive for the development of national power, and helps to interpret the divine directive that conscientiously burdened his hero with the painful dispute with Dido. To be sure, the poet must, in order to adapt classical theory to his national point of view, undertake a colossal adjustment: he removes the Trojan War, where the Greeks perceive an important moment precisely in their struggle with the Orient, from the traditional connections, blames Ilion's fall only on Laomedon and the Priamides ('*Laomedonteae luimus periuria Troiae*', *Georg.* 1.502;[22] '*culpatus . . . Paris*',[23] *Aen.* 2.602—Aeneas, as we know, belongs by lineage to an auxiliary strand of the royal house),[24] and, highlighting this artificially, has the Trojan people, after emigrating to Hesperia, appear to be the true bearers and shapers of the civic ideal ['Polisidee'] of the Occident. Yet even this very broad scope appears too narrow for the lofty flight of the poet; proof of the historical necessity and the beneficial effects of this new world regime, supplied (most insistently via Polybius) by political historiography, is not enough for him: he strives to make the case for transcendental justification of the events in order to prove for everyone the religious consecration of Roman political power.

In opposition to the early attempt at a historical synthesis, those old and new views on the cyclical course of world history attempted by Vergil (that is to say [in opposition to] the teachings [a] on ages of the world so different from each other and yet basically so insightful, [b] on the cataclysms periodically renewing the face of the earth, as Plato describes them in *Timaeus*,[25] [c] on the great year of the world and the ensuing return of all things—the *apokatastasis* of the Stoics,[26] and the expectations of the coming dawn of the '*aetas aurea*' [Golden Age] following the course of the first millennium since the destruction of Troy roused namely through the sibylline teachings) seemed [to be] more cosmological speculation than historico-philosophical insights, as they contained no rational explanation of the historical process, no matter how productive they seemed to be in forming the foundation of a mystical historiography.[27] Vergil had then listened to and pondered over the wisdom of his ancestors and over the oracles with precisely the same devout fervour as he was to have later made the legend (canonized in Rome) of the founding of Lavinium by Aeneas, which was to remove any doubts about the Trojan origin of the Roman polity, an object of a teleological re-creation interpreting both the legendary prehistory as well as the history that was to grow from it. That is to say, we see him in his first creative phase as a bucolic poet[28] enthused by eschatological ideas and dedicated to dreamlike messianic faces, traces of which he indeed already found in his pastoral poet-master, Theocritus ('Herakliskos', 86ff.);[29] however, in later years, without breaking with the inspirational premonitions of his youth, as he searches for material for a national epos, following the track of the publicly acknowledged myth linking Rome with Troy, he immerses himself in meditations on the fate of his people—a fate at once wonderful and yet evolving so logically—and then finds once again confirmation and inspiration in the model itself: he was of course also reading in his Homer (among numerous prophecies, all of which pointed to the basic notion of predestination) that famous prophecy of Poseidon about the rebirth of Troy and the descendants of Aeneas down to the latest generation to be promised political power (*Il.* 20.305ff.).[30] Could he at this point be unsure where he should begin in order to let Rome's destination shine forth most effectively in all its glory and holiness? Did not the words of that god, favourably inclined toward the Trojan name, but furious over the treason of Priam's ancient city, already contain the core of the entire future fateful development?

It was thus necessary to continue Homer's Bible, not, to be sure, solely as sacred history, in order to show how the word of the prophet had been fulfilled, but also as continuous prophecy so that, while seeing the past, one continuously has a view of the great future toward which the secretly working higher powers—'numina magna deum' ['the great powers of the gods'] (*Aen.* 2.623)—are wisely leading. To be sure, only in the light of this future was the reader able to assess the entire force of that which once was destined as rescue or as a test, and assess the complete value of that which was so laboriously achieved, by considering its most far-removed dire consequences for the fate of the world: '*tantae molis erat Romanam condere gentem*' ['of so great effort was it to found the Roman race'] (*Aen.* 1.33). Thus the Italic prophet's song of Aeneas' flight to Latium becomes a universal revelation of the divine plan of human history.

This expansion of the visual and mental sphere resulted, however, in its own retrospective force upon the mode of presentation, one that in no way represented a change for the better when seen and judged from a purely artistic point of view. The visage of the epic muse, who up to this point looked into the past without asking the Fata residing therein as to its meaning and purpose, now consciously averts its gaze to the things that then had to come—in fact, she conjures them up because she recognizes their essence—and now we, deeply touched, see as her face suddenly turns pale. Myth flows into history without becoming one with it—Torquato Tasso imitated this manner with the greatest enthusiasm—and we now stand precisely at the confluence of the two differently coloured streams. An artistic antinomy springs from the intuition transcending time, unable to overcome the latter despite the high mastery of the poet. He neutralizes the opposition by transforming mythology into teleology and theology; no surprise that their original abundance of life [*Lebensfülle*][31] is impoverished. The subjugation of the mythological under a notional heading that did not develop spontaneously from its original core resulted inevitably in a reduction of its fresh immediacy, of its naive joy in the 'free play of the living powers',[32] and resulted in a weakening of that poetic inhibition that we are accustomed to treasure as characteristic of 'pure poetry'; this is a congenital danger against which the organism of a work of art can protect itself as with an antidote by increasing the romantic element. One cannot avoid seeing the internal split between the muse and the sibylline in the final organic epic of antiquity: for, despite all the anguish and artificiality, this must indeed be considered an organically created product of its own dubious time, a time that had new meaning and that, in its own way, was one creating its own mythology. But is it not in the nature of things that a swansong should consist of something exaggerated that shows that a life is running dry? Thus it is no less beautiful because it no longer belongs to the earth, according to Plato, but glorifies Apollo, revealed to the dying in the glory of the eternal.

In this way, too, the hero's dehumanization[33] was predestined; this was so often blamed on the singer of the *Aeneid*, without properly appreciating his hieratic seriousness and his intention that reached almost beyond the limits of art: the intention aimed at presenting a being born on high, the son of a heavenly mother, indeed free of any individual desires, who finds his completely devout self anew in the fulfilment of his noble profession as bearer of the gods and saviour of his people.

In order to carry out his intention the poet had to know how to show the progression and the connections of the events in such a way as to be obvious at each step how each event—like a spark of electricity—results through contact with the earliest to the most remote promises and those occurrences only halfway revealed. To accomplish this, however, two theoretical conditions had to be met, and Vergil's drawing this double insight from the depths of his spirit capable of seeing the world in god is an irrefutable sign of his originality and the main reason for his historical impact.

He is probably the first classical poet to speak of national determination as a mission (and this was one of the two prerequisites). He claims that the individual calling of his people develops its own special idea, an idea indeed necessary to achieve economic entelechy, and [that the people] represents this idea in its historical essence. This is the intuition forming the foundation of the celebratory warning '*tu regere imperio populos, Romane, memento (hae tibi erunt artes)*' ['Roman, remember to rule the nations with your sway (these will be your arts)'] (*Aen.* 6.851ff.)[34] and combining the two opposing postulates—national self-determination, on the one hand; the universal, on the other—within one harmonious single entity.

The second prerequisite, closely connected to the first, was the belief in divine providence. If we look more closely at the content of this belief we can, at first, hardly deny the impression of a striking similarity between Vergil's ideas and the Stoic teachings of Pronoia.[35] So, for example, the Stoic Q. Lucilius Balbus' speech in Cicero ('*De natura deorum* II' ['On the nature of the gods']) seems to anticipate the poet's views on the methods, means, and goals of divine intervention in the course of history.[36] The gods take care of the human race; they desire its union with a society fulfilling the ethical ideal and especially favour those communities that contribute the most to that end. They lead and save the states and the statesmen whom they use for their high goal and teach them through inspiration and prophecies, dreams and wondrous signs. Without their help, even the greatest would not have been able to accomplish anything meaningful: '*nemo . . . vir magnus sine aliquo adflatu divino umquam fuit*' ['There was never a great man without some divine inspiration'] (II.66, 167). For this reason, Homer shows individual gods aligned with their favourite heroes as leaders and protectors. Providence directs the course of humanity towards the highest good. This is what the Stoa thought; the poet's pious notion was different. It [the Stoa] taught that the gods themselves, citizens along with humans in the common state called the Cosmos, were part of the cycle and realm of power of natural life. Stoic divination ('*anum fatidicam, Stoicorum Pronoian quam latine licet Providentiam dicere*' ['the fate bearing year, the *pronoia* of the Stoics which in Latin is called Providence']; I.8, 18) was thought to be pantheistic and derived from the perspective of a Logos immanent in nature. Vergil, however, still honouring Homer's '*Dios aisa*' ['divine fate'] and the monotheistic interpretation of this concept in Aeschylus,[37] understands '*deorum fata*' (and he already speaks of '*fatum*' in the first words of his heroic poem) as an absolutely transcendental effect of the supernatural powers that lead the select humans to their predestined salvation goal according to a preordained plan. All these beliefs were probably in agreement with native intellectual currents of his age that arose out of the mysterious Hellenistic religions. And once he has achieved this precise notion of divination he applies it to his own chosen people as a whole and to this people's individual male leaders.

And so in Vergil's presentation of the wanderings and warring struggles of *pater Aeneas* we have before us a kind of saint's life reminiscent of Bible stories—instead of a heroic saga of the classic mould full of fame and suffering resulting in a mythological justification of the respective heroic cult.[38] This life introduces an unpredictable series of deeds not all carried by that single hero, but at a later time by the inheritors of his mission. This life also merely functions as the beginning of an immeasurable exposition of fate, in the face of which Vergil sees himself more as precursor of that exposition and as God's tool than as the creator of the exposition. Like Abraham, Aeneas can only find solace during his tribulations in the distant vision of his lineage, numerous and glorious as the stars in the heavens.[39] For the *pater Indiges*[40] sees as his lineage not only his Trojan descendants, but the entire Roman people entrusted to his care. This is his state of mind in the Elysian 'Parade of Heroes' (*Aen.* 6.752–892), where he becomes acquainted face to face with the unborn succession of predestined multipliers of the Roman name, or while he watches the images presenting the future history of Rome, including the battle at Actium on the shield forged for him, as once for Achilles, by Vulcan: '*imagine gaudet, attollens umero famamque et fata nepotum*' ['he rejoiced in the imagery taking upon his shoulder the glory and the fates of his descendants'] (*Aen.* 8.730f.). Strange in all of this is that in the unworldly region of timeless being—as in God's thinking—all of these souls, chosen to carry out the divine plan and not yet become flesh, yes, even the events themselves that will only play out in long centuries to come, stand finished and firmly formed as ethereal images of light that Aeneas observes and the god of the arts depicts. And from the viewpoint of the poet there is no doubt that a determination so far-reaching is indeed reconcilable with human free will: so pure and complete is the conviction of the '*candida anima*' ['beautiful soul'], the good man being '*ut melior vir non alius quisquam*' ['such that no other man is better']—as Horace imagined and admired his character as the moral foundation of his '*ingenium ingens*' ['immense talent'] (*Sat.* 1.5.41; 1.3.32f.)[41]—that the free will of the chosen is seen as one with the will of God.

Still, not even the glory of the earthly realm, shown to the ancestor, is the bottom line of Vergilian historical wisdom. The visionary is able to see further; and his early, pleasing vision 'is ever present in his mind'. He sees a child of God in the cradle smiling at the pure mother and the whole of nature all around wondrously transformed. Who is the *puer* who causes the paradise of the Golden Age on earth to blossom anew? Is Aeon of the Greek-Egyptian mystery rites,[42] born of the virgin, whose happy news long echoes in the sounds of sibylline voices (as Norden, *Die Geburt des Kindes*, thinks),[43] probably the same young Aeon at play about whom Heraclitus (fr. 52) had whispered dark things, probably following the Orphic notion of the dallying child Dionysus-Zagreus and the representative of his father, Zeus, in ruling the world?[44] Whatever the case, in any event, Vergil is true to himself. Anchises' shadow is a reference to the final goal of the entire development in the *Aeneid*, in that he, in the 'Parade of Heroes', pointing to Augustus' shining image, says, '*hic vir, hic est ... aurea condet saecula qui rursus Latio regnata per arva Saturno quondam*' ['He is, he is the man ... who will establish again the Golden Age in Latium throughout the lands once ruled by Saturn'] (6.791f.).[45] The Pax Romana itself, according to the poet's innermost thoughts, is only a precondition and preparation for the return of the *Saturnia regna* ['the realm of Saturn'] (*Ecl.* 4.6): then 'the remaining tracks of our sins will be erased and the earth will be saved from eternal horror' (4.13ff., in Norden's translation[46]). It would hardly be possible to more precisely define in advance the teachings of the Christian era, beginning with the Golden Age of the Redeemer.

It would surely never have occurred to the Homeric Hephaestus to use his art for prophecies, something the *Aeneid* inappropriately entrusts to its journeyman's seriousness; however, no other fate was to be ordained to the author himself than that of an artist. Quite far away he [the artist] removes himself without notice from the epic military path, yes, from the whole classical view of *res gestae*, a view that up to then Mnemosyne alone had been responsible for along with her golden daughters. And the further he strays from the trodden path, the more obvious it becomes for us, who can see broader horizons, the basic convergence of his historiosophy, half concealed by the veil of poetry, with the first perfectly uniform and complete historiosophic system; a system, presented magnificently, that draws us into a long series of texts extending from the Book of Genesis to Daniel. Accordingly, Vergil's interpretation of history lies temporally between the Bible and St Augustine's masterpiece *De civitate dei*. The interpretation becomes the foundation of the medieval teaching about the meaning of Rome (cf. Dante's *Inf.* 2.20–4). It is only natural that the texts that led to this interpretation found their place in the literary treasure chest of the Christian era from the beginning. When Emperor Constantine begins the negotiations of the first ecumenical council in Nicaea by reading the messianic *Eclogues* in a Greek version, the translations of the *Aeneid* used by the oriental church fathers prove, on the other hand, that its universal meaning for Christianity has been grasped and honoured prophetically.

Following the collapse of the ecumenical ideal that fades out in Dante's treatise *De monarchia*, the newly born national consciousness mines from the same quarry, fulfilling its needs in accordance with its capacity. The songs of praise of Italy in the *Aeneid* and in the second book of the *Georgics* inspire Petrarch to patriotic hymns. Vergil's vernacular becomes a holy relic, a spiritual palladium of nations proud of belonging to the *genus Latinum* by descent, language, moral stance. If the feeling of ecumenical unity of Christian culture is to awaken anew as a stirring force, the forehead of the great poet—who combined through mediation the historical prerequisites of this comprehensive unity (Rome and the Greek Orient, classical heritage, and

New Testament hope) in his gentle sensitivity and even more gentle premonition—must be adorned with more abundant and more fragrant laurel branches than with wilted ones sprung up not in sacred groves, more abundant than our epoch—practising memory as archaeology, not experiencing time as the eternal present in the spirit—is able to weave.[47]

NOTES

The translation was first published in Jeep and Torlone (2009). It is appears here with minor modifications. The German text can be found in W. Iwanow, 'Vergils Historiosophie', in *Wege der Forschung: Wege zu Vergil*, ed. Hans Oppermann, (Darmstadt: Wissenschaftliche Buchgesellschaft, 1963), 19.220–32. It first appeared as 'Vergils Historiosophie', *Corona* 1.6 (May 1931): 761–74. Available at: <http://imwerden.de/pdf/wjatscheslaw_iwanow_corona_1931-37.pdf> [last visited 24 January 2014].

For the convenience of the reader the translation of Greek and Latin citations in Ivanov's and Fedotov's essays are provided inside the body of the text in square brackets. The latter are also used in the text of the translation to clarify some difficult passages by adding words that are not in the German text of Ivanov's essay and by including in the text of the translation German words that do not have an exact equivalent in English.

1. Here Ivanov probably alludes to the title of a novel by Goethe, *Die Wahlverwandtschaften*. Ellis Dye comments: 'It seems certain [. . .] that the chemical concept referred to in the work's title, imported from the arena of human relations into the natural sciences and here carried back into the world of human relations, refers to the unpredictable separations and realignments that may result when new personal encounters disturb an equilibrium.' 'Die Wahlverwandtschaften', *Literary Encyclopedia*, 5 December 2005. Available at: <http://www.litencyc.com/php/sworks.php?rec=true&UID=5600> [last accessed 21 January 2014].

2. Ivanov here refers to the hymn that commemorates the legend according to which St Paul visited the sepulchre of Vergil at Naples:

> Ad Maronis mausoleum
> Ductus fudit super eum
> Piae rorem lacrymae;
> Quantum, inquit, te fecissem
> Vivum si te invenissem
> Poetarum maxime.
>
> When he was led to the tomb of Maro
> He bedewed it with tears of piety

'How much would I have extolled you,'—
He said, 'if only I had found you alive,
The greatest of all poets.'

See Hare (1889), 154.

For some reason Ivanov misquotes the hymn above, replacing *maxime* (vocative case) with *maximo* (perhaps translating his own German dative 'dem größten unter den Dichtern').

3. Here Ivanov refers to the age-old comparison of the *Aeneid* with Homer's *Iliad* and *Odyssey*. For a long period of time, perhaps even well into the twentieth century, the *Aeneid* was considered inferior to its Greek epic predecessors. Even such fundamentally formative works as Richard Heinze's *Virgils epische Technik* (3rd edn, Leipzig, 1915) or the invaluable commentary of J. Conington and H. Nettleship (3rd edn, London, 1881–83) viewed Vergil to some degree as an epigone of Homer. A seminal study of V. Pöschl, *Die Dichtkunst Virgils: Bild und Symbol in der Aeneis* (3rd edn, Berlin, 1977), took a more revolutionary approach by interpreting Vergil's epic as a truly Roman poem which emulates rather than imitates Homer and which has a powerful dark undercurrent.

4. Servius gives Vergil's mother's name as Magia; Probus, as Magia Polla. For more information on Vergil's parents, see Levi (1998).

5. The lines in Dante's *Purgatorio* where Statius praises the *Aeneid* are 97–102: 'de l'Eneida dico, la qual mamma / fummi e fummi nutrici poetando: / sanz'essa non fermai peso di drama' ('I speak of the *Aeneid*; when I wrote / verse, it was mother to me, it was nurse; / my work, without it, would not weigh an ounce'; trans. A. Mandelbaum, *The Divine Comedy of Dante Alighieri*, Berkeley: University of California Press, 1980; available at: <http://dante.ilt.columbia.edu/books/dc_man delbaum/pur_21.html>) [last accessed 23 March 2014].

Publius Papinius Statius (40/50–96) is mostly known for his *Thebaid*, the subject of which is the Theban cycle of myths, famous from Sopho-cles' Theban plays (*Oedipus Rex, Oedipus at Colonus, Antigone*). It was above all in the Middle Ages that Statius achieved great popularity. One medieval legend had Statius converting to Christianity upon reading the Fourth Eclogue (Conte, 1994, 487). That legend found its reflection in Dante's words cited here by Ivanov. Pamela Davidson (1989), 44, also suggests that Statius presented special interest for Ivanov, because Thebes was the birthplace of Bacchus and centre of his cult. The figure of Statius then linked together 'the cult of Dionysus to Christianity through the intermediary of Vergil's influence'.

6. Daphnis' death and resurrection is the subject of Vergil's Fifth Eclogue. In this poem two shepherds, a younger and an older, Mopsus and Menalcas, compete in a singing contest. Mopsus performs a song about the death of

Daphnis, whereas Menalcas offers 'The Apotheosis of Daphnis'. The phrase 'world affairs of the present' ('Weltereignissen der Gegenwart') refers to an interpretation of Daphnis' resurrection in Menalcas' song in the light of Roman history. Menalcas was supposed to establish a cult in Daphnis' honour, and his altars were to be built together with the altars for Phoebus (*ecce duas tibi, Daphni, duas altaria Phoebo*, 'look, Daphnis, two altars for you and two for Phoebus': *Ecl.* 5.66). In Servius' commentary on this passage we read *et quibusdam videtur per allegoriam Caesarem dicere, qui primus divinos honores meruit et divus appellatus est* ('to some it seems that through allegory he [Vergil] is talking about Caesar because he was the first one who earned divine honours and was declared a god'). This interpretation is disputed by Clausen, who thinks that the identification of Daphnis and Caesar is rather 'grotesque' and does not do justice to the 'allusiveness and complexity of the poem' (Clausen, 1994, 152). Ivanov's evocation of and reliance on that interpretation serves his goal of viewing Vergil as a poet with prophetic vision.

7. A quote from Vergil *Ecl.* 4.4–5: 'Ultima Cumaei venit iam carminis aetas; / magnus ab integro saeclorum nascitur ordo' ('The last age of Cumaean prophecy is coming / A great succession of centuries is born anew').

8. Ivanov's own term.

9. Plutarch's *De defectu oraculorum* 419B ('On the failure of oracles') contains a story attributed to someone named Epitherses, a grammar teacher. He narrates how his ship sailing for Italy approached the small island of Paxi in the Ionian sea. A mysterious voice emanating from the island commanded the pilot of the ship, an Egyptian named Thamos, to sail to Palodes, another island nearby, where he was to proclaim that the great god Pan was dead. When the wind was favourable, Thamos drove the ship close to Palodes and shouted: 'The great Pan is dead (*Pan ho megas tethneken*)'. In response a great sound of lamentation resounded through the dark sky and the forests, although there was nobody seen on the shores of the island. Plutarch then relates that this story reached Rome and provoked the curiosity of Tiberius Caesar, who summoned Thamos to question him and then dispatched scholars to investigate the story further. This event occurred perhaps between 14 and 37 CE, though the Christian tradition makes it coincide with the birth of Christ. Eusebius Pamphili, fourth-century bishop of Caesarea, even suggested that Pan in the story stands for Christ. This view continued to gain faith and was strongly reinforced centuries later by Rabelais, whose Pantagruel in retelling the story promoted Eusebius' interpretation. Ivanov's interpretation of the story is consistent with his interpretation of the Fourth Eclogue. The

story and its meaning have attracted the attention of many modern writers since 1890. See Irwin (1961).

10. Aeneas utters these words in an attempt to console his comrades after a devastating storm which left them shipwrecked.

11. *Ecl.* 4.60.

12. Consistent with his overall perception of the Fourth Eclogue, Ivanov prefers to read these Vergilian lines as a metaphor for the Virgin Mary and Christ.

13. Ivanov most likely means here Odysseus' encounter with Nausicaa on the island of the Phaiakians in *Odyssey* 6. Just like Aeneas in Carthage, Odysseus finds himself shipwrecked on the island of Scheria, where he is welcomed by the princess Nausicaa, who expresses romantic interest in him. Unlike Aeneas, however, Odysseus wants to go home to his wife and does not encourage Nausicaa's advances.

14. *Aen.* 4.169. This line refers to the consummation of love between Dido and her Trojan guest in the cave where they had to hide during the hunt from the storm arranged by Juno, who wanted to delay Aeneas' arrival in Italy. Dido becomes a 'casualty' in the great divine design for the foundation of the Roman race. We might disagree with Ivanov's opinion that Vergil dismisses the whole episode with Dido with a reprimand. If anything Vergil feels enormous sympathy for the Carthaginian queen, whose love for Aeneas proves to be her undoing. See Ross (2007), 32–5, and Spence (1999), 94–5.

15. Apollonius of Rhodes was a Hellenistic poet, a contemporary of Theocritus, who lived in Alexandria at the court of Ptolemy III (246–222 BCE). He was the author of the *Argonautica*, the only epic poem that survived from Hellenistic times. The myth of Medea helping Jason to retrieve the Golden Fleece (especially the third book of the poem) might have influenced Vergil's depiction of Dido as a powerful queen in love with a foreign hero.

16. Camilla is a legendary Volscian maiden who supported Turnus in his fight against Aeneas and was killed by the Etruscan Arruns. Vergil narrates her story in *Aen.* 7.803; 11.539–828.

17. *Aethiopis* is a lost Greek epic poem of the eighth–seventh century BCE which supposedly covered the events of the Trojan War after the *Iliad*. The *Aethiopis* was sometimes attributed by the ancient writers to Arctinus of Miletus. According to a summary of the *Aethiopis* given by an unknown Proclus in his *Chrestomathy* and a few other references, Penthesilea, the Amazon warrior, arrived to help the Trojans fight the Greeks after Hector's death and was killed by Achilles, who then mourned her (*Aethiopis*, fr. I Allen, in N. G. L. Hammond and H. H. Scullard, eds, *Oxford Classical Dictionary*, 2nd edn, Oxford: Clarendon, 1970, 798).

18. Lausus, the son of Mezentius, the exiled Etruscan king, was killed by Aeneas in Book 10. It is noteworthy that Ivanov sees all these 'victims' of the *Aeneid* (Ross, 2007, 32) in the light that highlights and elevates the mission of Aeneas. It has to be noted, however, that Vergil requires more of his readers. In his epic the grief and loss of the young lives in the war is ubiquitously emphasized—see Galinsky (1996), 247, and Conte (1994), 283–4. Pallas, Dido, Camilla, Lausus, Nisys, and Euryalus: all of these 'casualties' of Aeneas' mission Ivanov prefers to interpret in the context of the great providential cycle of history whose harbinger is Aeneas.

19. Turnus, king of the Rutulians, led the Italian forces against Aeneas, since Aeneas claimed Lavinia, Turnus' betrothed. At the end of Book 12 Aeneas faces Turnus in the final battle closely fashioned on one between Hector and Achilles in the *Iliad*. Turnus admits his defeat and begs Aeneas not to kill him. Aeneas hesitates but then does go on to kill Turnus. It is not the gods, however, as Ivanov suggests here, that do not allow Aeneas to spare his arch-enemy. Rather, Aeneas catches a glimpse of the sword belt once won by his ally and protégé Pallas, who was killed and stripped of the belt by Turnus. The sight of the belt turns Aeneas' indecision into revenge for his slaughtered friend. The end of the *Aeneid* provoked much debate as to the meaning of that final and unnecessary killing for understanding Vergil's authorial intent: was it meant to glorify Roman valour or serve as a warning about the brutalizing effects of war? See Conte (1994), 284. For a comprehensive treatment of Book 12 and the final battle between Turnus and Aeneas, see Putnam (1999).

20. The context is the story of the sinner who anointed Jesus' feet.

21. The example from the *Aeneid* that Ivanov uses here to argue Vergil's anticipation of the Christian ideal of martyrdom is not very convincing. The story of the two Trojan youths Nisus and Euryalus is one of a romantic, homoerotic love and as such would hardly fit into the idea of Christian martyrdom. '*Nimium dilexit*' is a quote from Nisus' speech as he tries to protect his friend from the attack of the Rutulians, who catch Nisus and Euryalus leaving the Rutulian camp after a killing expedition where they snatched a bright enemy helmet and garments: '*me, me, adsum qui feci, in me convertite ferrum, / o Rutuli! Mea fraus omnis, nihil iste nec ausus / nec potuit; caelum hoc et conscia sidera testor; / tantum infelicem nimium dilexit amicum*' ('Against me, me, the one who did it, turn your sword, / Oh, Rutulians! Mine is the treachery, this one never dared / Nor was he able to commit it; I call the heavens and the stars as my witnesses: / That is how much he loved his unhappy friend). He says that Euryalus was too young to be the mastermind behind the attack and the plunder, and that his only fault was his

excessive love for him, Nisus. Rudich (2002b), 348–9, aptly points out that *fortunati ambo* should not be understood as a parallel to the envy-provoking ecstasy of a martyr's death but in terms of Platonic *eros*.

22. The full quote is: '*satis iam pridem sanguine nostro / Laomedonteae luimus periuria Troiae*' ('long since we have paid with our blood for the sacrileges of Laomedon's Troy'). Instead of using the neutral 'Trojan' or 'Dardanian' here, Vergil chooses to remind his readers of King Laomedon, Priam's father, who tricked the gods twice by perjuring himself and caused the first destruction of Troy. See Mack (1999), 140.

23. This quote is taken from Venus' appeal to Aeneas when he amid burning Troy sees Helen and wants to kill her for Troy's destruction. Venus in fact says: '*Non tibi Tyndaridis facies invisa Lacaenae / Culpatusve Paris, divum inclementia, divum, / Has evertit opes sternitque a culmine Troiam*' ('It is not the hated face of the Spartan daughter of Tyndareus that you must blame, nor Paris, but the cruelty of the gods, the gods, destroys these riches and topples Troy from its height'). Ivanov's choice of the first quote supports his argument, but this quote does not. Paris, according to Venus, his most eager supporter, should *not* be blamed for the Trojan disaster.

24. Aeneas was the son of Anchises, brother of Priam, king of Troy, father of Hector, the champion of the Trojans.

25. It is perhaps not surprising that out of all the Platonic dialogues Ivanov references only *Timaeus* in this essay. In the *Timaeus* Plato presents an elaborately wrought account of the formation of the universe. The universe, he proposes, is the product of the handiwork of a divine Craftsman ('Demiurge', *dêmiourgos*, 28a6), whose Intellect (*noûs*) fashions the perfect universe from the disorderly state initially prone to erratic movement. For more, see Tarán (1971).

26. *Apokatastasis* translated from Greek means 'a complete restoration, re-establishment'. In Stoic philosophy *apokatastasis* is reconstitution of the Cosmos by the perfect Logos (identified with Zeus) after the stars and the planets return to their original position aligned with Cancer. In Christian doctrine the concept was promoted by Origen of Alexandria, who understood it as a reunion of all souls with God.

27. This sentence presented a challenge in rendering it in English. Thus it is divided into constituent parts indicated by the letters in square brackets in order to clarify the meaning.

28. The *Eclogues* or *Bucolics* are Vergil's earliest surviving poetic corpus, written sometime between 42 and 39 BCE—see Conte (1994), 263. Closely fashioned after the bucolic idylls of the Hellenistic poet Theocritus of Syracuse (*fl.* third century BCE), it, nonetheless, included a wider range of specifically Roman experience such as politics, civil war, and contemporary poetic debates.

29. Ivanov is referring here directly to Theocritus of Syracuse and his *Idyll* 24. In this poem there are clear points of identification between Ptolemy Philadelphus and the ten-month-old baby hero Herakles (Herakliskos). Ivanov sees this as an inspiration for Vergil's 'messianic vision' of the miraculous child in the Fourth Eclogue. Theocritus is considered the father of the so-called 'bucolic' genre and his influence on Vergil's early poetic corpus is substantial. However, *Idyll* 24 does not strictly belong to Theocritus' 'bucolic' corpus, but is more of part of his 'court poetry'.

30. In *Il.* 20.302–4, 306–8, Aeneas is rescued by the gods from the murderous hands of Achilles. The following lines spoken by Poseidon decide his fate and might have been the starting point for Vergil's creation of his hero as the founder of the Roman race: 'It is destined that he shall be the survivor, / that the generation of Dardanos shall not die, without seed / obliterated... For Kronos' son has cursed the generation of Priam, / and now the might of Aineias shall be lord over the Trojans, / and his sons' sons, and those who are born of their seed hereafter' (*The Iliad of Homer*, trans. R. Lattimore, Chicago and London: University of Chicago Press, 1951; paperback edn, 1961). The evocation of this prediction in the *Iliad* by Ivanov demonstrates yet again his constant search for continuity and the syncretic view. Here he sees the relationship between the *Iliad* and the *Aeneid* as parallel to the one between the Old and New Testaments. See Rudich (2002b), 346–7.

31. Ivanov may have borrowed this term from Friedrich Schiller, who had a considerable influence on him. The Grimms' *Deutsches Wörterbuch* in fact has Schiller's poem *Götter Griechenlands* ('Greece's gods'), l. 11, as the first citation for *Lebensfülle* (q.v.). This entry represents the earliest use of the term maybe even coined by Schiller.

32. Ivanov puts 'freien Spiel der lebendigen Kräfte' in quotation marks, but does not indicate the source of the quotation. He most likely alludes here again to Schiller, who in a prologue to his play *Die Braut von Messina* writes: 'Der höchste Genuss aber ist die Freiheit des Gemüts in dem lebendigen Spiel aller seiner Kräfte' ('the highest pleasure is, however, freedom of the mind in the living play of all its powers'). See 'Über den Gebrauch des Chors in der Tragödie', <http://www.wissen-im-netz.info/literatur/schiller/messina/chor.htm> [last visited 23 February 2013].

33. The German word Ivanov uses here is 'Entpersönlichung'. We translated it as 'dehumanization' with an understanding that it is not quite what it means in German but suggesting that it is what Ivanov means to emphasize in Aeneas' transformation by the end of the *Aeneid*, which some critics found unsettling in Vergil's hero.

34. These words Anchises addresses in the underworld to his son in Book 6, making explicit the emblematic function of Aeneas as a Roman hero.

35. *Pronoia*, Roman *providentia*, is the Stoic concept of divine providence or fate. In Greek *pronoia* means 'planning in advance, foresight'. For the Stoics, unlike the Epicureans, the universe is made by the controlling power of God, who is equated to uncreated and imperishable nature or universal *Logos* (Reason). Humans merely act out the plan prescribed by Nature's *pronoia* (providence). See Long (1974), 168–9.

36. Ivanov recalls here a celebrated passage of Cicero's treatise *On the Nature of the Gods* which he places in the mouth of Lucilius Balbus as an exposition of Stoic theology.

37. Ivanov is most likely referring to Aeschylus' tragedy *Agamemnon*, the first play in his *Oresteia* trilogy, in which the chorus extols Zeus as the only powerful god who ordains everybody's fate.

38. This view of Aeneas' character is certainly in tune with Ivanov's overall reading of the *Aeneid* as a prophetic poem on the threshold of upholding Christian values. However, that view ignores (and knowingly so) the complexity of Vergil's hero and the ambivalence of the authorial intent. While Aeneas' heroic quest is a study in *pietas* ('devotion to his duty'), it is also contemplation on the brutalizing effects that war has on his character. See Putnam (1999), 223–5, and Ross (2007), 26–7.

39. In this parallel between Aeneas and Abraham we can undoubtedly detect the influence of Solov'ev's approach to Vergil.

40. According to Livy (Book 1) Jupiter Indiges was a name given to the deified Aeneas. Ovid in the *Metamorphoses* (14.581ff.) uses the term *Pater Indiges* or simply *Indiges*. The word *indiges* in Latin seems to be of doubtful meaning. What is beyond any doubt is that *indigetes* (the plural of *indiges*) means a certain class of Roman gods. Scholars have suggested several interpretations of what these gods actually represented: from deities of extremely limited function to native Roman deities as distinct from imported, foreign gods. Ivanov seems to support the latter interpretation and views Aeneas as a truly Roman god who extends and then converts his Trojan lineage in the 'promised land' of Italy. See N. G. L. Hammond and H. H. Scullard (eds), *Oxford Classical Dictionary*, 2nd edn (Oxford: Clarendon, 1970), *Indigetes*.

41. Ivanov is referring here to two of Horace's *Sermones*. The first one (*Satires* 1.5) tells the story of Horace's journey from Rome to Brundisium in 37 BCE, when the poet accompanied Maecenas with the goal (not explicitly stated in the poem) of achieving reconciliation between Antony and Octavian. The exact lines Ivanov has in mind here refer to Horace's meeting on the road with Plotius, Varius, and Vergil, to whom Horace refers with praise: '*animae qualis neque candidiores / terra tulit neque quis me sit devinctior alter*' ('persons of which kind the earth has

never carried anyone more beautiful and nobody else is closer to me'). The second poem (*Satires* 1.3) is primarily concerned with how to handle the shortcomings (*vitia*) of human beings and contains lines 32–4 that refer to the idea that looks can be deceiving: '*at est bonus, ut melior vir non alius quisquam, at tibi amicus, at ingenium ingens inculto latet hoc sub corpore*' ('but he is a good man, and no other man better, but he is your friend, and great talent hides underneath this coarse body').

42. The work of Johann Jacob Bachofen (1815–87) *Mutterrecht und Urreligion* may have influenced Ivanov also. Bachofen talks both about these mystery services and Aeneas claiming the centrality of the Trojan hero for the Romans as a representation of their emancipation from their oriental origins.

43. Eduard Norden (1868–1941) was one of the most influential scholars of his generation, whose work on Vergil influenced numerous classical scholars. His book *Die Geburt des Kindes: Geschichte einer religiösen Idee* ('The birth of the child: the history of a religious idea': Leipzig, Berlin: B. G. Teubner, 1924) was 'impressive and obscurely learned' (Clausen, 1994, 129) and without a doubt formative for Ivanov's reading of the Fourth Eclogue. Norden connected this poem with Eastern theology and ritual, especially with two religious festivals celebrated annually in Alexandria—that of Helios on 24–5 December (Christmas Eve) and that of Aeon on 6 January (Epiphany). See Clausen (1994), 129, who points out that Norden made 'a religious or mystical interpretation of the Fourth Eclogue seem intellectually respectable'. For more on Aeon, see note 44.

44. Fr. 52 of Heraclitus preserved by Hippolytus and confirmed by Lucian reads: 'Aeon is a child at play, playing draughts; the kingship is a child's.' The meaning of the word 'aeon' in this fragment presents some difficulty. G. S. Kirk (1954), xiii, maintains that 'in early contexts . . . the word is most likely to refer to human lifetime, perhaps with the special connotation of the destiny which is worked out by the individual during his lifetime'. The Orphic myth of Dionysus Zagreus that Ivanov refers to here presents some difficulty because we do not have anything approaching a complete narrative about it earlier than Olympiodorus, a Neoplatonic philosopher of the sixth century CE. Olympiodorus narrates the myth briefly in his commentary on a passage from Plato's *Phaedo*, in which Socrates and his friends are debating the justification of suicide. Many other authors—some as early as Pindar and Plato—offer details or variations of what Olympiodorus says. In sum the story of Dionysus Zagreus is a story of death and rebirth. According to this story Dionysus was the child of Zeus and Persephone who was to succeed Zeus and be declared the new king of the cosmos.

The jealous Titans, encouraged by Hera, killed and dismembered the god-child, cooked his flesh, and ate it. Zeus punished the Titans and brought the child back to life. For detailed discussion of the sources and variations of the myth, see Graf and Johnston (2007), 66–93.

45. In Vergil's *Aeneid* the myth of Saturn follows the traditional story of blending him with the Greek Kronos, Zeus's (Jupiter's) father (*Aen.* 8.319ff). In the mythological tradition Kronos (Saturn) was the ruler of the universe in the Golden Age. After being overthrown by Zeus (Jupiter), he came to Italy. However, the important feature of Vergil's Golden Age is that, as Karl Galinsky (1996), 93, has observed, it 'comes to connote a social order rather than paradisiac state of indolence' characteristic of the Golden Age before Jupiter and seen as a 'slothful existence that required no mental or physical exertion'. It is also noteworthy that Ivanov avoids any political interpretation of the passage, although it is a part of the panegyric to Augustus and his Pax Romana.

46. Norden: 'werden etwa noch vorhandene Spuren unserer sünde getilgt und wird die Erde erlöst werden von dem ewigen Graus'.

47. The final paragraph of Ivanov's essay on Vergil recalls Ivanov's and Gershenzon's *Correspondence from Two Corners*. See Davidson (2006).

Georgii Fedotov's 'On Vergil' («О Виргилии»), Translated from Russian

A century of French romanticism coincided with the 2000th anniversary of Vergil's birth. It allows us if not to see at least to palpably sense the significance of such phenomena as classicism and romanticism. Even now romanticism is already controversial, outdated, although not completely outlived. Will anyone ever celebrate Hugo's 1,000th anniversary? Romanticism is an episode, taste, perhaps even an illness of youth. Classicism is no longer a school or a tradition, but rather blood. It is the inherent sign of culture. Western culture is a culture that has grown out of Vergil. To be more precise: out of the Bible and Vergil. But today I am talking about Vergil.

The young Augustine recited, as a part of a school assignment, the monologue of the abandoned Dido, and her suffering moved him to tears. The mature Dante, a stern emigrant and a mystical lover, chose Vergil to be his guide in the Inferno, to be his teacher of ethics, a harbinger of Grace: *Tu duce, tu maestro*. The practical politician Pitt, justifying in the House of Commons his powerlessness to save the life and the throne of Louis XVI,[1] could not find more eloquent, more commonly accessible language than Dido's sorrowful lament over Priam's kingdom: *Me si fata meis* (4.340).[2] It is not a problem if Pitt stumbles in his citation; the whole auditorium can finish it for him.

In the Middle Ages, when Vergil was known by heart, it was customary to compose whole poems (cantos) from the verses and half-verses of the *Aeneid*. Thousands of young men in Oxford and Cambridge could do the same in our days. We Russians are not attentive enough to this most permanent fact of Western culture, and we are always amazed when we read that Spencer, for example, wrote poetry in Latin.[3] What do Spencer and poetry have in common? But Vergil is precisely the common language of the West—what unites St Augustine, Dante, Pitt, and Spencer. The Bible may be forgotten; Vergil remains.

That is why there is so much measured pace—the cadence of the hexameter—and so much virtue in the battle of Aeneas, and in Western history.

But what is Hecuba to us?[4] Are we, as Scythians, even invited today to the feast? It seems that Vergil was always foreign to the Russian soul. Out of millions of Russian youths who have gone through Vergil, how many grew to love him? Briusov, perhaps, is the only poet in Russia captivated by Vergil and able to adequately translate him. Fet's weak *Aeneid* testifies that even this poet brought up on classical antiquity found Vergil's spirit foreign to him.[5] However, let us not come to rushed conclusions. Psychological distance does not imply absence of love. The spirit looks for something alien to overcome itself. If Russian culture is not narrowly nationalistic but universal, if it is developed within the controversies of unusual breadth, it has to find a place for Vergil. And indeed it did find that place.

The shadow of Vergil—perhaps even invisibly—stood over the Russian Empire. In the classical era of its might Latin genius already palpably revealed itself. In the cold and lavish halls of the Hermitage, in the Pompeian frescos on the walls of Nicholas's palaces, in the measured weight of the *History of the Russian State*[6]—Vergilian copper resounds.

'*Tu regere imperio populos, Romane, memento*' ['Roman, remember to rule the nations with your sway'].[7]

The very conception of the empire was classical. The mission of Peter-Nicholas I repeated the mission of Augustus: to unite a number of nations under the rule of a crown-bearing nation, enlightened by a foreign culture—*excudent alii* ['the others will cast'][8]—but faithful to its religious treasures: the penates of mysterious Troy. Isn't it remarkable that the summit of the empire coincides with the age of classicism in Russia: the era of Batiushkov, Delvig, Pushkin?[9] Pushkin's verse can be understood only in the context of Latin verse.[10] Parny, Voltaire, or Byron cannot explain it. As Ovid resounds in the strophes of *Eugene Onegin*, so does Vergil in Pushkin's odes,[11] in that very high style which was later adopted by Briusov. Pushkin himself, of course, was much more indebted to Ovid and Catullus[12] than to Vergil. The youthful circle of classicism during Alexander's era was held captive by Augustan eroticism and through it longed for Greece.[13] That longing was satisfied only in our days by Viacheslav Ivanov. But the voice of Vergil began to sound every time a sentimental and romantic poet approached the theme of empire.

It is strange, but even before the Russian muse entered Vergil's school, the Russian Church did. During the long time of Kievan 'rule' the Latin school—from Vergil to Thomas—educated the Russian clergy. Only in the 1820s did the Russian language replace Latin in the seminary. Now the Russian Church remembers these days as 'Latin imprisonment'. But can the chiselled thunder of Philaretus'[14] word be imagined without Vergil? Up until the middle of the last century every page of Russian spiritual literature testified to the noble nature of that Latin school. From the middle of the century the degeneration of the language becomes unstoppable. The demise of the Latin spiritual school coincides with the extinguishing of the Gallic gentry, also raised on the old Latin yeast. As a result we see that onset of wildness, that barbarization of the Russian speech, which Symbolism found at the beginning of the twentieth century.

Let us agree that for Orthodoxy the Vergilian school was indeed a strange and inappropriate garment—not so with the Russian Empire, which it fits perfectly.

With the death of the Russian Empire will Vergil have any meaning for us?

Try to reread him and you will see how much closer and more beneficial his seemingly cold muse has become to us. Now, in inconsolable sorrow over our lost fatherland, we for the first time hear Aeneas' longing. We understand that the *Aeneid*, like any great epos, is a song about death, together with achieving the promise of salvation. 'Lost and regained homeland.' How can we without deep emotion read the second book—about the burning of Troy, about the last and hopeless battle of Aeneas? '*Vidi Hecubam centumque nurus Priamumque per aras / sanguine foedantem quos ipse sacraverat ignes*' ['I saw Hecuba and her hundred daughters and (I saw) Priam near the altars defiling with his blood the fires which he himself had consecrated'].[15]

Yes, we saw Priam, killed in the blood of his own son. Yes, we escaped the fire with the old man Anchises and the sacred treasures of Troy. It was we who fought with the Harpies for the meagre remnants of food. It was we who ate our 'tables'. We auspiciously passed by the Cyclopes and Scylla, but how many old men have we buried, how many friends are missing swept away in the waves. *Palinurus in undis*! ['Palinurus amid the waves'].[16]

Quae regio in terris nostri non plena laboris? ['What region in the world is not aware of our toil?'][17]

It was we who at Dido's feet repeated the now legendary story of Troy's demise, and no magic of foreign beauty can replace for us the image of our resurrected land.

Our sorrow is more painful, because we cannot, unlike Aeneas, detach ourselves from our native land. We cannot build Pergamum on the 'penates' alone. Our Hesperia is in the East. We are doomed, like shadows, to return to the smoking remains, and the horrors of the previous night do not leave our memory. But if only once we had dared in our travels with Vergil to step over the almost insurmountable threshold of the seventh book, perhaps we could have found a source of courage in the struggles and toils of the hero, who soars over his suffering.

The thousand-year-old Vergilian wine is like Auerbach's magic cellar:[18] everyone chooses a drink according to his own tastes—and there is no danger of burning oneself. That is the nature of classicism: Vergil, Pushkin, or the white ray of the sun.

Hardly any of us reads the *Bucolics* or the *Georgics*; almost nobody. That is understandable: the *Aeneid* cannot be replaced by Homer, but we prefer Hesiod and Theocritus to their Latin pupil. However, anyone unfamiliar with the *Bucolics* cannot even imagine how much tenderness and lyricism was hidden in Vergil's youthful muse, before he locked himself in the armour of duty and toil. The love complaints of the shepherds help us understand better the muffled moans of Aeneas and Dido. They give us a key to the mysterious fate of Vergil.

Its mystery is not in the superficial texture of life events—in fact his life was surprisingly uneventful—but in the difficulty to discern any personal sources of this objective, national epic. Vergil is inseparable from Rome, and his poetic oeuvre is inseparable from the political deeds of Augustus. It is easy to dismiss this mystery with a fashionable phrase: 'social commission'. It is on Pollio's commission that the poet sang of Arcadian love, and on Maecenas' commission of Italian agriculture; but on Augustus' commission he sang of piety and the feat of Aeneas. Agriculture, piety, and the feats of the legions were equally necessary to the growing structure of the empire. But is Vergil only a skilful craftsman, only a Roman Briusov,[19] whipping his dream like a mule to move it along?[20]

There is a troubling duplicity in his own personal fate, which perhaps explains the fate of his muse.

A son of a peasant from the environs of Mantua,[21] an awkward, shy provincial, he always retained his love of the land, and Maecenas was not wrong to entrust to his lyre the works and days of the farmer. The magnificence of Rome is forever linked with the Italian land and with the Italian gods. It is on the farmers' patriotism that Augustus, the reformer, is building the spiritual ideal of his empire.

But, strangely enough: that plebeian cannot stand the air of northern Italy. His weak health drives him south—'*Calabri rapuere*' ['The Calabrians took . . .'][22]—to Campania, to Sicily, to the sacred land of Magna Graecia. It is hard to believe that only the invasion of Augustan veterans would have chased him away from the shores of Mincio. The longing for Theocritus' Greece drove him south, that longing for the blessed, unreal land of love and song. The Lombard peasant[23] had his heart wounded with longing for Greece. He gives to it his ultimate sacrifice—his life—when, sick, he undertakes a journey to his promised land, so that he can burn out under the blazing sun of Megara. To Greece and to Troy he gave that sacrifice because his ultimate goal was to reach the Trojan shores.[24] But what are the ruins of Troy for him but a romantic ghost of the East rising for him as it does for us behind Hellas' shadow? That is how Vergil, a romantic, is revealed in the victorious classical poet.

However, his eternal life is connected precisely with the victory of a classic. Vergil brought his dreams to the altar of national gods. He killed in himself his pity for the Greeks—Aeneas' enemies. He forgave Augustus for the confiscation of his paternal land, just as Italy forgave him for stealing its freedom. Together with his people he sees in Caesar and Augustus gods, who granted everyone, after so many years of excruciating civil war, peace and glory. The genius of Rome awakens in his heart, and he devotes his life in its entirety to serving the Roman idea. His contemporaries Ovid and Horace, also summoned by the Muses, did not succeed in overcoming Epicureanism, careless eroticism, irresponsible scepticism.[25] That was done by a peasant poet connected with his native land in a very different way than Horace was. That is why he could become an educator not only of the last sons of Rome, but also of the new Israel, which shared Roman land.

I do not want to appear annoying, but how can one avoid saying that Vergil's fate was full of foreboding meaning for the fate of Russian culture, and especially for its present state?

One thing is certain: if the mysterious heart attuned to the voices and forebodings were not beating behind the shield and the armour of classicism, how could Vergil have become the Sibyl predicting Christ? The confusing secret of the Fourth Eclogue in its bucolic surroundings can be solved only through insurmountable romantic longing, open to the prophesy of dreams.

Jam redit et Virgo, redeunt Saturnia regna ['Now the Virgin returns and the reign of Saturn returns'].[26]

The political ideals, the awaiting of the Augustan *Pax Romana*, are whimsically combined with the eschatological dream of the Golden Age, where nature and man are in harmony, and where traces of the old sin are eliminated, *sceleris vestigia nostra* ['our traces of crime'].[27] It was not random and it was not artificial that the patristic and medieval theologians linked Vergil's prophecy with the Infant of Bethlehem. Vergil expressed all the longing of the ancient world for the Redeemer, all the vague expectations, condensed in the age of Augustus into one tense mystical invocation. The ritualistic piety of Aeneas in the end is nothing but a working transformation of the white coal in the Fourth Eclogue.[28]

Will Vergil ever be revived for Russia? I am afraid not. Our road is different—the broad, meted road of history from which ever since the time of Muscovy we have disobediently deviated. Our road does not go through Troy-Rome, but through Greece, which gave us the word, which gave us the prayer, and, in the last hour of our history, opened a mysterious depth of prophetic and eternally self-renewing beauty.

Let the poet who resurrected for us the mystical Greece be unfaithful to her for the sake of Rome. Only he showed us that renouncing Greece is renouncing Russia. For us Vergil will never replace Homer, whose delectable verses in Russian hexameter have lulled our hearing since childhood.[29]

But in the hour of a solemn feat, when we will be required to give up everything vital and dear, beauty itself, we can draw our inspiration from the toils of a hero wandering over all the seas and lands in search of his fallen homeland.

O patria, o divum domus Ilium et incluta bello moenia Dardanidum! ['O homeland, o gods' abode Ilium and the ramparts of the Trojans famous in war'].[30]

NOTES

First published in Paris in Числа ('Numbers') 2–3 (1930). The Russian text can be found in Fedotov (1952), 215–22. Available at: <http://odinblago. ru/o_vergilii> [last visited 23 March 2014].

1. Here Fedotov is referring to the British politician William Pitt (the Younger) who tried in the House of Commons to defend Louis XVI, toppled by the French Revolution, and expelled the French ambassador upon hearing of the king's execution in 1793. We can easily see why these events were in Fedotov's mind as he was writing in his forced emigration after the events of 1917.

2. Here Fedotov makes a mistake. The line he cites does not belong to Dido but to Aeneas, who in his response to her accusation of betrayal laments that he cannot live his life according to his own will (4.340ff.): *'Me si fata meis paterentur ducere vitam / auspiciis et sponte mea componere curas, / urbem Troianam primum dulcisque meorum / reliquias colerem'* ('If the fates were to allow me to lead my life / According to my own decisions and to settle my concerns by my own will, / I would first of all take care of the Trojan city and the sweet remains / Of my people').

3. This anxiety about Russia's lack of attention to the important figures of Western culture recalls Chaadaev. Fedotov seems to be making a pun on Spenser/Spencer (spelt the same in Russian): Edmund Spenser, the Elizabethan poet, who, despite his high canonical status in English literature, was relatively little known in Russia, and Herbert Spencer (1820–1903), the philosopher/biologist/political theorist, who was very popular and influential among Russian intellectuals in the late nineteenth century. The point of the pun is that Russians mostly know about Herbert Spencer, so when they hear/read something about Spenser and poetry in Latin, they are confused. I would like to thank Vitaly Chernetsky for clarifying this reference for me.

4. This phrase from Boris Pasternak's Russian translation of Shakespeare's *Hamlet* is taken from Hamlet's monologue about an actor who reads the words of Aeneas describing the sufferings of Hecuba upon seeing Priam's violent death. The phrase became a part of Russian idiomatic vernacular and often referred to a person or a matter that is irrelevant to a task of discussion at hand.

5. This opinion, as we saw in Chapter 6, differed from the way the Russian public reacted to both translations. Fedotov perhaps appreciated Briusov's faithfulness to the Vergilian text and thought of his 'foreignizing' tendencies as the way to revive interest in Roman antiquity among Russian readers.

6. Nikolai Karamzin (1766–1826), *Istoriia gosudarstva rossiiskogo*.

7. See Chapter 4 for the commentary on this quote.

8. The full quote is at 6.847: *Excudent alii spirantia mollius aera* ('The others will cast more skilfully the bronze statues that breathe') is taken from the speech of Anchises addressed to Aeneas in the underworld. The quote is used to convey the idea that each nation has its own destiny. In Vergil's sentence the *alii* refers to the Greeks, who were hailed for their ability in the arts, but the Romans had a different mission.

9. It is not clear why Fedotov terms Pushkin's era as 'the age of classicism' unless he means it in a completely different way, as an era that produced the most classic examples of Russian poetry.

10. This statement of course is an exaggeration, as I tried to demonstrate in my chapter on Pushkin, who was little indebted to the precepts of classicism.

11. Both of these comparisons are rather vague. I found little trace of Ovid in *Eugene Onegin*, and even less of Vergil in Pushkin's odes.

12. This statement is true: Pushkin's Ovidian and Catullan allusions in his lyric poetry are much more pronounced.

13. I fail to understand this connection Fedotov makes between Augustan erotic poetry and the Russian fondness for Greece, which at Pushkin's time was primarily fostered by Lord Byron's romantic death there. This statement could have been engendered by the overall direction of this essay to prove that Greece for Russia came to mean after the Revolution significantly more than Rome and by extension Vergil.

14. Philaretus (Drozdov), Metropolitan of Moscow, was the most influential figure in the Russian Orthodox Church for more than forty years (1821–67).

15. *Aen.* 2.501–2, taken from Aeneas' narration to Dido about the destruction of Troy (see Chapter 4).

16. Reference to 6.337–9, where Aeneas meets the former pilot of his ship, Palinurus.

17. *Aen.* 1.460, where Aeneas addresses his friend Achates upon seeing the murals depicting the scenes of the Trojan War in the Temple of Juno in Carthage.

18. Fedotov makes a reference here to Goethe's *Faust*, where Mephisto takes Faust to Auerbach's tavern in Leipzig.

19. This is a somewhat strange and perhaps biased opinion, putting Briusov and Vergil on the same scale of poetic achievement. While Briusov

undoubtedly was a great poet, he by no means can be seen on the Russian literary landscape as important as Vergil was on the Roman.

20. Here Fedotov makes a reference to a stanza in Briusov's sometimes-mocked poem «В ответ» ('In response', 1902): «Вперед, мечта, мой верный вол! / Неволей, если не охотой! / Я близ тебя, мой кнут тяжел, / Я сам тружусь, а ты работай!» ('Plough ahead, oh dream, my eternal ox! / Against your wish, if not willingly! / I am near you, my whip is heavy, / I work myself, and so should you!'). Original available at: <http://www.world-art.ru/lyric/lyric.php?id=11121> [last visited 22 January 2014].

   This poem provoked some criticism from Briusov's fellow poets, such as Marina Tsvetaeva, who questioned whether or not Briusov can be considered a poet in a true sense of the word. See M. Tsvetaeva, 'Vospominaniia', <http://www.classiclibr.ru/lib/sb/book/1430/page/3> [last visited 26 September 2013]. For a more positive interpretation of this poem see Mochul'skii (1962), 100, who suggests that Briusov saw poetry not merely as a result of uncommon talent but as hard work.

21. Here, as noted in Chapter 4, Fedotov does not deliver an accurate account of Vergil's origins. See Levi (1998).

22. The epitaph on Vergil's tomb in Posilipo near Naples was: '*Mantua me genuit; Calabri rapuere; tenet nunc Parthenope. Cecini pascua, rura, duces*' ('Mantua gave birth to me, the Calabrians took me, now Naples holds me; I sang of pastures [the *Eclogues*], country [the *Georgics*], and leaders [the *Aeneid*]').

23. Again Fedotov misrepresents the facts here to add more force to his argument.

24. According to tradition, Vergil travelled to Greece to revise the *Aeneid*. After meeting Augustus in Athens and deciding to return home, Vergil caught a fever while visiting a town near Megara. After crossing to Italy by ship, weakened with disease, he died in Brundisium harbour on 21 September 19 BCE. It is not clear what is the source of Fedotov's statement here that Vergil was trying to reach Troy: he may simply have been aiming to romanticize Vergil's death and connect it with the fate of the Russian exiles who also looked to the East (Russia) with longing.

25. Fedotov's take on Roman poetry is of course rather subjective. While he finds both Ovid and Horace to be frivolous, in Vergil he sees, as does Ivanov, the messianic tendency, which he then connects with Vergil's presence in Christianity despite his pagan origins.

26. *Ecl.* 4.6. This line was used by Christian apologists as proof of Vergil's prophetic powers, and Fedotov most certainly prefers that interpretation. However, Vergil here refers to the story of Aratus describing the constellation of the Virgin, who once was called Justice and mingled with the men of the golden race (see Clausen, 1994, 120). The reign of Saturn

was also synonymous with the Golden Age, which the ancients conceived of as a mythical paradise irretrievably lost.

27. *Ecl.* 4.13. Clausen (1994), 133, suggests that in this line Vergil is referring in *sceleris* to the Roman civil wars.

28. I am not sure what 'coal' («уголь») Fedotov has in mind in the Fourth Eclogue. Vergil describes the abolition of the practice of dyeing wool with the restoration of the Golden Age, because the white wool of sheep grazing in the meadows will spontaneously assume the colours produced by dye. Perhaps that is what Fedotov is misremembering.

29. An interesting observation in support of the argument I advanced in Chapter 6 that there is no canonical translation of the *Aeneid* that matches the translation of the *Iliad* by Gnedich.

30. *Aen.* 2.241–2. The line is from Aeneas' narration about the sack of Troy where he bewails the Trojan mistake of opening the city walls to lead in the Trojan Horse.

Bibliography

Primary Texts

Briusov, V. (1933) 'O perevode Eneidy russkimi stikhami', in *Vergilii, Eneida*. Trans. V. Briusov and S. Soloviev. Moscow: Academia: 39–45.

Brodsky, J. (1981) 'Virgil: Older Than Christianity, a Poet for the New Age', *Vogue* 171 (October): 178–80.

Brodsky, J. (1995) *On Grief and Reason: Essays*. New York: Farrar, Straus and Giroux.

Brodsky, J. (2000) *Collected Poems in English*. New York: Farrar, Straus and Giroux.

Brodsky, J. (2001) (Brodskii, Iosif). *Sochineniia Iosifa Brodskogo*. Ed. Ia. A. Gordin. 7 vols. St Petersburg: Pushkinskii Fond.

Brodsky, J. (2011) (Brodskii, Iosif). *Stikhotvoreniia i poemy*. Introduction, text, and commentary by L. Losev. 2 vols. St Petersburg: Izdatel'stvo Pushkinskogo Doma.

Fedotov, G. P. (1952) *Novyi grad: Sbornik statei*. Ed. Iu. P. Ivask. New York: Izdatel'stvo imeni Chekhova.

Fedotov, G. P. (1996–), *Sobranie sochinenii v dvenadtsati tomakh*. Moscow: Martis.

Fet, A. (1888) *Eneida Vergiliia*. Introduction and commentary by D. I. Naguevskii. Moscow: Tipografiia A. I. Mamontova.

Ivanov, V. (1971–9) *Sobranie sochinenii*. Ed. D. V. Ivanov and O. Deschartes. Brussels: Foyer Oriental Chrétien. Vol. 1, 1971; vol. 2, 1974; vol. 3, 1979. Available at: <http://www.rvb.ru/ivanov/> [last visited 23 March 2014].

Kniazhnin, Ia. B. (1961) *Izbrannye proizvedeniia*. Leningrad: Biblioteka poeta.

Kotliarevskii, I. (1969) *Sochineniia*. Introduction and notes by I. Ia. Aizenshtok. Leningrad: Sovetskii pisatel'.

Lomonosov, M. V. (1959) *Polnoe sobranie sochinenii*. Moscow, Leningrad: Izdatel'stvo Akademii nauk SSSR: vols 6, 7, 8.

Osipov, N. (1933) *Iroi-komicheskaia poema*. Introduction by B. V. Tomashevskii. Leningrad: Biblioteka poeta.

Petrov, V. (1781) *Enei: Geroicheskaiia poema Publiia Vergiliia Marona*. Trans. V. Petrov. St Petersburg: v Tipografii Akademii nauk.

Pushkin, A. S. (1949) *Sochineniia*. Ed. M. A. Tsiavlovskii and S. M. Petrov. Moscow: Gosudarstvennoe izdatel'stvo khudozhestvennoi literatury.

Rydel, C. ed. (1984) *The Ardis Anthology of Russian Romanticism*. Ann Arbor: Ardis.

Scarron, P. (1858) *Le Virgile travesti en vers burlesque*. Ed. Victor Foumel. Paris: Garniere Frères.

Solov'ev, V. S. (1970) *Pis'ma*. Ed. S. M. Solov'ev and E. L. Radlov. 4 vols. Brussels: Zhizn's Bogom.

Starikovsky, G. G. (2012) *P. Vergilii Maron: Eclogi*. Toronto: Aeterna.

Sumarokov, A. P. (1957) *Izbrannye proizvedeniia*. Leningrad: Biblioteka poeta.

Critical Bibliography

Akhmatova, A. (1990) *Sochineniia v dvukh tomakh*. Ed. and commentary by M. M. Kralin. 2 vols. Moscow: Pravda.

Allworth, E. A. (2003) 'Russia's Eastern Orientation', in C. H. Whittaker with E. Kasinec and R. H. Davis, Jr (eds) *Russia Engages the World*. Cambridge, MA: Harvard University Press: 139–61.

Alpers, P. (1979) *The Singer of the Eclogues*. Berkeley: University of California Press.

Alpers, P. (1996) *What is Pastoral?* Chicago: University of Chicago Press.

Anderson, T. (1967) *Russian Political Thought: An Introduction*. Ithaca: Cornell University Press.

Armstrong, R. H. (2008) 'Classical Translations of the Classics: The Dynamics of Literary Tradition in Retranslating Epic Poetry', in A. Lianeri and V. Zajko (eds) *Translation and the Classic: Identity and Change in the History of Culture*. Oxford: Oxford University Press: 169–202.

Arnold, B. (1994) 'The Literary Experience of Vergil's Fourth "Eclogue"', *Classical Journal* 90.2: 143–60.

Arnold, M. (1905) *On Translating Homer (1861)*. London: George Routledge: 1–111.

Austin, R. G. ed. (1955) *P. Vergilii Maronis Aeneidos Liber Quartus: Edited with a Commentary*. Oxford: Clarendon.

Averintsev, S. S. (1996) 'Dve tysiachi let s Vergiliem', *Poety*. Moscow: Shkola Iazyki russkoi kul'tury: 19–42. Available at: <http://ec-dejavu.ru/v-2/Virgil_Averintsev.html> [last visited 11 March 2013]. Reprinted in Averintsev, S. S. (2004) 'Dve tysiachi let s Vergiliem', *Obraz antichnosti*. St Petersburg: Azbuka-klassika: 202–24.

Baehr, S. L. (1991) *The Paradise Myth in Eighteenth-Century Russia: Utopian Patterns in Early Russian Literature and Culture*. Stanford: Stanford University Press.

Bakhtin, M. (1981) *The Dialogic Imagination: Four Essays*. Trans. C. Emerson and M. Holquist. Austin: University of Texas Press.

Bassin, M. (1991) 'Russia between Europe and Asia: The Ideological Construction of Geographical Space', *Slavic Review* 50.1: 1–117.

Batalden, S. K. (1982) *Catherine II's Greek Prelate Eugenios Voulgaris in Russia, 1771–1806*. New York and Boulder: East European Monographs.

Becker-Cantarino, B. (1973) *Aloys Blumauer and the Literature of Austrian Enlightenment*. Bern: Herbert Lang.

Belinskii, V. G. (1953) *Polnoe sobranie sochinenii*. Moscow: Akademiia nauk: 1.164.

Belinskii, V. (1955) *Polnoe sobranie sochinenii*. Moscow: Akademiia nauk 7.110.

Bethea, D. M. (1994) *Joseph Brodsky and the Creation of Exile*. Princeton: Princeton University Press.

Blok, A. (1958) *Dvenadtsat': Skify*. Moscow: Izd-vo khudozhestvennoi literatury.

Bloom, H. (1976) *Poetry and Repression*. New Haven: Yale University Press.

Bojanowska, E. (2007) *Nikolai Gogol: Between Ukrainian and Russian Nationalism*. Cambridge, MA: Harvard University Press.

Bono, P. and Tessitore, M. V. (1998) *Il mito di Didone: Avventure di una regina tra secoli e culture*. Milano: Bruno Mondadori.

Bowra, C. M. (1945) *From Virgil to Milton*. London: Macmillan.

Braginskaia, N. (2004) 'Slavianskoe vozrozhdenie antichnosti', in *Russkaia teoriia 1920–1930-e gody: Materialy 10-kh Lotmanovskikh chtenii*. Moscow: RGGU: 49–80.

Braund, S. (2010) 'Mind the Gap: On Foreignizing Translations of the *Aeneid*', in J. Farrell and M. C. J. Putnam (eds) *A Companion to Vergil's Aeneid and Its Tradition*. Oxford: Wiley-Blackwell: 450–64.

Briggs, W. W. (1981) 'A Bibliography of Vergil's "Eclogues" (1927–1977)', *ANRW* II.31.2: 1267–1357.

Briusov, V. (1955) 'Ovidii po-russki', in *Izbrannye sochineniia v dvukh tomakh*. Moscow: Gos. izd-vo khudozhestvennoi literatury: 2.250–7.

Brooks, R. A. (1953) '*Discolor Aura*: Reflections on the Golden Bough', *American Journal of Philology* 74: 260–80.

Brower, R. A. ed. (1959) *On Translation*. Cambridge, MA: Harvard University Press.

Brumm, A. (2002) 'The Muse in Exile: Conversations with the Russian Poet Joseph Brodsky', in C. L. Haven (ed.) *Joseph Brodsky: Conversations*. Jackson: University Press of Mississippi: 13–35.

Bufalini, R. (2006) 'The Czarina's Russia through Mediterranean Eyes: Francesco Algarotti's Journey to Saint Petersburg', *Modern Language Notes* 121: 154–66.

Burrow, C. (1997) 'Virgil in English Translation', in C. Martindale (ed.) *The Cambridge Companion to Virgil*. Cambridge: Cambridge University Press: 21–37.

Capern, A. (2008) *The Historical Study of Women: England, 1500–1700*. Basingstoke and New York: Palgrave Macmillan.

Chlodowski, R. I. (1984) 'Russia', in *Enciclopedia Virgiliana*. Roma: Istituto dell'Enciclopedia italiana: 608–17.

Cioran, S. D. (1977) *Vladimir Solov'ev and the Knighthood of the Divine Sophia*. Waterloo, Ont.: Wilfrid Laurier University Press.

Clark, K. (2011) *Moscow, the Fourth Rome: Stalinism, Cosmopolitanism, and the Evolution of Soviet Culture, 1931–1941*. Cambridge, MA: Harvard University Press.

Clausen, W. (1964) 'An Interpretation of the *Aeneid*', *Harvard Studies in Classical Philology* 68: 139–47.

Clausen, W. V. (1994) *A Commentary on Virgil: Eclogues*. Oxford: Clarendon.

Coleiro, E. (1979) *An Introduction to Vergil's Bucolics with a Critical Edition of the Text*. Amsterdam: Grüner.

Conington, J. (1898) *The Works of Vergil*. Vol. 1. *Eclogues and Georgics*. London. Revised by H. Nettleship. 4th edn.

Connolly, J. (1992) 'The Nineteenth Century: The Age of Realism', in C. A. Moser (ed.) *The Cambridge History of Russian Literature*. Cambridge: Cambridge University Press: 333–86.

Conte, G. B. (1986) *The Rhetoric of Imitation: Genre and Poetic Memory in Virgil and Other Latin Poets*. Trans. C. Segal. Ithaca: Cornell University Press.

Conte, G. B. (1994) *Latin Literature: A History*. Trans. J. B. Solodow. Revised by D. Fowler and G. W. Most. Baltimore and London: Johns Hopkins University Press.

Covi, M. C. (1964) 'Dido in Vergil's *Aeneid*', *Classical Journal* 60: 57–60.

Cracraft, J. (1973) 'Feofan Prokopovich', in J. G. Garrard (ed.) *The Eighteenth Century in Russia*. Oxford: Clarendon: 75–105.

Cracraft, J. (2003) 'St. Petersburg: The Russian Cosmopolis', in C. H. Whittaker with E. Kasinec and R. H. Davis, Jr (eds) *Russia Engages the World*. Cambridge, MA: Harvard University Press: 24–49.

De Armas, F. A. (1972) *Paul Scarron*. New York: Twayne.

Davidson, P. (1989) *The Poetic Imagination of Vyacheslav Ivanov: A Russian Symbolist Perception of Dante*. Cambridge: Cambridge University Press.

Davidson, P. (1996a) 'Hellenism, Culture, and Christianity: The Case of Vyacheslav Ivanov and his "Palinode" of 1927', in P. I. Barta, D. H. J. Larmour and P. A. Miller (eds) *Russian Literature and the Classics*. Studies in Russian and European Literature 1. Amsterdam: Harwood Academic: 83–116.

Davidson, P. (1996b) *Viacheslav Ivanov: A Reference Guide*. New York: G. K. Hall.

Davidson, P. (2000) 'Vladimir Solov'ev and the Ideal of Prophecy', *Slavonic and East European Review*, 78.4: 643–70.

Davidson, P. (2006) *Vyacheslav Ivanov and C. M. Bowra: A Correspondence from Two Corners on Humanism*. Birmingham: Centre for Russian and East European Studies, University of Birmingham.

Davidson, P. (2007) 'Between Derzhavin and Pushkin: The Development of the Image of the Poet as a Prophet in the Verse of Zhukovsky, Glinka, and Kiukhelbecker', in C. O'Neil, N. Boudreau and S. Krive (eds) *Poetics, Self, Place: Essays in Honor of Anna Lisa Crone*. Bloomington: Slavica: 182–214.

Egunov, A. N (1964) *Gomer v russkikh perevodakh XVIII–XIX vekov*. Moscow and Leningrad: Indrik: 40–9.

Ekaterina II (1901) *Sochineniia imperatritsy Ekateriny II*. St Petersburg: Imperatorskaia Akademiia nauk: 7.256.

Elder, J. P. (1961) '*Non Inussa Cano*: Virgil's Sixth Eclogue', *Harvard Studies in Classical Philology* 65: 109–25.

Etkind, E. (1973) *Russkie poety-perevodchiki ot Trediakovskogo do Pushkina*. Leningrad: Nauka.

Figes, O. (2002) *Natasha's Dance: A Cultural History of Russia*. New York: Picador.

Florenskii, P. A. (1914) *Stolp i utverzhdenie istiny*. Moscow: Sergiev Posad.

Forrester, S. (2004) 'Sons, Lovers and the Laius Complex in Russian Modernist Poetry', *Slavic Review* 63: 1–5.

Frajlich, A. (2007) *The Legacy of Ancient Rome in the Russian Silver Age*. Studies in Slavic Literature and Poetics 48. Amsterdam and New York: Rodopi.

Freidin, G. (1987) *A Coat of Many Colors: Osip Mandelshtam and His Mythologies of Self-Presentation*. Berkeley: University of California Press.

Friedberg, M. (1997) *Literary Translation in Russia: A Cultural History*. University Park, PA: Pennsylvania State University Press.

Frolov, E. D. (1999) *Russkaia nauka ob antichnosti*. St Petersburg: Izd. S.-Peterburgskogo universiteta.

Galinsky, K. (1996) *Augustan Culture: An Interpretive Introduction*. Princeton: Princeton University Press.

Garrard, J. G. (1973) 'Introduction: The Emergence of Modern Russian Literature and Thought', in J. G. Garrard (ed.) *The Eighteenth Century in Russia*. Oxford: Clarendon: 1–21.

Gasparov, M. L. (1971) 'Briusov i bukvalism (po neizdannym materialam k perevodu "Eneidy")', *Masterstvo Perevoda* 8: 88–128.

Gasparov, M. L. (1979) 'Vergilii: Poet budushchego', in *Istoriia vsemirnoi literatury v deviati tomakh*. Moscow: 1.5–34. Available at: <http://www.philology.ru/literature3/gasparov-79.htm> [last visited 10 April 2013].

Gasparov, M. L. (1997) 'Briusov-perevodchik: Put' k pereput'iu', *Izbrannye trudy*. Moscow: Iazyki russkoi kul'tury: 2.121–9.

Gaut, G. (1998) 'Can a Christian Be a Nationalist? Vladimir Solov'ev's Critique of Nationalism', *Slavic Review* 57.1: 77–94.

Gill, C. (1997) 'Passion as Madness in Roman Poetry', in S. M. Braund and C. Gill (eds) *The Passions in Roman Thought and Literature*. Cambridge: Cambridge University Press: 213–41.

Gillespie, A. D. (2004) 'Joseph Brodsky (Iosif Aleksandrovich Brodsky)', in M. Balina and M. Lipovetsky (eds) *Russian Writers since 1980*. Dictionary of Literary Biography 285. Detroit: Gale: 17–39.

Ginzburg, L. (1987) 'Iz zapisei 1950–1970-kh godov', *Literatura v poiskakh real'nosti*. Leningrad: Sovetskii pisatel': 98–138.

Gleason, A. (1972) *European and Muscovite: Ivan Kireevsky and the Origins of Slavophilism*. Cambridge, MA: Harvard University Press.

Graf, F. and Johnston, S. I. (2007) *Ritual Texts for the Afterlife: Orpheus and the Bacchic Gold Tablets*. London and New York: Routledge.

Greenfeld, L. (1992) *Nationalism: Five Roads to Modernity*. Cambridge, MA: Harvard University Press.

Gregg, R. (1977) 'The Nature of Nature and the Nature of Eugene in the Bronze Horseman', *Slavic and East European Journal* 21.2: 167–79.

Griffiths, T. and Rabinowitz, J. (1990) *Novel Epics: Gogol, Dostoevsky and National Narrative*. Evanston: Northwestern University Press.

Griffiths, T. and Rabinowitz, J. (2011) *Epic and the Russian Novel from Gogol to Pasternak*. Boston: Academic Studies.

Gukovskii, G. (1927) *Russkaia poeziia XVIII veka*. Leningrad: Akademiia: 45–6.

Gustafson, R. F. (1996) 'Soloviev's Doctrine of Salvation', in J. D. Kornblatt and R. F. Gustafson (eds) *Russian Religious Thought*. Madison: University of Wisconsin Press: 31–48.

Hammond, P. (1999) *Dryden and the Traces of Classical Rome*. Oxford: Oxford University Press.

Hardie, P. (1997) 'Virgil and Tragedy', in C. Martindale (ed.) *Cambridge Companion to Virgil*. Cambridge: Cambridge University Press: 312–26.

Hardwick, L. (2004) *Translating Words, Translating Cultures*. London: Duckworth.

Hardwick, L. (2006) 'Greek Drama as Diaspora in Performance', in C. Martindale and R. F. Thomas (eds) *Classics and the Uses of Reception*. Oxford: Blackwell: 204–15.

Hare, A. J. C. (1889) *Cities of Southern Italy and Sicily*. New York: Routledge.

Harrison, E. L. (1989) 'The Tragedy of Dido', *Echos du Monde Classique / Classical Views* 33.8: 1–21.

Hayes, J. C. (2009) *Translation, Subjectivity, and Culture in France and England, 1600–1800*. Stanford: Stanford University Press.

Hosking, G. (1997) *Russia: People and Empire, 1552–1917*. Cambridge, MA: Harvard University Press.

Hubbard, T. (1998) *The Pipes of Pan: Intertextuality and Literary Filiation in the Pastoral Tradition from Theocritus to Milton*. Ann Arbor: University of Michigan Press.

Hughes, L. (1998) *Russia in the Age of Peter the Great*. New Haven and London: Yale University Press.

Jeep, J. M. and Torlone, Z. M. (2009) 'Viacheslav Ivanov's *Vergils Historiosophie*: Background, Translation, and Commentary', *Toronto Slavic Quarterly* 27. Available at: <http://www.utoronto.ca/tsq/27/jeep-torlone27.shtml> [last visited 10 September 2013].

Johnson, W. R. (2001) 'Imaginary Romans: Vergil and the Illusion of National Identity', in S. Spence (ed.) *Poets and Critics Read Vergil*. New Haven: Yale University Press: 3–18.

Jones, W. G. (1976) 'A Trojan Horse within the Walls of Classicism: Russian Classicism and the National Specific', in A. G. Gross (ed.) *Russian Literature in the Age of Catherine the Great*. Oxford: W. A. Meeuws: 95–120.

Irwin, W. R. (1961) 'The Survival of Pan', *Publications of the Modern Language Association of America* 76.3: 159–67.

Kagarlitsky, B. (2008) *Empire of the Periphery: Russia and the World System*. London: Pluto.

Kahn, A. (1993) 'Readings of Imperial Rome from Lomonosov to Pushkin', *Slavic Review* 52.4: 745–68.

Kalb, J. (2003) 'Lodestars on the Via Appia: Viacheslav Ivanov's "Roman Sonnets" in Context', *Die Welt der Slaven* 48: 23–52.

Kalb, J. (2008) *Russia's Rome: Imperial Visions, Messianic Dreams (1890–1940)*. Madison: University of Wisconsin Press.

Kallendorf, C. (2005) 'Vergil's Post-classical Legacy', in J. M. Foley (ed.) *A Companion to Ancient Epic*. Oxford: Blackwell: 574–88.

Kallendorf, C. (2007) *The Other Virgil: 'Pessimistic' Readings of the Aeneid in Early Modern Culture*. Oxford: Oxford University Press.

Kara-Murza, A. A. (2006) *Intellektual'nye portrety: Ocherki o russkikh politicheskikh mysliteliakh XIX–XX vv.* Moscow: Russian Academy of Sciences.

Karamzin, N. M. (1848) *Polnoe sobranie sochinenii russkikh avtorov*. St Petersburg: Sobranie Smirdina: 1.591.

Karlinsky, S. (1985) *Russian Drama from Its Beginnings to the Age of Pushkin*. Berkeley: University of California Press.

Karsai, G., Klaniczay, G., Movrin, D. and Olechowska, E. (2013) *Classics and Communism: Greek and Latin behind the Iron Curtain*. Ljubljana, Budapest, Warsaw: University of Ljubljana.

Kirin, A. (2010) 'Eastern Nations, Western Culture, and the Classical Tradition', in S. A. Stephens and P. Vasunia (eds) *Classics and National Cultures*. Oxford: Oxford University Press: 141–62.

Kirk, G. S. ed. (1954) *Heraclitus: The Cosmic Fragments*. Cambridge: Cambridge University Press.

Kiselev, A. F. (2004) *Strana grez Georgiia Fedotova: Razmyshleniia o Rossii i revoliutsii*. Moscow: Logos.

Klimoff, A. (1986) 'The First Sonnet in Viacheslav Ivanov's *Roman Cycle*', in R. L. Jackson and L. Nelson, Jr (eds) *Viacheslav Ivanov: Poet, Critic and Philosopher*. New Haven: Yale Center for International and Area Studies: 123–33.

Knabe, G. S. (2000) *Russkaia antichnost'*. Moscow: Russian State University for the Humanities.

Knight, J. W. F. (1944) *Roman Vergil*. London: Faber and Faber.

Kornblatt, J. D. (2009) *Divine Sophia: The Wisdom Writings of Vladimir Solov'ev*. Ithaca and London: Cornell University Press.

Kostalevsky, M. (1997) *Dostoevsky and Solov'ev: The Art of Integral Vision*. New Haven: Yale University Press.

Kreps, M. (1984) *O poezii Iosifa Brodskogo*. Ann Arbor: Ardis.

Kulakova, L. I. (1951) *Ia. B. Kniazhnin*. Moscow and Leningrad: Iskusstvo.

Kulakova, L. I. (1959) 'Ia. B. Kniazhnin', in G. P. Berdnikov et al. (eds) *Russkie dramaturgi*. Leningrad and Moscow: Iskusstvo.

Laruelle, M. (2008) *Russian Eurasianism: An Ideology of Empire*. Baltimore: Johns Hopkins University Press.

Leach, E. W. (1974) *Vergil's Eclogues: Landscapes of Experience*. Ithaca: Cornell University Press.

Lednicki, W. (1978) *Pushkin's Bronze Horseman: The Story of a Masterpiece*. Westport: Greenwood.

Levi, P. (1998) *Virgil: His Life and Times*. New York: St. Martin's.

Lim, S. S. (2008) 'Between Spiritual Self and Other: Vladimir Solov'ev and the Question of East Asia', *Slavic Review* 67.2: 321–41.

Linderski, J. (1990) 'Mommsen and Syme: Law and Power in the Principate of Augustus', in K. A. Raaflaub and M. Toher (eds) *Between Republic and Empire: Interpretations of Augustus and His Principate*. Berkeley: University of California Press: 42–53.

Long, A. A. (1974) *Hellenistic Philosophy: Stoics, Epicureans, Sceptics*. 2nd edn. Berkeley: University of California Press.

Loseff, L. (1990) 'Politics/Poetics', in L. Loseff and V. Polukhina (eds) *Brodsky's Poetics and Aesthetics*. New York: St. Martin's: 34–55.

Losev, A. F. (2000) *Vladimir Solov'ev i ego vremia*. Zhizn' zamechatel'nykh liudei. Moscow: Molodaia gvardiia.

Losev, L. (2006) *Iosif Brodskii: Opyt literaturnoi biografii*. Zhizn' zamechatel'nykh liudei. Moscow: Molodaia gvardiia.

Lotman, Iu. M. and Uspenskii, B. A. (1984) 'Echoes of the Notion of "Moscow as the Third Rome" in Peter the Great's Ideology', in Ann Shukman (ed.) *The Semiotics of Russian Culture*. Trans. N. F. C. Owen. Ann Arbor: Dept of Slavic Languages and Literatures, University of Michigan: 53–67.

Lotman, Iu. M. (1996) 'Ocherki po istorii russkoi kul'tury', in *Iz istorii russkoi kul'tury (XVIII–nachalo XIX veka)*. Moscow: Iazyki russkoi kul'tury: 13–337.

Mack, S. (1999) 'The Birth of War: A Reading of *Aeneid 7*', in C. Perkell (ed.) *Reading Vergil's Aeneid: An Interpretive Guide*. Norman: University of Oklahoma Press: 128–47.

Mackiw, T. (1983) *English Reports of Mazepa, Hetman of Ukraine and the Prince of the Holy Roman Empire, 1687–1709*. New York: Ukrainian Historical Association.

Maguire, R. A. (1994) *Exploring Gogol*. Stanford: Stanford University Press.

Maiorova, O. (2010) *From the Shadow of Empire: Defining the Russian Nation through Cultural Mythology*. Madison: University of Wisconsin Press.

Malia, M. (1999) *Russia under Western Eyes: From the Bronze Horseman to the Lenin Mausoleum*. Cambridge: Harvard University Press.

Mandel'shtam, O. E. (1974) *Stikhotvoreniia*. Ed. N. I. Khardzhiev. Biblioteka poeta: Bol'shaia seriia. Leningrad: Sovetskii pisatel'.

Mandel'shtam, O. E. (2001) *Stikhotvoreniia: Proza*. Ed. S. Vasilenko and M. Gasparov. Moscow: Ripol Klassik.

Manning, C. A. (1923) 'The Classics and Russian Literature', *Sewanee Review* 31: 474–85.

Marlowe, C. and Nashe, J. (1968) *Dido, Queen of Carthage, and the Massacre at Paris*. Cambridge: Methuen.

Matual, D. (1982) 'Solov'ev's Translation of Virgil's Fourth Eclogue: Afterword to *The History and Future of Theocracy*', *Slavic and East European Journal* 26.3: 275–86.

McElduff, S. and Sciarrino, E. (2011) *Complicating the History of Western Translation*. Manchester, UK, and Kinderhook, NY: St. Jerome.

McLeish, K. (1990) 'Dido, Aeneas, and the Concept of *Pietas*', in I. McAuslan and Peter Walcott (eds) *Virgil*. Oxford: Oxford University Press: 134–41.

Meerson, O. (1999) 'Review of Tomas Venclova's *Sobesedniki na piru: Stat'i o russkoi literature*', *Slavic and East European Journal* 43.4: 718–19.

Mersereau, J. (1999) 'The Nineteenth Century: 1820–40', in C. A. Moser (ed.) *The Cambridge History of Russian Literature*. Cambridge: Cambridge University Press: 136–88.

Mikhalchi, D. (1944) 'Ancient Literature in Russian Translations', *Modern Language Review* 39: 63.

Mochul'skii, K. (1962) *Valerii Briusov*. Paris: YMCA Press.

Molodiakov, V. E. (1994) 'Rasskazyvai, pamiat'', in the afterword to *Valerii Briusov: Iz moei zhizni*. Moscow: Terra: 258–68.

Molodiakov, V. (2010) *Valerii Briusov. Biography*. St Petersburg: Vita Nova.

Monas, S. (1983) 'St. Petersburg and Moscow as Cultural Symbols', in T. G. Stavrou (ed.) *Art and Culture in Nineteenth-Century Russia*. Bloomington: Indiana University Press: 26–39.

Monti, R. C. (1981) *The Dido Episode and the Aeneid: Roman Social and Political Values in the Epic*. Mnemosyne Supplement 66. Leiden: Brill.

Munteanu, D. L. (2009) 'Placing Thebes and Ithaca in Eastern Europe: Kundera, the Greeks, and I', *Arion* 17.1: 1–16.

Myers, D. (1992) '"Hellenism" and "Barbarism" in Mandelshtam', in Arnold McMillin (ed.) *Symbolism and After: Essays on Russian Poetry in Honour of Georgette Donchin*. London: Bristol Classical: 85–101.

Newlin, T. (1996) 'The Return of the Russian Odysseus: Pastoral Dreams and Rude Awakenings', *Russian Review* 55.3: 448–74.

Newman, J. K. (1972) 'Pushkin's "Bronze Horseman" and the Epic Tradition', *Comparative Literature Studies* 9.2: 173–95.

Norden, E. (1924) *Die Geburt des Kindes: Geschichte einer religiösen Idee*. Leipzig: Teubner.

Otis, B. (1964) *Virgil: A Study in Civilized Poetry*. Oxford: Clarendon.

Pappaioannou, S. (2009) 'Eugenios Voulgaris' Translation of the Georgics: An Introduction to the First Modern Greek Translation of Vergil,' *Vergilius* 54: 97–123.

Parry, A. (1963) 'The Two Voices of Vergil's *Aeneid*', *Arion* 2: 66–80.

Peace, R. (1989) 'The Nineteenth Century: The Natural School and Its Aftermath, 1840–55', in C. A. Moser (ed.) *The Cambridge History of Russian Literature*. Cambridge: Cambridge University Press: 189–247.

Perkell, C. (1981) 'On Dido and Creusa and the Quality of Victory in Vergil's *Aeneid*', *Women's Studies* 8: 201–23.

Perkell, C. (1999) 'Aeneid I: An Epic Program', in C. Perkell (ed.) *Reading Vergil's Aeneid: An Interpretive Guide*. Norman: University of Oklahoma Press: 29–49.

Perkell, C. (2001) 'Pastoral Value in Vergil: Some Instances', in S. Spence (ed.), *Poets and Critics Read Vergil*. New Haven: Yale University Press: 26–43.

Petrovskii, F. A. (1966) 'Russkie perevody "Eneidy" i zadachi novogo ee perevoda', in *Voprosy antichnoi literatury i klassicheskoi filologii*. Moscow: Nauka: 293–306.

Platonov, R. (2007) 'Remapping Arcadia: "Pastoral Space" in Nineteenth-Century Russian Prose', *Modern Language Review* 102: 1105–21.

Poe, M. (1995) *Foreign Descriptions of Muscovy: An Analytic Bibliography of Primary and Secondary Sources*. Columbus: Slavica.

Poe, M. (2000) '*A People Born to Slavery*': *Russia in Early Modern European Ethnography, 1476–1748*. Ithaca: Cornell University Press.

Poe, M. (2003) 'A Distant World: Russian Relations with Europe before Peter the Great', in C. H. Whittaker with E. Kasinec and R. H. Davis, Jr (eds) *Russia Engages the World*. Cambridge, MA: Harvard University Press: 2–23.

Polukhina, V. (1989) *Joseph Brodsky: A Poet for Our Time*. Cambridge: Cambridge University Press.

Polukhina, V. (1992) *Brodsky through the Eyes of His Contemporaries*. New York: St. Martin's.

Proskurina, V. (2005) 'Peterburgskii mif i politika monumentov: Petr Pervyi Ekaterine Vtoroi', *Novoe Literaturnoe Obozrenie* 72. Available at: <http://magazines.russ.ru/nlo/2005/72/pro6.html> [last visited 23 March 2014].

Putnam, M. C. J. (1965) *The Poetry of the Aeneid*. Cambridge, MA: Harvard University Press.

Putnam, M. C. J. (1970) *Vergil's Pastoral Art: Studies in the Eclogues*. Princeton: Princeton University Press.

Putnam, M. (1987) 'Daedalus, Vergil, and the End of Art', *American Journal of Philology* 108.2: 173–98.

Putnam, M. C. J. (1999) '*Aeneid* 12: Unity in Closure', in C. Perkell (ed.) *Reading Vergil's Aeneid: An Interpretive Guide*. Norman: University of Oklahoma Press: 210–30.

Pym, A. (2003) 'Introduction: On the Social and Cultural in Translation Studies', in A. Pym, M. Shlesinger and Z. Jettmarova (eds) *Sociocultural Aspects of Translating and Interpreting*. Amsterdam: John Benjamins: 9–35.

Pypin, A. N. (1902–13) *Istoriia russkoi literatury*. Vols 3 and 4. St Petersburg: Tipografiia M. M. Stasiulevicha.

Quint, D. (1992) *Epic and Empire: Politics and Generic Form from Virgil to Milton*. Princeton: Princeton University Press.

Raeff, M. (2003) 'The Emergence of the Russian European: Russia as a Full Partner of Europe', in C. H. Whittaker with E. Kasinec and R. H. Davis, Jr (eds) *Russia Engages the World*. Cambridge, MA: Harvard University Press: 118–37.

Raeff, M. ed. (1999) *Russian Intellectual History: An Anthology*. With introduction by Isaiah Berlin. Amherst: Humanity.

Ram, H. (2003) *The Imperial Sublime: A Russian Poetics of Empire*. Madison: University of Wisconsin Press.

Reyfman, I. (1990) *Vasilii Trediakovskii: The Fool of the 'New' Russian Literature*. Stanford: Stanford University Press.

Reyfman, I. (2003) 'Catherine II as a Patron of Russian Literature', in C. H. Whittaker with E. Kasinec and R. H. Davis, Jr (eds) *Russia Engages the World*. Cambridge, MA: Harvard University Press: 50–71.

Reynolds, A. (2005) 'Returning the Ticket: Joseph Brodsky's "August" and the End of the Petersburg Text', *Slavic Review* 64.2: 307–32.

Reynolds, A. (2007) 'Feathers and Suns: Joseph Brodsky's "Dedal v Sitsilii" and the "Fear of Replication"', *Slavic and East European Journal* 51.3: 553–81.

Riasanovsky, N. (1952) *Russia and the West in the Teaching of the Slavophiles*. Cambridge, MA: Harvard University Press.

Riha, T. ed. (1969) *Readings in Russian Civilization*. 2nd edn. Vol. 2. Chicago and London: University of Chicago Press.

Rogger, H. (1960) *National Consciousness in Eighteenth-Century Russia*. Cambridge, MA: Harvard University Press.

Ronen, O. (2008) 'Vergilii u akmeistov', in E. A. Takho-Godi (ed.) *Antichnost' i russkaia kul'tura Serebrianogo veka: XII Losevskie chteniia*. Moscow: Volodei: 106–17.

Rosenshield, G. (1996) '*The Bronze Horseman* and *The Double*: The Depoeticization of the Myth of Petersburg in the Young Dostoevskii', *Slavic Review* 55.2: 399–428.

Rosenthal, B. G. (1993) 'Lofty Ideals and Worldly Consequences: Visions of *Sobornost'* in early Twentieth Century Russia', *Russian History* 20.1–4: 179–95.

Ross, D. (2007) *Virgil's Aeneid: A Reader's Guide*. Malden, MA, and Oxford: Blackwell.

Rudich, V. (1986) 'Vyacheslav Ivanov and Classical Antiquity', in R. L. Jackson and L. Nelson, Jr (eds) *Vyacheslav Ivanov: Poet, Critic and Philosopher*. New Haven: Yale Center for International and Area Studies: 275–89.

Rudich, V. (2002a) 'On Pushkin and Vergil', *Arion* 10.1: 35–53.

Rudich, V. (2002b) 'Vergilii v vospriatii Ivanova i T. S. Eliota', *Europa Orientalis* XXI. 1: 339–51.

Rzhevsky, N. (1998) 'Russian Cultural History: Introduction', in N. Rzhevsky (ed.) *The Cambridge Companion to Modern Russian Culture*. Cambridge: Cambridge University Press: 1–18.

Sandler, S. (2004) '"Pushkin" and Identity', in S. Franklin and E. Widdis (eds) *National Identity in Russian Culture*. Cambridge: Cambridge University Press: 197–216.

Saunders, T. (2008) *Bucolic Ecology: Virgil's Eclogues and the Environmental Literary Tradition*. London: Duckworth.

Scherr, B. P. (2008) '"Don't Shield the Original from the Reader": Mikhail Gasparov on the Art of Translation', *Slavic and East European Journal* 52.2: 235–52.

Schimmelpenninck van der Oye, D. (2010) *Russian Orientalism: Asia in the Russian Mind from Peter the Great to the Emigration*. New Haven and London: Yale University Press.

Segal, C. (1990) 'Dido's Hesitation in *Aeneid 4*', *Classical World* 84.1: 1–12.

Segel, H. B. (1973) 'Classicism and Classical Antiquity in Eighteenth- and Early-Nineteenth-Century Russian Literature', in J. G. Garrard (ed.) *The Eighteenth Century in Russia*. Oxford: Clarendon: 48–71.

Seleznev, I. Ia. (1861) *Istoricheskii ocherk Imp. Litseiia, 1811–1861*. St Petersburg.

Serman, I., and Kochetkova, N., eds (1973) *Poety XVIII veka*. Leningrad: Biblioteka poeta: 1.325.

Serman, I. (1989) 'The Eighteenth Century: Neo-classicism and the Enlightenment, 1730–90', in C. A. Moser (ed.) *The Cambridge History of Russian Literature*. Cambridge: Cambridge University Press: 45–91. Repr. 1992.

Sforza, F. (1935) 'The Problem of Virgil', *Classical Review* 49.3: 97–108.

Shliapkin, I. (1885) 'Vasilii Petrovich Petrov, "karmannyi" stikhotvorets Ekateriny II (1736–1799),"' *Istoricheskii Vestnik* 23.11: 381–405. Available in online version by I. Remizov, 2007: <http://memoirs.ru/texts/Schl_P_IV85_23_11.htm> [last visited 27 March 2013].

Sinitsyna, N. V. (1998) *Tretii Rim: Istoki i evoliutsiia russkoi srednevekovoi kontseptsii (XV–XVI vv)*. Moscow: Indrik.

Smith, G. S. (2005) 'Joseph Brodsky: Summing Up', *Literary Imagination: The Review of the Association of Literary Scholars and Critics* 7.3: 399–410.

Snell, B. (1953) 'Arcadia: The Discovery of a Spiritual Landscape', *The Discovery of the Mind*. Trans. T. G. Rosenmeyer. Oxford: Blackwell: 281–310.

Sobolevskii, A. (1889) 'K iubileiu I. P. Kotliarevskogo', *Bibliograph* no. 10–11: 190.

Spence, S. (1999) '*Varium et Mutabile*: Voices of Authority in *Aeneid 4*', in C. Perkell (ed.) *Reading Vergil's Aeneid: An Interpretive Guide*. Norman: University of Oklahoma Press: 80–95.

Spence, S. (2001) 'Introduction: After Grief and Reason', in S. Spence (ed.) *Poets and Critics Read Vergil*. New Haven: Yale University Press: xiii–xx.

Sutton, J. (1988) *The Religious Philosophy of Vladimir Solovyov*. New York: St. Martin's.

Tairova-Iakovleva, T. G. (2007–) *Getman Ivan Mazepa: Dokumenty iz arkhivnykh sobranii Sankt Peterburga*. St Petersburg: Izd-vo S-Peterburgskogo universiteta.

Tarán, L. (1971) 'The Creation Myth in Plato's Timaeus', in J. P. Anton and G. Kustas (eds) *Essays in Ancient Greek Philosophy*. Vol. 1. Albany: SUNY Press.

Terras, V. ed. (1985) *Handbook of Russian Literature*. New Haven: Yale University Press.

Thomas, R. (2001) *Virgil and the Augustan Reception*. Cambridge: Cambridge University Press.

Tolz, V. (2001) *Russia: Inventing the Nation*. New York: Oxford University Press.

Toporov, V. N. (1990) 'Italiia v Peterburge', in *Italiia i slavianskii mir: sovetsko-italiianskii simposium.* Moscow: Institut slavianovedeniia i balkanistiki: 49–81.

Toporov, V. N. (1996) 'U istokov russkogo poeticheskogo perevoda', in *Iz istorii russkoi kul'tury (XVIII–nachalo XIX veka).* Moscow: Iazyki russkoi kul'tury: 589–635.

Torlone, Z. M. (2009) *Russia and the Classics: Poetry's Foreign Muse.* London: Duckworth.

Torlone, Z. M. (2011) 'Vasilii Petrov and the First Russian Translation of the *Aeneid*', *Classical Receptions Journal* 3.2: 227–47.

Uspenskii, B. (1984) 'The Language Situation and Linguistic Consciousness in Muscovite Rus', in H. Birnbaum and M. Flier (eds) *Medieval Russian Culture.* Berkeley: University of California Press: 365–85.

Venuti, L. (1998) *The Scandals of Translation: Towards an Ethics of Difference.* London and New York: Routledge.

Venuti, L. (2008) 'Translation, Interpretation, Canon Formation', in A. Lianeri and V. Zajko (eds) *Translation and the Classic: Identity and Change in the History of Culture.* Oxford and New York: Oxford University Press: 27–51.

Verheul, K. (1973) 'Iosif Brodskii's "Aeneas and Dido,"' *Russian Literature Triquarterly* 6: 490–501. Repr. in Russian translation (1986) in *Poetika Brodskogo*, ed. L. Losev. Tenafly: Ėrmitazh: 121–31.

Vitale, S. (2000) *Pushkin's Button (Bottone di Puskin).* Trans. Anne Goldstein and Jon Rothschild. Chicago: Chicago University Press; 1st edn: New York: Farrar, Straus and Giroux, 1999.

Vorms, A. E. (2003) *Beseda s L. N. Tolstym o Vergilii.* Tula: Iasnaia Poliana.

Wachtel, M. (1994a) *Russian Symbolism and Literary Tradition: Goethe, Novalis, and the Poetics of Vyacheslav Ivanov.* Madison: University of Wisconsin Press.

Wachtel, M. (1994b) 'Viacheslav Ivanov: Student Berlinskogo Universiteta', *Cahiers du Monde Russe et Soviétique* 35: 353–76.

Wes, M. A. (1992) *Classics in Russia, 1700–1855: Between Two Bronze Horsemen.* Brill's Studies in Intellectual History. Leiden, New York, Cologne: Brill.

Westbroek, P. L. (2007) *Dionis i Dionisiiskaia tragediia: Viacheslav Ivanov. Filologicheskie i filosofskie idei o Dionisiistve.* Dissertation, Amsterdam.

Wolf, R. L. (1960) 'The Three Romes: The Migration of an Ideology and the Making of an Autocrat', in Henry A. Murray (ed.) *Myth and Mythmaking.* New York: George Braziller: 174–98.

Wortman, R. (1995) *Scenarios of Power: Myth and Ceremony in Russian Monarchy.* Vol. 1. Princeton: Princeton University Press.

Wortman, R. (2003) 'Texts of Exploration and Russia's European Identity', in C. H. Whittaker with E. Kasinec and R. H. Davis, Jr (eds) *Russia Engages the World*. Cambridge, MA: Harvard University Press: 90–118.

Wright, M. R. (1997) '*Ferox Virtus*: Anger in Vergil's *Aeneid*', in S. M. Braund and C. Gill (eds) *The Passions in Roman Thought and Literature*. Cambridge: Cambridge University Press: 169–84.

Zaitseva, N. V. (2001) *Logika liubvi*. Samara: Samarskii universitet.

Zelinksii, F. F. (1916) 'Viacheslav Ivanov', in S. A. Vengerov (ed.) *Russkaia Literatura XX Veka*. Vol. 3. Book 8. Moscow: T-va Mir: 101–13.

Zernov, N. (1944) *Three Russian Prophets: Khomiakov, Dostoevsky, Soloviev*. London: S.C.M.

Zetzel, J. (1982) 'The Poetics of Patronage in the Late First Century B.C.', in B. K. Gold (ed.) *Literary and Artistic Patronage in Ancient Rome*. Austin: University of Texas Press: 87–102.

Zverev, A. (2001) *Nabokov*. Moscow: Molodaia gvardiia.

Zyla, W. T. (1972) 'A Ukrainian Version of the Aeneid: Ivan Kotljarevs'kyi's Enejida', *Classical Journal* 67.3: 193–7.

Index